Mastering Search Analytics

Brent Chaters

O'REILLY®

Beijing · Cambridge · Farnham · Köln · Sebastopol · Tokyo

Mastering Search Analytics

by Brent Chaters

Copyright © 2012 Brent Chaters. All rights reserved.
Printed in the United States of America.

Published by O'Reilly Media, Inc., 1005 Gravenstein Highway North, Sebastopol, CA 95472.

O'Reilly books may be purchased for educational, business, or sales promotional use. Online editions are also available for most titles (*http://my.safaribooksonline.com*). For more information, contact our corporate/institutional sales department: (800) 998-9938 or *corporate@oreilly.com*.

Editors: Mike Loukides and Mary Treseler	**Indexer:** Seth Maislin
Production Editor: Jasmine Perez	**Cover Designer:** Karen Montgomery
Copyeditor: Rachel Head	**Interior Designer:** David Futato
Proofreader: Jasmine Perez	**Illustrator:** Robert Romano

October 2011:   First Edition.

Revision History for the First Edition:

2011-10-07   First release

See *http://oreilly.com/catalog/errata.csp?isbn=9781449302658* for release details.

ISBN: 978-1-449-30265-8

[LSI]

1317919765

*This book is dedicated to my late mom,
Mary-Lea (Rivet) Chaters, who always wanted to
write a book, as well as my sister, Tricia,
my father, Gary, and the rest of my family
for their support. Lastly, a special thanks to my
better half, Caroline, who has helped me keep
my sanity, supported my late nights, and made
sure I found time to eat and socialize.*

Table of Contents

Preface

This book is designed to fill a gap in the search world. While there have been many books on website analytics, search engine optimization (SEO), and paid search (and even some on site search), this book looks at bringing these disciplines together as search engine marketing (SEM), as originally conceived by Danny Sullivan (*http://searchengineland.com/does-sem-seo-cpc-still-add-up-37297*). Solid search programs are driven by data and analysis, and combine both SEO and paid search tactics. Site search is an oft-forgotten source of mineable data, and should be included as part of your overall SEM program.

 Nowadays, SEM has been co-opted to define paid search. When Danny Sullivan first coined the term, his intent was to illustrate that SEO was part of a search strategy and that the newly defined space of paid search was another part of a total search strategy. Search engine marketing referred to the overall search program.

My goal is to get you thinking about how to segment your data, as well as to show you how to use some of the available tools that can help you think of ways SEM can be used to improve revenue. We will also discuss how to measure the health of your current search programs: how to identify bottlenecks, whether you can compete against other sites, and what you need to consider if you do decide to compete.

The truth of the matter is that there are many websites and software options that enable search gurus to do what they do. The exciting thing about search analytics is that it's still very much like the Wild West. There are many solutions, from self-service pieced-together options to enterprise-level solutions such as those offered by Covario and Adobe. Regardless of scale, the analytics and analysis side should be driven by human interpretation and thought. Avinash Kaushik, author of *Web Analytics 2.0* (Sybex), is famous for stating that 90% of your investment should be in the people and 10% in the tools. While I don't think this should be a hard and fast rule, its spirit holds true: action comes from insights, and those insights are derived by the people using the tools.

Lastly, this book leans a bit more to the SEO side of measuring marketing tactics, both due to the impact SEO can have on a site—SEO is responsible for 80% or more of search traffic to most sites today, with paid search responsible for the remaining 20%—and because the topic of measuring paid search has been highly covered in many other books. However, to have a true marketing presence, you must consider both SEO and SEM as tactics that work together to bring customers to your website and drive value to your business.

Audience

This book has three audiences in mind: the search specialist, the marketer, and the executive. For the search specialist, this book will provide the information needed to improve site traffic (in terms of quantity, quality, and goal completion) through the use of analytics tools and measurements. For the marketer and executive, this book will provide information on establishing what sort of market share an organization has, and evaluating how well that organization performs in a given market compared to competitors.

An online presence is an almost mandatory part of any business today. Search ensures that your business can be found online. This book is for anyone who is looking to understand how search can be used to drive incremental revenue and opportunity: you will learn how to measure the success of your search programs to allow for benchmarking against other online strategies, as well as how to derive insights to improve revenue and value through search marketing.

Because every company is different, each one will have different needs. Different companies may have disparate methods to generate revenue or reduce costs. Some examples include:

Transactional sites
> Users come to these websites to purchase a product. The company generates revenue by the products it sells.

News and information sites
> Typically, these sites generate revenue through display advertising, such as banners.

Support sites
> Revenue is realized by reducing costs through self-service forums and FAQs.

Customer data sites
> These sites tend to gather customer data, such as email addresses, mailing addresses, and other contact information, so that customers can be marketed to at a later date.

While this book provides different tactics and suggestions, there is no one-size-fits-all solution. Instead, by the end of this book, you should be able to develop a framework of measurements and analytical thinking that will help you make decisions, as well as establish some ground in how best to approach problems you may see in search—or, more importantly, how to poke holes in the data and interpret what the results may mean or indicate.

There is a gap between many new search specialists and the senior managers who rely on the data they provide. The data your senior management—what Avinash Kaushik refers to as the HiPPO (highest paid person's opinion)—needs is very different from the data that a search specialist would require. Typically, the HiPPOs will be senior marketers or executives who do not speak the language of title tags, URL formats, canonicalization, or other common terminology search experts use daily. What they do speak and understand is ROI, revenue growth, and time to profitability. Analytics and data help to bridge the gap that can make decision making easier for both the search expert and the executive.

Why Measuring Search Is Important

In today's market, search can be responsible for driving anywhere from 10% to 90% of traffic for websites. Google serves 34,000 searches per second, while Yahoo! and Bing serve 3,200 and 927 searches per second, respectively (*http://searchengineland .com/by-the-numbers-twitter-vs-facebook-vs-google-buzz-36709*). With Facebook, Google, Yahoo!, and MSN vying for the most visited site each month according to ComScore (*http://www.comscore.com/Press_Events/Press_Releases/2011/4/comScore _Media_Metrix_Ranks_Top_50_U.S._Web_Properties_for_March_2011*) and Netcraft (*http://toolbar.netcraft.com/stats/topsites*), many user experiences will involve more than one search at some point each day.

Search optimization, be it organic or paid, is as much about delivering traffic as it is about what the traffic does once it gets to your website. In fact, I personally feel that the most important search optimization activity is often simply to understand what users are actually doing when they come to your site. Often, when they see large volumes of traffic going to their sites, many organizations believe they should continue to focus on increasing site traffic, as opposed to improving the experience of the site. With this in mind, I will focus a great deal on not just measuring the traffic that gets to your site, but what users do once they are there. My approach is to optimize the user experience, while maintaining an open and friendly site for search engines.

Search is a developing field that is growing rapidly and at a highly competitive pace. Companies are taking note and investing in search, be it paid, organic, or site search. As companies invest in search, they will expect to see results. The easiest way to show results is by defining and measuring what are often referred to as key performance indicators (KPIs).

A recent study from Conductor (*http://www.conductor.com/news/unoptimized-seo*) shows that those who practice SEO can spend 4 out of every 10 hours on tasks that involve measuring, monitoring, and analyzing results and content. This information should not be all that surprising, as the best way to optimize is through measurement and monitoring.

Understanding how to utilize resources to automate, capture, and track these elements can increase the time allotted to link building, content creation, and improving your customer experience.

Ask yourself how well you are doing in the search market. Can people find you? What volume of traffic is SEO driving to your site? When people get to your site from a search, do they stay or leave right away? When people look for your brand in a search engine, what is that experience like? Do you run paid search campaigns? Do you spend more per word than you recover in sales for your paid words? How frequently are people using your own site's search? How many sales does your site search contribute to? How much is all this work costing your company, and how much revenue is it pulling back in? A company's online success is powered by findability and relevance. The goal of most search engines is to provide the most relevant piece of information in response to a query that is put into a little box like the one in Figure P-1.

Figure P-1. The search box

Assumptions This Book Makes

This book expects that if you are a search specialist, you understand the basics of SEO, SEM, and site search (meaning you understand how to set up a paid search campaign, you understand that organic search cannot be bought, and you understand how your site search operates and works).

This book will try to use the lowest-cost tools available to ensure accessibility to as many people as possible. Most examples for clickstream analytics will use Google Analytics, although Adobe SiteCatalyst or any other clickstream tool will work just as well. When there are major differences between the enterprise-level analytics packages, I will try to explain them. The most common tools used will be Google Analytics and spreadsheets, but there are many options and many software choices available to you. Feel free to try any number of them. Good tools are measured not by how expensive they are but by how effectively you, the analyst, wield them. This holds true regardless of business size. Many free tools provide the same insights you would find with "enterprise-level" software. Find the tools that are right for you.

While tools are important, this book's focuse is mostly on getting you to think strategically about search—to get you to think about how and why you should make a decision. Tools provide data, but you provide the insights, interpretations, and recommendations. This means there will be some discussion about how to set up certain tools, and examples of how to do so, but the primary reason for reading this book should be to improve your strategizing and decision making.

To maintain accessibility, I have done my best to simplify any mathematics required so that you can perform the calculations quickly on paper or with a basic calculator or spreadsheet. The scale of your business will influence how complicated some of these calculations may become. However, in the spirit of KISS (Keep It Simple, Stupid), I have done my best to provide the simplest formulas possible.

Anyone who is involved in paid search will also know that today this is a very process- and tool-driven SEM tactic. There are many great books on paid search, and they go through these tool sets very deeply. Also, the use of paid search to measure many data points has historically been well documented. The purpose of this book is not to show you how to measure everything, but to show you how to measure the effectiveness of your search campaigns and how to use this data to coordinate and improve those campaigns.

For anyone looking for deeper insight on SEO, SEM, site search, or statistics in general, I highly recommend the following books:

For SEO:	Eric Enge et al., *The Art of SEO: Mastering Search Engine Optimization*. O'Reilly, 2009.
For SEM:	Brad Geddes, *Advanced Google AdWords*. Wiley, 2010.
For site search:	Peter Morville and Jeffery Callender, *Search Patterns*. O'Reilly, 2010.
For statistics:	Sarab Boslaugh and Paul A. Watters, *Statistics In a Nutshell*. O'Reilly, 2009.

When we look at search engines, for the most part we will be looking at Google to keep things simple. Where there is greater variance between the major engines, I'll call that out.

Contents of This Book

Each chapter will cover different sets of metrics and questions that all tie back to search. In some cases, we will look at how to monitor offsite metrics, such as rankings and presentation in search results, while in other cases, we will be looking at measuring the effectiveness of the search page once a user is delivered to it. Improving the search experience should not simply be about delivering people to a site, but ensuring they are delivered the optimal experience.

Chapter 1, *Introduction to Search Analytics*, is an introduction to why search analytics is different from traditional web metrics; we'll also look at some of the more popular programs and software in use today. You should, by the end of this chapter, have an understanding of some basic analytics concepts, and it will prepare you for the journey ahead by introducing you to a variety of sources for data collection.

Chapter 2, *Establishing ROI*, gets at what everyone who runs a business would like to know: what is the return on investment (ROI)? It will also dispel some myths about the

ROI of SEM versus SEO. At the end of this chapter, you should have the knowledge needed to provide justification for your search programs.

Chapter 3, *Tracking and Optimizing SEO and Paid Search Traffic*, explores traffic from search. You will learn how to measure, analyze, capture conversions, and establish values for tasks your customers may perform that may not be easily identified as resulting in monetary gains.

Chapter 4, *Tracking Words—SEO and Paid Search*, dives into exploring how to track words and establishing plans for both SEO and SEM to improve and modify your keywords, as well as understand words that may have issues or be virtually impossible to rank on.

Chapter 5, *Coordinating SEO and Paid Search*, explains how to tie your SEO and SEM programs together and how to look for opportunities in each of your search strategies to improve the other. You will also learn how to test out theories and ideas in either program, and how to determine which of the two (i.e., SEO or SEM) is the better choice for your site. You will learn how to coordinate the data you are seeing to improve both programs.

Chapter 6, *Site Search Analytics*, will show you how to capture the value of your own site search and how to look for ways to improve it.

Chapter 7, *Correlating SEO/Paid Search and Site Search*, will bring all three search disciplines together: SEO, SEM, and site search. You will learn how to look for patterns that can indicate issues or disconnects between programs, as well as getting some ideas on how to improve the customer experience by using the data your customers are already providing you on the fly.

Chapter 8, *Competitor Research and Competitor Tracking*, looks at techniques you can use to track and monitor what your competitors are doing. You will learn how to monitor and understand their campaigns, as well as how effective they may be in relation to yours.

Chapter 9, *Tracking Off-Site Trends*, explores all the offsite indicators for SEO and SEM. It looks at how to explore what may cause bumps and spikes in the data you see, as well as how to track external influences on your rankings and positions.

Chapter 10, *Tracking Mobile Search*, focuses on mobile search, a relatively new area of search that is generating lots of discussion in the field. You will learn how to track and understand the differences between mobile and desktop users, and we will explore where mobile search may go.

Chapter 11, *Social Media and Search*, looks at how social media is impacting search rankings and results. This chapter explores some basic KPIs you can leverage to measure how socially engaged your website is.

Chapter 12, *Webmaster Tools—Data Direct from the Engines*, zeros in on search spiders, discussing tracking and measuring what they are doing, what they see, and how to make sure your site is as indexable as possible.

Chapter 13, *An SEO Audit (On-Page Factors)*, explains how to audit your site for issues that may cause problems for spiders or users. You will learn how to establish some key performance indicators (KPIs) to watch for on your site to ensure proper site health.

Chapter 14, *Dashboards and Reports*, starts to tie everything together, as you are shown how to create dashboards and expanded reports using all the data points you have learned along the way.

Chapter 15, *Building Your Own Audit Tools and Enabling Others*, provides information on some auditing tools you may want to create on your own, as well as how to enable others, build out timelines, and scale your search analytics program.

Conventions Used in This Book

The following typographical conventions are used in this book:

Italic
> Indicates new terms, URLs, email addresses, filenames, and file extensions.

`Constant width`
> Used for program listings, as well as within paragraphs to refer to program elements such as variable or function names, statements, and keywords.

> This icon signifies a tip, suggestion, or general note.

> This icon indicates a warning or caution.

Using Code Examples

This book is here to help you get your job done. In general, you may use the code in this book in your programs and documentation. You do not need to contact us for permission unless you're reproducing a significant portion of the code. For example, writing a program that uses several chunks of code from this book does not require permission. Selling or distributing a CD-ROM of examples from O'Reilly books does require permission. Answering a question by citing this book and quoting example code does not require permission. Incorporating a significant amount of example code from this book into your product's documentation does require permission.

We appreciate, but do not require, attribution. An attribution usually includes the title, author, publisher, and ISBN. For example: "*Mastering Search Analytics* by Brent Chaters (O'Reilly). Copyright 2012 Brent Chaters, 978-1-4493-0265-8."

If you feel your use of code examples falls outside fair use or the permission given above, feel free to contact us at *permissions@oreilly.com*.

Safari® Books Online

Safari Books Online is an on-demand digital library that lets you easily search over 7,500 technology and creative reference books and videos to find the answers you need quickly.

With a subscription, you can read any page and watch any video from our library online. Read books on your cell phone and mobile devices. Access new titles before they are available for print, and get exclusive access to manuscripts in development and post feedback for the authors. Copy and paste code samples, organize your favorites, download chapters, bookmark key sections, create notes, print out pages, and benefit from tons of other time-saving features.

O'Reilly Media has uploaded this book to the Safari Books Online service. To have full digital access to this book and others on similar topics from O'Reilly and other publishers, sign up for free at *http://my.safaribooksonline.com*.

How to Contact Us

Please address comments and questions concerning this book to the publisher:

O'Reilly Media, Inc.
1005 Gravenstein Highway North
Sebastopol, CA 95472
800-998-9938 (in the United States or Canada)
707-829-0515 (international or local)
707-829-0104 (fax)

We have a web page for this book, where we list errata, examples, and any additional information. You can access this page at:

http://shop.oreilly.com/product/0636920018094.do

To comment or ask technical questions about this book, send email to:

bookquestions@oreilly.com

For more information about our books, courses, conferences, and news, see our website at *http://www.oreilly.com*.

Find us on Facebook: *http://facebook.com/oreilly*

Follow us on Twitter: *http://twitter.com/oreillymedia*

Watch us on YouTube: *http://www.youtube.com/oreillymedia*

Acknowledgments

A special thanks goes to Philip Wong, Georgia Sievwright, Mike Sandhu, Joanne Doucette, Jassie Aujla, and Mark Scholz for the support in my career and for opening up doors for me, as well as to all the other fine folks at Hewlett-Packard. Thanks also to:

- Mike Loukides, Mary Treseler, and the rest of the O'Reilly folks for their support throughout the writing of this book, as well as their wisdom, guidance, editing, and patience

- Rachel Head for the skill and depth she brought to editing, and providing clarity when clarity was needed

- Rand Fishkin for his kind insights and the team at SEOmoz for answering all my questions

- David Fahey and the folks at AdGooroo for taking the time to talk and provide some deeper insights into their products

- Justin Cutroni for providing some last-minute insights and updates

- Bill Barnes of Mediative for providing updated user experience information with Google Instant

- AJ Kohn for the GA hack on tracking SERPs

Finally, a very special thanks to the technical reviewers:

- Jill Kocher for the details in the review, and for keeping me on the straight and narrow path for SEO

- Sean Power for helping me find clarity and some great insider tips, as well as for the background on some updates to recent analytics tools

- Alex Cohen for making sure every "i" and "t" was crossed, and for the paid search insights

- Chris Knoch for the push to get more social

- Daryl Acumen for offering up his time, and for being a super smart analytics guy

CHAPTER 1

Introduction to Search Analytics

To define success, you must be able to measure it.
To improve upon your success, you must be able to measure it.

Successful search campaigns are won by those who know where they are weak and where they are strong. To be a winner in search, you need to have a solid metrics foundation. There isn't any magic solution or formula; it comes down to measuring, testing, analyzing, and interpreting data. If you want to improve your search campaigns, you will need to exhaust all the data you have, beginning with the data closest to the user or customer and then expanding out.

Fix and improve what you can control first (your website and the customer experience), then try to fix the larger issues (competing and moving up the rankings by building more links for competitive words). A good approach to working with data is to look at data about the user (words and searches bringing them to your site), data throughout your site (what they are doing on your site), and off-site data (influence over offline actions such as buying a product in a store), and then to tie all of this back to data from the search engine (determining whether the engines are interpreting your site's content as you feel it should be interpreted). The success of your search campaigns depends on recognizing that you have access to user behavior as well as user intent. The engines try to understand user intent in order to provide the best experience possible and pass this along every time a user comes to your website through the referring URL. Knowing the users' intent should help us shape our entry points, as well as the overall experience that people have when engaging with our sites.

Search—be it SEO, SEM, or site search—is a very simple concept. The search engine's goal is to deliver the right content to the right person in the right place and at the right time. The engines are always looking to perfect this. The question is, how do you know if your business is a winner?

Tools you will need in this chapter:

- Clickstream tracking package (Google Analytics, Adobe SiteCatalyst, etc.)
- Google Keyword Tool or some other keyword research tool
- Spreadsheet program (Excel or something similar)

How Is Search Data Different from Clickstream Data?

Search analytics introduces some qualitative data from the search term coupled with many quantitative data points in the form of click-through rates, traffic volume, conversion rates, and more.

> *Qualitative data* measures behavior and the reasons driving that behavior. For example, surveys and questionnaires can provide qualitative data; in our case, this may also come from search parameter patterns over repeat sessions.
>
> *Quantitative data* is numerical data. Examples of this are the number of visits to a website, or the number of people who purchase a product.
>
> *Clickstream data* measures the actions users take on your website by tracking what and where they click.

You can get some insight into users' intent and decision-making processes by looking at groups of search terms as qualitative data points. For example, if a user comes to your site from three different search terms, looking at those terms may show some of the decision making that has occurred. For instance, if the search pattern looks like "ACME widgets"→"ACME widget reviews"→"ACME widget sale", we can see that the user started out looking for a product, was then influenced by the reviews, and then looked for a discounted price. You can further amplify this qualitative data with site surveys. By bringing together qualitative data and quantitative data, we can start to get a better idea of the intent of our users, and optimize their experience.

You can get better ideas of "intent patterns" through search when you merge your external search data with your on-site search data. Perhaps many users come to your site through branded terms, meaning words that are specific to only your brand. An example of this would be a search for "iPhone": that is specific to Apple, and there is a brand association there. When users show up from a branded term, what secondary searches do they perform on your site?

Have you enabled your clickstream analytics to capture the referring search terms and the associated site search terms? Are you recognizing that many users who come to your site on branded terms are looking for a specific product? Or perhaps there are a great number of support searches. If you have paid for the click-through SEM, maximize the value by learning what users are looking for and develop landing pages to bring this needed information closer to the user. In the case of SEO, you cannot always dictate what page will rank, but you can improve your site's general navigation to include links to these deeper pages. Recognizing your customers' needs and providing content that helps them will in the long run also help improve your business.

Search also gives you insight into the language of your customers. The goal of keyword research is to understand the language landscape of the search engines. What are the search volumes like, and how competitive are other sites on these terms? This is data that can be fed to other marketing channels. Why not apply this keyword research to your email deployments or your in-store flyers, bringing online and offline insights together to create subject lines and in-store banners with the language customers use?

When we talk about branded versus nonbranded words, I see all too often a confusion with internal versus external language. Internally you may want to call your product "the super best product ever!" while users may simply call it "widget." Unless you have the dollars and branding resources to get people to change their language, you may need to recognize that it is easier to get people to think about your product by creating at least a small word association to the word "widget." Ignoring the elephant in the room and calling your product anything but may result in people not having that "ah ha!" moment and realizing that your widget is really also "the super best product ever." Search is as much about measuring word use and linguistic needs as it is about measuring clicks, inbound links, and other data points.

Beyond these factors, SEO has unique challenges in that all the major search engines operate as black boxes. The search engines do not let anyone know the recipe for their secret sauce, or in this case the algorithm that makes them run. To better understand these algorithms, SEO specialists have had to try to reverse engineer them. It's also important to understand that each engine runs different algorithms—for example, Bing runs a different algorithm than Google. Each engine's algorithm is proprietary to that engine; in some cases, other engines may lease these algorithms (as Yahoo! now leases Bing's algorithm), but each major algorithm will have its own quirks and issues to test against.

The best way to reverse engineer something such as a search algorithm is to look at data points, examining them to try to determine which return positive feedback and which return negative feedback. Analytics help take a lot of the guesswork out of the SEO's job.

Search analytics is not just about measuring traffic delivered, but also about *landing page optimization* (LPO) and *conversion rate optimization* (CRO). LPO is focused on retaining and moving people through your site; it acknowledges that not everyone comes to your site through the home page. You typically start by optimizing your high-volume entry pages and work down from there. CRO is focused on moving people through a funnel to a goal. This conversion may occur over several visits as part of the overall life cycle and decision-making process of purchasing a product. CRO takes into account the stages of this process and the needs of a user to help that user make a decision as quickly as possible.

A search strategy is not concerned simply with delivering traffic to a site; it must take into consideration the handoff of that traffic, as well as the pathing of that traffic to each goal and objective. Site search also helps facilitate the measurement of on-site navigation issues and needs. Think about moving beyond measuring traffic volume, and measuring business objectives and goals. Think about measuring to improve those objectives and goals.

Who Are You Optimizing For?

First, let me come right out and say it: why do SEO and SEM people always have to prove which is more important? Why can't we just all be search people? A well-defined search program should utilize both SEO and SEM tactics to provide maximum coverage and exposure to the right person at the right time, to maximize your revenue. I do not believe that SEO and SEM should be optimized separately from each other; in fact, there should be open sharing and examination of your overall search strategy. With that said, each practice has its own needs and methods that may be unique to it. Still, remember that the goal is to maximize your revenue by investing smartly. This means that you should invest in traffic that will convert at the maximum value for you.

Search optimization—particularly SEO—is traditionally thought of as improving the rankings of pages. Therefore, pages are optimized for search engines. My personal opinion on this is that if this is your only objective, you are doomed to fail. The simple fact is that the engines are changing every day. There are no "rules," just best practices that have been adopted because they show positive results in rankings and can have positive results for the end user. To me, it's not how much traffic you get that counts, but what you do with the traffic.

Your goals in improving search results should include positive impacts to your customers, and ultimately, positive impacts to your revenue streams. Optimizing entry pages for SEO is about improving the flow of traffic into your site to achieve a positive outcome for both your customers and your business. Users arriving from search should have an even better customer experience than those who enter through your home page. Search analytics are just as much about what happens on your site as what drives people to your site.

On top of all this, the online world has brought us an overwhelming multitude of information points. SEO in particular moves at such a rapid pace of change that keeping up with changes in the algorithms is practically impossible. Eric Schmidt, former CEO of Google, claims Google uses over 200 ranking factors to establish what shows up on every organic search result (*http://searchengineland.com/schmidt-listing -googles-200-ranking-factors-would-reveal-business-secrets-51065*). On top of this, there are over 500 tweaks made to the algorithm every year—more than one change per day. Optimizing to the engines is not a game you can win, but optimizing to people and their behaviors is.

Relevancy can also have an impact on paid search. Google AdWords (the largest of the paid search options) measures relevancy through *Quality Score*, a metric that takes into account the click-through rate (CTR) of the keyword, the historical CTR of all ads and keywords in your account, the CTR of the display URL in the ad group, the quality of your landing page, the relevance of the keyword both in the ad group and to the search query, and other factors. The better your Quality Score is during each search, the less you will pay per click. It should also be noted that the Quality Score used to determine the cost per click is generated for every search and is not a direct reflection of the Quality Score you see in AdWords (*http://adwords.google.com/support/aw/bin/answer.py?hl=en &answer=21388*).

Beyond this, the real power of paid search is that you have *full* control over the user experience: everything from what copy and text the users will see to what pages they will be directed to. You can control the time of day results will be displayed, and you can even target specific device types (mobile or desktop) or geographies (particular cities or countries). The amount of direct and immediate control you have over your paid search campaigns means a greater opportunity to optimize and improve results.

Site search can vary from site to site. How effective is your site search? How frequently is your site search used? There are a great deal of data points specific to search; the challenge is figuring out what points need to be used to answer specific sets of questions. Data only has value if it enables someone to do something.

For those of you used to practicing website measurement through Google Analytics or other clickstream tools, there will be some familiarity, though search analytics also use off-site factors, as well as user experience (UX) and information architecture (IA) factors. This book will introduce several programs that will enable you to capture data and explain how to use some of these programs. Some are paid and some are free, but the most important things to consider will be which tools enable you to make insights that help you meet your business needs, and which ones you feel most comfortable using. Sometimes the free options can be just as good as an enterprise-level paid option, and whenever possible, this book will use the lowest-cost option in each example. An extensive list of tools is provided in the Appendix.

Search analytics requires a bit of psychology; because we are dealing with words and people, we are given partial insights into our users' thoughts. Think of a search box as a word association test. People provide a word or a group of words describing or identifying what they are looking for. The engine's job is to interpret the user's intent and match that word or words to the page or pages it thinks will best serve the user.

Further, a great deal of data aggregation is carried out to identify patterns that groups of searchers follow. At times you may need to make some assumptions. When you find this to be the case, I strongly urge you to use surveys to help eliminate this guesswork.

Qualitative data can go a long way. For example, you can ask people on the page with the highest abandonment rate, "What are you looking for?"

When you need to make an educated guess, it's important to remember it is just a guess. It can act as a starting place, but it's only ever a hypothesis. Be prepared to follow a different avenue if it turns out that you are wrong. Like a good detective, you should be able to use your analytics to eventually answer questions or support theories you may have, but until you have supporting data, your hypothesis will only ever be an unproven guess. Also, because people change, you will never be able to stop measuring your site if you plan on improving sales and the user experience.

What Are Others Trying to Measure?

A recent SEMPO and Econsultancy report (*http://econsultancy.com/us/reports/sempo -state-of-search*) revealed that both SEO and SEM are in conflict with what the engines tell us to do—namely, "provide good content." Instead, what most are trying to do is "drive traffic," without regard for the quality of that traffic. The report shows that over 40% of companies cite driving traffic as the main objective for their SEO programs. This a pretty vague goal, and we can assume websites are already getting traffic from search engines, even if they are not optimized. It's not only volume that counts, though: it's important that conversion rates remain the same and that the additional traffic is as engaged as the current traffic. Why not set some deeper action than simply driving traffic as your goal for SEO? That is, assuming your site does not generate revenue only through display ads—and if it does, why not set your goal to be driving more repeat traffic? Keep them coming back for more!

The rest of the goals for SEO traffic in the report read as follows: generating leads, selling products, increasing brand awareness, and, lastly, improving customer satisfaction and customer service. Only 2% of companies cited improved customer satisfaction as their main goal. At least they are defining more actionable goals, but what about the lifetime value of the customer? Where is the foresight for long-term value?

Even as a secondary objective, improved customer service still ranks as the lowest goal for SEO, cited by only 5% of companies. Agencies also fell into a similar pattern, although their primary objective was to generate leads, followed by driving traffic.

If the search engines tell us that we must create great content and provide good customer experiences to rank well organically, but our primary goals are instead driving traffic or creating leads, how do we bridge this gap? Is an improved customer experience mutually exclusive of driving traffic or generating leads? I would suggest not, but where should the priorities be placed?

Speaking from my own experience, metrics that bring together both voice-of-the-customer data (for example, where customers are given a questionnaire and provide written feedback) and clickstream data that tracks conversion and site usage show that improved customer satisfaction measured through the customer surveys has typically led to improved site usage, improved conversions, and, more importantly, longer repeat customer relations. Avinash Kaushik echoed this point in a post on his web analytics blog (see the entry *http://www.kaushik.net/avinash/2007/04/the-three-greatest-survey-questions-ever.html*) where he cited the advice he had given to a Fortune 100 company looking to improve its website and increase sales.

One of the first things I ever discovered that was cool about voice-of-the-customer data was how it made segmenting and thinking about site data so much cleaner. I used to look at the data as a whole, thinking "My god, we only have a conversion rate of 3%" or whatever the conversion rate was.

Then one day when I was looking at a voice-of-the-customer survey, I realized that not everyone is coming to buy products. Some are coming for support, some are coming to download software, some are coming to purchase, and others are simply coming to learn about a product.

This got me to thinking that if I know that only 35% of the site visitors are potential paying customers, our 3% conversion rate is most likely misrepresentative. If I were to filter out the 65% of site visitors who have come with little or no intention of making a purchase, our conversion rate would suddenly jump up to 8.5%.

The voice-of-the-customer survey also showed me that to maintain long-term relationships with existing customers, I must make sure that the website fulfills the needs of the other 65% of the site visitors.

Voice-of-the-customer surveys allowed me to better illustrate what our conversion rate was with users who intended to purchase (8.5%) and, with refinements, how many intended to purchase online versus offline. Filtering out the customers who intended to purchase offline made that 8.5% increase significantly. This finding prompted me to ask the rest of the team, "How can we get people who intend to purchase offline to commit to an online sale?" We decided to focus on the users closest to making the jump to a purchase first.

The point of this is not to show you how to boost your numbers, but how to make sure you are spending your time smartly. In our case, once I realized that not all of our visitors were coming to the site looking to make a purchase, I saw that we no longer had to worry about getting all the traffic to convert; instead, we could focus on making sure that the traffic that intended to purchase was converting. More specifically, when I saw that we were doing fairly well with users who intended to purchase online, I realized we could boost our conversions by focusing on the users who were looking to purchase offline.

In contrast to the results for SEO and SEM, the SEMPO and Econsultancy report showed that paid search's primary goals are generating leads and selling products, with

75% of companies citing these as their main goals. Driving traffic was the third highest ranking goal, with 19% of companies striving for this. Improved customer service was the objective of only 2% of these campaigns.

It is interesting to see that when dealing with paid search, the goal is tied to something more tangible than simply driving traffic. Perhaps because you have to pay for these ads, companies feel they must show a more palpable result. Again I have to ask, why not also look at creating a great customer experience and working at making that dollar last longer by trying to increase repeat business and focusing on retaining your customers?

What Do Companies Most Want to Measure?

The SEMPO and Econsultancy study also asked the companies and agencies surveyed what they considered to be the three most important metrics for search and SEO. Table 1-1 shows how they broke down and identifies the chapters in this book where you can find information on the metrics identified.

Table 1-1. Most important SEO and SEM metrics (data from 2011 SEMPO and Econsultancy survey)

Metric	Percentage of responses for SEO by companies	Percentage of responses for SEO by agencies	Percentage of responses for SEM by companies	Percentage of responses for SEM by agencies	Chapter covered in
Site traffic	57%	43%	14%	11%	Chapter 3
Conversion rate	33%	40%	59%	50%	Chapter 3
Click-through rate	28%	20%	37%	34%	Chapter 2
Page rank	28%	18%	N/A	N/A	Chapter 9
Position	27%	37%	N/A	N/A	Chapters 2 and 4
Number of sales/leads	25%	34%	40%	33%	Chapters 2 and 3
Brand awareness	22%	14%	12%	7%	Chapter 8
Return on investment	15%	28%	31%	33%	Chapter 2
Customer engagement	13%	9%	5%	5%	Chapter 3
Number of links	10%	9%	N/A	N/A	Chapter 9
Cost per sale/Cost per acquisition	8%	11%	23%	38%	Chapter 2
Value of sales/leads	8%	10%	12%	10%	Chapters 2 and 3
Customer satisfaction/ advocacy	6%	1%	3%	1%	Chapter 1
Cost per click	5%	5%	26%	29%	Chapter 4
Cost of generating sale offline	2%	3%	4%	3%	Chapter 3

Metric	Percentage of responses for SEO by companies	Percentage of responses for SEO by agencies	Percentage of responses for SEM by companies	Percentage of responses for SEM by agencies	Chapter covered in
Profitability of sales	2%	7%	9%	11%	Chapters 2 and 3
Return on ad spend	2%	6%	17%	27%	Chapter 2
Other	1%	1%	1%	1%	—

Interestingly, across the board, conversion rate ranks fairly high in terms of what is being tracked, yet customer satisfaction ranks low. Also, the importance of ROI increases as spend awareness increases. ROI is given more weight when agencies are involved, and with paid as opposed to organic search. Site traffic remains the top metric measured for organic search, which indicates to me that organic campaigns have not reached the same level of metrics engagement as paid search campaigns.

I also fear that in this case, site traffic metrics are simply measuring how much traffic was delivered to a site. This is a largely worthless metric. If your site is monetized through traffic, how is it monetized? Through ad impressions? If so, you should measure number of ad impressions served as opposed to traffic. Site traffic is an archaic metric with little actionable value. The same can be said for click-through rate (CTR). Again, this metric is worthless on its own. What I would rather know is what percentage of the CTR traffic bounced, and whether that is good or bad. This indicates how successful I am at retaining users—that is, whether I am helping them to complete their objectives and meet their goals.

What Challenges Do Companies Face?

The last piece of the SEMPO and Econsultancy study we will consider is what challenges companies identified in relation to their search programs. The report indicates that 44% of companies have difficulty measuring ROI for SEO and 40% of companies for SEM. Beyond this, obtaining executive buy-in, getting budget allocations, and making the business case for investment account for 53% of the challenges SEO marketers face and 45% of those faced by paid search marketers.

I believe these challenges can be overcome by presenting clear and concise metrics that show ROI, share of voice, and lifetime value. These are all issues that typically are raised either by more senior people or people in other departments who have to decide where is the best area to spend the budget. These other departments are accountable for what they spend, so when investing in search there should be an expectation to have a measurable data point.

Lastly, 40% of companies identified optimizing destination pages as an SEO challenge, and 42% as a paid search challenge. This is a somewhat vague description that may refer to optimizing either to rank well or to push traffic further into the site. Both of these issues are very relevant and real concerns, each of which can be addressed through analytics and landing page optimization. By defining the goal of a page and what action a user may take on that page, and also by understanding the overall business objectives of the company, you can begin to define what you need to track beyond traffic volumes.

Business Objectives

Every business has a reason for being. It has a goal. It has a market. Before you even begin to build a metrics program, conduct interviews throughout your business to find out what the goals are. Find out what your customers need. Set up voice-of-the-customer surveys: iPerceptions offers 4Q, which is free and an excellent start if you are working with a limited budget.

Learn what your business is attempting to do both online and offline. While you may not be able to easily measure offline results, you should do your best to translate those into online goals.

To capture offline goals in online instances, you will have to think outside of the box. In some cases, you can capture offline results through coupon codes by using custom URLs that append tagging, such as *www.acme.com/promotion* redirecting to *www.acme.com/directory/some-promtion.html?cid=campaign-variable*. Tagging and marketing URLs that redirect to longer URLs can help you track an offline campaign back to an online action. In this example, the variable that comes after "cid=" is used to identify a specific marketing campaign that is tied to a business objective.

By clearly setting out the business objectives, understanding what your customers see as issues today, and knowing your market and who your competitors are, you will ensure that you are better informed as you start to establish an analytics-driven strategy. You should be aiming to develop a plan that will encompass these needs and provide ways to translate online actions into measurable events.

Beyond setting business objectives, you will also have the task of improving your search programs. These programs should be tuned to deliver results that help you meet your business objectives. There are some basic business objectives that will come out early, the first of which will likely be ROI. To impact this, you will have to look at improving what happens on your site. Your job is not to simply deliver traffic to a site, but to ensure that traffic is successful in meeting the goals of your business.

You will use data to answer the question of how successful your search programs are. To optimize your programs, you will need to make data-driven decisions. Part of your responsibility may be keeping the big bosses (HiPPOs) happy, or you may be the big boss yourself. Often, the data they or you need is much different than the data your marketing person needs, and it will be very different than the data the person running your SEM, SEO, or site search program needs.

What Auditing Tools Should I Be Using?

The software, browser plug-ins, and websites you select should be items you are comfortable with, or are able to utilize efficiently. The important thing to remember is that you do not have to spend a lot of money to get the best auditing tools. As you will quickly discover, there is great variance in cost. The tools you select may depend on the scale of your programs or the size of your company. For example, Kenshoo, Marin Software, Adobe, and ClickEquations all provide very powerful SEM tools to manage and track paid search campaigns with budgets ranging from $25,000 to millions of dollars a month; however, these may not be the best solution for a small business. Do not get caught up in individual software or tools; instead, learn what data points and information will help you further understand any holes or issues in your search strategies and focus on those.

The following sections provide a brief summary of the types of tools you will come across. Specific packages will be introduced in later chapters as examples demand, and a full list is provided in the Appendix.

Website Analytics

Having some way to track traffic through your site will be critical to success. Website analytics tools typically provide clickstream tracking. Data from these tools shows where and how customers move through your site. Today, most are implemented through tagging. The problem with tagging is that it does not always capture what search spiders do on your site. Clickstream tracking tools that rely on tagging usually require a JavaScript tag or a beacon, such as an image, to be placed on every page to capture actions. JavaScript tagging only captures the actions of users that can execute JavaScript. This excludes visits from users on screen readers, users who prefer to disable JavaScript, and most search engines. The use of image tagging allows for some information to be captured should JavaScript tagging fail.

To capture the search spider, you need to look at options such as log analyzers that parse your website's log files to pull data from all visitors to your site, including search spiders. They can usually be configured to exclude or include certain user data.

One final note to point out about relying on clickstream data from tagging solutions is that because this technology relies on cookies, the numbers can be inaccurate. For example, a recent ComScore study (*http://www.comscore.com/Press_Events/Press _Releases/2011/5/Impact_of_Cookie_Deletion_on_Website_Audience_Measurement _in_Latin_America*) showed that 33% of Internet users in Latin America delete their first-party cookies. This figure is, however, much higher than that reported by some experts (*http://www.kaushik.net/avinash/2008/07/web-analytics-visitor-tracking-cook ies.html*) and ComScore does have a bias because of its business model. These results may also be isolated to the Latin America audience.

For more on website analytics, see Avinash Kaushik's *Web Analytics: An Hour a Day* (Sybex), and for some history, see Chapter 5 of Alistair Croll and Sean Power's *Complete Web Monitoring* (O'Reilly).

Link Tracking

Link tracking tools can be used to give you an idea of who is linking to your domain and its individual pages. Their output can vary in detail, trying to list every page that links to some page on your site or simply listing the domains linking to your domain. In some cases, you may only get a total number of links, without knowing what domains or pages are linking to your site. Some tools will also identify internal links, monitoring which pages of a site link to other pages on the same site. This data is useful in analyzing IA and UX as well as SEO.

Page Authority

Page authority is a measurement first made popular with Google's PageRank, which assigns a level of authority to a page or domain based on a combination of factors, the most predominant of which is number of inbound links. Pages with a higher PageRank are more likely to show at the top of search results, though Google has made some comments indicating that PageRank is not as important a factor now as it once was.

The folks at SEOmoz have also created some of their own tools to learn about the authority of pages and sites: MOZ Rank and MOZ Trust. Authority and trust are used when looking at links from other sites. Basically, links from pages or sites with higher levels of trust and authority are assigned greater value.

Ranking Position

Most likely, one of the first questions anyone running a search program will need to answer is "what position do we rank in for some word or term?" This is also known as the search engine result page (SERP) position. Ranking position tools provide a way of capturing either SEO or SEM rankings (or, in some cases, both).

One more thing to keep in mind is that a trend is emerging for the search engines, or at least Google, to pass along the ranking position of the clicked-on link for some searches. If this trend continues, you may be able to get an idea of SERP position based on referred traffic. The upside of this is that you will be able to determine the impact that position has on traffic to your site.

Keyword Search Volume and Competition

Sometimes, the best battle to fight is the one no one is fighting. Understanding the volumes of searches on particular terms as well as the number of competitors can help you understand if it's a fight you want to take on. In some cases, it may be better to try going up a slightly less steep mountain. Keyword search volume and competition tools pull their data from exclusive sources; for example, Google uses its own data set, while Trellian uses numerous sources. There may be great variance between tools with regard to the anticipated search volume on any given word, so take the expected volumes with a grain of salt.

Social Links and Social Noise

Social media activity (such as Facebook likes and tweets that contain links) has been confirmed as a factor in search rankings by both Google and Bing. The suspicion is that right now it has a lower impact than some other indicators, but this may change over time. Social media sites also have a propensity to push links out to third-party sites, such as blogs, if the noise gets loud enough, or if you are fortunate enough to connect with a well-known blogger.

Social media is still a developing space that is changing rapidly. Not only is it important to monitor the social space from a search perspective, it is also important to know what people are saying about you and your products and to be able to engage in these discussions where they take place. The tools for this category, which are listed in the Appendix under "Social Links and Social Noise" on page 345, offer some monitoring capabilities to help you with this.

Keyword Volume or Keyword Density on Page

Keyword volume is the measurement of words and terms on a page. Most tools look at the terms as a list of single, double, and triple word combinations. Keyword volume does not take into account meaning or any of the semantics associated with the words on the page. It simply gives you an idea of whether you repeat certain words or sets of words over and over in your pages (which may actually be bad in some cases). Some of the tools help you identify a weight based on words and HTML tags. Note that these tools do not tell you if the text is readable by a human or if it makes any sense. The onus for clear content is always on the author of the text.

Mobile and Geographic Traffic Estimations

Recently, one of the larger shifts for Google has been an emphasis on local search results (for example, returning local business results based on the location of the searcher). Smaller companies are able to rank much more highly on local results, whereas larger companies would dominate otherwise. Furthermore, searches are happening on mobile devices that are becoming even more location-aware, down to specific longitude and latitude values. These types of tools will help you learn about opportunities in different geographies, as well as mobile search volumes, which may differ greatly from PC search volumes on some words or terms.

Competitor Insights

The search landscape is highly competitive—so much so that you may have competitors in the search results you didn't even know existed. You will not only be competing against companies that may compete in the same markets offline, but also against information sites like Wikipedia or online stores like Amazon. Tools in this category will offer you some insights into who your competitors may be. Sites ranking higher or generating more traffic may be doing something that you are not. You will also be able to see how they trend over time and where you trend against them.

Multiuse Tools and Sites

There are several solutions that offer multiple data points. SEOmoz, Web CEO, and SEO Book each provide a selection of excellent SEO-related tools for keyword research, link building, competitor tracking, auditing, and more. There are also several large-scale enterprise options available that enable you to tie together search, other digital marketing, and offline marketing measurement points.

Spreadsheets

Before we end this section, there is one other piece of software you will need: a spreadsheet program. You will likely spend lots of time pulling data into spreadsheets to help you keep track of this information, and if you are not putting information into spreadsheets yourself, you will find that many of these tools output into spreadsheets. You don't need to be a spreadsheet wizard, but you should be prepared to be dealing with them in some form or another.

An Explanation of Macro, Micro, Value, and Action Metrics

One of the first things you need to do for any analytics program is define your *key performance indicators* (KPIs). KPIs should be objectives and results, sometimes referred to as OKRs (*http://blog.anthonyrthompson.com/2010/01/objectives-and-key-re sults/*). The simple idea is to define what and where positive results happen on your site. Objectives help keep your eye on the ball and results help tell you if you got a touchdown. Measuring KPIs can typically be classified into four silos: macro, micro, value, and action metrics. These are defined as follows:

Macro metrics

Macro metrics look at a large subset of information. In the realm of SEO metrics, examples might include the total number of inbound links to a page, average keyword position for a group of keywords, or total number of visitors from search. These analytics are often useful when meeting with upper management, when responding to marketing requests, and for understanding general ROI values.

Micro metrics

These metrics examine the smaller parts of a macro metric. For example, if you were looking at the total number of links to a page, the micro metric would look at what domains are linking to that page. Often, these analytics are great for understanding where certain SEO or SEM elements need to be tweaked. Macro metrics often drive the micro metrics that are examined.

Action metrics

Action metrics capture a user's input or response (for example, clicking deeper into your website or interacting with 3D demos). Testing out different ad copies to see which one results in the most clicks is an example of an action metric, measuring when the user takes action. Action metrics are an excellent way to measure the usability and experience of your site.

Value metrics

Value metrics are tied directly to revenue or other goals that are considered the core driving forces of your website. These metrics might include clicking on web banners that create revenue for you, purchasing from an ecommerce engine, or subscribing to your newsletter. Value metrics may be a subgroup of action metrics. Value metrics are also the touchdowns. These are your goals and conversions.

Value and action metrics were first introduced to me by one of my senior executives. It didn't take me long to realize that he was not only interested in conversion rates and the bottom line; he also wanted to measure the use of the site.

Our site did a lot more than just sell products, and he recognized this through key performance indicators that measured the actions users took that might not be directly related to sales or value. He referred to them as "volume metrics," but I thought "action metrics" sounded more appropriate, and it was easier to explain the difference to stakeholders.

As for micro and macro analytics, when presenting data I always had two approaches: top-down or bottom-up. Which one I used would change from audience to audience, but when I was presented with a hard question, such as "Why is traffic down for such and such a segment?," my approach was consistently the same: start at the top and work my way down. First I compared the data to see if traffic really was down, and if so, I checked whether I could see a dip from any specific source. Was search traffic down? Was display banner traffic down? Was bookmarked or direct traffic down? Were there any pages whose traffic suddenly dropped from one month to the next, or year to year? The big question triggered all these little questions and made problem solving much easier.

If you take one thing away from this discussion, it should be to think about how you can segment traffic and then segment it again. When answering questions, smaller portions of data are always easier to deal with and dissect than larger chunks of data, which are usually much better for reporting to executives on.

As Avinash would say, all of these metrics are "data puke" if you cannot make them actionable. Say, for example, you had 1,000,000 visitors to your site, 50% of whom added a product to a shopping cart, 25% of whom began to check out, but only 3% of whom actually did check out.

The 1,000,000 is your macro metric. You would then want to segment this group into better-defined categories, such as users looking for support, users with strong buying intent, and users with weak buying intent. Where do you get the data to segment these users? In the world of search, we can look at how many users have come to the site on keywords that indicate a need for support versus keywords that include product terminology and keywords that have purchase phrases in them.

We can eliminate the traffic that came in on support terms as likely purchasers of our products, and conversely we can say that anyone who came in on terms with "buy," "deal," or "offer" in them likely had high intent to purchase. Suppose this group represented 10% of our traffic. We now have a micro metric, which is 10% of 1,000,000, or 100,000.

The users that added a product to their cart can be segmented by the action metric "users that added something to a cart." This group could then further be segmented into "users who started to check out" to provide us with better insight into how much our "high intent" segment overlaps into these two segments. If there is high overlap, we are likely doing a good job of getting interested buyers through our site. However, what happens at the checkout? Why do we have such a drop-off?

We can track the folks that check out as a conversion or value metric, and again we'd want to see the overlap in our micro metric, but also we want to know how to get more of these people through the full checkout process.

At this point, we have done a fair amount of data analysis: we have identified segments of people, we have identified where people are failing to complete an action, and we have identified a potential untapped area for revenue improvement if we can just figure out how to get users who come to our site on high-intent-to-purchase keywords through the checkout. To that end, I would resort to a simple questionnaire presented to users before they leave the site, which should include the question: "What can we do to improve your experience next time?"

As you develop your analysis strategy, it helps to think of what you are measuring and at what level of detail you are measuring. Referring back to these four groups of metrics will also help you think about your audience and whether you can drill deeper into any information available to you. It will also help you select the right tool for the job when you need to pull data from a resource.

Presenting Search Analytics—Who's Your Audience?

Chapter 14 is dedicated to this subject, but before we dive into any analytics, it's important to think about who will be looking at the data. The most important questions to ask are "Why should they care?" and "Why do I care?" More often than not, people want more data than they ever use.

In the case of presenting the data, sometimes less is more. When there are too many data points, your audience can become overwhelmed or run into what is called "data paralysis," which is when a decision can't be made because there is too much data to absorb or comprehend. This is why you will need to think, "Segment! Segment! Segment!" Present data that is actionable, not fascinating.

Before you begin pulling data, make sure you fully understand what question whoever will be taking action on the results wants answered. Work to answer that question as best you can. It doesn't hurt for you to look at deeper data, and if you see something that indicates deeper analysis is needed, by all means keep digging. Also remember that the data you present will raise questions; if you don't have the data you need at your fingertips, know where you can find that information to ensure you can get answers quickly to whomever it is that is asking the questions.

Finally, you should also keep in mind that being presented with lots of numbers can sometimes become *boring*! Yes, I know this is a book on analytics and numbers, and I personally love looking at numbers, but not all people do. Chapter 14 gives some examples of how to improve the display of numbers and data.

Setting Expectations

Before we even look at a single number, I want to set some expectations and prepare you for some speed bumps you may come across. The first is that numbers can be pulled out of thin air—4 out of 5 people know that. In fact, I don't know if that is true, but I do know that including numbers in a statement can make it seem more credible. When pulling your numbers, don't make anything up; the integrity of the data and your own personal integrity should be upheld regardless of any pressures to show improvements even if there are not any.

If you aren't getting a result that is positive, be prepared to report on something negative. From time to time, you may see a decrease in something where an increase was hoped for, and you may be tempted to fudge the numbers to make the results appear better. Don't do this! At some point, it will catch up to you. It is better to fail quickly and learn from your mistakes than to misrepresent numbers. Integrity is what makes analytics reliable.

This leads to my second point. As the expression popularized by Mark Twain states, "There are three kinds of lies: lies, damned lies, and statistics." Just because they are numbers does not mean they are facts. Numbers and analytics can be manipulated to appear both positive and negative. We will see examples of this in the next chapter, where the same statistically correct data is presented in different lights.

Some data sources you use to pull your data may contain sampled data. For example, in Google Analytics, the message "This report is generated in fast-access mode" (Figure 1-1) indicates that the data is sampled and not comparing the same data sets anymore. Most data we will work with is intended not to provide exact numbers but to provide us insights, and therefore we will not have to rely completely on exact data. It is, however, to your benefit to inquire if any of the data sources you use are using sampled data. If you are not familiar with averages, medians, and percentiles, I suggest you take a look at Bruce Fey's *Statistics Hacks* (O'Reilly) to learn more about data and sampling.

When comparing two related data sets, I suggest that you use the same tool. For example, if you want to compare your site traffic to your competitors', do not attempt to compare your clickstream data with their ComScore data, as the results will be misleading. While the ComScore data is less accurate, it is at least comparing the same sampling of users, and your goal should be to compare apples to apples as closely as possible. By consistently using the same sources, you will find less fluctuation in

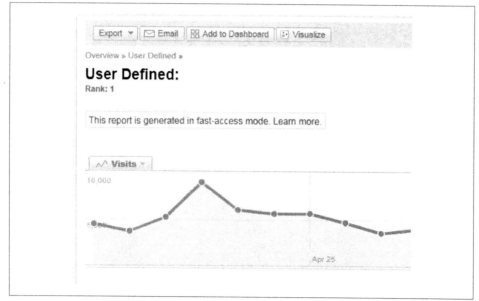

Figure 1-1. Google Analytics report that indicates data is being sampled

numbers. This also means you will get fewer questions about data integrity and you can focus more on acting on the data.

As another example, you would not want to compare web analytics from two different JavaScript-based sources, such as Adobe SiteCatalyst and Google Analytics; it would be an even worse idea to compare a JavaScript-based source to a log-based source. Different analytics tools use different rules internally to measure a variety of data points, and there may also be gaps, such as JavaScript-based tracking not capturing activity from bots. Remember, settle on one source and establish that as your baseline source when comparing analytics across multiple sites, words, or campaigns.

Establishing What You Will Track

Before you go any further in this book, try to answer a few of these questions:

- What website or websites do you want to monitor?
- What keywords do you want to track?
- What keywords are considered branded terms? That is, what words are specific to your brand alone?
- What keywords are considered nonbranded terms?
- What is the goal of your business?
- What is the goal of your website?
- What one thing should a customer be able to do on a specific page?

- What pages are considered success pages (meaning if a customer gets to it, he has completed a task that has a positive impact for your business)?
- What are the values of these success pages? Is there a monetary value directly tied to them? If not, can you develop some sort of value estimate for them?

We look at a few of these questions in more depth in the following sections.

What Website or Websites Do You Want to Monitor?

While you can find all sorts of sites online, these are the five most common types of websites today:

- Media sites (CNN, Wall Street Journal, etc.)
- Transactional sites (Amazon.com, Zappos, etc.)
- SaaS (Software as a Service) (salesforce.com, etc.)
- Collaboration sites (Facebook, etc.)
- Affiliate sites (shopping.com, Groupon, etc.)

Each site has its own unique needs and challenges. Each site also has a different way of producing revenue. Revenue is typically generated directly online in three ways:

- Advertising (the selling of advertising space, as Google does with AdWords)
- Product sales
- Signing up users to a service

Media sites and collaboration sites typically generate revenue through ad impressions. When advertising is sold by impressions instead of clicks, it is to that company's benefit to drive as many people to their site as possible. In these cases, you can find the value of a user based on the average number of impressions you can generate. For example, every ad may be worth 5 cents an impression. If you can generate 10 impressions, then you have earned 50 cents. If that is your average value earned, then each customer is worth 50 cents.

Monetary transactions and subscriptions are typically the driving force on transaction sites and SaaS sites. That is, they generate revenue by selling or getting subscribers to opt into a product or service.

When dealing with product purchases, you will have an *average order value* (AOV). The average value is calculated by adding up the number of orders and the total amount of revenue, then dividing total revenue by the total number of orders.

AOV = Total Revenue / Total Number of Orders

The last way of generating revenue is through *affiliates*. Technically, Groupon is not a true affiliate, but it does act on behalf of other companies, selling products and receiving a commission for each sale. In a traditional sense, affiliate sites make money by marketing and creating leads or selling products through a storefront for another company. Affiliates, such as product sales sites, can track average lead value. This is typically the average amount of money each lead to the parent site is worth. This value may be based on actual transactions occurring on the parent site, or it may be good enough simply to generate the lead. Amazon offers an affiliate program rewarding leads based on purchases that happen on its site.

To add more complexity to tracking affiliate sites, if you are the parent company, you may want to get reports and data back from the affiliates. You may want to know how many impressions your products get on these sites, or how many people click on a product on an affiliate site but do not come to your site. You also will want to track which affiliate sites refer more traffic, and which refer the best-converting traffic.

You should have an idea of what type of website you are responsible for. You should also consider any competitor websites you would like to monitor. Deciding which websites you want to track may impact what is measurable. An affiliate site should provide much more data than a competitor site, but regardless, know who you want to track, and build those lists up.

If your business is based on referrals from other sites, such as affiliate sites or affiliate marketing, reach out to your affiliates and request weekly, monthly, quarterly, or annual reporting. If you have the option to install your own tracking methods, ask for your affiliates to set those up too if it will help provide a better picture of what is happening. With affiliates, there are also several pitfalls to watch out for. It is usually in their best interest to report higher volumes, as that is usually what determines if they get paid. Establish some key affiliates to work out pilot programs with, and build from there. It is also key to note that tracking beacons may create privacy issues for some websites.

The impact of privacy on metrics is another important issue you need to be aware of. Today there is talk of "do not track" legislation, and of companies implementing do-not-track technology and opt-outs (*http://donottrack.us/*). Google has made its own announcement on this, which impacts personalized advertising but not all analytics directly as of yet (*http://googlepublicpolicy.blogspot.com/2011/01/keep-your-opt-outs .html*). Tracking people through your site needs to be done in a way that respects their privacy, providing you with insights through anonymous data, and there are legal implications that are beyond the scope of this book. Most off-the-shelf software does not cross the privacy lines, but with constantly changing legal stances and concerns, it is a hotly discussed topic.

When dealing with tracking competitor sites, be prepared to get sampled data and estimates. Unless you have a very generous competitor, most numbers you will be able to get will be based on sampling and panels. This means that data on your competitors may be more or less accurate, but you will never get exact numbers, and the degree of variance is unknown. ComScore and Nielsen are examples of sources for this type of data.

What Keywords Do You Want to Track?

Begin to think about what keywords you want to track. You should have some idea of what words you feel best represent your website. Start with that list, and add words to or remove words from it as needed. If you are launching a website with no history at all, you will need to consider what words you think people should use to find your site. Later we'll explore how to validate whether these are good words or bad words, but for now make that list, keep it close at hand, and be prepared to build it up. You may also want to think about negative words, or words you do not want to be associated with. These could be vulgarities, politically incorrect terms, or words that may create confusion about your site. For example, if your company sells red bicycles as opposed to motorbikes, you may want to add words like "motorbike" and "motor" to your negative list (Table 1-2).

Table 1-2. Keyword list and negative keyword list

Keywords	Negative keywords
Bike	Motorcycle
Red bike	Motorbike
Bike shop	Motor
Austin bike shop	Harley
Tom's Bike Shop	Chopper

It's usually best to keep each of these sets of words in a spreadsheet; it will make manipulating and tracking them easier later on. Also, some PPC campaigns allow for bulk uploads of words in spreadsheet format.

What Keywords Are Considered Branded Terms?

Now that you have your word list, go back through it and pick out the terms that are specific to your company, website, or brand. These can also be word pairings, like "Nike shoes." Separate these terms from the other terms (Table 1-3). If you don't have any branded terms in your list, sit down and think about what words you might like to trademark. This will be the start of your branded list.

Table 1-3. Keyword list with branded terms added

Keywords	Branded terms	Negative keywords
Bike	Tom's bike shop	Motorcycle
Red Bike	Tom's bike	Motorbike
Bike Shop	Tom's bike repairs	Motor
Austin Bike Shop		Harley
Sport Bike Shop		Chopper

If you have other people to poll, go out and ask them for feedback as well. You can interview people in your company, customers, or partners to find out what terms they link the most to your company and brand.

What Keywords Are Considered Nonbranded Terms?

Take a look at the words still remaining in your list; these are your nonbranded terms (Table 1-4). These should be terms that your competitors would compete on. Later on we'll try to figure out how competitive the market for those terms is, but for now you should have several ways to segment your keywords besides branded and nonbranded (for example, by product line, or geography, or eventually by the revenue they drive).

Table 1-4. Keyword list changing remaining keywords to nonbranded terms

Nonbranded terms	Branded terms	Negative keywords
Bike	Tom's bike shop	Motorcycle
Red Bike	Tom's bike	Motorbike
Bike Shop	Tom's bike repairs	Motor
Austin Bike Shop		Harley
Sport Bike Shop		Chopper

You may also want to build similar word lists for your competitors, partners, and affiliates. As you develop your word lists, over time you will notice that some words constantly bubble to the top; you may also see some words overlap across partners, affiliates, and competitors. They may be words that are highly competitive, or words that convert extremely well. Make mental notes of these words, as we will look to develop strategies around these terms in later chapters.

Concluding Thoughts

A good analyst is always looking for patterns and anomalies. An anomaly may even be the fact that nothing has changed, or that a pattern is too consistent. As someone reading the data, you have to be willing to ask questions and also to recognize when something doesn't seem right. It's better to look into a question than to be silent and realize later something has gone very wrong. The best analyst is the one who asks a lot of questions. The following chapters should give you a start in determining what these questions are, and how to best answer them. To become a true master, you will need to learn how to ask the kinds of questions that will help you segment your data and also how to find the answers to those questions.

While we are looking at these problems, I also encourage you to ask yourself questions about other anomalies you might see. Try to figure out how you might solve the problems in the examples with other tool sets. Do not simply limit yourself to the tools reviewed in this book; be willing to try new tools. The search field is only just beginning to develop some sophisticated search analytics tools. If you see something new, take the time to compare it to what you are familiar with. Look at the data; look at how easy it is to use or not use. The tools will enable you to manipulate data, but it will be your brain and inquisitive mind that will provide the insights. Avinash's rule of investing 10% in your tools and 90% in your people is a good one to live by. Insights are driven by analysts, not tools, regardless of how automated they claim to be.

CHAPTER 2

Establishing ROI

Follow the money.

Good businesses can project how much they expect to make in a quarter, and expect to report a positive profit, or return on investment (ROI), at the end of each quarter. You need to learn how to measure, estimate, and calculate ROI to be successful.

In simple terms, positive ROI is achieved in three different ways:

- By increasing revenue
- By decreasing costs
- By increasing customer loyalty

To see this positive growth, you must also assume that margins stay the same as revenue increases or as costs decrease. Increasing revenue can be done by driving more sales, increasing average order values, or upselling products. Decreasing costs can be achieved by driving more people to self-service venues such as online support forums or online research. So, even activities that may not have a direct cost, such as selling a product, may impact revenue by decreasing overhead if online support is offered. Increasing customer loyalty is really retaining value over a prolonged period. You can sell to a person once, or you can sell to them many times—increasing loyalty is about repeat business.

The SEMPO and Econsultancy survey we looked at in Chapter 1 showed that over 50% of search managers struggle to get budget, secure executive buy-in, or make their business case. Clearly they are not speaking the language of those controlling the flow of money. Establish the value of your department or your program early, and ensure that it aligns with the overall goals of your business. Most businesses do not operate on "gut feeling"; they require data and research before investing into most programs. ROI is a universal language spoken across business units and groups, as well as companies.

If you are thinking about setting up a search program, whether paid search, SEO, or site search, you will likely need to justify how this will help your company. If you are the owner of the company, you will want to know if the effort you put in will generate a sufficient return on that investment. Even if you have already established some search programs, you will want to know if you are getting a good ROI. Your gut may tell you your programs are good, but do the facts and figures support this? Is there an opportunity to improve your programs further?

 Years ago, when I first got involved with search, it was on the paid side. One of our VPs was very smart, and also highly supportive of the decisions I made in my career. I was fortunate to not have to make a business case to invest into paid search.

Once the campaigns started, he began to review this data with me on a biweekly basis. He would review the cost per click of every campaign and keyword, and circle the ones that were "too expensive." Every couple of weeks he would tell me to remove those words because they cost too much, and every couple of weeks I would explain that the words were important because our competitors were bidding on them. This was before I realized that you don't have to be everywhere your competitors are. However, he would agree and we would let them run. I also argued to keep some of these words in play not just because competitors were bidding on them, but because they served a purpose in helping to assist in sales and building awareness.

Finally, one day I sat down and said, "OK, how much should we be bidding on per word?" He replied, "Less than a dollar, and I want the same quality of traffic and volume to keep coming." "When we get to that figure," I asked, "will you invest more?" He answered, "No."

To cut a long story short, we did get to that magic number. At our next meeting I said, "OK, we're at the magic number. I need to ask though, how much do you spend per click on display advertising?" When he told me the cost per click we averaged for display advertising, knowing how it converted on our site, I had no problem asking for a higher investment, and suggested it come from the display budget. He looked at the numbers and agreed, because I could show him a better return was happening on his paid search spend than on his display spend. This budget helped partially fund the salary for a dedicated person to work on search auditing and metrics, adding to our small team of search experts. All it took was understanding his goals, and then being able to compare his return by channel and spend. As they say, "money talks!" I just wish I had asked more questions about where we spent our budget a lot sooner.

Do you know how to estimate how much you are leaving on the table by not expanding your efforts? ROI should be about maximizing return while minimizing investment. In some cases, there may be a high initial investment with a long-term return that can be well worth the effort. Knowing your ROI is also a nice way to make the people who say "you are wasting your time" go away and encourage the people who control the purse strings to continue to invest in your programs. Having the value of what you do at hand through ROI calculations means you can stop worrying about justifying what you are doing and focus on getting it done.

Tools you will need in this chapter:

- Clickstream tracking package (Google Analytics, Adobe SiteCatalyst, etc.)
- Google Keyword Tool or some other keyword research tool
- Spreadsheet program (Excel or something similar)

ROI—The Universal Metric

There is one language that is understood universally across companies, and that is the language of finance. Every company is working to maximize its potential value and each one will have a different strategy for achieving this, but at the end of the day, a company can only be considered successful if it can afford to keep the lights on.

Every company has to pay taxes and every company has bills to pay. Some companies may believe in producing products that they want to use, while other companies may strive to provide the best customer experience and service possible—whatever their goals are, companies can only meet them by generating revenue.

ROI provides insights into the overall cost of an investment, taking into account everything from the marketing budget to the costs of equipment and software. There are other variations of ROI where the investment is defined differently. One of the more common variations you may see is return on ad spend (ROAS).

ROI and ROAS are calculated as follows:

ROI = ((Revenue - Cost) / Cost) × 100.

ROAS = ((Revenue - Advertising Cost) / Advertising Cost) × 100

Both ROI and ROAS are expressed as percentages, hence the multiplication by 100.

Here is the best way to think of the two. Suppose you are selling lemonade and you spend $25 on flyers that you put up around your neighborhood. Further suppose it costs another $25 to make that lemonade. The money you spend on flyers would be your ad spend, so you would need to make at least $25 to get a positive ROAS, while you would need to make $50 to get a positive ROI. To make this even more interesting, suppose you paid someone $25 to sit at your lemonade stand to sell the lemonade. That is another $25 that may not come out of your ad spend. Now you need to make $75 to have a positive ROI, but still only $25 for a positive ROAS.

For simplicity's sake, I will use the term ROI to talk about measuring the value of an investment. Understand, however, that there are several ways to measure this, and your own organization may have a specific way as well, depending on how budgets are split and defined.

As part of your measurement model, it is best practice to establish baselines. One of the first baselines you should establish is your ROI value. To do this, you will likely run through several stages of your analytics program. Bruce Clay uses the following framework (*http://www.bruceclay.com/web_analytics.htm*) that I think works very well:

> Determine Needs → Identify Goals → Define Metrics → Collect Data → Record Baseline → Test Improvement Strategies → Implement Improvements → Measure Results → Repeat Process Periodically

In Chapter 1, we talked about understanding your business needs and goals. At this point, we are starting to define our metrics. The first metric we want to define is how to capture an ROI value. We understand how to calculate this, but now we must capture and collect it.

Because ROI is tied to monetary value, we must identify actions that generate measurable revenue. There are two approaches: actual and estimated. Actual ROI is measured when you have direct access to purchase data and the referring lead. For example, offline you can use coupons to measure the direct impact of the source of those coupons.

Capturing Actual ROI

Online you can use clickstream data to track the impact certain web pages have on online sales. Capturing actual monetary values allows you to be much more specific about the return of an action. Discovering where sales happen, be they on or off your site, enables tracking of sales, providing instant insight into revenue. Further, capturing more granular data, such as information on products that are added to or removed from users' carts but never purchased, allows you to track opportunities you may be missing out on by not improving your checkout process or other sections of your site. Understanding what roadblocks are preventing people from making purchases is critical to finding ways to enable more purchases to happen. That said, actual revenue is a great number to have access to, and most clickstream tools, such as Adobe SiteCatalyst and Google Analytics, have the ability to capture this data. Spending the time to set this up can result in valuable insights that can target revenue specifically.

Your actual ROI will be captured as the revenue spent directly online or directly measurable to an action on your website. The ROI formula remains the same.

Capturing Estimated ROI

Estimated revenue or revenue influence is calculated by "guessing" how much revenue an action will generate. There are several online models where you do not have a direct line to impact ROI. You do, however, have influence. The following list shows direct and indirect actions that can impact ROI. Understanding attribution models such as direct influence versus indirect influence will enable you to have a much deeper understanding of your impact on ROI. Direct influences are measurable and attributed to sales through very clear channels (such as coupons, or referral IDs). Some actions may fall into both categories, depending on whether you apply a cost to them online:

- Offline sales (indirect or direct)
- Lead generation such as email opt-ins (indirect or direct)
- Relationship management such as PR and influential marketing (indirect)
- Purchases (direct)
- Downloading software (indirect or direct)
- Downloading a white paper (indirect or direct)
- Using a specific tool on your website (indirect or direct)
- Sharing content through social media (indirect or direct)
- Clicks on an ad (indirect or direct)
- Referrals to other sites (indirect or direct)

Using the example of selling products offline, you may need to make an estimate as to how many of your users will actually make a purchase offline. To arrive at this estimate, you can partner with a company such as ComScore or Compete to get industry analysis based on user panels, or you can gather data yourself by conducting surveys on your site (there are any number of online survey options, such as Survey Monkey). Surveys are a good way to find out about your users' buying intent. You can trigger surveys after specific actions, such as using a "help me choose" tool or an interactive demo, and you can ask the respondents targeted questions such as whether they intend to purchase a product, if they found the demo useful, how much they are planning to spend, in what time frame they plan on purchasing a product, and if they have purchased anything recently. Surveys are a very useful tool when used well.

The feedback you get from survey questions such as "Do you plan on making a purchase?," "How much do you plan to spend?," and "When do you plan on making the purchase?" will allow you to create some estimates. Based on sampling data, you can derive the average expected spend, and how close your customers are to making a purchase. This latter point allows you to identify whether a particular action is more likely to be taken by people closer to or farther from making a purchase.

Using this data, you can also see if there is a variance in average estimated revenue based on how close the customers are to making a purchase. The closer to purchase a customer is, the more likely it is that she has an idea of her budget; however, this number is typically on the low side, as the customer is shopping around and looking for the best deal. This is actually a good thing, as it's better to use conservative estimates when setting expectations. It's usually better to overperform than underperform.

In the case of email opt-ins or other lead-generation activities, you can establish a value per lead or name captured. Dividing the total number of leads by the average revenue generated by the leads will provide you with an average cost per acquisition.

It can be trickier to attach a monetary value to PR and marketing efforts, but it is still possible to establish an estimated impact to revenue. In very simple terms, advertising spend is typically based on the number of people it can influence—meaning that for each set of eyeballs there is a positive value or potential influence. If you understand the value of the eyeballs, you can create an online strategy that has an ROI comparable to that of your offline strategies. Consistently benchmarking across all routes to market allows for informed decision making.

Your estimated ROI will be captured as the revenue estimated through surveys and panel data to be based on an action on your website that influenced a sale that was not trackable directly by your metrics suite. The ROI formula remains the same.

Presenting ROI Data

Businesspeople understand dollars much better than they will ever understand inbound links, HTML tags, duplicate content issues, or any number of other issues you may feel are important. If you are lucky, you will be supported by people who trust you. Often, you will need to make a business case. When presenting your ROI data, you must make clear whether you are using direct or estimated values. Setting expectations clearly builds trust. Further, once you have an ROI value, you can begin to do some really neat stuff with this data.

The best search strategists focus on conversion. Having identified your key revenue points, you have also discovered what your top-line KPIs should be. These are the points you will want to optimize and improve upon with the traffic your search programs bring in.

When we talk about actionable analytics, optimizing against data points is a big one. Successful search marketers will think like salespeople and try to move people through to success events (e.g., sales). If you identify three or four different conversion points, and you know the different values of each of them, you can look at each point, start to build up ideas on how to improve them, and begin to make informed decisions based on revenue impacts.

By estimating the extent to which you can improve each point, you can begin to figure out where to attack first to improve the bottom line. For example, if today's revenue sits at $1,000/month, based on 10 users converting each month, you can project that doubling the number of conversion will also double the revenue each month, thus effectively doubling your investment. You can now present a current ROI and a projected ROI that will result from improving a conversion point or increasing traffic (that is, assuming that traffic converts at the same rate as before). By projecting estimates as to what you can do with your search program, you can create a better story about the opportunity that exists with the right investment. Most of this book will be dedicated to how to more accurately estimate the ROI and make decisions based on the impact it will have to your bottom line.

These improvements will come from improving your external search rankings, keywords, and targets, as well as what happens when users get to your site. While you do not have to be a user experience expert, you do need to understand how people move through your site, and what the goals of your site are.

Why Search Matters to Sales Online and Offline

To help you understand the impact search has on business, here are some quick facts on sales, user behavior, and search based on some recent survey data (*http://www.glob alspec.com/advertising/wp-detail/WP_BuyCycle* and *http://www.dhcommunications .com/2010/03/no-surprise-b2b-buyers-need-to-find-your-content/*):

- When searching for products and services to purchase, the top three resources people make use of are search engines, supplier websites, and online catalogs.
- 62% of people will type the company names they know into a search box rather than typing in the company URLs directly.
- 69% of people use social media to find information during their research phase.
- During the initial research phase, 42% of buyers evaluate four or more suppliers.
- When buyers move closer to finishing the deal, only 26% get quotes from those four suppliers.
- The 74% that cut their initial group of four down do so because those eliminated did not provide the right level of information.

Information on a website whose value is typically measured as driving "awareness" or "engagement" often has real-world impacts. Identifying the content on your site with the highest impacts to revenue through surveys, as discussed in "Capturing Estimated ROI" on page 29, will set you apart from your competition.

If 74% of purchasers eliminate potential sites to buy from because those sites do not provide enough information, it is clear that you will miss out on opportunities if your information is not open, accessible, and findable through search. Identifying the content on your site that works as a deal closer will help you identify which content needs to be monitored and, more importantly, indexed by search engines. Do you know what content helps close sales? Can you take the risk of turning business away because your site offers a poor web and search experience? The survey data also indicated that 69% of people use social media to find information during their "needs awareness and research" phase. Does your company show up in social circles? The more findable your business is, the more business opportunities you will have. Your website is the invisible sales rep that can stay with the customer and be called upon at any time.

Let us recap: search is not about marketing first, it is about being findable, because being findable leads to sales. Sales pay your check. Your check helps you maintain your standard of living. Improve your site's sales and be able to show the impact your work has had, and you will be more likely to get a "yes" than a "no" when you ask for improvements to your department. Build your ROI case first and figure out how to improve upon it, and you will be amazed at how quickly support comes your way. When they say "keep your eye on the ball," in this case the ball is sales. Try to keep that in mind as we look at other analytics throughout the rest of this book.

The Problem of Only Capturing ROI

ROI is a key measurement and the first thing you should look at, but how do you measure ease of use? How do you know if your online experience is a positive one for most of your customers? ROI won't tell you these things. If you plan on growing ROI, you need to understand the factors that will help you move the ROI needle. ROI is a dollar value; further analytics are needed to understand how to optimize your ROI values. These typically come in the form of measuring the user experience. Further, not all sites derive their revenue directly from sales. Facebook, for example, generates revenue through advertising, as does Google, and both have worked to create a great user experience, striving to maximize this user experience and increase profit. There is a reason why Google is the most-used engine while Overture is a thing of the past. It's why Facebook now rules, while MySpace is circling the drain. Connecting with users, and building experiences and communities, has helped these sites grow bigger than any competitor around them.

The goal of your analytics should be to improve the overall experience for your customers. A happy customer is a good customer. In some cases, a happy customer may simply be one who finds support quickly. There isn't direct ROI in this case; instead, you're looking at cost savings or customer satisfaction, both of which are part of the lifetime value of a customer. If you can show that improving self-support services on your website reduces costs, you have an ROI figure you can use. And even if it doesn't reduce costs on the support side, it may improve long-term customer loyalty. In these cases, you may need to estimate what the long-term value of a customer is. You may not be able to get an exact ROI, but you will be able to estimate the value of improving your customer experience.

Beyond ROI, you should also be looking to use your website to foster communication and dialog with your customers. People who find your site may have come with a specific intent and found that you don't offer what they are looking for. Running voice-of-the-customer surveys on your site can help you get feedback on what you can do to improve the site experience. Dialog may not have any direct ROI attached to it in this case, but you will get an idea of what people want, and that can drive improved ROI. You may get some ideas you can use to improve your customers' experience. You may also find that what your customers want is not what you think they need.

ROI is a value and it helps you to know if you will be profitable or not, but it can't tell you if customers are satisfied with the service you are providing. Ideally, customers will provide feedback to help you improve the overall experience.

As we look at ROI, keep in mind that to improve it you will need to look at many other metrics and analytics, related not only to increasing traffic to your site but also to improving the user experience once people have arrived. You need to start thinking beyond delivering users, and start to think about outcomes for users. Your job is to look at this data to figure out how to maximize profit. I see this being achieved by delivering more of the right people to the right web pages, improving what people currently do when they get to your pages, and making sure your site is as findable as possible by as many people as possible.

Interpreting Data and Studies to Build a Case

Many companies have split up their SEO and paid search strategies, which I think is a bad idea. The smart companies work to leverage paid search to fill holes in their SEO strategies, while also using SEO best practices to further improve their paid search campaigns. There are many studies that show the value of search, but the only study that really matters is the study of your website. I do not think that SEO is more important than paid search, or vice versa. I have worked on both sides of the search spectrum, and each has distinct advantages that complement the other. Looking to maximize both strategically is the best option.

Where Do People Click in the Search Results?

Historically, rankings have been important for organic search. Personalized search results are changing how sites rank in the first position organically, but from an estimate standpoint, we can use click data to help make informed decisions and to project and forecast ROI and the value of those positions.

Typically, the higher you rank, the more traffic you will get per term. Interestingly, I have also observed that a better rank on a term also results in an increase in time spent on the site, pages viewed, and goals or objectives completed by users. Further, I have observed that in a given time period, the engagement of people referred to the same page by the same word varies as a function of the page's ranking position. In this case, however, correlation does not equal causation.

I cannot say that higher rankings cause these effects. I cannot tell if these increases in user engagement are because the search engine is doing a better job at getting the right people to the right pages, or because changes made to the pages have resulted in improvements to the customer experience, or simply because the pages now rank better (and users trust higher rankings). I would assume it is a combination of all three. By creating content that is relevant to a search term, we increase the likelihood of our pages ranking well, and as a result of the relevancy and the rank, users are more likely to engage and complete goals on these pages.

In today's search environment, we have several sources of data that can help us understand how important position, ranking, type of search result, and more are related to *click-through rate* (CTR). Click-through rate is measured by taking the total number of times a search result is presented and the total number of times that link is clicked on. By dividing the number of clicks on a link by the total number of impressions, you will get the percentage of the total clicks that link got. That is your CTR.

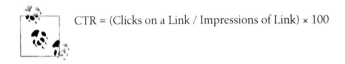 CTR = (Clicks on a Link / Impressions of Link) × 100

Knowing CTRs for rankings is important because it will allow you to project your ROI. By estimating traffic based on ranking and estimated search volumes, we can estimate how much of the volume we can capture by ranking in different positions. Having estimates of CTRs will help with our estimates as well as with making decisions about what words to optimize.

In August 2006, AOL released a large set of user data that had been analyzed to determine the average CTR of each position on Google's results pages (*http://bizthoughts .mikelee.org/the-click-through-rate-of-googles-search-results-page.html*). The results of this analysis continue to be reinforced today by newer studies (*http://searchenginewatch .com/article/2049695/Top-Google-Result-Gets-36.4-of-Clicks-Study*). These studies provide insight into how important a search engine result page (SERP) spot is. Figure 2-1 shows a breakdown of the positions, with the range of CTR percentages each position receives.

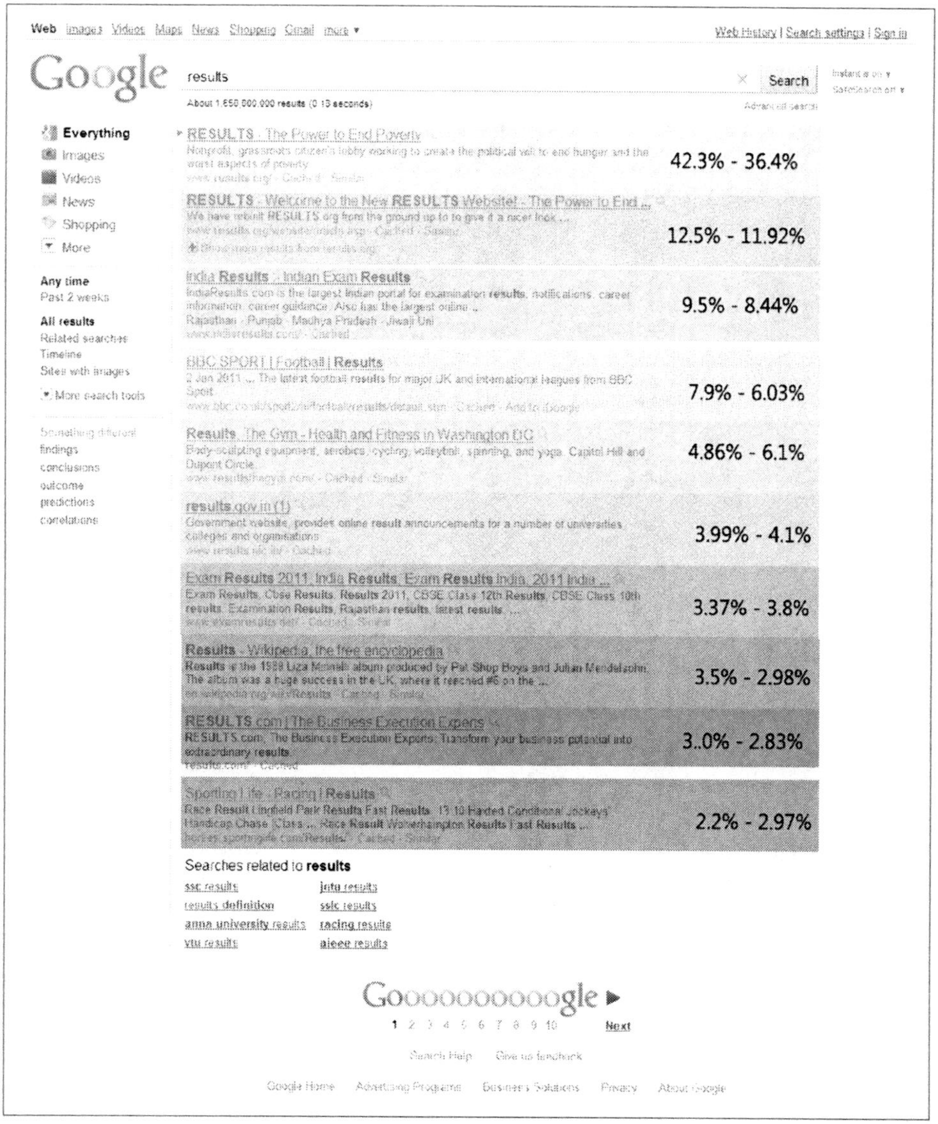

Figure 2-1. *CTR of organic search positions*

Eye tracking data from Mediative (*http://www.mediative.ca*) has also provided insights into user awareness of positions based on what rankings users look at (Figure 2-2). Analysis of this data showed that searchers typically begin by looking at the upper-left corner of search result pages, with some scanning to the right and downward. This results in an "F"-shaped pattern, also known as the "golden triangle."

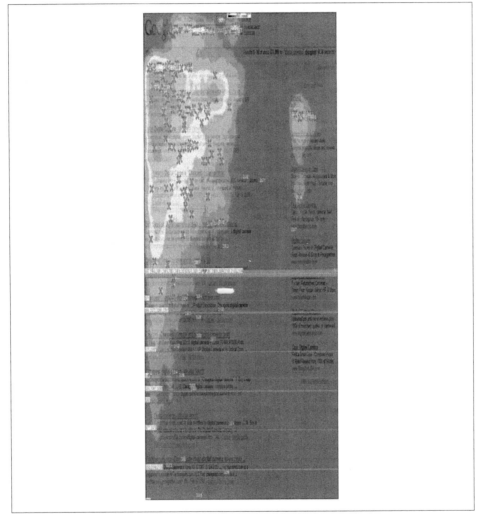

Figure 2-2. Eye tracking based on static results courtesy of Mediative

Recent changes in the user experience—such as the launch of Google Instant, which enables the page to be dynamically updated as a user types—have resulted in some changes to users' scanning behavior (Figure 2-3). There is less scanning down the page and less scanning to the right of the page, impacting the visibility of paid links as a user types. The visual focus is much more on the top results and the suggestions made as a user types. This shows that interface changes to a search engine can impact visibility—and potentially click-through rates as well. Decreases in traffic from search may be caused by changes in the interface of the results page, showing that while the algorithms used by search engines are important, how the results are displayed can be equally important.

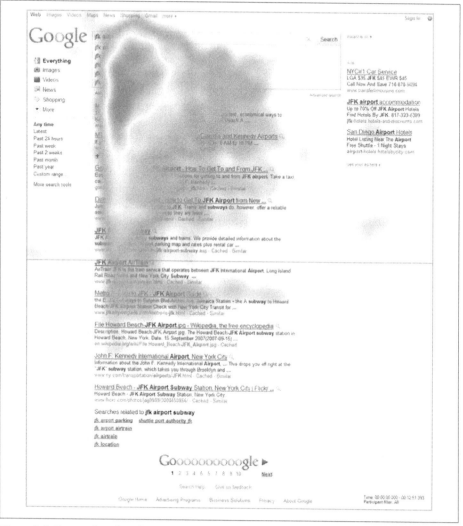

Figure 2-3. Eye tracking based on Google Instant results courtesy of Mediative

Universal search result click patterns

The term "universal search results" refers to content within the search results page that is called out separately—for example, videos, news results, weather forecasts, maps, and showtimes. This content is displayed very differently from typical search results (Figure 2-4). Universal results account for about 33% of search results on Google and 54% of searches on Bing. Universal results impact the CTR of regular links negatively, as the universal results receive more clicks than the other links (see *http://blog.com-Score.com/2010/10/universal_search.html, http://blog.comscore.com/2010/10/universal_search.html* and *http://searchengineland.com/iprospect-blended-search-resulting-in-more-clicks-on-news-images-and-video-13708*).

Universal or "blended" search result CTRs typically break down, as Table 2-1 shows. Some results have a CTR of over 100%, as a user may click on more than one search result in a single session (say, when comparison shopping). Essentially, universal or blended results end up skewing the data of simple searches toward these additional segments. This means a number 1 rank on a search result may not result in as high a CTR as you might expect if the SERP contains blended results. Now that Google Webmaster Tools can provide you with data on the number of impressions and CTRs of some of your organic keywords, you can verify whether your words are on track against these numbers based on position. If you are not trending well on some terms, it may be due to blended results hijacking your clicks.

Table 2-1. Universal search result CTRs (source: http://blog.comscore.com/2010/10/universal_search.html)

Universal type	SEO results—universal search
Shopping results	127%
Local results	107%
Dictionary definitions	80%
Maps	73%
Stock quotes	66%
News results	36%
Images results	31%
Video results	17%

Figure 2-4. Example of a universal search result

Paid search result CTRs

The last part of the puzzle is to know how many clicks you receive due to paid search versus SEO. The Mediative eye-tracking study shows us that side sponsored ad visibility is 50% for a number 1 position, while SEO rankings one through three get 100% visibility. The difference is even greater when we look at Google Instant. Further, comScore data reveals that paid search results receive about 22% of clicks on a SERP. In other words, SEO drives about three-quarters of the clicks.

However, paid search is a bit of a weird animal in that ranking, and while important, is not the only factor to consider: ad copy also plays an important role. Highly engaging, relevant ad copy and headlines can sway clicks, as well as the relevancy of the word being bid on. I have seen CTR on paid search go from 1% up to 15% or 20% depending on the term. For estimating ROI, we can use some baseline knowledge to understand how ads may perform based on position, with everything being equal. This also allows us to set a target to benchmark how well we expect our paid search campaigns to perform in terms of traffic volume.

The company First Rate conducted a study (*http://www.firstrate.com.au/blog/ctr-of-top-paid-ad-positions-revealed/*) to estimate CTR based on ad position. The results are presented in Table 2-2.

Table 2-2. Search result CTRs

Paid search SERP position	CTR of paid search based on position
1	17%
2	13%
3	7%
4	5%
5	5%
6	3%
7	5%
8	2%
9	1%

Comparing CTRs across all types of search

Table 2-3 shows the breakdowns of these results side by side. Universal search is a bit different in that it returns a group of results, so if shopping results were to show up, it is almost guaranteed that a user will click on one of these. Usually, when universal search results are returned, the search term was specific to something that could have a visual representation or content in another format, such as shopping results or videos.

Table 2-3. Search results CTR

SERP position	SEO results—no universal search	Universal type	SEO results— universal search	Paid search SERP position	Paid search CTR
1	42.3%	Shopping results	127%	1	17%
2	11.92%	Local results	107%	2	13%
3	8.44%	Dictionary definitions	80%	3	7%
4	6.03%	Maps	73%	4	5%
5	4.86%	Stock quotes	66%	5	5%
6	3.99%	News results	36%	6	3%
7	3.37%	Images results	31%	7	5%
8	2.98%	Video results	17%	8	2%
9	2.83%			9	1%
10	2.97%				
11 and beyond	0.66%				

Knowing each of these CTRs will help you estimate the traffic you can expect from search terms. Once you have estimates for all of your terms, you can estimate an ROI value based on position and ranking to build a business case. You can estimate the volume of traffic you expect to see, and using clickstream data from Adobe SiteCatalyst, Google Analytics, or whatever else you use, you can estimate based on traffic increases to certain pages how many additional goals will be completed. Finally, having assigned a value to those goals, you can estimate the projected ROI for your program.

Let's look at an example of estimating ROI from CTR. Assume you can get 100 people to your site through improvements to search, and assume that 10% of people on your site today complete a goal with a value of $10 each. The extra 100 people should mean an increase of 10 more goal completions per day (10% of 100), for an increase of $100 total. If it only costs you $20 to make this improvement, you can then estimate your ROI as:

(($100 -$20)/$20) × 100.

for an estimated ROI of 400%.

You should note in Table 2-3 that the second and final columns do not add up to 100%. This is because clicks may happen on secondary pages, or after new search terms are entered. Finally, Figure 2-5 shows us what search CTRs are like when both SEO and paid search results are returned. The paid search results may change based on if you receive a number 1 result above the SEO results or to the right of the SEO results. When situated to the right of the SEO results, a number 1 paid search result gets only about

3% of clicks; more clicks go to the number 1 SEO result. Thus, it's not only position that's important, but location on the page as well. As we'll see shortly, there are sources we can use to help us predict search volumes.

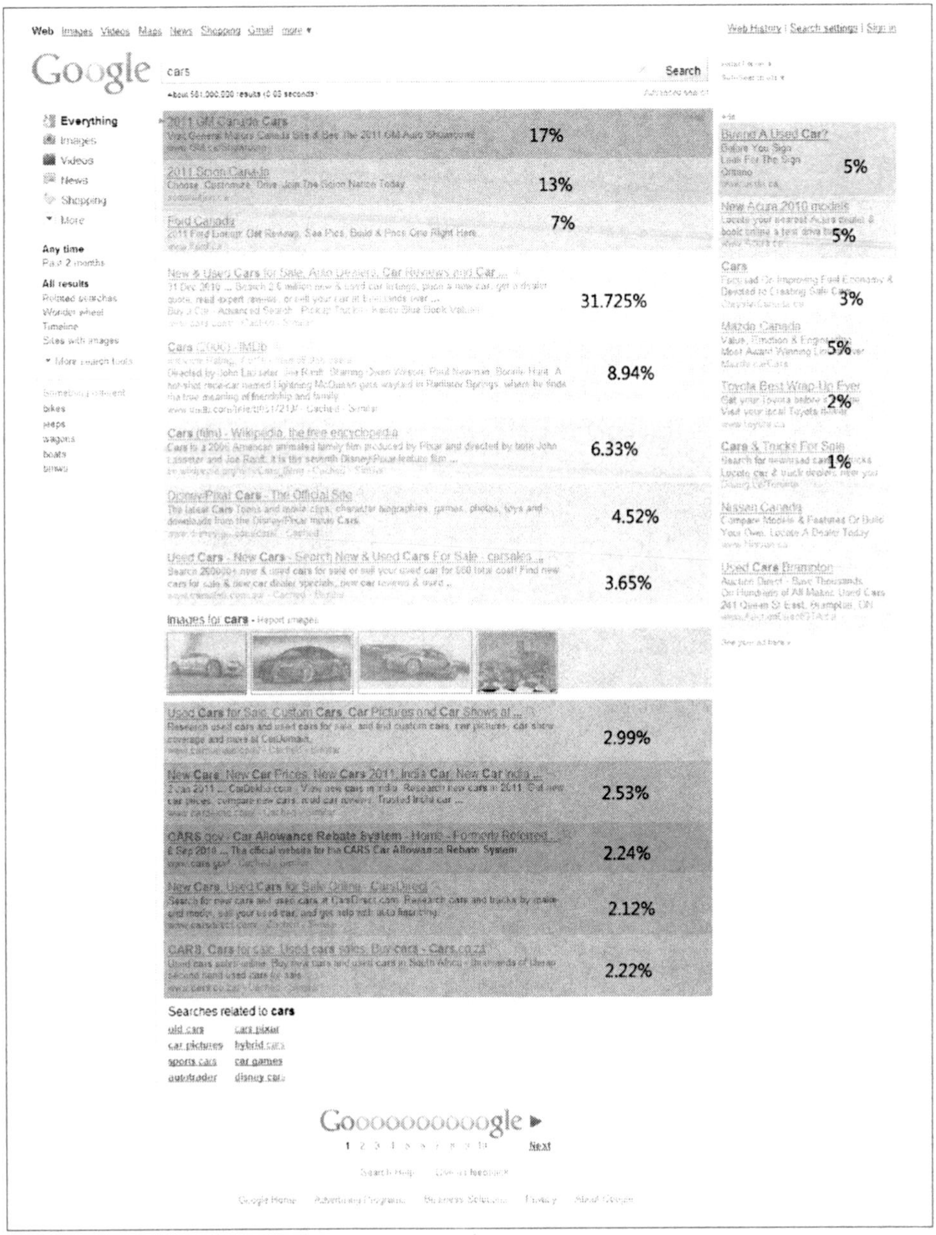

Figure 2-5. Search results with scattered CTR across paid and organic results

What's the Average Spend of SEO and Paid Search?

Engine Ready conducted a study that compared many interesting data points to show how SEO and paid search stack up (*http://searchenginewatch.com/article/2051411/SEO -vs.-PPC-Heavyweights-Duke-it-Out-at-SES-Chicago-2009*). As I've said, I think they should be viewed as complementary, but this study does provide some data that it will be useful to investigate:

> The second study scrutinized the order-value to see if users coming from paid ads were buying more or less than organic search referrals. It turns out that people coming from paid ads spend an average of $117 compared to $106 via organic.

While organic search referrals may result in a lower average spend, if we quickly apply what we know about the volume differences of traffic (25% of traffic comes from paid search and 75% from SEO) we can see if the lower spend actually means less money. Table 2-4 illustrates this.

Table 2-4. Comparing average spend values

Source	Total visits	Average spend value	Total spend of all orders
SEO total	9	$106	$954
Paid search total	5	$117	$585
SEO position #1	4	$106	$424
Paid search position #1	3	$117	$351

As you can see, SEO generates more revenue than paid search, even with a lower average spend by customers. Keep in mind that while you can use average spend for other great insights, it is not a good metric to use to identify which of your campaigns are generating better overall returns.

> The formula to calculate average spend per visit is:
>
> Average Spend = Sum of Revenue Generated / Number of Visits with a Spend

Wal-Mart is a good example of the power of low prices and high volumes. Stores like this don't look to make large volumes of money by selling highly priced products; instead, they look to do large volumes of sales of heavily discounted products. If we think about search as a whole in the same way, SEO should drive more overall sales based on volume, while paid search may generate more revenue because it can be highly targeted.

What's a Visit Worth?

Knowing how much each visit is worth, or the value per visit, allows you to get a very granular value for the worth of each customer. This in turn helps you identify how much you should invest into acquiring each new visit. The same study from Engine Ready cited the following as a trend for value per visit:

> On average a [visit] from a paid ad is worth $2.38 while [its] organic counterpart is worth $1.35.

Table 2-5 shows that if we assume the same segmentation patterns we have seen between SEO and paid search exist and we look only at total visits, SEO will be responsible for a larger portion of the traffic than paid search. If we assume again 1,000 visits to the site, approximately 750 will be from SEO and 250 from paid search. We are looking at the value of the average visit, so we just want to look at the totals, without taking into account positional ranking. We know that SEO typically generates three times as much traffic as paid search. The average value of a visit from paid search, however, isn't even twice as much as the average value of a visit from SEO. Just knowing this, we can tell that SEO will provide more value overall than paid search, due to the larger traffic volume. We also can see that our total values are pretty close to the paid search and SEO total values we calculated in the preceding section.

Table 2-5. Differentiation of SEO and paid search when looking at absolute total values

Source	Total visits	Average value of a visit	Total value of visits
SEO total	750	$1.35	$1,012.50
Paid search total	250	$2.38	$595

Knowing the average value of a visit is important if you want to figure out how much you can spend per visit before running into a negative ROI or if you want to compare this value to the average cost per acquisition (CPA).

The formula to calculate value per visit is:

Value per Visit = (Conversion Rate of Visits / 100) × Average Spend

We divide the conversion rate by 100 to convert percentages to decimal points. If you know your margins and can use them in calculating the average spend, that can allow for a much more accurate number to work with.

The formula to calculate average cost per acquisition for SEO and paid search is:

SEO Average Cost per Acquisition = Any Monetary Investment / Total Number of SEO or Paid Search Conversions

Recall that an acquisition may be anything from purchasing products to signing up for a newsletter; it will not necessarily have a direct revenue attached to it.

An Example of Calculating Values

If we had 750 visits come from SEO and converted 9 of them, and we spent 4 hours working to get that traffic and were paid $10 per hour, we would have spent $40 to get 9 people to our website who actually bought something from us via SEO. This means we would have spent $4.44 per acquisition ($40 spent in man hours / 9 conversions = $4.44 per acquisition).

This means that we are spending more per acquisition than the average visit is worth ($1.35). We now know we need to get either our number of visits up or our conversion rate up, so at least 30 conversions happen for every 4 hours of work we put into acquiring customers. At this point, we would just be breaking even.

Here's how we would calculate the cost per acquisition for paid search, again assuming nine conversions and a labor cost of $40 (4 hours work at $10 per hour):

1. If we had an average cost per click (CPC) of $1.25 and had 250 visits come from paid search, this means the total spent on clicks was $312.50.
2. If we add this figure to the labor cost, we get $352.50 as our total investment.
3. Dividing our total investment by the total number of paid search conversions (9) gives us an average cost per acquisition of $39.17.

Again, we have a few options to improve our average cost per acquisition here: we can try to get our average CPC down, or we can attempt to improve the conversion rate on our site.

Quickly Identifying Bad Investments

With new search campaigns, you should expect to see small returns at first, but be able to optimize your campaigns to meet your targets and get a positive return very quickly. Still, there is a point where it is just a bad decision to make the effort or investment. We can find this point quickly with our cost per acquisition: the break-even point should be greater than or equal to the CPA.

 The formula to calculate the break-even point is:

Break-even Point = Net Profit × Conversion Rate

Break-even Point ≥ Cost per Acquisition

To calculate the break-even point for your search campaign, either SEO or paid, you need to know the average value of your sales. Say you're selling bikes for $400 and you make a net profit of 20% for every bike sold, or $80 per bike. This means you have $80 to spend on marketing before you start losing money on every sale.

Assume you see an average conversion rate of 2.03% from your paid search campaigns. Your break-even point, or the maximum cost per click you should be paying to ensure you don't lose money is $80 × 2.03%, which gives you $1.62. This means you should not be bidding on words worth more than $1.62. Anything above this and you will be running the risk of seeing a negative ROI.

Compound this with other marketing activities you may want to run, such as web banners, and this break-even point comes down even more. If you wanted to allocate only half of your profit margin to paid search, you would be looking at an even further reduced value to play with. A key part of your paid search campaign strategy is knowing the maximum that you should spend per lead, on average. As long as the overall average cost per click from paid search is less than the $1.62, you can run a profitable program even if some words are more expensive than the cost per acquisition.

You can also calculate how much you would have to increase your profit margin to justify bidding on higher-cost terms. For example, changing your average bid from $1.62 to $1.80 would mean that you would be looking at $1.80 divided by 2.03%, giving you a new total price of $88.67. Thus, you would need to increase the cost of your bikes by $8.67 to increase the cost per click by 18 cents. In the world of search, profitability is measured by pennies.

Paid Search and ROI

Now that you have some background on understanding the value of your SEO and paid search campaigns, we'll dive deeper into some of the nuances of each type of campaign, as you will have different concerns for your SEO and paid search programs. We will look at this at both a macro level and micro level of detail, as well as action and value analytics.

How to Estimate ROI for Paid Search

Tracking your goal conversions for both SEO and paid search can help you to identify where one program is more successful than the other, and possibly to apply that success to the other program, if it's relevant. Due to the tighter control over paid search, from the search experience down to the website experience, my expectation is that paid search will have a higher conversion rate.

Testing the effectiveness of your paid search campaigns is a quick and easy way to spot where you can make targeted improvements to optimize your conversion rate.

As I've said before, the first thing you will need to do is figure out what you define as a conversion goal or "lower funnel activity" on your website.

You can attach values to different kinds of conversion actions. For example, you can figure out the value of an opt-in to your email newsletter by tracking the emails you send out and the average value of orders made by customers who come to the site through a link in the newsletter. You can also attach a dollar value to the action of users contacting a sales associate, by having associates document how many sales they close from web leads. At this point, we are only looking at the general conversion rate or baseline for your website. If you have set up a clickstream tool for capturing conversion statistics, you may be able to pull the data directly out of it (as shown in Table 2-6, for example).

The three metrics in Table 2-6 can be utilized in a great number of ways. Average spend value—or in the case of direct ecommerce, average order value—tells us how much a single user will spend when making a purchase. Average conversion rate lets us know how strong a lower funnel activity is at closing a deal, and average value per visit tells us how much perceived value there is in getting someone to accomplish the lower funnel activity. By segmenting out each of our goals and capturing these metrics, we can see which lower funnel activity provides the highest chance of a sale happening (average conversion rate), as well as which has the highest value (average value per visit). It is the average value per visit that we will use to estimate our ROI.

Table 2-6. Value of different conversions

Conversion action	Average spend value	Average conversion rate	Average value per visit
Purchase product	$520	2.03%	$10.56
Sign up for email	$268	5.1%	$13.69
Contact sales associate	$700	1.2%	$8.40

Search engines make it easy to track metrics such as ROI with free tools provided through Google AdWords and Microsoft AdCenter. It only takes a few minutes to set up an account. You can sign up for Google AdWords at *https://adwords.google.com/* and Microsoft AdCenter at *https://adcenter.microsoft.com/*.

Once you have an account set up at Google, you can find the Traffic Estimator shown in Figure 2-6 by going to *https://adwords.google.com/select/TrafficEstimatorSandbox*. Here, you can input what your maximum CPC and daily budget will be. The tool will provide estimates of average CPC and estimated ad position. The tool does for you a lot of the work that we were doing before. Remember that these are estimates, and the numbers may be different when applied to a real campaign.

Using the terms "bikes" and "red bikes" on broad match, we see an estimated average CPC of $0.73 and $0.00, likely due to low search volumes. These are very loose estimates, but for exploratory purposes they will work for us. We can also set our own max CPC. Knowing our break-even point, we can use that value to see what volumes of traffic we could expect for these terms. If we just want a quick check that this term isn't going to be costing us money per search, we can verify that the CPC doesn't ever

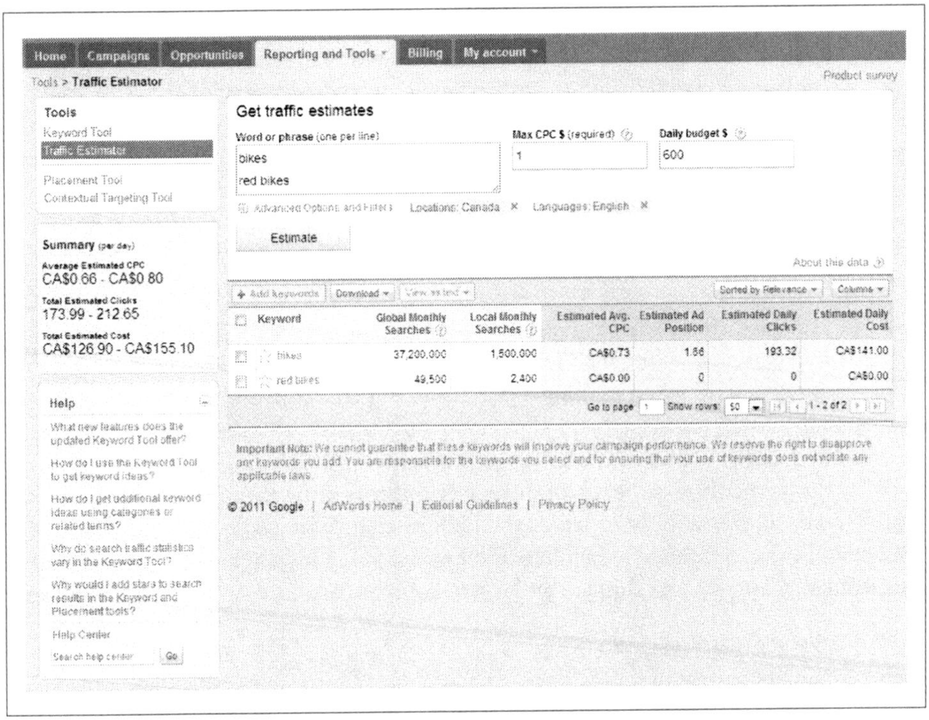

Figure 2-6. Traffic and CPC estimates from Google Traffic Estimator

go over our break-even point. If we really want to do our job well, we may look at multiple words to figure out which sets will provide us the best ROI. We want to maximize clicks while minimizing CPC.

A term you will hear in the search landscape over and over is the *long tail*. Originally popularized by Chris Anderson in *Wired* magazine, and later in his book *The Long Tail: Why the Future of Business Is Selling Less of More* (Hyperion), the term essentially refers to the fact that there are more searches on unique or smaller groups of search terms than there are on the most popular terms. A good example of the *long tail* is that in total, Amazon sells more books not in its top 100 list than all the books in its top 100 list combined. More action happens in the long tail than in the short head. Figure 2-7 shows an example of the short head, the midtail, and the long tail. The further you move to the right, the further into the long tail you get. Midtail terms are usually the sweet spot we are looking for. They are words with enough search volume to drive traffic, but not enough competition to have multiple bids on them. These terms should offer the best combination of affordability and results.

You will need to do keyword research, in the paid search tools provided, and look at the estimated CPC and estimated traffic. You will likely find out that bidding on four terms is better than bidding on one term. Think of it this way: if the term "bike" has an average CPC of $1.25 and will generate an estimated 100 clicks, this means we'll

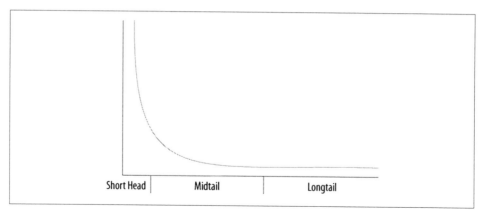

Figure 2-7. *The long tail and the short head*

spend $125 on that one word. In contrast, the terms "red bike," "blue bike," "green bike," and "purple bike" each have an average CPC of $0.50, and each generates 25 clicks. We will still see our 100 clicks, but we will only have spent $50. Looking at this strictly in terms of traffic volume, this is clearly a better spend.

Now we can use the data from Table 2-6 to calculate estimated ROI values for both the term "bike" and our long-tail variations. This will give us a better idea of which program should work better for us. The results are presented in Table 2-7.

Paid Search ROI = (Average Value per Visit - Average CPC) × Estimated Traffic

Table 2-7. *Value of different conversions*

Conversion action	Average value	Average conversion rate	Average value per visit	Estimated ROI on "bike"	Estimated ROI on long-tail terms
Purchase product	$520	2.03%	$10.56	$931	$1,006
Sign up for email	$268	5.1%	$13.69	$1,244	$1,319
Contact sales associate	$700	1.2%	$8.40	$715	$790

How to Capture and Track ROI for Paid Search

Now that we have our estimates, we want to validate whether they hold true. Google and Bing each provide conversion tracking functions within their ad bid tools. Conversion tracking is implemented through a generated JavaScript that is placed on your conversion page. The tracking is getting more robust, but it currently only provides insights into conversions; you may also want to look at pathing and other clickstream data. For this reason, I suggest you spend some time configuring your clickstream tool of choice, be it Adobe SiteCatalyst or Google Analytics, to capture and track the results of your paid search campaigns. If you use the same account for both Google Analytics and Google AdWords, you can capture data from AdWords in the analytics tool by clicking Edit on the overview page beside the appropriate report, then clicking "Edit" in the "Main Website Profile Information" section, and finally clicking "Apply Cost Data."

In Adobe SiteCatalyst, you can capture paid search data by creating variables that are captured in a custom insight variable (sProp) by keyword, and then capturing each campaign in an eVar to segment based on campaigns. This is perhaps the simplest option. You can then segment some clickstream data by keywords, by setting the values of your sProp and eVar variables in the referring URL from the paid search tool.

You can also combine SiteCatalyst data with SearchCenter+ data to gain deeper insights, and to manage your keywords based on these insights. Because SearchCenter+ has access through APIs both to the clickstream data that includes your conversion events and to the keyword data (including cost per click), you can set up alerts based on keyword performance, perform attribution modelling, and even include organic search data. The challenge of SearchCenter+ is that because it can easily be automated without an understanding of what your CPA and CPC are, you may find that your campaigns run you, instead of the other way around. For this reason, I will focus not on specific tools but instead on fundamental ideas, which should be platform-agnostic. Our examples use the free tool Google Analytics simply due to its accessibility to a wide audience.

Conversion Rates by Keyword

The first thing we want to figure out is what our actual conversion rates are. We will also want to conduct some experiments. Remember that when we estimated our ROI, we used the site's average conversion rate. What we find with search, though, is that different words can have different conversion rates. While we saw that our four mid- to long-tail terms were cheaper to purchase than one short head term, we don't know if they will convert as well as our site average. We will want to keep track of our terms in a spreadsheet so we can see which terms truly have the best conversion rates. In some cases, you may be able to get this information directly from your web analytics tool. For example, in Google Analytics, you can set up goals and track words to goals, as shown in Figure 2-8. You can find this feature in Google Analytics under Traffic Sources→Keywords. If you have already set up site goals and words to show, you will see tabs such as "non-paid," "paid," and "total," which is both combined. This can make tracking conversion rate per word much easier.

Figure 2-8. An example of Google Analytics tracking words by conversion rate

If you have not yet set up site goals and you are running an instance of Google Analytics with ecommerce not selected, take a few minutes to set up some site goals (if you are running a commerce site, you will need to enable commerce tracking and tagging, which is much more complex than the process described in the following steps):

1. Click on "Analytics Settings," in the upper-left corner.
2. Select the profile you want to set up an action on and click "Edit."
3. You will see a section titled "Goals." You can set up to 20 goals. Go to your first goals set, and click "Add goal."
4. Give the goal a name.
5. Make sure the goal's active state is set to On.
6. Set the goal position you want it to be in.
7. Select the Goal Type (in most cases this will be a URL Destination).
8. Set up your URL to track.
9. Click on "Save Goal."

Once you have goals, setting up tracking of conversion rates and profits happens automatically. You will also be able to export your lists to CSV format to make sorting and manipulating the data easier in spreadsheets. What you will be looking for is whether your keyword sets convert at better or worse than the site average. You may also decide early on to test your short tail words against your long tail words; a short tail word may or may not have a better conversion rate than the long-tail terms.

When it comes to tracking referral data such as clicks from search campaigns, there are three different methodologies. They are referred to as "first-click," "last-click," and "multiclick" or "multiple-click" tracking:

First-click attribution
> In this method, the first click that leads someone to your website is attributed the conversion. It is known that before buying something, a customer may view your site multiple times. The first click is the one that initially brought them to your site, on their first visit.

Last-click attribution
> The most popular form of tracking; as you may have guessed, the last click that brought the user to the site is awarded the conversion attribution, regardless of any previous visits or referrals.

Multiple-click or multiclick attribution
> The most sophisticated form of tracking: multiple-click tracking attributes the conversion to the last click, but also provides each of the past clicks that are considered assists.

Each of these forms of attribution has its pluses and minuses. Google Analytics currently provides only last-click tracking, although there are hacks available to enable first-click attribution. Typically, you will see that the last clicks are branded words as opposed to generic words. Adobe SiteCatalyst and other enterprise-level analytics tools can be configured for multiclick tracking and may be worth checking out if you have the budget and sophisticated enough programs to warrant this. Google Analytics has only recently begun to explore this space, with Multi-Channel Funnels (Figure 2-9) currently in beta with some users. Multi-Channel Funnels allow you to track assists and last clicks, as well as to look at how different channels mix with each other.

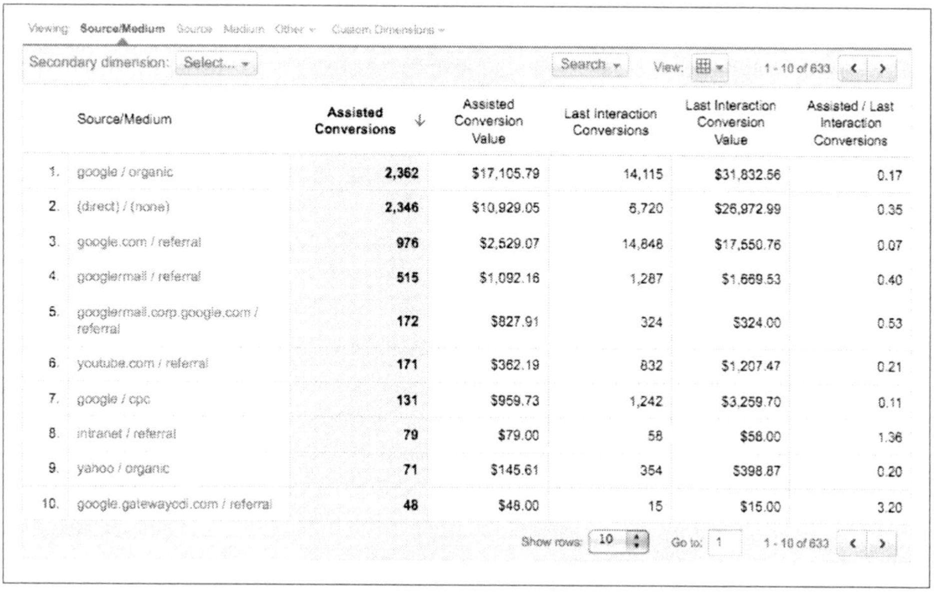

	Source/Medium	Assisted Conversions	Assisted Conversion Value	Last Interaction Conversions	Last Interaction Conversion Value	Assisted / Last Interaction Conversions
1.	google / organic	2,362	$17,105.79	14,115	$31,832.56	0.17
2.	(direct) / (none)	2,346	$10,929.05	6,720	$26,972.99	0.35
3.	google.com / referral	976	$2,529.07	14,848	$17,550.76	0.07
4.	googlermail / referral	515	$1,092.16	1,287	$1,669.53	0.40
5.	googlermail.corp.google.com / referral	172	$827.91	324	$324.00	0.53
6.	youtube.com / referral	171	$362.19	832	$1,207.47	0.21
7.	google / cpc	131	$959.73	1,242	$3,259.70	0.11
8.	intranet / referral	79	$79.00	58	$58.00	1.36
9.	yahoo / organic	71	$145.61	354	$398.87	0.20
10.	google.gatewaycdi.com / referral	48	$48.00	15	$15.00	3.20

Figure 2-9. An example of Google Analytics Multi-Channel Funnels, courtesy of Justin Cutroni

It is worth looking into eventually getting into tracking the first and last and each assist along the way, but for now we will address the last click (Table 2-8), as you may run into some issues calculating ROI by tallying up first and last clicks.

Table 2-8. Value of different conversions based on first or last click

Keyword	First-click attributes	Last-click attributes
Bike	58	6
Red Bike	15	20
Green Bike	10	30
Blue Bike	8	22
Purple Bike	18	14
Totals	109	92

Many paid search programs are built with last click in mind, as it has the lowest cost per click. Looking at this data, though, we see that while the term "bike" may not have accounted for many of the last clicks, it had a very strong influence on early decision making. Basically, it is the term that introduced the customers to our website. This is not to say this is the pattern you will always see, but this is a key analytic to look at. Now that we know the term "bike" is sending us more traffic than we may have thought if we only looked at last-click attribution, we want to know if we are getting a positive ROI from this term. The challenge is that the term "bike" may have resulted in a last click on the term "red bike" or another click on the term "bike." We can therefore run into a double counting issue if we cannot tie visit sessions to unique users. We also know that in some cases, a first click can also be the last click, which means we will always have more first clicks in total than last clicks.

Some paid search programs will track their own attributions to sales or other success events (e.g., Google AdWords Conversion Tracking: see *http://adwords.google.com/ support/aw/bin/answer.py?hl=en&answer=115794*). The challenge of relying on attributions from these services is that they do not consider any other media that may have resulted in conversion. They essentially only track their own programs, so if an email campaign closes the deal for a particular user, this will result in an attribution to the last keyword that delivered that person to the site, while truthfully it should have been counted as an assist.

We also should know the total number of clicks from all paid search campaigns, regardless of whether they resulted in a conversion or not. The total number of clicks (refers) will likely be higher than either your first or last click attributions, because:

- Some first clicks are also last clicks, which also means some last clicks are also first clicks.
- Some first clicks are followed by a second click that is a last click.
- Some first clicks are followed by one or more intermediate clicks (assists) before the last click.
- Some clicks will never result in a conversion.

Those intermediate clicks will not be captured as first or last clicks. If your web tracking software allows for it, you can track these clicks as assists. You should also start to see that sales attribution is not a simple matter of the last click being the only influencer in creating a sales opportunity.

Like some sales folks, there are strong openers and strong closers. We want to be able to figure out which of our terms are strong openers, as well as which are strong closers. To figure this out, we need to calculate an average value per customer for both openers and closers (Table 2-9). We'll assume an average order value of $520 for each word, though in the real world you may find that some words produce higher and lower average order values. Looking at only last-click conversion rates may be misleading. For example, in Table 2-9 we see that "bike" as an opener has a very strong average value per visit. On the other end of the spectrum, we see that "green bike" is a very strong closer. While the term "bike" may have opened a lot of doors, it certainly didn't close many deals, finishing with the weakest average value per visit.

Table 2-9. Comparing terms based on first and last click value

Keyword	First-click attributes	Average CPC	Conversion rate	First-click average value per visitor	Last-click attributes	Conversion rate	Last click average value per visitor
Bike	58	$1.28	29%	$150.80	6	3%	$15.60
Red Bike	15	$1.17	7.5%	$39.00	20	10%	$52.00
Green Bike	10	$0.98	5%	$26.00	30	15%	$78.00
Blue Bike	8	$2.03	4%	$20.80	22	11%	$57.20
Purple Bike	18	$1.14	9%	$46.80	14	7%	$36.40
Totals	109	$1.32	10.9%	$56.68	92	9.2%	$47.84

Based on the totals, we can also see that our first clicks as a whole produce a higher average value per visitor. This is to be expected, as we are tracking any first click from paid search. We now have enough information to decide if each of these keywords are effective in our campaign. By subtracting the average CPC from the average value per visitor, we can see if these words are creating a negative ROI when tracking either first- or last-click attributions. If our example had resulted in last clicks showing a negative return for a particular word, we might have thought about pulling that word from our campaign, but if that same word was shown to be a very strong opener, we might have reconsidered that strategy, or perhaps decided to pull the word but measure the impact the removal has on other channels that are closing deals for us.

You now have one more powerful piece of information in your toolbox. If you find that your paid search keywords are simply not converting to sales, you might want to go back and look at first-click attribution. You may discover that many leads come from paid search, but that the deals are closed with emails or banner campaigns instead.

The challenge you will have is to figure out what your spend should be on first-click terms with high average value per visitor numbers. If you know that these are not strong closers, you will have to reduce this figure to allow budgeting for a greater spend in the areas further down the purchase funnel that are driving the close of the deal, just as you would need to reduce this value for last-click terms if you found out that the sales they were closing were affected by other factors at the top of the funnel. Looking at our total average values per visitor, we can see that for first click we sit at around $56.68, and for last click at $47.84. This means our campaign's average CPC as a whole should not be more than $47.84, or the lowest total overall value for our campaign.

This kind of analysis lets us justify spending more on a term like "bike," which we know is a big contributor earlier in the funnel, even if later in the funnel it may actually result in what appears to be a loss per click (say, if the word sells for $20 per click). In this case, we know our campaign can support the CPC of this word because the campaign total average value per visitor sits at $47.84, so some words will pick up the slack that this word may appear to have when looking at last clicks. You may also experiment with your terms and try pausing some of your low-closing last-click terms, even if they have high first-click average value per visitor. You may find that this will have a negative impact later on your last clicks and that their conversion rates drop. However, you may discover that your brand is strong enough that your last-click conversion rates remain the same, and that you are spending money on a term that appears to be assisting later sales but in actuality has no influence.

So far, we have not identified what kind of influence a first click will have on a last click; we have only identified that our paid search campaigns may have more value in different parts of the buying cycle, and we are trying to assess which parts those may be. If a last-click strategy does not make sense for your business, you may end up instead using the first-click average value per visitor when trying to establish if the words you are bidding on have a positive or negative ROI.

SEO and ROI

We know how to predict ROI for our paid search terms, and we can utilize the same or similar data for our SEO terms. There are a couple differences when looking at SEO versus paid search, though. The biggest difference is that SEO does not have any CPC. We will instead only need to worry about time invested in our SEO work. We also may see that SEO changes in one place have unpredictable changes in another place. Say, for example, we have a site that ranks number 1 for the term "bike shops," but we also want to rank on the term "bikes." We might find that our "bike shops" ranking starts to dip because of the work we are doing to improve our ranking on the term "bikes." Changes in one location for SEO may have a trickle-down effect to other pages. Conversely, the SEO work you do may also have an overall uplift on the *long tail* volume of search you see. Because of these complexities, when looking at SEO you will want to establish how to capture ROI for a word as well as how to track ROI for your overall SEO program.

How to Estimate ROI for SEO

The first thing we will need to do is build up a list of words for which we want to establish an ROI. We want to know if these are words that will be worth pursuing financially. We begin by building out a keyword list like the one in Table 2-10, where we capture for each term the total number of searches and the current and target ranking position (later, we will look at how to capture position and monitor it automatically; for now, you can pull this information manually).

If you are trying to pull ranking results from Google, you need to append *&pws=0* to the URL and ensure that instant search is turned off. This disables personalized results, which are created based on your search history and, if your account is tied to social networks such as Twitter, Google Plus, or other social websites that share data with the search engines.

The external Google Keyword Tool (*https://adwords.google.com/select/KeywordToolEx ternal*), shown in Figure 2-10, provides us with search volume estimates. Uncheck "only show ideas closely related to my search terms" and plug in your terms. Once you have results, uncheck Broad on the left and check [Exact]. If you are targeting a specific country, you should also update the location and language under "advanced options." This will ensure that you are provided with the exact number of searches on the exact pairing and order of words for the specified country and language. In a paid search world, these settings let you define what variations of pairings your ad will show up in. In SEO, where we are targeting a specific word or set of terms, it lets us know how many times that word or set of terms has been searched in a specific country or language.

Table 2-10. Current position of words, targeted position, and estimated traffic increase

Keyword	Total searches	Current ranking position	Current traffic	Targeted ranking position	Estimated traffic	Change in traffic volume
Bike	33,100	10	690	6	989	43%
Red Bike	260	7	7	4	11	57%
Green Bike	210	12	1	10	4	300%
Blue Bike	390	—	—	10	8	—
Purple Bike	170	4	8	1	54	500%

You will also note that we are not trying to get a number 1 position for everything: we have made attainable targets, which should be based on who our competitors are and which sites are ranking ahead of us. We will also see later in this book that sometimes it is little fixes that are needed to move up in rankings, and other cases it is big fixes. Another option would be to build a grid like in Table 2-11, where we simply take a term and show what each position is worth for the top 10 organic spots. As we discussed in Chapter 1, the CTR of organic positions differs when paid search results are also presented. To future-proof us, we will use the mixed SEO and paid search results, as I prefer to underreport and set expectations low than overreport and set expectations high.

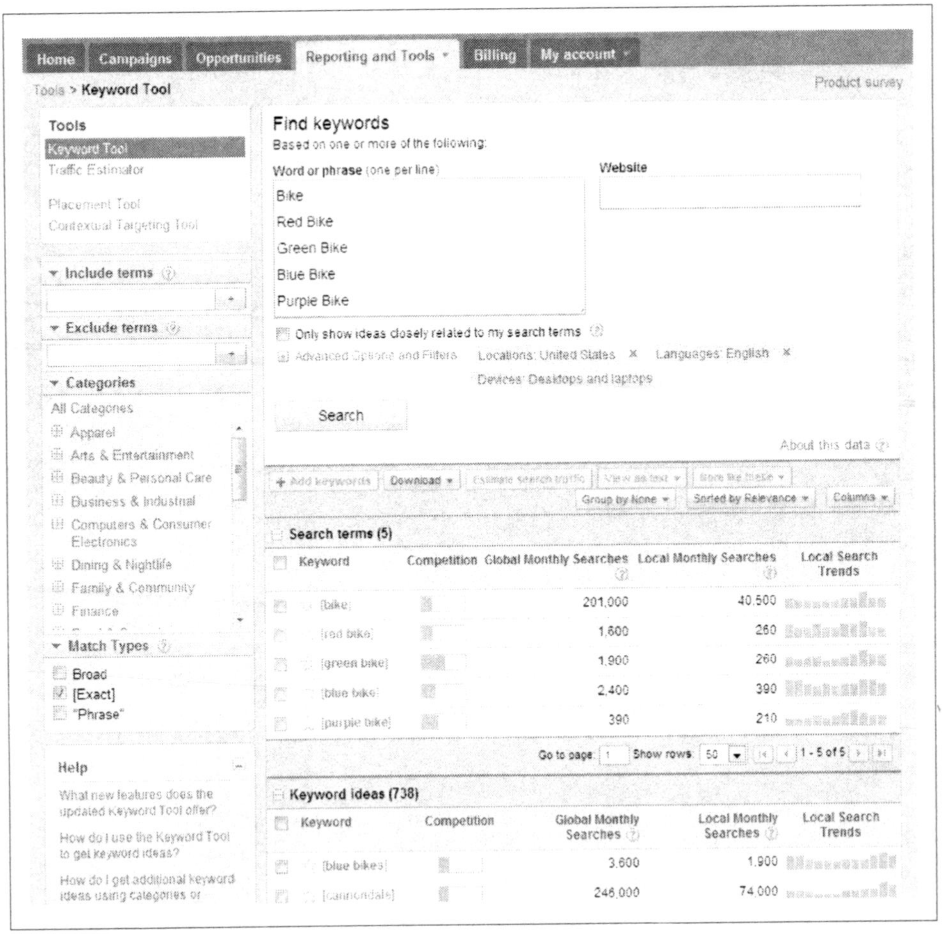

Figure 2-10. List of words from Google Keyword Tool to perform general research

Table 2-11. Value of position by ranking in top 10

	Total searches	#1	#2	#3	#4	#5	#6	#7	#8	#9	#10
Bike	33,100	10,500	2,771	1,962	1,496	1,208	989	837	741	701	734

Table 2-10 shows us that meeting our goal to improve our ranking on "bike" would increase the volume of traffic by 43%, while improving our ranking on "green bike" would increase traffic by 300%. That 300% increase sounds really good until you realize that it would only add three more visits to the site. In contrast, the improvement on the term "bike" would increase traffic by 299 visits. At this point, it would be really handy to know which of these terms does a better job at converting. We can get that information from Google Analytics the same way we pulled our paid search report, filtering instead on "non-paid." Knowing which terms convert better may also help us make our decision as to which words to focus on first.

If "bike" converts at .1% and "purple bike" converts at 3%, improving our ranking on "purple bike" will actually result in more conversions, even though it will drive fewer new customers (only 46) to our site. The rate at which terms convert impacts the overall number of new sales we will see, therefore indicating which terms will provide a better return on our investment of time. We would project that increasing our ranking on "bike" will bring us 0.299 new sales (299 × .001 = 0.299), whereas increasing our ranking on "purple bike" should bring us 1.38 new sales (46 × 0.03 = 1.38). It would make sense for us to look at the conversion rate for each term to understand how much further we could move the bar.

 This discussion makes the assumption that we are not looking at improving the user experience. Search is not just about improving traffic to your site; it's about improving findability. This means that as you move up the rankings you should also be trying to make it easier for customers to find what they need on your website.

If you're planning on targeting a term to improve your ranking, you should also be thinking of how to improve the page that word will take the customer to. Don't try to get a page selling a product to rank well on terms emphasizing support for that product. This will likely end in poor customer satisfaction and high bounce rates, and over time the search engine will likely recognize the irrelevancy of your page and push it down the rankings. Good search programs don't do a bait and switch; they should deliver on the promise of the search term entered.

If we have the average order value (which we have been giving as $520), which for SEO should be net profit, then we have enough data points to calculate how much more we can expect to make by increasing our position. We first calculate our average value per visit; we need to assume that our conversion rate will not change for now, so we will continue using $520 as our average value. If we assume "purple bike" converts at 3%, our average value per visit is $15.60. If we multiply this by the number of new visits we can expect for our work, which is 46 in this case, then we can anticipate a total increase in net profit of $717.60 for the month. This means the total number of hours we invest in improving our ranking on this term should not exceed a value of $717.60 per month. Any spend above that each month on this term and we will see a negative total value for SEO.

 Total Value for SEO = Current SEO Value - (Average Value per Visit × Number of New Visits)

The neat thing about SEO, though, is that if we do improve the rank of that term, the following month we may not need to invest nearly as much. That is, although the initial investment for SEO may be high, it typically decreases over time. Suppose that after analyzing our data, we decided that we could not move that term up to position 1 in a month; instead, we would need five months to do this. We do expect some positional gain over time—you don't just go from position 4 to position 1 overnight. However, there is also a risk that we will slip in the rankings, in which case we will see a negative ROI (Table 2-12). Feeling any pressure yet?

Table 2-12. ROI changes by position

Position in SERP (starting from position 4)	Change in traffic	Total value for SEO change	Incremental items sold
5	-1	-$15.60	-0.03
4	0	$0	0
3	3	$46.80	0.09
2	7	$109.20	0.21
1	46	$717.60	1.38

Knowing that our ROI can go down can be a bit intimidating. This is why when dealing with SEO you need to give careful consideration to any changes. Getting back to our five-month commitment to go from position 4 to position 1, we need to make some projections. We plan to make it to position 1 in our fifth month, so we'll aim to move up a position each month but leave some room in the schedule to allow for a possible period of slower growth.

In month 1, we see a profit increase of $46.80 as we move from ranking 4 to ranking 3. The next month, we see a profit increase of $109.20, as we move from ranking 3 to ranking 2. Now we expect to stay in rank 2 for the next two months, so for three months in a row we expect to stay at the increased level of $109.20. Finally, in the fifth month, we expect to jump to position 1 and see a profit increase of $717.60.

We can average this out as follows: ($46.80 + ($109.20 × 3) + $717.60) / 5 months = $218.40. So, we can expect our average profit over those five months to be $218.40. The longer we retain that number 1 position, the more our average ROI will increase. Now let's assume the time commitment required decreases after the first month, so we spend $400 in the first month but only $40 in each of the following months. Our average investment over this time is ($400 + ($40 × 4)) / 5 = $112 per month, attenuating the one-time cost of the initial investment. Our ROI over time for a position 1 ranking would be 540% [((717.60 − 112)/112) × 100], while the ROI for a position 2 ranking would be −2.5%. This means if we're not first, we're last, and we're losing money during our first four months. So how long will it be until we break even?

Break-even Point = Fixed Costs / Unit Net Profit Selling Price – Variable Costs)

Fixed costs are costs that are the same regardless of how many units you sell. This may be the initial investment you need to make to get to a higher ranking.

Variable costs are recurring costs that you must absorb—e.g., the investment you need to make to sustain that ranking.

To figure out our break-even point for the above example, we would take our fixed cost of $400, divide it by our unit selling price of $520, and subtract our variable cost of $40. We end up with 400 / (520 – 40) = 0.83. This tells us that we will need to sell 0.83 units above our current sell level throughout this search campaign in order to break even.

 Time to Break Even in Months = Break-even Point / Positional Increase in Items Sold per Month

By estimating the increase in number of items sold, we can calculate how long it will be until we break even.

If we managed to improve our ranking only to position 3, and continued to invest $40 per month, we would break even on our investment in about nine months. If we managed to improve our ranking to position 2 and continued to invest $40 per month, we would break even on our investment in about four months. For every month after that that we managed to retain that position, we would make an additional $100.80—but wait, that is less than the $109.20 we originally projected in Table 2-12! That is correct, because we must subtract the $40 we are spending each month from the $520 average order value net profit we've been using. Our net profit now is $480. The same rule should hold true if you incur labor costs in managing your paid search programs; you will need to factor these in there as well.

The key to ensure you don't go into a negative ROI is to keep your fixed costs reasonable, and to make sure that your variable cost is not more than your unit's net profit selling point. If your variable cost is ever more than your unit's net profit selling point (or in our case, net average order value), you will run into a problem reaching profitability. The fixed cost part of the equation will influence how long it takes you to get profitable. If this gets too high, it may take a very long time to get to a positive ROI, and you may not be able to hold out long enough if your pockets are not deep enough.

Accounting for the Butterfly Effect in Your SEO

Unlike with paid search, if you make changes or improvements to your site to improve SEO, you may see a butterfly effect: the flapping of wings may create a hurricane on another page or even on the current page you are editing. SEO is all about change, and the search engine can interpret every change you make as positive or negative. We want to make sure that the changes we make on the microscopic level do not impact our larger ecosystem. What good is it to rank well on a high-value nonbranded term if you suddenly stop ranking on five of your high-profile branded terms? While that is an extremely unlikely case, changes you make in one place can impact other areas of your site positively or negatively. For example, a change in linking structure may indicate to the search engines that a page you have edited is now no longer important.

Something else to keep in mind is that *not* making changes may also impact ROI. The search engines for SEO sort of have us in a catch-22 here. As the engines modify their search algorithms frequently, by changing nothing we run the risk of sliding in the ranks simply by being stagnant. If your site has enough content, some moves up will likely be offset by some small moves down. We also expect to see some fluctuation—say, a change of 5% up or down—each month. Major changes up or down may indicate either that something very wrong has happened, or that there has been a major algorithm change on the engine side. Your first duty should be to figure out which is the case. Major updates are typically announced, or discussed very quickly as others see changes in rankings. The three metrics you will want to look at are total SEO traffic value, total SEO traffic visits, and total bounce rate.

To get the total SEO traffic value, you capture all the clicks from SEO and measure the total value of sales—basically, you take all the sales from each SEO term and add that up into one giant number. Ideally, you can use multiclick tracking so you can get a better idea of your site flows as a whole; however, whichever form of tracking you use (multiclick, last click, or first click), once you commit to that measurement, you must stick with it. If you change this each month, you will see greater fluctuations.

Total SEO traffic visits is a measure of how much traffic SEO has driven to your site. We don't care what the words are or what the terms are; we just want to know how much traffic they have driven to the site. We also want to look at the bounce rate to verify that SEO isn't driving lots of nonrelevant traffic to the site. In other words, people come to our site with certain expectations, and we want to make sure we are delivering on those expectations. If our content is relevant to the searchers, they will travel deeper into our site.

What we are looking at is a very high-level view of our sales value, general traffic volume, and bounce rate. By looking at all three of these, we should see some natural trends. You also should be comparing year-over-year data if you have it.

Looking at month over month means looking at trends from month to month. Looking at year over year means looking at January 2010 compared to January 2011. The reason we want to look at year over year is that it will eliminate some seasonality effects we may see based on holidays, weather, or other transient factors. What we should be looking for is consistent year-over-year growth. If each month is up by 5% on average, then any months above that 5% are the months we moved the bar more significantly. Month-over-month data can give us hints about any major changes, but before interpreting them, you should also look at your previous year's month-over-month changes. If last year you went up 5% month over month and this year you are up only 2% month over month, you may want to ask yourself why. What happened last year to grow traffic that didn't happen this year? A good example of this could be December sales or traffic. If last year sales were up 25% month over month and this year they are up 20%, we may still have more traffic year over year, but it may be that this December we did not maximize value like we did the year before. Due to these being macro analytic values, we can't answer why that is with our current data sets; we simply know that it is. By segmenting and investigating historical data, we should be able to identify the why. This is an excellent example of how macro and micro data can provide differing insights, letting us first look at the larger picture and then drill down into the details.

When optimizing a single web page, you may also wish to look at the total set of words driving to a page you make a change to. If you plan to modify a page to capture a short head term, you should be aware of what the long-tail terms also driving to that page are. If there are many long-tail terms, the modifications you make to that page to gain short head rankings may have negative impacts on those terms that outweigh any gains. If, for example, you know you rank in position 5 on a term and want to move to position 3, but you have 20 more words that rank in position 7, modifications to that page for that one term need to be performed carefully to ensure that the changes do not negatively impact a significant portion of those 20 words. In Chapter 4 we will cover how to develop word clouds grouping the terms that drive to your page. Right now, we want to ensure we do a proper risk assessment. By figuring out the volume of traffic each of those words drives, you will be able to verify that any change up in ranking will drive enough traffic to compensate for each word or term that drops. The easiest way to do this is to create a simple chart to see what each additional word contributes to overall sales (Table 2-13).

Table 2-13. Sample traffic from terms to a single web page

Keyword	Keyword position	Clicks	Conversion rate	Average order value	Average value of a visit	Total value of term
Bike	3	180	4%	$380	$15.20	$2736
Red Bike	6	37	2%	$260	$5.20	$192.40
Green Bike	6	56	1%	$180	$1.80	$100.80
Purple Bike	6	48	3%	$690	$20.70	$993.60
Yellow Bike	6	85	5%	$553	$27.65	$2,350.25

From Table 2-13, we can see that moving the term "bike" up a position or two will have an impact; however, "yellow bike" and "purple bike" drive some significant revenue on the same page. You must be cognizant of the overall impact of any changes you make and monitor the effects on terms that rank lower but still drive some significant revenue. Losing those ranking may not be worth the gain in position for a single term, and you may need to revert any changes you have made back to what was originally there.

Understanding how your sales, traffic, and bounce rates change year over year and month over month will ultimately ensure that you are not caught by surprise at the end of the year or in a few months where you experience drops in traffic, due to obsession over ranking on a single term.

Capturing ROI for Site Search

To capture ROI from site search, you should utilize the same methodologies used in both paid search and SEO. Site search only differs in that we want to know how relevant our own algorithm is to what our users search for. When looking at site search, we are not just looking at how optimized our pages are, but also at how optimized our own index is; in this case, we own both sides of the search equation.

There may also be one more upside, depending on how your site search is implemented: you may be able to control the results. In these cases, you will want to look at how changes to site search will impact your ROI. In some cases, you may be able to include forced links or recommended links. If you have this capability, think of these as paid search links, only without the cost per click.

All the formulas we have used so far apply to site search just the same, though you may see a decrease in effort or time spends depending on how much control you have over your site search. You also have access to the number of total searches through your site search engine, meaning you can calculate conversions much more accurately. You can also capture abandonment from site search to measure the effectiveness of your site search.

 Here are the formulas for site search conversion and abandonment:

Site Search Conversion = Number of Orders by Users of Site Search / Number of Searches on Site Search

Site Search Abandonment = Exits from Site Search / Number of Searches on Site Search

Site search is a very valuable tool, and later on we will see how data from site search can help us improve our other search campaigns by giving us leads on ways to improve conversions. For now, site search should be treated as a specialized variation of SEO or paid search. Your goals for site search should be decreasing abandonment and increasing conversions. Your first metric for site search should also be improving results. Getting people to the right page on your site (a page as close to conversion opportunities as possible)—and then having that page become the conversion funnel—is the best strategy. Site search should improve the usability and navigation of your website; by doing so it will positively impact ROI.

Site search also provides insights into opportunities. By mining site search keyword data you can identify "hot" products or content that people frequently search for on your site. Elevating the visibility of this hot content is a quick way to positively impact ROI—it may actually result in fewer site searches being done, but it will mean more satisfied users.

While the use of site search may grow as you drive more traffic to your site, you should leverage the data you gather to try to reduce the number of searches to improve the experience of the users. The positive ROI of site search is mostly derived from the insight it provides that is directly related to your customers and their behavior.

Because of this function of site search, you may want to measure assists. If you can track pathing and referring pages, capturing whether site search has a role in purchases is usually going to be your best ROI analytic. We can track this in Google Analytics (Figure 2-11), using the following steps:

1. Click on "Analytics Settings."
2. Click on "Edit" for the profile you wish to track this in, or, better yet, create a new profile for only tracking site search by clicking "+Add new profile" in the actions column.
3. Select the goal you want to track site search impacts on, or create the goal you want to track.
4. Once you've done this, click "+Yes, create a funnel for this goal" under "Goal Funnel."
5. Input the URL of your site search page and name the funnel "site search." Leave "required step" unchecked.

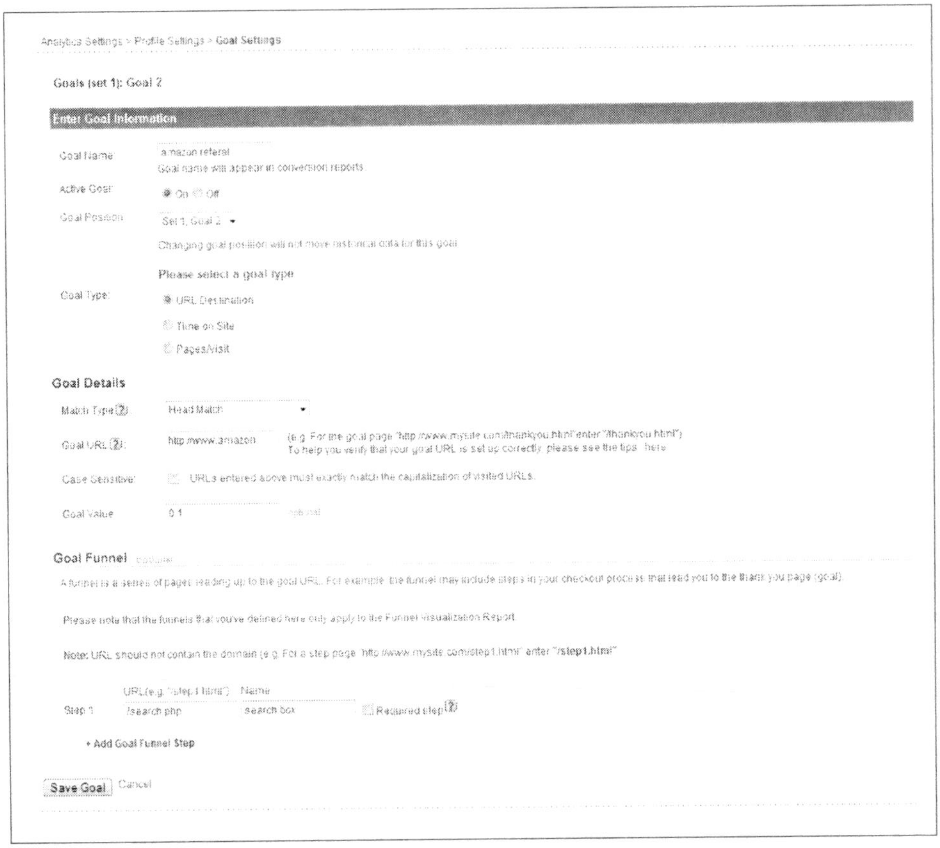

Figure 2-11. Google Analytics interface for setting up capturing goals

Once you've built this funnel, you can get to it from your analytics by selecting Goals→Funnel Visualization. You will then be able to track how many of your customers funnelled through site search at some point to complete a transaction, as shown in Figure 2-12. Knowing this will enable you to see how often site search plays a role in purchasing, regardless of the number of clicks made between the site search and goal completion.

Site search is a valuable tool, and you want to ensure you are tracking the role it plays on your site. Does it contribute highly to sales? Is it used frequently or infrequently? How efficient is it at getting people to the right pages? If you lease or pay for your site search technology, you will want to use our break-even point calculation to determine whether you're losing money on site search. The cost of site search may be a fixed cost if you paid only once for its use, or a variable cost if you pay for it every month.

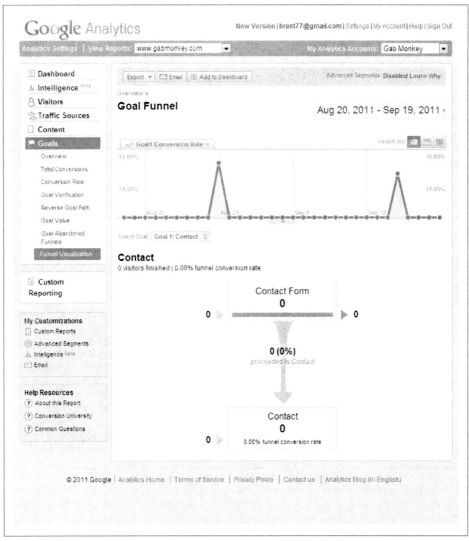

Figure 2-12. An example of a Google Analytics funnel report

To get an idea of the value of your site search, go to Content→"Content by Title" in your Google Analytics report and filter page title (Figure 2-13), or go to Content→"Top Content" and filter by page name. In either of these reports, the "$ Index" value will provide you with the average value of your conversions.

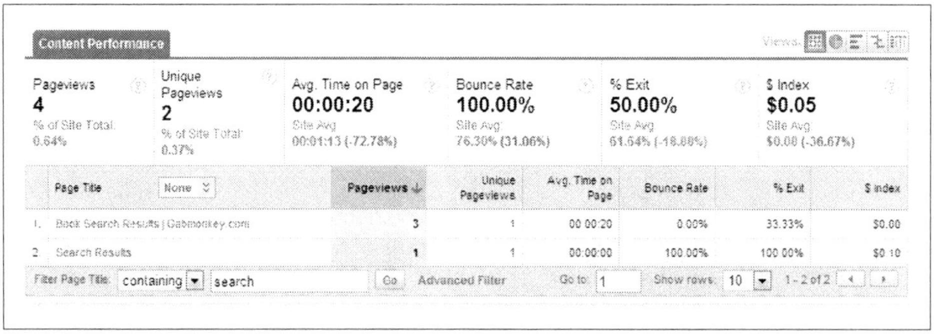

Figure 2-13. An example of Google Analytics tracking words by conversion rate

To get the total value of sales site search participated in, multiply this number by the number of page views. You may not be able to calculate if this is net or not, so you will need to figure that out. In a simple world, if site search's earned value is more than your monthly fee, it has recouped its value. In reality, what you will find is that some sites are willing to rent this technology even if they lose money on it, because it ultimately improves customers' satisfaction and experience with the website, which increases the likelihood of them returning. A repeat customer is typically worth more than a one-off customer, so site search can be a great investment.

Tracking Offline Sales

Tracking offline sales may be a crucial part of your road to market. It is also the hardest segment of sales to track. You may only be able to calculate an ROI for offline sales through proxies and estimates. You may have access to some data points that can help you estimate the influence your website has on offline sales. You may need to coordinate with other departments to get the data you need, but if you are in the business of selling things, the data should be there.

The key factor in tying online data to offline data is finding unique identifiers. These may be anonymously generated user IDs; coupons; or phone numbers, email addresses, or some other information that can identify users, with the caveat that you are not breaking any privacy laws by storing this data.

Once you have the unique identifier captured online, you can store it in Adobe Site-Catalyst as a transaction ID. When this transaction ID is used offline to complete a purchase (the coupon is redeemed, a phone call is made, etc.), you can import this data back into Adobe SiteCatalyst and merge your online and offline data.

Let's take a business that sells clothes. It may not sell direct online, but rather will use its website to drive people to a store. You can capture data regarding the website's role in several ways. For example, you can offer coupons that can be printed off your website, but this will only provide a small sampling of people who visit your site and then purchase offline, as not everyone may print or redeem the coupon. Another option is to use surveys to understand more about your customers. These are typically referred to as *voice-of-the-customer* surveys. By asking site visitors if they plan on visiting a store in the next week, two weeks, or month to purchase something, you can establish some baseline averages as to how often and when users of your site plan to visit your offline store. You may not be able to establish baseline average order values, but you may be able to use offline average order values.

You will also have a hard time getting exact conversion rates unless you have a very narrow and specific funnel to move people through. For example, if you have one phone number set up specifically to deal with online customers, you may use that to identify leads through anonymous data.

As you build up your data points, you will find you get a bigger picture of how your website influences offline sales. Through surveys, you may end up learning that 30% of people who come to your website plan on purchasing from your offline store. You may capture their email addresses during the process, and send a follow-up email to confirm the actual number of people who did purchase. These two numbers may be very different, and will be based on sampling, meaning the numbers are not exact but approximates. Because we are looking at tracking search, you can use the email addresses that you have captured as unique identifiers to store the referral agent against, and then import their answers into your existing data set to better understand the influence search has on offline sales.

Establishing offline trends early will help you develop a full picture of what role your search campaigns and website play in the purchase life cycle. If your site is simply based on impressions, you may still use surveys to learn more about this segment as a tool to help sell ads. Knowing that the information you give people on your site heavily influences their subsequent actions can be a very powerful sales tool as you establish rate cards.

Concluding Thoughts

What we learned about capturing ROI in paid search can be applied to SEO, and vice versa. What we have at this point is a good set of formulas and sources to pull data from so that we can capture and track values that are tied to dollars and cents. To justify your campaigns, as well as to ensure you are spending money wisely, you will want to make sure you run a positive ROI. To maximize your ROI, you will need to use the skills you will learn later in this book to figure out what needs to be changed, how it needs to be changed, and how to build a plan to target specific pages and sections of your website.

CHAPTER 3

Tracking and Optimizing SEO and Paid Search Traffic

The goal of SEO and paid search campaigns is to generate relevant traffic to your site.

As a search strategist, one of the challenges you will run into is when someone tells you to figure out how to get more traffic to your website. At the highest level, your SEO and paid search strategies should be about acquiring customers and being found by people who are in need of what your website provides (be it products, services, connections with others, etc.). Key to this is understanding your traffic: who is coming to your site, how they found you, what they are doing on your site, what the value of that traffic is, and how to improve the user experience.

Tools you will need in this chapter:

- Clickstream tracking package (Google Analytics, Adobe SiteCatalyst, etc.)
- Google Keyword Tool or some other keyword research tool
- A/B or multivariate testing tool (Google Website Optimizer, Adobe Test & Target, etc.)
- Spreadsheet program (Excel or something similar)
- Google and Bing Webmaster Tools
- Google Global Market Finder

Tracking Visitors and Segmenting Traffic from Search

Separating people coming to your site from search versus other avenues is the first key to understanding how searchers may differ from users who may already be aware of your brand. Searchers are different in that they may not know anything about your brand, what you do, and what other services you may offer or have any sort of loyalty to you. Fortunately, most clickstream packages allow for the segmenting of users coming to your site from search, and some clickstream tools can further segment traffic coming from paid and organic search.

You can further segment traffic from your paid search campaigns by appending tracking codes to your URLs. When creating the URL your paid search campaign will link to, you have the ability to inject into the link some data that will allow you to segment by ad group, keyword, engine, and so on. Figure 3-1 shows an example of a URL with a tracking parameter appended to it. The "TRK" part changes from tool to tool, as some may have set up the variables in a specific way. What you should be able to alter is the parameter.

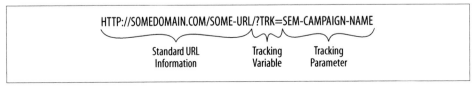

Figure 3-1. Example of a URL with a tracking code

A well-defined parameter can be set up based on a taxonomy and rule set, or it may be autogenerated by another data source or tool set, as is the case with some enterprise-class solutions. A taxonomy for a parameter may include the following:

- Start and end date of campaign
- Campaign name
- Campaign type (paid search, email, etc.)
- Targeted segment
- Internal business segment
- Anything else that makes it easy for you to identify the who, what, and why of the campaign later

Another neat trick with campaign tracking is that you can hide internal data by creating a map of codes to meanings. For example, you may not want to expose internal business segments, so you can change these to map against codes that are deciphered later on, either through your clickstream tool or through manual intervention.

It's important to establish your taxonomies early on, as some clickstream tools only provide a limited number of variables that can be tracked. By creating a well-defined parameter taxonomy, you ensure that you can track many pieces of information in one variable and are still able to segment your data.

Once you have enabled and created a tag for your paid search campaigns, you can pull this data directly from your clickstream software of choice—typically there will be a section called "campaigns" (Figure 3-2), usually in your sources section. When campaigns are set up, you cannot only view them but you use them to filter as well. For example, you can use campaigns to filter time on site, bounce rates, or, most useful of all, events, goals, and sales. This is the data that will be useful in tracking users and traffic through your site and tracking goal completions.

Segmenting SEO traffic into campaigns is a bit trickier. You can use Custom Segments in Google Analytics to segment based on keywords, and SAINT classifications in Adobe SiteCatalyst. The nice thing about this approach is that it is also retroactive, meaning you can use it not just to classify your content moving forward, but also the data you have already captured.

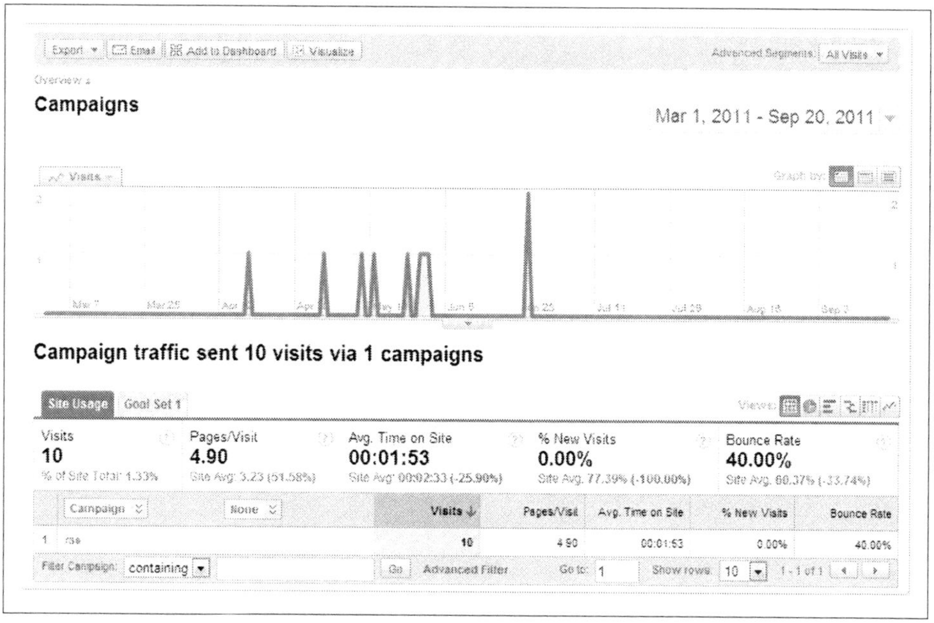

Figure 3-2. Example of campaign tracking

Beyond your clickstream data, the engines also provide ways to track success events for paid search. Google has a feature in AdWords called AdWords Search Funnels (*http://adwords.blogspot.com/2010/03/new-reports-adwords-search-funnels.html*) that allows you to see which words were clicked on, which appeared in search results, and which led to a conversion. If you think of it in sports terms, the conversion is the goal, and each of the other elements are assists.

While the Search Funnel tool is not perfect—it does not take into account organic listings you may show up on, or organic clicks that end up in conversions—it does provide some insight into what is happening through the funnel.

In Google Analytics, you can build a custom filter using the term you want to track by following these steps:

1. Click on "Advanced Segments" on the left.
2. Click on "Create New Custom Segment" at the top right.
3. Click on "Traffic Sources" on the left.
4. Select "Keyword" and drag it over to the right side.
5. Depending on if you are looking at one or many terms, build your filter accordingly. For this example, we'll assume one word, so use "matches exactly" as the condition and put the word in the "value" box.
6. Name the segment and test and then save it.
7. Return to your keyword report, locate your filter at the top right under "Advanced Segments," and check it.
8. You can now filter data based on the activity around this keyword.

The difference between building a taxonomy for campaign tracking codes and segmenting via filters is that you must think about how you are already capturing your data. For example, when we look at the different stages of the purchase funnel (Figure 3-3), we may group sets of words together to represent different spaces. We can use these words to build our filters, but it is much more time consuming, and greater thought is required to ensure coverage of all the important terms. You may also need to think about inclusion and exclusion rules; for example, if your company sells shoes, you may want to capture all terms for "shoe" as a top funnel awareness activity, and more specific terms such as "Nike shoe" as a lower funnel activity. This means that you will want to include all variations of the word "shoe" in an awareness segment but exclude any instance where it is paired with the word "Nike."

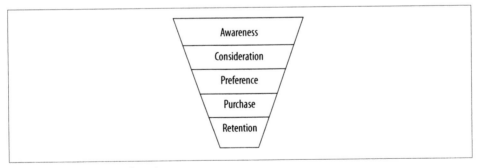

Figure 3-3. The purchase funnel

Segmenting and Tracking Offline Transactions

Beyond simple campaign tracking, you can also develop sophisticated tracking mechanisms that assign a unique ID to each user that accesses your site from search based on type. For example, organic traffic may be identified by "seo" and paid traffic by "paid-search", and you can get as sophisticated as we just got with our URL parameters. You would then have a code that might look something like seo-000234323, where the numbers identify the user (say, with the first five digits being a unique user identifier) and the campaign.

This code could then be captured dynamically for each user in a cookie or the URL, as well as in your clickstream tool, enabling you to track campaign data and to identify single users anonymously. This is a very powerful set of data to have, as it means you can track the users' paths through the site. You may also be able to take this into the offline space. For example, if your site is only informational, you may be able to track users offline by creating coupons or other items that require users to identify themselves. Say, for example, you allow users to configure a product online and then get it at a store. Having a printed page with the tracking code on it means you can capture the conversion at the offline point of sale.

Depending on how sophisticated your clickstream tool is, you may then be able to import this data back into it to get ROI numbers. Unica, Adobe SiteCatalyst, and Webtrends all have features that allow for data import in some form or another, while Google Analytics requires you to do this work by hand. That is, Google Analytics doesn't allow you to import offline data (like which coupon codes were printed off, and when); instead, you must export your clickstream data and then combine it with your offline data manually in a spreadsheet or database.

Once you have access to this off-site data, you will begin to get a richer picture of the influence your site and your different campaigns actually have on users taking action. Before you use this data, however, you will also want to know what the redemption rate is—that is, how many users may be printing off data versus taking action on it.

You can capture an estimated number of pages printed by tagging a print button with a JavaScript call to create a virtual page view, or store the action in another variable that you define for your clickstream tool. Your code will end up looking something like:

```
Function capture-prints(){
virtual page view code;
window.print();
}
```

The line of pseudocode that reads "virtual page view code" is where you inject your own code to generate a virtual page view when the print button is clicked (alternatively, you may opt to capture this in a variable, so as not to inflate the number of page impressions).

You will now be able to track approximately how many users print your code. You can also gather data on redemptions, and use this data to capture a conversion rate.

 To calculate redemption rate offline using your print tracking code and feedback from the redemption source, your formula should look as follows (where redemption rate is expressed as a percentage):

Redemption Rate = (Redemptions / # of Print Actions) × 100

Offline data, like online data, can and should be segmented and applied so you can understand the influence of your investments. As we begin to look at user behavior and actions, it will quickly become clear that once you understand how to segment your data, you can begin to measure not just opportunities that are closing deals, but also success events that move users toward purchases or other task completions that result in profit for you. As you work with integrating offline data, think about how you may want to segment that data against your search campaigns. You may want to segment down to the level of a single keyword or a set of keywords, or to specific pages you are looking to optimize. Unique IDs can be generated in a number of ways for offline tracking based on user behavior; tap into this opportunity to really leverage the value of offline data tracking.

 We first started to realize we had control over our campaigns (instead of our campaigns having control over us) when we were able to articulate and show how different keyword groups aligned to different stages in the customer purchase cycle.

We moved from trying to own every word, and the full page, and began to focus on maximizing the depth and quality of traffic we were receiving. We found we could group keywords and campaigns into different segments before they went to market.

We thought of words in groups of opportunity, such as high value and low value. We could also see how different sets of words were impacting sales, by creating our own proxy values based on voice-of-the-customer data, data from our channels, and data from third-party surveys.

We also came to find that at some point in the customer purchase cycle search played a role, in one form or another. In some cases, we discovered that words we had thought of as low-value actually did have a value to us, as they created opportunities for us to foster different relationships with different customers—and depending on what our objectives were, we could turn these on and off as needed.

Using Campaign Segmentation Data

Regardless of your website's goal, be it transactions, repeat visits, social engagements, or anything else, there will be different groups of users. From a transactional standpoint, these users may fall into different groups based on where they are in the purchase funnel (Figure 3-3). On the other hand, if your focus is on support, you may group your users into those looking for answers to FAQs, those seeking software updates, and those with unique issues.

We know that users may make several clicks before a purchase, and seeing the assists along the way helps us segment out marketing activities and how they align to the purchase funnel. We can identify different tasks for each action within a customer cycle segment. For example, we can define the following goals for users as they move down the purchase funnel:

Awareness
> Viewing a specific page about a new product (or a series of connected pages about new products), downloading a brochure on a product, and so on.

Consideration
> Looking at a product on the website and perhaps adding it to the cart, but not buying; reading a product specification page; calling a 1-800 number to learn more about a product

Preference
> Reading an article that compares us to our competitors, using a product configuration tool to build a product

Purchase
> A sales transaction, either online or offline

Retention
> Any repeat visit where there is high intent to purchase or where a purchase is made

Once you define the goals, you will want to associate values with them. Ideally these are monetary values, where you can say, for example, that every brochure read is worth $2.50 or every product configuration interaction is worth $4.68. The closer a user is to a purchase or a revenue action, the higher the value becomes, and the more accurate the data becomes.

Accuracy is important, and it's another way you can segment your traffic. You can create two buckets of revenue tracking: estimated or projected, and actual. Actual revenue tracking would pull data in only from actual transactions, while estimated or projected revenue tracking would use the values you've associated with the funnel activities.

Segmenting programs by actions

Once you are able to segment your programs by different actions in the customer's life cycle or needs, and you are able to segment by revenue and projected revenue, you can begin to refine your search programs.

When we begin to think about goals and assists, we begin to think about our ability to support the overall customer life cycle. We also begin to understand where we can add value and support to the needs of our business and customers (Table 3-1).

Table 3-1. Example of campaign comparison in the customer life cycle

Life cycle stage	Goal	Value	Supporting search program	Total spend	Total value
Awareness	White Paper Download	$180.56	SEO Technical Program	$689.69	$1,8056.00
	White Paper Download	$180.56	SEO Executive Program	$3,058.56	$9,028.00
Consideration	Product Engagement	$230.89	Branded Product Names Paid Search	$689.98	$2,3089.00
Preference	Product Comparison Engagement	$293.75	Branded Product Names SEO	$489.68	$4,406.25
	Competitor Comparison Engagement	$263.75	Competitor Keyword Campaign Paid Search	$4,359.45	$1,318.75
Purchase	Purchase a Product	Actual Revenue	Paid Search Coupon Campaign	$3,256.36	$38,987.90
	Purchase a Product	Actual Revenue	Paid Search Instant Savings Campaign	$3,986.36	$69,895.68
Retention	Repeat Visit to Accessory Page	$189.96	Paid Search Accessory Campaign	$395.69	$6648.60
	Accessory Purchase	Actual Revenue	SEO Branded Accessories	$569.37	$2896.36

In Table 3-1, actual revenue represents data that comes only from true sales. This can include online and offline data. For offline data, it should include only sales involving coupons or other trackable codes that can be associated to a specific campaign and merged with our clickstream data.

Looking at Table 3-1, we can begin to make some decisions about our search campaigns and strategy. In some cases, we have more than one campaign supporting a single goal, while other goals are supported by specific targeted campaigns.

Here are some insights we can gain from this data now that it is segmented:

- Our SEO Executive program is significantly outperforming our Technical program in terms of white paper downloads. We should ask why this is. Are we targeting the wrong people? Or is our Technical program not driving as much traffic as the Executive campaign? Are the entry pages not as compelling for technical people?

- Our SEO branded keywords are outperforming our paid search competitor keywords. We also see that our competitive keyword campaign is losing money. This may or may not be OK. The lower cost of our branded strategy can offset the loss of our competitor strategy, and the competitor strategy may have additional value that allows this to be a loss leader.

- Our Paid Search Instant Savings campaign drives a significant volume of actual purchases. We may consider whether there is more room to grow this campaign: are there more words we could bid on? Can we improve daily coverage of our keywords? Are there other geographies that we are not targeting that might help increase our sales?

- From a retention perspective, we see that we are influencing repeat customers, but we are not closing as many repeat deals. Do people prefer to shop offline for their accessories? Can we track this through coupons that can be used offline? Can we help drive more offline sales by providing a phone number to call?

This top-level analysis has provided a great deal of insight into questions we should be asking, and how to better improve the revenue we realize. There are two approaches to improving a campaign: looking at off-site factors and on-site factors. Off-site factors include optimizing and improving the traffic to your site, as well as offline purchases. As we are looking at traffic, we will assume the campaigns are delivering the volumes of users we expect, but we need to understand how to optimize for these users.

Tracking Pathing Through the Site

Now that we have segmented our traffic, we want to start to understand how this traffic engages with our site. Once a user gets to our site from search, we need to know where that user goes. Search, unlike other sources of traffic, provides us with users with very clear intentions and needs. We want to understand first if these needs are being met, and secondly if there is anything we can do to meet them better.

We can use large segments of keywords to get general ideas, and then we can use specific keyword filtering to see if there are some words that perform better at driving traffic through our site than other words. Using the information in Table 3-1, we may want to answer the question of why our SEO Technical program is not performing as well as our SEO Executive program. A quick look at traffic data may provide us with some insights, such as:

- In the awareness stage, technical traffic has a high bounce rate, while executive traffic does not
- Technical traffic does not have a high bounce rate but does have high on-site search volume, followed by an exit in the awareness stage
- Technical traffic does not have a high bounce rate, but user pathing shows that in the awareness stage, there is high abandonment on another page that is not our entry page

High Bounce Rates

Bounce rates, also referred to as *exits*, are tracked in most clickstream tools. To find your bounces, locate your Entry Page or Landing Page report. If your reporting tool does not have bounce rate tracking set up by default, you can use Single Access/Entries to get your bounce rate.

Bounce rates are usually a first stop for me when I'm trying to figure out why people are not completing goals. This is the easiest way to find out if we are delivering on expectations when someone comes through our front door. It also allows us to validate the quality of our entry page and the first impressions we're creating.

Once you've found your bounce rate report (or created it), simply apply your campaign filter and you should be able to see bounces specific to the campaign you are tracking. If the bounce rate is low relative to your site average, that means the page is engaging with users in some aspect, so you need to look for something else that may be impacting goal completions.

Low Bounce, High Site Search

If bounce rates are low, my next stop is to check the quality of the page itself. Sometimes our users are forgiving and really want what we have to offer even when our pages are not very good, so they will try our site search.

Site search is a great tool, but it also leaves us with a lot of unknowns in terms of where a user will go, and it implies that our entry page is not capturing the needs of our users. So we want to make sure that there is not an abnormal site search volume as well.

Almost all clickstream tools require site search tracking to be set up. You should capture the site search query, as well as which page the search occurred on. By segmenting to campaign and looking at the specific pages that triggered site searches, you can figure out which pages may be confusing or require improvements. Even better, if you can capture what the users searched for and you identify common patterns, you may be able to include some content specific to those searches on the page so that your users don't need to do a site search for it.

Low Bounce, High Pathing Exit

Pages with low bounces but low goal completions may indicate that users are getting lost in the path. Most enterprise-level clickstream tools provide a *pathing report* that shows an entry point and the next several pages viewed after that page, in order of popularity. Google Analytics is experimenting with this type of report in its version 5 code release. The nice thing about pathing reports is that you are not limited to creating a predefined funnel; instead, you can see what users are doing organically through your site, and follow branches to understand their pathing better.

I prefer a pathing report over a funnel fallout report for this very reason. I find they are more flexible, and allow me to explore the data more intimately. A funnel fallout report will only show me how many users moved on to the next stage, which is rather limiting.

Again, you need to filter this based on your campaign segment data to derive insights specific to your search strategy.

Using Pathing and Bounce Data

Pathing and bounce data is important, as it enables you to find out where the exits occur. To maximize return on your campaigns, minimizing early or low-value exits is a good strategy. Usually it is a better strategy than throwing more traffic at the problem, unless revenue is generated based on sheer number of eyeballs; even in this case, though, lowering bounces and understanding pathing data is still important, as you will want to increase repeat visits and know which pages are your high-value pages (high-value pages being pages that people naturally migrate toward, that you may be able to sell as a premium, or where you can include additional offering information).

Once you understand where the exits happen—your leak in the dam, if you will—you can begin to build up a strategy to fix it. Landing page optimization and conversion rate optimization are the best tools we have access to. We already have a general idea of user intent based on the search query provided. We also know what we see as the objectives and goals of our website, in each stage of the user funnel.

As part of your CRO, you should begin to think about search intent optimization. Most users will not complete a transaction from start to finish in one go, but rather will do so over several iterations and experiences with a site. How can you influence their next decision? Can you provide information that will push customers who are in the early stages of the decision-making process a bit further toward your brand? Having a user enter your site from a nonbranded generic word and leave thinking about your brand and using your brand terminology is what search intent optimization should be about. For example, say a user searches for "laptop" and ends up on the Apple.com website. This user then leaves that site, but the next time he searches for product information, he searches for "MacBook." This user has moved from a nonbranded generic word to a branded term that Apple is strong on.

Landing Page Optimization

Using on-page copy is but one way we can help influence the next search. To really get into landing page optimization, we want to know what keywords are driving people to a specific page. You can build keyword clusters by pulling data from your site analytics to see which keywords are referring people to a specific page. You can think of a keyword cluster like a cloud tag, only it's based on words and terms that deliver traffic to your site from the search engines, and the larger words will be bigger in the term cloud (Figure 3-4). This makes for great data visualization, and a feature of Google Analytics v5 is that you can change your view to "term cloud" when looking at any of the keyword reports.

Figure 3-4. Search traffic keyword cloud tag

Once we know what keywords are driving people to the page, we can start to assess what we can do to improve the on-page findability. If we see a large volume of searches for the term "pretty websites" driving traffic to our page, we need to ensure we have some quick visual hints to identify the relevancy of this page to that term. Figure 3-5 shows an example of this. The term "pretty websites" is predominant in the header of this page, as well as the lead-in to the article. It's also important to note that I am not talking about using H1 tags to optimize, but visual cues. The text could be wrapped in any HTML element; what we are looking at here is styling the content to "pop" on the page.

Figure 3-5. Optimizing visual cues

It's important to provide people coming in from search with visual cues, as they expect to quickly be able to find what they are looking for. When optimizing pages, there is the code side, where you look at HTML elements, and the findability side, where you look at how scannable a page is to the human eye. A well-designed page should have topics clearly separated and labeled, as well as images with clear positioning and descriptions if applicable.

Making sure that the page is quickly scannable is a great start. After this, we want to track how deep people are going into our site, and what other pages they are going to. What is the abandonment rate like? Are we providing clear options to drive users deeper into our site? If you are running a blog, as in the example for "pretty websites," abandonment rates being high may be OK. But why not look at improving the promotion of other content related to your article? Let people know there is deeper content on your site. If you are running a commerce site, ensure you have clear calls to actions to get people to products, support, or services you may offer. Do not bury all your links at the bottom of the page; plot and lay out the page to improve the visibility of the things people can click on.

Landing page optimization is perhaps the most important tool you will have in your toolkit, be it for SEO, paid search, or site search. Learning how to track and understand what people do on a specific page will enable you to make the correct decisions on what elements need to be changed or tweaked. It will also be the best way to maximize revenue, but keep in mind that any sort of optimization you perform is to ultimately improve the experience of your customers.

The selection of section headers (H1 through H6) that should "pop" on the page will also help influence potential follow-up searches. Lead with headlines that are strong and reflective of terms that other pages on your site rank well for. If you use "running shoes" instead of "running sneakers," the next search may be influenced to focus on "shoes" rather than "sneakers."

Sophisticated landing page optimization comes down to A/B and multivariate testing. This allows you to test and modify elements on a page in different combinations to see which ones improve goal or task completion rates. These may be complex changes, such as removal or inclusion of navigation elements, or simple changes, such as a color adjustment.

A/B and Multivariate Testing

There are a variety of options for A/B or multivariate testing, including Google Website Optimizer and Adobe Test & Target. They all have the same outcome: improving visitors' engagement with your web pages, as well as your site's overall usability.

A/B testing in a nutshell

The principle behind A/B testing is to serve different versions of content to a randomly split group. This split may be 50/50, 80/20, 60/40, or some other variation that you determine is appropriate based on your audience and testing group. You may want to test with a smaller pool in order to limit negative impacts on a larger selection of traffic. You can also A/B test paid search ads on the search engines, as well as the content on your site.

When running A/B testing, you may test entirely different pages against each other, or pages that differ in only a single element. The choice is yours. Do bear in mind, though, that by splitting traffic across different pages you may cause your analytics tools to register a dip in traffic. You'll need to account for that as you run your tests on the different pages, if this is how your A/B testing script works.

Multivariate testing in a nutshell

Multivariate testing is similar to A/B testing, but includes changing multiple elements on a web page in different combinations. Think of it as A/B testing on steroids, where you have lots of little changes all being tested at once.

Multivariate testing usually uses one single page where different elements are changed through the use of JavaScript. The scripts will populate different content elements that you define in different variations and determine which is the most successful combination of elements.

For landing page optimization, I prefer multivariate rather than A/B testing for the simple fact that you are refining a page more surgically, looking at each individual small change instead of larger sweeping changes across an entire page. Multivariate testing is also very flexible; you can use it to test a single element (as with A/B testing), or multiple elements on a page all at once.

Running a Multivariate Test

Configuring these tests is pretty simple. Regardless of the tool you use, they all run in a very similar fashion, and most require some JavaScript code to be placed on your web page. Be sure to include a `noscript` tag to handle browsers with scripting turned off, as well as to accommodate users with accessibility issues.

For our example of setting up a multivariate test, we will use Website Optimizer. When you first log in to Optimizer, you will be presented with a screen (Figure 3-6) that has "Create another experiment" at the top. Click this to set up your first experiment.

Figure 3-6. Creating an experiment in Website Optimizer

You will get a screen that asks you if you want to run an A/B test or a multivariate test (Figure 3-7). For our example, choose multivariate.

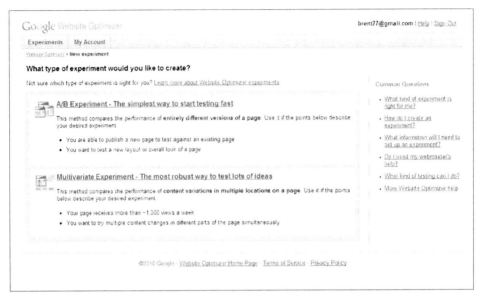

Figure 3-7. Choosing A/B or multivariate testing

The next screen is an informational screen instructing you to choose a page to test, figure out which sections of the page you'll be modifying and then identify the conversion/success or goal page (i.e., where you want users to end up).

The last setup screen (Figure 3-8) is where you input the data for your test. You need to:

1. Name your experiment.
2. Identify the page being tested.
3. Identify your conversion page.

Once you have completed these steps, you must identify who will be implementing the code (you or someone else). Select yourself for this example.

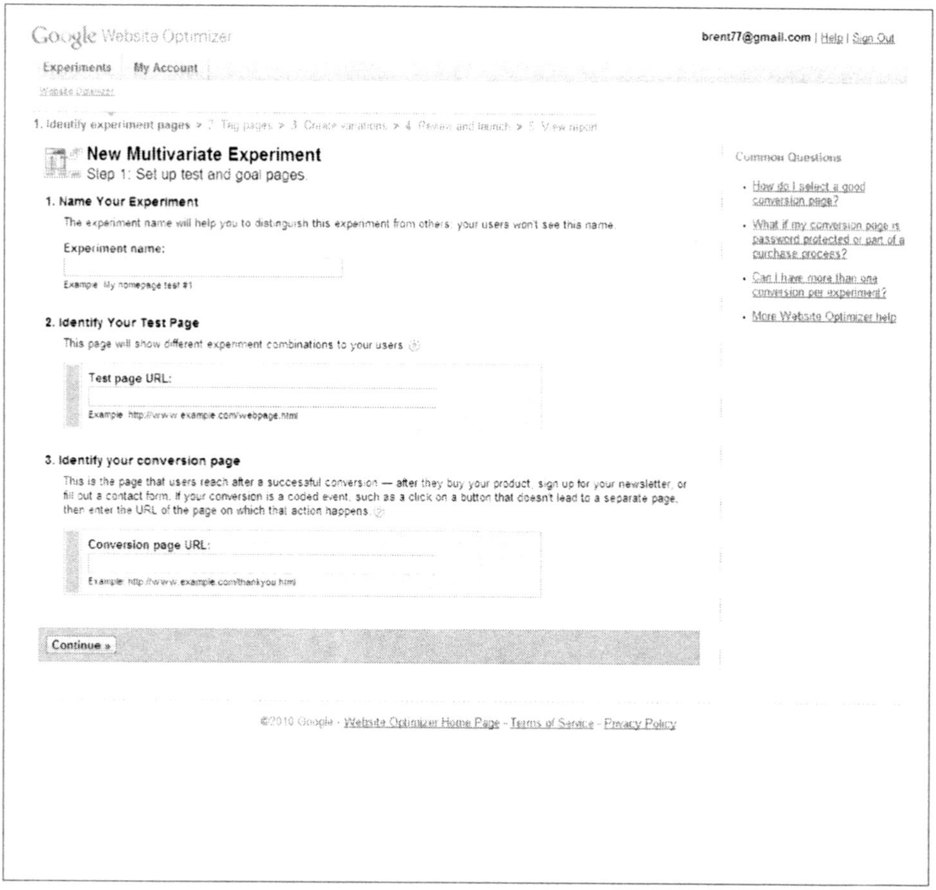

Figure 3-8. New multivariate setup

When you move to the next screen, you will be provided with the JavaScript needed to run the experiment (Figure 3-9). Place these scripts on the appropriate pages, as per the instructions on the screen, and validate the pages.

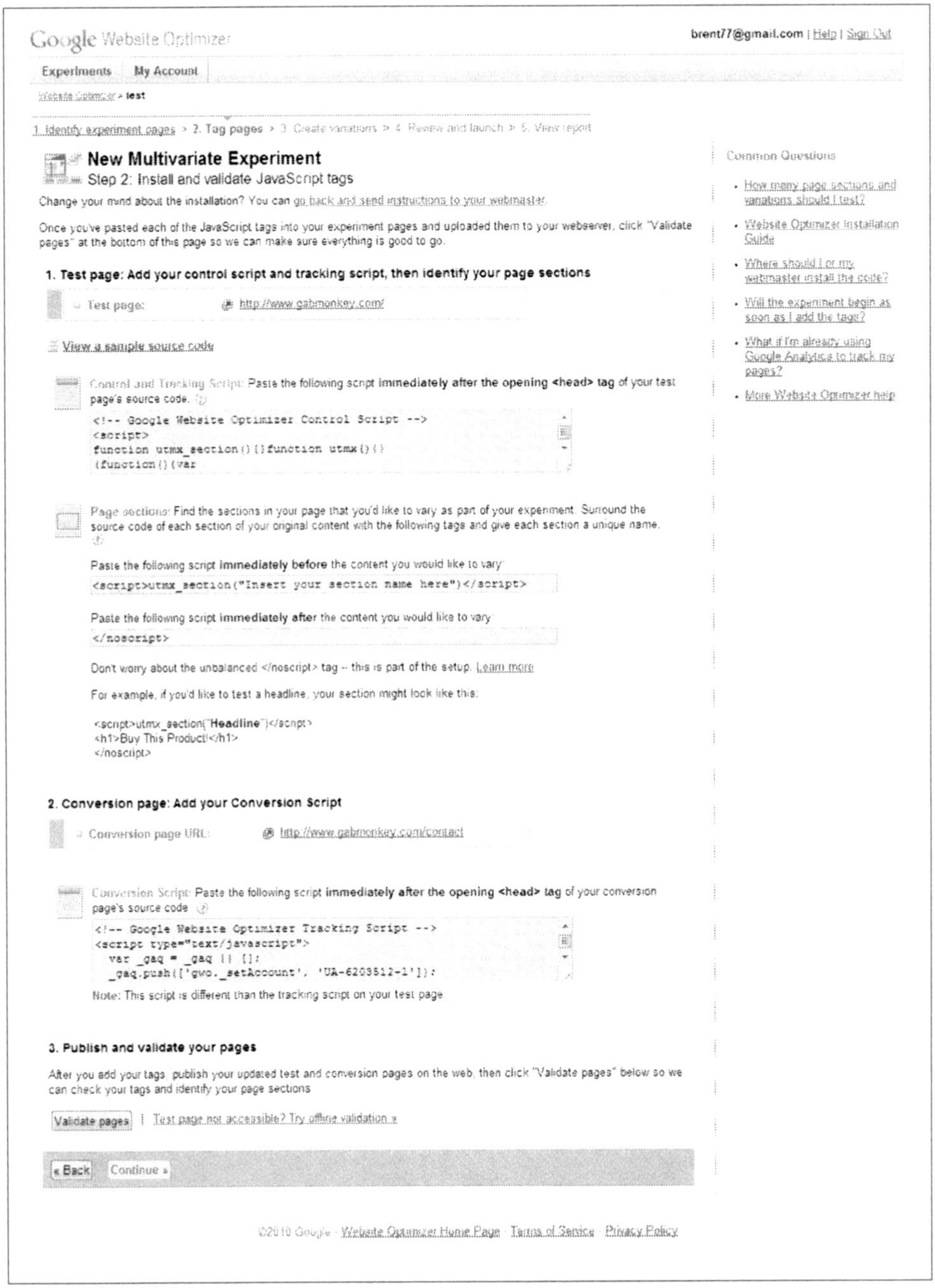

Figure 3-9. JavaScript code for a multivariate test generated by Google

Place the following code in each section in which you want to test an element, replacing "Insert your section name here" with a meaningful ID for that section (each location will need to be uniquely identified in order to inject your variations):

```
<script>utmx_section("Insert your section name here")</script>
</noscript>
```

Once your code is in place, you can begin to create variations of the different elements you have tagged on each page (Figure 3-10). Simply click "Add new variation" and give it a name. You can use HTML or plain text. The elements you create will be run in a variation of patterns and combinations. If you are just learning, start with one variation and slowly work up to bigger projects with multiple variations and elements that are being tested.

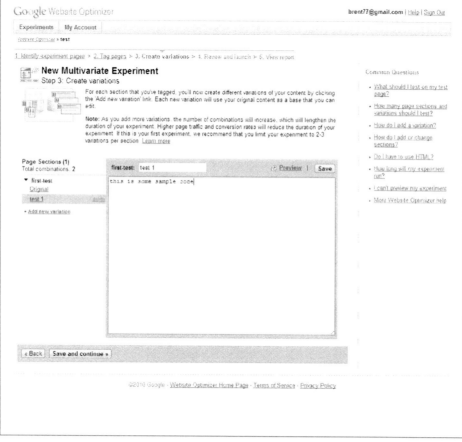

Figure 3-10. Creating the variations

Next, you will be asked to review and launch your test (Figure 3-11). You can also include comments about what you are testing, or why this test is important. This will help you remember the purpose of the test if you end up with many tests all running at once, or if you have tests that may run over extended periods of time.

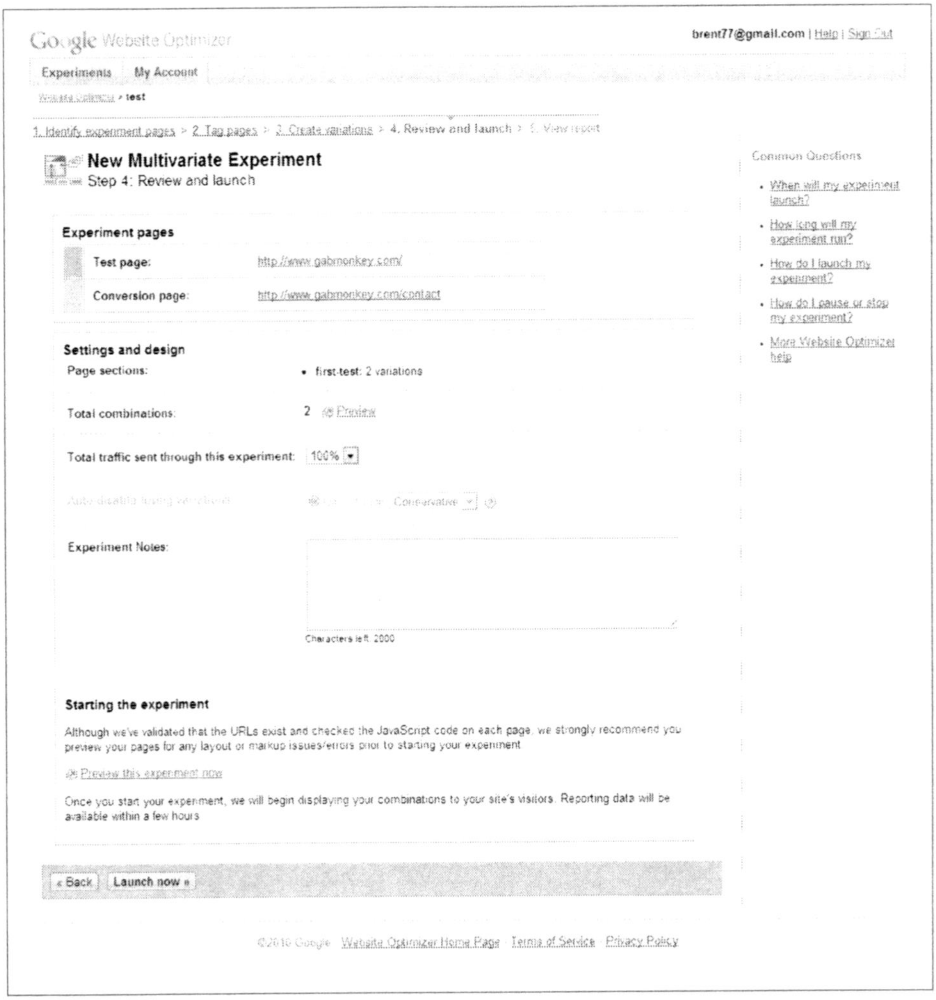

Figure 3-11. Reviewing and launching your test

As your test runs, you can follow along to see which combination performed better and what the improvement to goal completion was (Figure 3-12). Once you are satisfied with the results of your test, you can implement the successful page with the new permanent elements and, if you so choose, run another set of tests to continue your improvements.

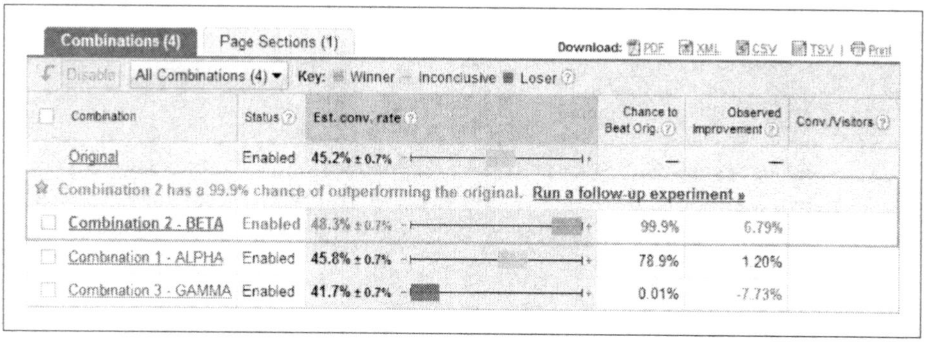

Figure 3-12. Results of a multivariate experiment from http://websiteoptimizer.blogspot.com

You may see changes in test results over time. As you run a test, depending on the elements modified and the goals defined, you may run into seasonality effects, or you may find that the phenomenon of "newness" impacts changes either positively or negatively. Some testing suites allow you to account for this and show the interactions over time as well, so you can rule out effects like seasonality and newness.

How Testing Improves Your Search Campaigns

Running A/B or multivariate tests is simple. As we just saw, it should only take a few minutes to set up the code to test. The hardest work is coming up with the different pages or elements to test. Testing is critical to the success of search. The effectiveness of search as a traffic delivery mechanism is significantly improved by taking action and being accountable for what happens with that traffic once it is delivered.

At this point, you should be thinking about goals for all your search campaigns, and simple testing can move the bar by significant leaps. In Figure 3-12, the successful page resulted in an improvement of 6% in our conversion rate. If the page receives 100,000 visitors per month and originally had a conversion rate of 10%, this means that 10,000 success events happened each month on the original version of the page. An observed improvement of 6% would mean that 10,600 conversions were happening on the more successful page.

Now suppose you also improved the volume of traffic to that page. Not only would you have the 6% improvement from page modifications based on testing, but you would also have improved volumes of traffic from search.

The caveat is that as search is all about relevancy, so too must your testing be about relevancy. If you modify a page to push in new traffic that it was not originally designed for, you may see impacts to your testing.

Esentially, if you plan on optimizing a page for new terms from search, you can run multivariate tests to see which variations of the page will not only work well for the current traffic, but also for any net new traffic you hope to generate.

If you are including new words in a paid search campaign or modifying a page to include new targeted organic words, doing A/B or multivariate testing at the same time will show how the page handles these changes, and the impact they have on the customer experience. In essence, when trying to improve traffic, also think about the impact this traffic may have on a page, and how you can measure the success of the traffic you generate in engaging with the page.

Measuring Engagement

Engagement is a measure of the experience and interaction a person has with your website or web page, and it goes hand in hand with A/B testing and multivariate testing. When running these tests, you should consider engagement with your page or website. Engagement metrics may include complex math that uses time on site, page views, and more to come up with a single number. The most common version of this is RFM (recency, frequency, monetary value). It is very complex to measure, and it can come in different formats for different companies. Further, I don't think any single site has one single measure of engagement. Here are two different examples of engagement for two different websites.

Example 1 of Engagement

When measuring engagement on my blog, I consider it a success if I can get people to: (1) read an article (measured by average time spent on the articles); (2) even better, comment on an article; or (3) best of all, sign up for RSS or email notifications of new content. Each of these engagement elements has a higher success level in my mind, and they are all measurable.

Time on site is "soft," meaning it doesn't tell me much about whether people are impacted positively or negatively by the content of the site, or if they are truly reading anything. All I know is that they've spent enough time on the page to have read something.

Comments provide me with more meat. I can now see how many people are commenting, and what they are thinking—do they agree or disagree? I can measure success here as a ratio of visits to comments, so I can easily see which articles are more successful, or at least which provoke more reactions from people to get them engaged with my blog.

RSS and email opt-ins tell me people have found my content worthy and they want to read more. This is the ultimate feather in my cap for my blog. It tells me that the readers are interested in coming back, and that I've now developed a relationship or opened up the lines of communication more freely.

Example 2 of Engagement

Google, as a search engine, is in the business of providing users access to content as quickly as possible. Google has made changes to the results it presents over time, including adding features such as local results, page previews, and instant results. Usually, when a new change is made—instant results, for example—Google also pulls up some user statistics that show how this feature has decreased search times. It may also cite how searches are now more complex, using more words per search.

If I were to guess at what Google was measuring for engagement, it would be search volume, search complexity (number of words per search), number of search sessions, and time to search.

Search volume provides Google with a general idea of how many users are actively searching at any given time. Every search is considered an engagement with Google, and a success. Some may argue that clicks on paid ads would be considered the primary engagement, but I suspect Google uses its economics of size to generate its revenue. That is, more searches means more opportunities to generate paid ads that may get clicked. If Google was to use paid ads as its main measurement, it would likely skew the results to always show ads, which would diminish trust in the results it presents.

Search complexity, as a measure of engagement, is a way to measure how well Google is doing with interpreting and building trust with users as they input searches. The more complex my search is, the more likely I think it is that the engine will provide me with a result. Search complexity has been shown to increase over time as users become more trusting due to positive results from the engine's algorithm.

Number of search sessions can be measured as how many search sessions a user performs around the same topic. Performing several very similar searches (say, for closely related terms such as "dog," "dog breed," and "dog type") indicates that the user's engagement with the results is not a positive one. Similarity in searches in a single session can therefore indicate how well the engine is doing at returning results, and if users feel these results are useful.

The last measure of engagement is time on site. For my blog, two to three minutes on a page is considered a good amount of time; for search engines, the quicker they can deliver results and get you onto another website, the better they have done in completing their task. So, positive user engagement with an engine is actually measured by reducing time on site, but increasing frequency of use.

Engagement and Search Campaigns

As we talk about traffic from your search campaigns, you will need to think about user engagement. As we saw from these two examples, a greater "time on site" can be either a positive or negative measurement. Studying engagement metrics means moving beyond page views and time on site, and thinking about what people should be doing on your site.

Engagement metrics provide a way to study the actions people take, regardless of their overall goals, to try to measure user satisfaction with your content or your online presence. I wish there was a simple one-size-fits-all solution, but part of the fun of analytics is learning how to measure behaviors.

All Traffic Is Not Created Equal

As we look at user engagement, we need to consider search as the source of traffic. We will notice that in some cases there are pages that simply have high bounce rates because they are successful one-stop shops. It is not always "I came, I saw, I puked," as Avinash Kaushik is famous for saying about bounces. It may be "I am learning, I came, I read, I wanted to learn more so I searched again."

Consider a student writing a paper. She may search on a topic, open three or four pages from a search result to pull together three or four different views on a subject, and repeat this process several times. Variety of sources is important to this user; she likely will not drill down any further, but there may be an offline component such as citation in a piece of work. This kind of user behavior can indicate that the site was successful at delivering educational content, which may be its primary goal.

What needs to be understood with traffic from search is that it can fall into the bucket of highly relevant, highly engaged traffic, or nonrelevant and nonengaged traffic. You could, in theory, run a paid search campaign and drive tons of traffic to your website, but the quality of this traffic can be just as important as the quantity. Let's assume your site has an average conversion rate of 3% and you average about a million visitors per month. This means 30,000 conversions per month.

Let's assume now that you're asked to get another 500,000 users to your website. If they all convert at the same rate as before, you'll be looking at 45,000 conversions per month. However, if the traffic is poor and your conversion rate slips to 1.5%, you'll be looking at 22,500 users converting per month. This is actually lower than the figure you were getting before you adjusted your site to drive more traffic to it.

Why might something like this happen? There are number of reasons. For one, by modifying your landing page to drive traffic from search terms with higher search volumes, you may end up alienating existing users of the page (remember when we talked about using multivariate testing to offset this?). That is, your original audience may feel this page is no longer relevant to them. You have certainly increased traffic, but due to the new page design, you may now be attracting people who are too high up in the purchase funnel.

Let's take the same scenario again, and focus not on driving large volumes of traffic but very specific traffic lower in the funnel. Let's assume we drive an additional 100,000 users, which is one-fifth of what we drove before. Let's also assume that these users are highly engaged and convert well. We see our conversion rate increase to 4%, which means we now see a total of 44,000 users converting each month. A smaller, more targeted increase in traffic results in almost the same number of users converting as in our previous example, when we increased traffic by 500,000 visits per month but did not improve the conversion rate.

Further, we may start to break down this traffic and find that some traffic generates higher average order values. This is traffic we want to segment off so we can figure out how to further optimize and increase revenue with this particular segment. Certain terms may generate higher average order values, and focusing on these terms may yield a significant ROI.

The downside is that there is no way to predict exactly what a segment of traffic will be like until you become familiar with the rest of the traffic driven to your site. There will be times when you think a segment or target should be highly valuable and it turns out to be a dud. This happens from time to time, but it should not deter you from applying this strategy whenever possible. In the long run, you will learn how to maximize revenue both with existing traffic and by creating more traffic. The main thing to keep in mind is that you can control any factor on your website; what you cannot control is what the search engines do.

For this reason, I always recommend looking at your site first and figuring out what you can fix and control there before worrying about external factors and attempting to gain lots of new traffic that may not convert.

Volume of Traffic Versus Number of Conversions

As we just saw, volume of traffic and conversion rates do not always correlate. While we may not be able to predict exactly what will result in good-quality traffic, we do have some tools at hand to help us figure this out.

If we have developed a search strategy where we have bucketed our words into sets based on position in the conversion funnel—as we looked at briefly with our shoes example and is also illustrated in Table 3-2—we can start to figure out which words it will be best to expand on to generate more conversions.

Table 3-2. Engagement matrix

Awareness	Consideration	Preference	Purchase	Retention
shoe repairs	shoes	steel toe boots	discount boots	shoe repairs
boot laces	boots	running shoes	discount shoes	boot laces
running equipment	heels	black running shoes	best price on shoes	
gym membership		acme running shoes	lowest price on shoes	
		basketball shoes	coupons for shoes	
			shoe store location	

The terms in our preference and purchase funnels are likely to have the highest conversion rate, while the terms in our awareness and consideration funnels are likely to drive the most traffic per term. What we are looking for is to create a balance between traffic and conversions.

When we are told to try to get more sales, we should be focusing on the words that bring in users lower in the purchase funnel. However, we also know that for some of these terms, we need to first show up in the consideration phase of a search. So, we need to make sure our strategy to get words to rank covers terms in both the consideration phase and the preference/purchase phase. By focusing on only one part of the purchase cycle, we may ultimately end up driving large volumes of poorly converting traffic, or only small volumes of traffic that converts well.

Having your keyword lists sorted in such a way that you can see what parts of the purchase cycle they are relevant to will make your optimizing job easier and help you strike a good balance. In Table 3-2, we lumped these words into different categories, with some overlapping. There may actually be even more overlap. Table 3-3 shows how better to keep track of our keywords.

One thing you will notice is that, when I reclassified these words into a matrix, I included the most words in the awareness and retention funnels. The reason for this is that even though a customer may have already chosen a brand or store, there is still an opportunity for us to sway his decision. Some terms are much stronger awareness terms than others, and the same applies to retention; thus, you may want to subdivide the terms in these categories into strong and weak. The rest of our words are easily categorized and some may show up in different parts of the funnel, which is OK.

Table 3-3. Engagement matrix

Keyword	Awareness	Consideration	Preference	Purchase	Retention
shoe repairs	yes	no	no	yes	yes
boot laces	yes	no	no	yes	yes
running equipment	yes	no	no	no	no
gym membership	yes	no	no	no	no
shoes	yes	yes	no	no	yes
boots	yes	yes	no	no	yes
heels	yes	yes	yes	no	yes
steel toe boots	yes	yes	yes	no	yes
running shoes	yes	no	yes	no	yes
black running shoes	yes	no	yes	no	yes
acme running shoes	yes	no	yes	no	yes
basketball shoes	yes	no	yes	no	yes
discount boots	yes	no	yes	yes	yes
discount shoes	yes	no	yes	yes	yes
best price on shoes	yes	no	yes	yes	yes
lowest price on shoes	yes	no	yes	yes	yes
coupons for shoes	yes	no	yes	yes	yes
shoe store location	yes	no	yes	yes	yes

Seeing our words split out like this allows us to now target certain terms more accurately. For example, the term "shoe store location" may be a good word to aggressively optimize. It has coverage in many buckets; it is also a potentially stronger awareness term and may generate good volumes of traffic. We will also want to look at all of the terms in the purchase funnel as words likely to increase conversions.

When we start to see a slip in traffic volumes, this may indicate we are slipping in our awareness terms. Tossing ground here may hurt us in the long run, and we need to assess whether the slip is due to more competition, loss of rankings, or simply changes in the volumes of search in general on our awareness terms. Changes in traffic from these terms may be predictive of dips in other terms further down our timeline; these changes may show up in days, weeks, or months, depending on our business, but awareness and consideration terms can usually act as indicators of what is happening in a segment and can allow you to explain why certain traffic may be expected to decrease when you must forecast what sorts of traffic volumes and sales you can expect to see in the future.

Traffic from Search Engines: Not All Engines Are Created Equal

Having our words sorted in a matrix will also allow us to begin to track patterns from different engines. I've often observed that Bing tends to deliver lower volumes of traffic that converts well, whereas Google can send larger volumes of traffic that does not convert as well. Establishing our keyword matrix and setting up analytics to track differences in the behavior of users coming to us from different search engines can help us refine our search strategies.

Most site analytics programs allow you to filter based on source. If there is a specific engine you would like to know more about, simply build a filter specific to that engine. In Google Analytics, this is done through the Advanced Segmenting area. However you go about segmenting based on source, here are the key elements you will want to look at:

- ROI
- Abandonment rate
- Average order value
- Cost per acquisition
- Return frequency (how often people come back from the same engine)
- Conversion rate
- Total sales volume
- Total number of referrals

With this information, we can surmise which engine delivers us more qualified leads, as well as estimating the scale and volume of these leads. Most folks focus on Google due to the sheer volume of traffic it can provide. However, when you're dealing with millions of searches per day across all the engines, even within the 20% market share between Bing and Yahoo! there is great opportunity. Even better, because most people focus on optimizing for Google, the competition to rank well on Bing is lower. This means you have a better chance of improving your rankings with less competition.

A well-optimized search practice can and should be easily transferable from one engine to another. While each engine runs a different algorithm, the general theories are the same across the board. For paid search, you may find that your CPC is less on one engine than another, and that the ROI is higher for a specific campaign or ad group.

Numerous studies have been run to show how users engage differently on Bing and Google, and how the types of searches differ. Bing is more focused on tasks and portal-like activities (booking trips, getting weather updates, etc.), while Google focuses on information searches (and, more recently, local search results). Each engine provides slightly different results, and each engine may drive different types of traffic to your site. The only way to be certain is to test the traffic from each engine.

Furthermore, if you are looking at a global scale, you will need to take into account other engines besides Bing and Google. Local or regional engines such as Yandex and Baidu target specific markets and regions (Russia and China, respectively), while Yahoo! has a large following in Japan. Market considerations and the engines driving this traffic will both impact the quality, type, and quantity of users who are sent to your site.

Typically, when dealing with regional engines, there will be significant biases and changes in user behavior. If you want to get traffic from Yandex, which typically serves the Russian market, you may need to have your site translated into Russian; more importantly, you'll need to be sure you can serve that market, so if you are in direct commerce you may want to rethink your strategy. Experience has shown that online shopping is not as prevalent in Russia as it is in the West, so you'll need to make sure you simplify the online experience for these users, as they may be new to online shopping, or provide access to your products in local brick and mortar stores.

If dealing with Baidu, you may also run into issues with the government or other policies that are in place in the Chinese market. We will talk more about locality later; for now, the key is to understand that user behavior and patterns can change. You may also consider optimizing for online buying engines, or other vertical search engines.

If you are investing heavily into paid search, you will want to think of multiple bid strategies to use across multiple engines and how you will manage these. Running paid search programs directly through Google or Bing is simple for smaller campaigns, but as you grow in scale, or look at inclusion across multiple engines, you may need to consider solutions such as Clickable (*http://www.clickable.com/*), which allows for multiple account management and multiple bid strategies.

Strategically speaking, from a paid search perspective, you may begin to think of your search strategy like an investment banker. You will invest in keywords not only across different ad groups, but across different engines and languages, each with different costs and ROI. Segmentation of traffic by engine will be important to measuring the success of your campaigns.

Seasonality and Traffic

Tracking seasonality can be critical to business, and it can help explain trends and increases and decreases in traffic. If your site has been running for more than a year, you can easily capture the effects of seasonality. If, however, you are entering a new market or pursuing keywords that are new to your business, you may want to do some research in this area. The Google Keyword Tool and Google Trends can provide insights into seasonal effects on terms and words (Figure 3-13).

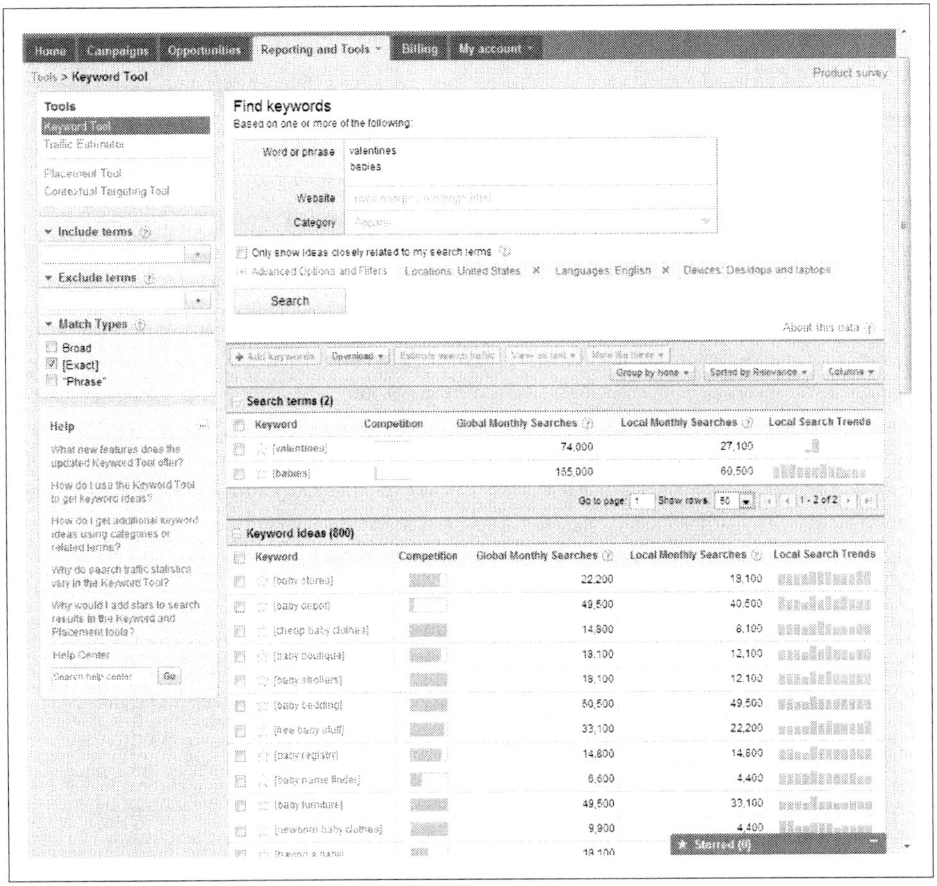

Figure 3-13. Monitoring seasonality in Google Keyword Tool

Terms such as "valentines" and "babies" both show some seasonality. "Valentines" naturally displays an uptick in February; "babies," on the other hand, sees a strong uptick in March. Is this because more people find out they are pregnant in March, or do we see more births in this month? There may be any number of reasons for this, but the term certainly shows some seasonality. Using the Google Keyword Tool allows us to predict these sorts of seasonality trends.

More important is when we can track seasonality based on our own numbers. There are several ways of tracking growth; the most common are *month over month* (MoM), *year over year* (YoY), and *quarter over quarter* (QoQ). Year-over-year tracking allows us to compare growth based on the season; when we track it month over month, we can start to see how we are truly trending from an analytics standpoint. Table 3-4 illustrates the raw data, while Figure 3-14 shows a chart of this same data for visualization purposes.

Table 3-4. Month-over-month and year-over-year tracking

Metric	Jan 2010	Feb 2010	March 2010	Jan 2011	Feb 2011	March 2011
Visits	265,895	286,448	245,896	269,684	356,266	265,598
% change MoM	—	7.7%	-14.2%	—	32.1%	-25.4%
% change YoY	—	—	—	1.4%	24.3%	8.01%

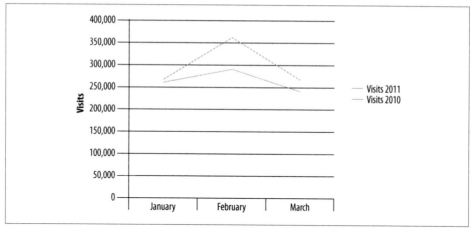

Figure 3-14. Data from Table 3-4 displayed visually in a chart

Our chart shows us that while March 2011 figures were down from the last month, they were still up year over year; further, February 2011 saw a dramatic increase both month over month and year over year. Most likely, February is the anomaly. We may want to ask if there were any additional search campaigns run during this month, or if there were any terms that spiked significantly in February 2011. March's numbers month over month look bad but actually return to a more normalized pattern of growth compared to year-over-year trends.

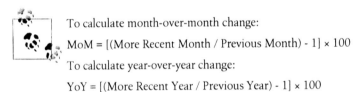 To calculate month-over-month change:

MoM = [(More Recent Month / Previous Month) - 1] × 100

To calculate year-over-year change:

YoY = [(More Recent Year / Previous Year) - 1] × 100

Understanding seasonality may help predict when to expect growth and decline. It should not come as a surprise that March dipped again for us, though we are suspect of the massive growth in February. The seasonality of this business may certainly be a factor, or it may be related to something that is not specific to seasonality.

Tracking year over year and month over month can't tell us for certain that spikes and declines we see are due to seasonality; what it can do is point out abnormalities we should investigate. Trends through the rest of the year should become predictable for well-run campaigns. If you are able to, you may also keep a log sheet of activities for each month. You may track what paid search programs you turn on and off, and when, as well as any changes to your search programs or any announcements from the search engines on algorithmic changes. This data can help you explain spikes and changes in your analytics over time.

We could also apply this theory to link building, where we see increases in links over time during certain activities. For example, you may run several successful social media campaigns where you see surges of links, or run annual offers that continue to drive and build links. Seasonality can apply to many different analytics and metrics, and it's always something worth investigating if you have the capability to do so.

Is There Value in CTR?

Click-through rate, or CTR, is a highly utilized metric in many reports. From a paid search perspective, CTR is important, as it will impact the Quality Score of your paid search campaigns. A low CTR is perceived as indicating irrelevant content that will likely result in additional costs over time. Further, from an organic standpoint, decreases in CTR may impact your organic rankings. Strictly speaking, from an engine perspective, CTR is relevant simply because the engines say so.

From a reporting standpoint, however, what does a 50% click-through rate really tell you? This could mean that 2 out of 4 people clicked a link, or 1,000 out of 2,000. CTR really doesn't provide a very useful value most of the time. CTR actually has much more value when you have established a value for something you are looking to track.

For example, suppose we discover a set of keywords that generate a great deal of traffic to our site, but that currently have a low CTR. Knowing our baseline, we can now use CTR as a usable metric, as long as we realize that our general traffic volumes are not decreasing. We would want to measure CTR against traffic volume changes month over month or year over year, whichever is more relevant to our business.

Measuring and monitoring CTR can be a quick way to assess the validity of changes you make, but it should not be the sole metric used to confirm the value of a program. Further, high CTRs do not always correlate to high conversion rates. CTR is an action analytic, not a value analytic. Action analytics typically don't have a dollar value associated with them and therefore are used when we want to measure or monitor changes and improvements. They may sometimes be tied to revenue, though: an example would be a high CTR on a word that appears very high in our keyword funnel but does not result in a lot of immediate sales. CTR should be used to measure only when you are looking to improve a known section of your search campaign or strategy.

Capturing Traffic Volume Based on Positioning

In Chapter 2, we showed how you can estimate traffic based on SERP position. You can find keyword search volumes through Google's Keyword Tool (*https://adwords .google.com/select/KeywordToolExternal*). When using this tool to find SEO traffic volumes for a specific term, you must always use the [Exact] match option on the lefthand side after making a selection. You can then estimate traffic volumes by multiplying the volume of traffic by the click-through rate associated with that position, as we saw in Chapter 2.

Being able to estimate traffic is a fantastic tool to help define your search strategy and the value of a position. Once you achieve a certain position or rank, or even when you've been holding it for a while, you will want to validate what that position value is truly worth. Both Google (Figure 3-15) and Bing (Figure 3-16) provide a webmaster suite that shows you impressions as well as clicks for terms that drive traffic to your site. Knowing the actuals of these numbers will help you understand if your words are performing at an expected average, or if something seems off. For example, say you have a first-place ranking on a term but are only getting a 15% CTR. Looking at the search result page, you may find there are image results returned with that search that are eating into your overall traffic. You may consider optimizing for images, or running a paid campaign concurrent with your SEO campaign.

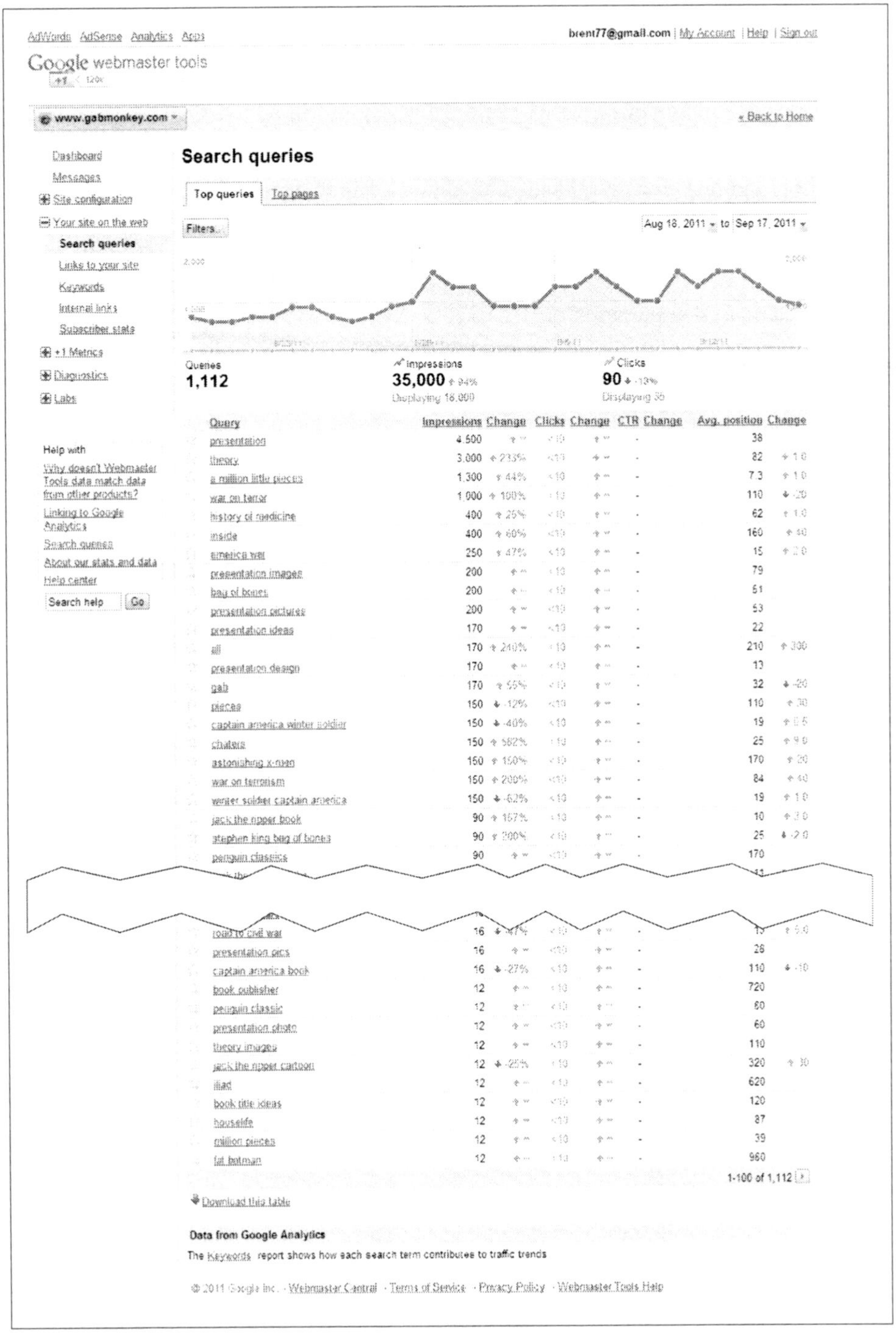

Figure 3-15. Google Webmaster Tools impressions and clicks

Figure 3-16. Bing Webmaster Tools impressions and clicks

Understanding actuals is important, as this is what we actually work with. The data provided in these reports can be applied to your campaigns as well to understand which are the high-volume terms that are truly driving traffic. Further, you can now track position based on information passed in the URL string from Google results in most cases. This is passed as the "cd" value in the referring query string. Basically, Google tells you what position the search result a user clicked on to get to your site was in. If you can build filters in your site analytics tool, you can capture and track this data. There are a number of ways to do this in most search analytics programs, as long as you pull the value of the constant width cd parameter from the referring query string.

A. J. Kohn has a great tutorial on how to set up SERP tracking in Google Analytics (*http://www.blindfiveyearold.com/track-keyword-rank-in-goo gle-analytics*). There are different ways to do this, but I prefer this version due to the ways you can drill down through the data in Google Analytics:

1. Create a new account profile (always do this when creating new filters in Google Analytics).

2. Click the "Edit" link next to the new profile.

3. Create a new filter to report on organic traffic only. Name it "Report Organic Traffic" and apply the following settings:

   a. Filter Type: "Custom filter", "Include"

   b. Filter Field: "Campaign Medium"

   c. Filter Pattern: "organic"

   d. Case Sensitive: "No"

   e. Save your changes.

4. Create another new filter to report on Google traffic only. Name it "Report Only Google Organic Traffic" and apply the following settings:

   a. Filter Type: "Custom filter", "Include"

   b. Filter Field: "Campaign Source"

   c. Filter Pattern: "google"

   d. Case Sensitive: "No"

   e. Save your changes.

5. Create another new filter to capture the keyword rank using a regular expression. Name it "Capture Google Keyword Rank" and apply these settings:

   a. Filter Type: "Custom filter", "Advanced"

   b. Field A → Extract A in the drop-down choose: "Referral"

   c. In the text field beside where you selected "Referral" put: \?| &)cd=([0-9]+

   d. Field B → Extract B in the drop-down choose: "-"

   e. Output To → Constructor choose: "User Defined"

   f. In the text field beside where you selected "User Defined", put: Rank: $A2

   g. Field A Required: "Yes"

   h. Field B Required: "No"

   i. Override Output Field: "Yes"

   j. Case Sensitive: "No"

   k. Save your changes.

This data lets you see not only how important rankings are, but also what effect position has on engagement. Do people coming from a first-ranked position stay on your site longer, look at more content, or complete more transactions than people coming from other positions? You will likely find that the answer to most of these questions is yes, as a well-optimized page is also a useful page. The search engines are in the business of providing the best pages and experience possible to a user, which is why this book focuses so heavily on monitoring and measuring what happens beyond the search page.

Tracking Mobile Traffic—SEO Versus Paid Search

In Chapter 10, we will dive deeper into mobile traffic, but while we are on the topic of tracking traffic, you will want to look for some of the differences between your mobile and desktop users. While the search algorithms do not change much based on device type, user behavior can. For example, with mobile users, you may see more local searches and results showing up than with desktop users. People coming to your site on a mobile device may also gravitate toward other sections of your site than traditional desktop users. Log and track what parts of your site each segment of traffic is going to, and what sorts of tools they utilize on your site. For example, you may find that a store locator is heavily used on mobile devices. To improve this experience for users, you may try to implement geolocation detection.

We're already seeing changes in search results in response to the proliferation of mobile users. Google will use your location to drive some searches to provide relevant results. This occurs today in Google Places. The same functionality occurs for desktop users as well, but the experience becomes more seamless for mobile users, as the engine is able to return results for locations close to the user, whose location is determined based on IP address and other geospecific information. These sorts of personalization may help significantly in retaining the users that come to your site through the search engines.

Tracking International Searches and Linguistics

International searches are another thing that you should keep an eye out for on your site. You can track searches from foreign locations, as most search engines have different geographic variations—for example, *google.com* comes in flavors, such as *google.fr* for France, *google.co.uk* for the UK, and many other variations. You may find that you have a larger international audience than you thought, particularly if you have content offered in multiple languages.

Within your clickstream analytics package, you should be able to filter based on geography. This report will tell you how much traffic is coming from other countries, and if you have a high volume of traffic from these countries. What this report will not do is identify areas it might be worth targeting if you want to improve your international traffic volumes. Further, the report only provides geographical information, not linguistic insights.

As search is heavily language-focused, you may discover that if you are a US-based company, you are excluding a significant portion of your audience by not including Spanish terms in your list of keywords. Google's Global Market Finder (Figure 3-17), which you can find at *http://translate.google.com/globalmarketfinder/index.html*, allows you to take a word in English or any other language and have it auto-translated into most major languages. In addition to providing translations, the tool reports on competitive opportunity and search volumes worldwide.

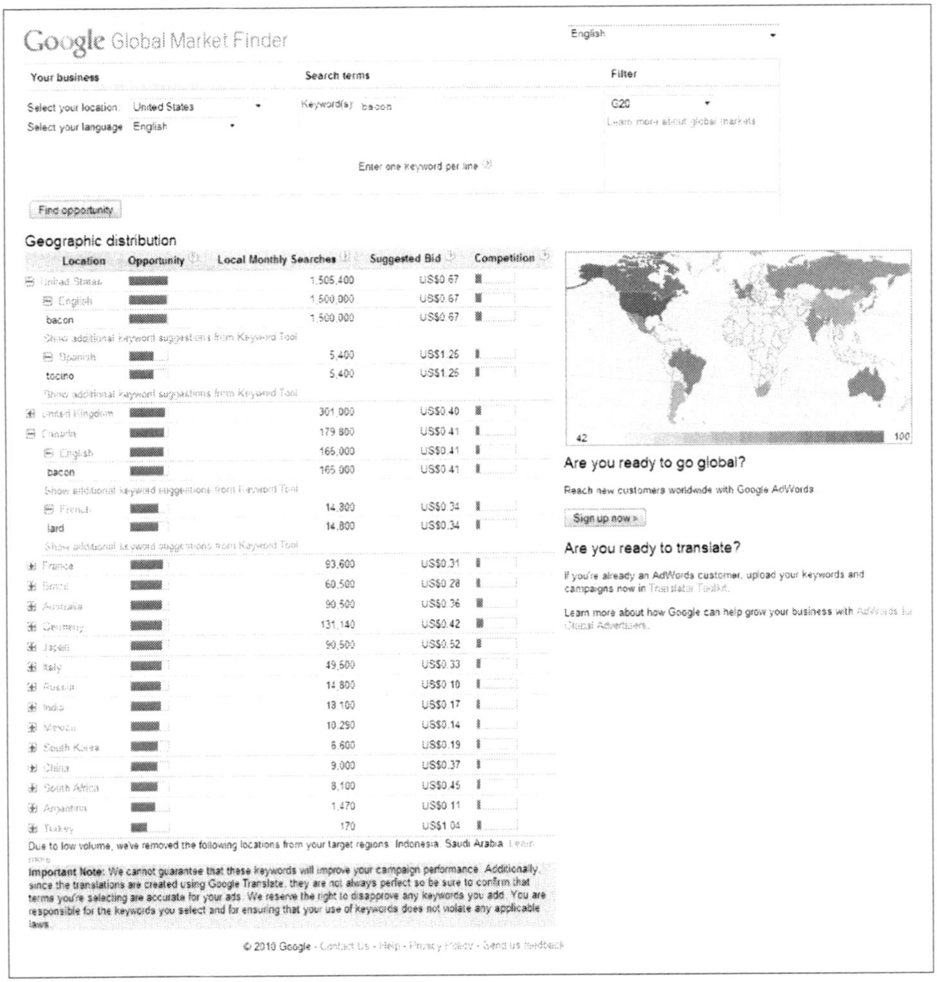

Figure 3-17. Google Global Market Finder

Running the example "bacon" on the G20 countries shows that, at the time of writing, there are 8,100 searches in the United States each month on the Spanish word "tocino." While this volume is low compared to the 1.8 million searches on "bacon" in the United States each month, it indicates some opportunity. The downside to using a tool like this is that not all translations are created equal, and auto-translation tools may miss other variations of words or terms that a natural speaker of the dialect would understand. If you're looking into this, you will want to engage with a professional translation company that understands not just the language but also some of the dialects, including slang, and is familiar with local traditions and culture.

Optimizing Conversion Rates for SEO and Paid Search

Before we conclude this chapter, let's take another look at CRO, as this is perhaps the most important analytic to track. By now, you should be able to define what are considered conversions on your site, associate dollar values with them, understand the differences between your mobile and desktop users, and have an idea of what sorts of international market opportunities you have. Further, you should be able to segment your search traffic based on location in the funnel, and understand why some traffic converts better than other traffic.

This all brings us back to improving these conversion rates. You should now be able to estimate the volume of traffic you can expect based on SERP position, understand what the current conversion rates are for pages you are looking to optimize, and build a strategy that will improve both your rankings and your conversion rates. SEO and paid search are not just about position in the engines; when evaluating your search campaigns, you must look beyond rankings to the landing and entry pages. When designers develop new pages, they should work with both the search and usability teams to ensure an optimal result. In fact, in a well-defined organization, the search team is an extension of the usability and user experience team.

Having your search team work closely with your user experience and usability team will ensure that they understand when user experience cannot be compromised for the sake of traditional search best practices. For example, when thinking about page titles, it may be more important to go with what delivers the best experience for users by clearly identifying the topic of the page, even if other words may be more relevant from an SEO perspective. Search should not be about a fanatical race to get a top ranking; it should be about helping your customers find what they're looking for.

Conversion rate optimization is the art of ensuring that customers can transition easily from a search term to finding what they are looking for. This may be in the form of more information, which they seek either through your site search or by going back to a search engine; as we discussed earlier, you should consider how the content on your pages may be able to influence secondary search terms. By developing sets of pages together, you can create pages with keyword clusters, as well as idea clusters. An *idea cluster* is much like a set of chapters in a book. They should all be thematically similar, but on slightly different topics. By building out these sets of idea clusters, you can cover a wide set of topics and ensure that you rank across several terms for a specific segment, product, or idea. For example, a company selling sports equipment might have a general page on sports, as well as separate pages on hockey, football, surfing, and golf. Each of these would then have its own set of associated pages—for example, on how to get a proper fit with your equipment, how to use it safely, how to care for it, and how to store it during the off-season. Beyond these pages, there would also be the pages specific to the products. The surrounding pages would all drive to the product pages and build a more thematic idea around these pages. Some people call these *value-add pages* and put a lot of effort into them, while others see little benefit and only want to see their product pages listed. By building up these pages, in addition to providing core product information and specs, you can help customers understand the value of your products and what makes them different from your competitors' products.

Concluding Thoughts

As we wrap up this chapter, I hope it has become apparent how important on-page optimization is not just for search, but to improve your sales and customer retention. The biggest lesson to take away from this chapter is that you should focus on fixing and influencing the items that you have direct control over, which are your own site pages. If you focus on conversion and usability when building your pages, you will have much greater success than if you focus simply on driving bigger volumes of traffic. Anyone can drive traffic over the short term; it's achieving good conversion rates and sustaining that traffic over the long term that is difficult.

If you find you are under pressure to drive traffic regardless of bad content, then your company may need to assess what its goals and targets are. Developing a sustainable plan includes creating good content and improving the user experience.

CHAPTER 4

Tracking Words— SEO and Paid Search

Search, whether SEO, paid search, or site search,
is a word problem.

While in the previous chapters we have looked at some mathematical formulas you can use to capture and track the results of your various search activities, search is really a very complex word problem. When you think about it, it's actually pretty amazing what the search engines do, how well they do it, and how frequently. Consider how much content the search engines have indexed. There are over one trillion unique URLs on the Internet (*http://googleblog.blogspot.com/2008/07/we-knew-web-was-big.html*), and from that content, the search engines are able to pluck out the best page that represents a given term in the blink of an eye. When I put the term "coffee" into Google's search box, it returns that result in 0.16 seconds—that's pretty impressive (Figure 4-1). Not only that, but the search engine also maps where the nearest coffee shops to me are located. Unreal.

Suppose your website is all about coffee. If one of your pages appears in the results list when someone types "coffee" into a search engine's query box, you have already accomplished a lot. As you can see in Figure 4-1, there are some 230,000,000 other pages also competing on this one word. That's a lot of pages about coffee! When you see those results you may say to yourself, "But I've got the best page ever on coffee, and Wikipedia ranks number 1?" Yes, yes it does, and for a number of reasons (with the biggest most likely being the number of inbound links that page has and the authority of the site).

For organic rankings, the search engines use both on-page and off-page indicators. If you feel you should be present on this word, I suggest now is the time to begin a paid search campaign. As you set up that campaign, ask yourself, "How much is this click worth to me?" In this chapter, we'll be looking at tracking the words you think you should be ranking on so you can decide if you have a problem (say, if Wikipedia is

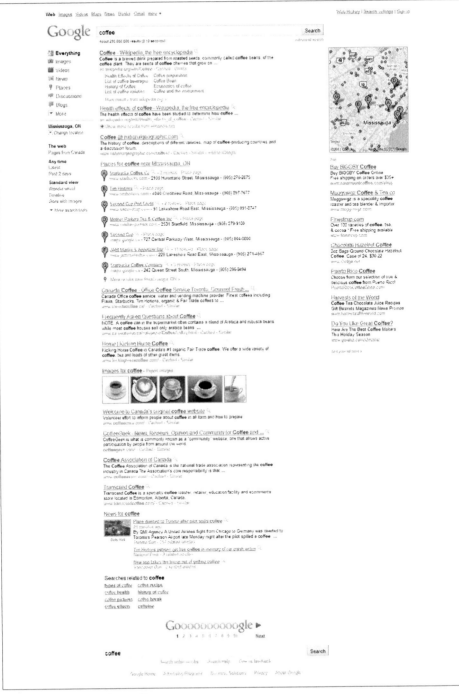

Figure 4-1. Searching for "coffee"

ranking ahead of you), or if you are lucky and already rank very well on those terms. We will also be looking at how to tell how much you are paying per word, and if you feel it is worth more or less.

Words and terms people use to find your content that result in positive ROI and engagement are ultimately what you want to be measuring. There are a number of ways to track words, and the strategies for SEO and paid search vary in terms of how you will want to manage your word lists. In this chapter, we will look at determining which are your top-performing words and which are underperforming, deciding what words have potential (do you really think you will rank on "coffee" if you sell tea?), clustering words around your pages, and creating whitelists and negative keyword lists. We'll also explore some specific metrics to look at for paid search campaigns.

Lastly, when selecting your words, you will need to use some judgment as to whether a term is really relevant. Just because you have the choice of tea or coffee in the morning doesn't mean pages about tea should rank in a search for coffee, and vice versa. When people search for a term, they want to find the pages that are most relevant to that term. The search engines rewards you for relevancy: if you get to the top of the rankings and the engines start to notice a lot of people coming back and searching on the same term again, the odds are they will pick up a signal that your page is simply not relevant. Do you really feel like spending all that time to get to the top of a search only to find you have a high bounce rate? I guess that depends on whether you can make a profit that way, but generally speaking it's not ideal.

Tools you will need in this chapter:

- Clickstream tracking package (Google Analytics, Adobe SiteCatalyst, etc.)
- Google Keyword Tool or some other keyword research tool
- Spreadsheet program (Excel or something similar)
- AdWords or some other paid search tool
- Keyword tracking program (e.g., WebPosition)

Tracking SEO Keywords

Understanding what words are driving people to your website—and more specifically, what words are driving people to a particular page on your site—is the first step to understanding opportunity. There are two components to consider: what words currently drive traffic, and what words you think should drive traffic. Further, the choice of words you use on a web page can impact SEO factors on that page.

As we saw in Chapter 2, when looking at ROI, improving the ranking of a page on one term can impact the volume of traffic to the site, which should drive incremental ROI. Typically, when optimizing a site for SEO, there are site-wide tactics and page-level tactics. Page-level tactics usually involve mapping keywords to a page and then saying that page should rank on those words.

On more than one occasion, I have been asked how to improve the ranking of a page on a very aggressive word. Particularly when dealing with large enterprise sites, you can end up with several departments and teams all competing over the same keywords, each with its own page.

This quickly becomes counterproductive, as instead of working together to build a unified front, these organization are fracturing and splitting their SEO efforts to see minimal gains. At an enterprise-level, if you plan on targeting an aggressive keyword, you cannot expect the search engines to reward you with relevant rankings if you can't send positive on-site signals (such as well-developed inbound links and site information architecture), let alone trying to build links off-site.

If you can't fix the things you have direct control over, you can't ever expect to rank on a high-value nonbranded term. Experience has shown me that sometimes it's not a technical issue that needs to be resolved but an organizational thinking and strategy issue, especially when bonuses are based on success and the bonuses force organizations to fragment their SEO strategies.

This approach of assigning words to a page seems a bit backwards to me, in that you should know what top-level words are already driving traffic to a page. You can find this out by examining your clickstream data and building a keyword cloud or keyword cluster.

Keyword clustering is a very simple process of taking a targeted page on your website and understanding what traffic and terms already drive traffic to that page.

Developing Keyword Clusters and Finding the Short Head and Long Tail

To develop our keyword clusters, we must first identify a page in our clickstream tool. As a heads up, when you run this report, you may find that the words that drive traffic to your page are not the words you think should be driving traffic to that page. The top words should be relevant to the content.

In Google Analytics, our first step would be to find the page we want to optimize under Content→"Top Content" and click on it. Under "Analyze," select "Entrance Keywords" and you will be presented with a list of all the words that have driven traffic to your page (Figure 4-2). To filter only for the organic words, click "Advanced Segments" in the upper-right corner and select "Non-paid Traffic." In Google Analytics v5, you can generate a keyword cloud by changing how reports are visualized when viewing the keyword report—you can also filter based on page, if you operate on a more visual level.

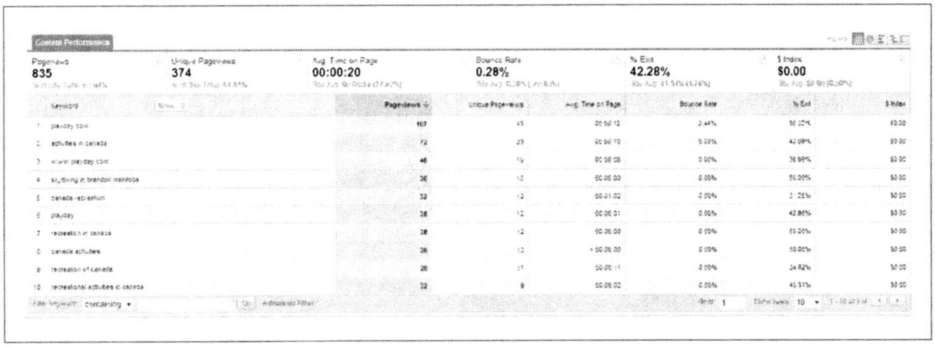

Figure 4-2. Google Analytics report for referring keywords to a page

You should be able to see the number of page views, number of unique page views, bounce rate, exit rate, and average value of the page. Table 4-1 shows a sample of the data from Figure 4-2. Also take note that there are over 130 terms driving traffic to this page. Remember when we talked about the long tail? This is a perfect example of this in action. The top term, "playday.com," drives only 29% of the traffic; all the other terms combine to create more traffic than that one term. Optimizing that term in ways that impact the other terms may have dire repercussions. Also surprising is the volume of searches on "skydiving in Brandon Manitoba"—a term that most likely was not intentionally optimized for, but a term that drives some significant traffic on its own.

Table 4-1. Adding in page views to keyword clustering

Keyword	Page views	Unique page views	Bounce rate	% Exit	$ Index
playday.com	107	45	2.44%	38.2%	$0.00
activities in Canada	72	33	0%	43.06%	$0.00
www.playday.com	46	19	0%	36.96%	$0.00
skydiving in Brandon Manitoba	36	18	0%	50.00%	$0.00
Canada recreation	32	12	0%	31.25%	$0.00
playday	28	12	0%	42.86%	$0.00
recreation in Canada	26	12	0%	50.00%	$0.00
Canada activities	26	13	0%	50.00%	$0.00

Looking at this data set, we see that we don't have an indexed value to derive an ROI value from. The real world will often throw us curveballs like this. For this case, I would suggest estimating an ROI value by determining which words achieve success based on other measurable activities. For example, which words deliver more traffic to a page with a high-value goal or activity? This would be an ideal time to use a pathing report and filter by individual keywords. This process can become laborious, and you may choose to look only at the top 10 words driving traffic to your site, as they will likely be the highest sources of revenue. You'll want to build your strategy to revolve around the words with the highest conversions and goal completions, relative to the customer's stage in the conversion funnel.

Once we know what keywords are driving traffic to our home page, we can also better decide if perhaps we should look at pushing some of this traffic into other sections of our site, by modifying links on the home page, utilizing some of these top keywords and pointing further into the site. By doing this, we indicate to the search engines that our site contains another page on this topic. If we build up enough of these links on our site, we may be able to transfer that traffic from the home page to a deeper page that may be better able to serve the needs of the customers, improving both traffic and bounce rate. We only want to do this if we expect to see a positive ROI on this effort, though. We can take this data and use it to project which words would be the best to try to further optimize and move up the rankings, to bring in more traffic.

Segmenting Keywords in Clusters

Through our keyword clustering, we can also look at segmenting words. There may be groups of words that can be further grouped together: for example, in Table 4-1, we see that we could potentially segment our keywords based on geography or activity.

 The concept of clustering keywords around pages was first introduced to me by Bill Hunt. He's a super-smart guy, and has really led the way in the paid search and SEO field. What I like about this concept is that it makes you realize that you are not looking at a one-page–to–one-keyword mapping; instead, you are looking at sets of words that play off each other.

If you think about mapping one page to one keyword, you end up very focused on a short-head objective. By building up keywords in clusters, you start to think of words in relation to each other, and you start to think about the midtail and beyond. Further, it is much more manageable to think of keywords in terms of concepts and ideas and relevancy. My spin on this concept is that I like to think of one lead word that is the target word, and several supporting words around that word. You want to maximize your optimization to cover all those words, but you may find the cluster has more value for increasing ROI than the single lead word does.

The lead word keeps you focused on the overall concept and idea of the page and helps you quickly sum up what the page should be about.

Segmentation helps to make large groups of words more manageable (e.g., as in Figure 4-2, where we have 134 different terms driving people to one page). By segmenting words in such a way, we can refine our CRO strategy by looking at whether each of these segments has appropriate space on the page and can serve the needs of people likely coming in on these search results, and considering whether it would be appropriate to split the content across several pages rather than leaving it all on one page.

You also want to find out how these words currently rank, as well as the specific page in the search results. To find your ranking, you can use WebPosition (Figure 4-3) or any other rank checking program.

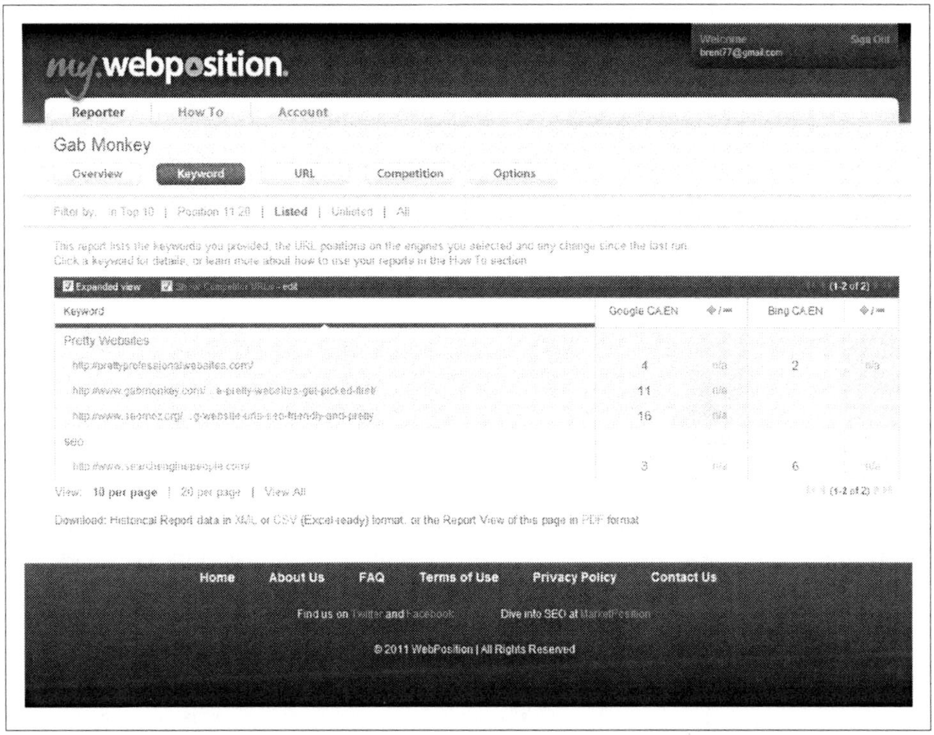

Figure 4-3. WebPosition keyword report

We can also look at segmenting our words into long tail and short tail terms; that is, our top 5 or 10 driving terms and then the subset of terms that drive further traffic. This can help us identify terms that are positionally weak in the rankings. Table 4-2 shows the SERP positions for each of the keywords we identified earlier.

Table 4-2. Keyword clustering against our homepage

Keyword	SERP position	Page views	Unique page views	Bounce rate	% Exit	$ Index
playday.com	1	107	45	2.44%	38.2%	$0.00
activities in Canada	5	72	33	0%	43.06%	$0.00
www.playday.com	1	46	19	0%	36.96%	$0.00
skydiving in Brandon Manitoba	8	36	18	0%	50.00%	$0.00
Canada recreation	12	32	12	0%	31.25%	$0.00
playday	2	28	12	0%	42.86%	$0.00
recreation in Canada	7	26	12	0%	50.00%	$0.00
Canada activities	18	26	13	0%	50.00%	$0.00

By adding in the SERP position, we can identify the terms where we have the greatest opportunity to improve traffic. We may also find that some of these terms are very difficult to compete on.

Creating our keyword cluster has given us a better idea of what exactly is happening with this page in terms of its SEO value. We can see both the short head and long tail impact, and what terms convert well and do not convert well. Also, we now know which terms have the greatest room for improvement.

Knowing the potential of these terms will help us to build out our ROI formula to figure out which of these terms are the ones that will have the greatest impact on our ROI. The words that will generate the greatest revenue changes are the words that we should target first. In this case, because we do not have an average customer value, we will assume the goal of the site is simply to drive traffic to generate advertising impressions. In Table 4-3, we include another column called "Potential traffic increase." We will use what we know about ranking position to estimate how much additional traffic we could drive to each section by moving each term up three spots or to a number 1 position (whichever is less). This doesn't mean these changes will be easy to achieve. To measure feasibility, we will have to build out a competitor analysis, which we will cover in Chapter 8.

Table 4-3. Adding in growth potential for keywords

Keyword	Avg SERP position	Page views	Unique page views	Bounce rate	% Exit	$ Index	Potential traffic increase
playday.com	1	107	45	2.44%	38.2%	$0.00	0
activities in Canada	5	72	33	0%	43.06%	$0.00	53
www.playday.com	1	46	19	0%	36.96%	$0.00	0

Keyword	Avg SERP position	Page views	Unique page views	Bounce rate	% Exit	$ Index	Potential traffic increase
skydiving in Brandon Manitoba	8	36	18	0%	50.00%	$0.00	23
Canada recreation	12	32	12	0%	31.25%	$0.00	0
playday	2	28	12	0%	42.86%	$0.00	71
recreation in Canada	7	26	12	0%	50.00%	$0.00	20
Canada activities	18	26	13	0%	50.00%	$0.00	0

To figure out the change in traffic volumes you are likely to see if you move up or down a position, use the following formula:

Expected Total Page Views – Current Page Views × (1 + Projected SERP CTR % Converted to a Decimal)

Finally, to calculate the potential traffic increase, use:

Potential Traffic Increase = Expected Total Page Views – Current Page Views

Here, we can see that our best improvements in traffic volume will come from improving the rankings of the terms "playday" and "activities in Canada." Knowing this, we can now start to explore how difficult it would be to improve these terms in the rankings based on an analysis of our competitors (we'll return to this in Chapter 8).

Another analytics tool you might want to consider is Wordtracker Strategizer. It provides insights into the click-through share you have on a word, as well as an idea of some of the better opportunities you may have for improving your ROI. Strategizer imports Google Analytics keyword reports and also incorporates Google AdWords data to give you an idea of the click share you have per word (*http://www.wordtracker .com/academy/automatic-seo-case-study-tahoe-mountain-sports*). Strategizer allows you to look at the data in a number of ways, so you can figure out if it is worth going after terms with high volumes and low conversions or high conversions and low volumes. You may still need to do some of your own math, but Wordtracker is working on making the tool simpler to use and making it easier to spot opportunities. With the integration of Google Analytics, Wordtracker Strategizer has the potential to be a very powerful tool in your kit if you take the time to sit down and understand it. It may save you significant time trying to figure out what words have the best value.

Keyword Research for New Opportunities

Understanding what we want to optimize on for currently ranking words is a start in identifying opportunities, but we also need to look at what we are *not* ranking on, and if it is worth investing time and effort pursuing rankings on new terms or words. This requires keyword research.

No tool will tell you exactly how much traffic will come from a word. I have used the Google Keyword Tool for research on keywords and been told that the traffic volume is too low to measure, and yet in my clickstream data, I see significant volumes of traffic from these terms. This means the keyword research tools are good for estimates only.

The Google Keyword Tool was designed to support paid search activities, but it can be leveraged for organic research as well. The tool provides some insights into search volumes (Figure 4-4). When using the Keyword Tool for organic keyword research, make sure that you always have [Exact] match selected. This option will only be available (on the lefthand side) after you enter the words you are looking for. Selecting [Exact] will provide data for a specific search on a specific term.

The Keyword Tool also allows you to filter based on geography and language, as well as device type, should you want to see the difference between searches on desktop and mobile devices. The tool provides global and local monthly search statistics, so you can get an idea of a specific geography, as well as the global volume if your brand reaches across borders.

Using the tool is very simple: just put in the words you want to learn more about, and it will return information on those words, as well as suggesting other similar search queries. With the estimated traffic volume you can project a volume of traffic based on targeted position. Take the estimated volume and multiply it by the percentage based on organic ranking position to determine approximately how much traffic opportunity may exist for you on a word or term.

As an example, consider the word "cereal." If it has roughly 34,000 searches a month, and you feel you can capture the 8th ranking spot, you are likely to receive 1190 visits from that word (34,000 × 0.035 = 1,190). Based on your site's average conversion rate, you can then project approximately how many of these customers you expect to convert to a sale. If we assume a 3% conversion rate, this means 1190 × .03 = 35.7 conversions. Knowing you would have 35.7 conversions, you can project an approximate revenue by multiplying the number of conversions by the average order value.

It will likely take more effort and time to capitalize on opportunities for keywords that you do not rank on, which you will also have to take into account. Most of the time, you will find yourself looking to improve organic rankings for terms you currently rank on, which makes sense. As you already have an established traffic base, and some insights into behavior, you can compare how you currently rank to how your competitors rank and determine if you have a chance of beating those competitors. Further, you have the opportunity to optimize your page for traffic already coming in on that

Find keywords

Based on one or more of the following:

Word or phrase (one per line)   Website

Bike

Red Bike

Green Bike

Blue Bike

Purple Bike

☐ Only show ideas closely related to my search terms ⓘ
☐ Advanced Options and Filters

Locations and languages ⓘ

All Countries		All Languages	
United States		English	
United Kingdom		Japanese	
Japan		German	
Germany		Portuguese	
Brazil			

Include specific content ⓘ   ☐ Include adult ideas

Show Ideas and ⓘ   All mobile devices
Statistics for

Filter keywords ⓘ   Local Monthly Searches ▼ >= ▼ [   ] Remove
+ Add another

Search

About this data ⓘ

✚ Add keywords | Download ▼ | Estimate search traffic | View as grid ▼ | More like these ▼

Group by None ▼   Sorted by Relevance ▼   Columns ▼

☐ Search terms (5)

☐	Keyword	Competition	Global Monthly Searches ⓘ	Local Monthly Searches ⓘ	Local Search Trends
☐	[bike]		90,500	9,900	
☐	[red bike]		210	36	-
☐	[green bike]		170	36	-
☐	[blue bike]		210	45	

Figure 4-4. Keyword research on all mobile devices

term, meaning that even with the same traffic volume, you can improve conversion rates and on-site activities as you work at pushing up the rankings.

Working to rank on terms you don't currently rank on will be a much more involved process, and you may want to consider looking at paid search to bridge the gap and build awareness of content you have that is related to certain terms. To understand how to improve rankings on new terms, you need to understand how people find you today.

How Are People Finding Me Today?

The first question you should be asking is how people are finding your site today. What words are already driving traffic to your site? What words might a search engine see as the most relevant to a page that you're developing? These are important questions, and ones that can be answered. First, though, you should understand some basic theories around the search engine algorithms. The terms *latent semantic indexing* (LSI) and *latent Dirichlet allocation* (LDA) are often bandied about when looking at keyword relevancy in a document. LDA can be seen as a sort of extension of LSI. The goal of both is to provide some semantic context to terms, words, and groups of words. In layman's terms, the search engine algorithms try to provide context to words, to understand synonyms, and to recognize that some word pairings have different meanings when together than they do separately.

The engines try to create an association or understanding of the context of the words based on use patterns they see. Without knowing for sure, SEO people need to guess at which models best match what is used by the engines. LSI has been ruled out, as it doesn't scale well. LDA is a possible option, as is the Hidden Topic Markov Model (HTMM). Then there is certainly a great likelihood of something unique to each subsystem. In Google's case, this may be its proprietary "phrase-based information retrieval" system. The larger body of work (the Internet) and all the data it contains also plays a big role in the algorithm.

In a *Wired* article published in 2010, Google admitted to using user behavior as a way to "educate" its algorithm even further about variations in synonyms; the article also discussed how important the proximity of words to each other is to understanding the differences in context of a set of words (*http://www.wired.com/magazine/2010/02/ff_google_algorithm/all/1*). So, what we do know is that frequency and context within a page play a role in determining on-page factors. For example, use of the term "hot dog" alongside terms such as "ketchup" and "relish" indicates a food-based context. The algorithms used in both Google and Bing are much more sophisticated than simply looking at how many times a word appears in a document. Feel free to go out and learn more about these topics if you are interested in understanding search patterns. For our purposes here, we do not need to get any deeper into the algorithms. The point is that, as we look at words and groupings, we may see some oddities in words linking to pages; also, when using keyword density tools and keyword volume tools, we should bear in mind that they are simply very basic tools that can provide some limited insight into how frequently a word appears in a page.

Knowing that there are algorithms that look at synonyms and other word variations, we do have a limited set of tools we can use to measure relevancy to a specific word. There are several options for measuring keyword density and volume, as reviewed in the Appendix. Each of these has its pros and cons: the value of a keyword density or volume checker is not to check the *relevancy* of a term on a page, but to help identify if there is a word or term that is significantly over- or underused. When trying to determine the relevancy of a page using an LDA tool (it may be worth keeping an eye out for the one SEOmoz has in the works (*http://www.seomoz.org/blog/content-optimization-revisiting-topic-modeling-lda-our-labs-tool*)), you may use a density check to see if a certain term may be in use that is bringing down your LDA score. Using the LDA score to determine relevancy and then a volume or density tool to check the frequency of terms in a document can provide you with much better insight into the differences between your page and a page ranking higher than you in the search results on a specific term.

For our purposes, we want to know what words are bringing people to the content on our site. Secondly, we want to know what the likelihood is of any new content we create being found. That latter point is key, as it allows you to start thinking about the search process before content is created. If you can enter this mind-set when creating content, you will start to realize that it's not all about keywords; including images or video that can also be indexed may help drive traffic and improve the findability of your site and content. You will also come to really understand how important the long tail is compared with the short head in terms of driving traffic by the end of this chapter.

For organic optimization you will also need to consider how you will build awareness of new pages to generate new links from other sites, as well as raising social awareness and building social links to your site. These are all off-site factors that significantly help improve rankings, and they are all things we can measure. We will look at these issues further in Chapter 9.

For paid search, we want to know which words are driving traffic that converts, and how to maximize good terms and minimize bad terms. Essentially, we will be creating "whitelists" and "negative keyword lists"—terms that should be familiar to most paid search folks—and setting up proper tracking and auditing of these terms. We also want to be able to predict seasonality effects and understand when some words will go big, and we will look at building keyword clusters for our paid search pages, as we did for our SEO pages.

Tracking Paid Search Keywords

Paid search is a different beast from organic search when it comes to making decisions about keywords. When you're setting up a paid search campaign, there are different types of matches you can set up for keywords, and these match types differ between Bing and Google. The following sections provide definitions of these match types directly from the engines[*] and examples of when ads will run. Because there are different types of matches and they are interpreted in different ways, a given word can be either a drain on your budget or a great revenue generator, depending on the match type. Match types will impact how quickly you burn through money, and how targeted your ads are.

---

[*] For more information, see *http://adwords.google.com/support/aw/bin/answer.py?hl=en&answer=6100* and *http://adcenterhelp.microsoft.com/help.aspx?project=adcenter_live_std&market=en-us&querytype=topic&query=moonshot_conc_matchoptions.htm.*

Broad Match

Google approaches broad match as follows:

> This is the default option. If your ad group contained the keyword *tennis shoes*, your ad would be eligible to appear when a user's search term contained either or both words (*tennis* and *shoes*) in any order, possibly along with other terms. Your ads could also show for singular/plural forms, synonyms, and other relevant variations.

Bing, on the other hand, handles broad match a bit differently:

> [It] triggers the display of your ad when individual words in your keyword appear, in *any* order, in a customer's search query. For example, your keyword *red flower* would match search queries that include *red flower*, *flower is red*, and other variations, and not just *red* or *flower*.
>
> Broad match can expand to include words that are closely related to your keywords. For example, a search query for *red carnation* might result in your ad being displayed, because adCenter automatically identifies carnation as a type of flower. Use broad match to expose your ads to a wider audience.

Table 4-4 compares the way broad match is handled by Google and Bing.

Table 4-4. Black Cats on broad match

Search query	Google	Bing
Cat	yes	no
Black	yes	no
Black Cat	yes	maybe
Black Cats	yes	yes
Free Black Cats	yes	yes
Cats that are Black	yes	yes
the Black Cat	yes	yes

Phrase Match

Phrase match is handled by Google in the following way:

> If you enter your keyword in quotation marks, as in "tennis shoes," your ad would be eligible to appear when a user searches on the phrase *tennis shoes*, with the words in that order. It can also appear for searches that contain other terms as long as it includes the exact phrase you've specified.

In this area, Bing is quite similar to Google, as illustrated in its documentation:

> [It] triggers the display of your ad if the word or words in your keyword appear in a customer's search query—even if other words are present in the typed query. Your keyword *red flower* would match searches for *big red flower* and *red flower*, but not *yellow flower* or *flower red*.

Table 4-5 shows a comparison of how phrase match is handled by Google and Bing.

Table 4-5. Black Cats on phrase match

Search query	Google	Bing
Cat	no	no
Black	no	no
Black Cat	no	no
Black Cats	yes	yes
Free Black Cats	yes	yes
Cats that are Black	no	no
the Black Cat	no	no

Exact Match

Google explains its approach to exact match as follows:

> If you surround your keywords in brackets—such as [tennis shoes]—your ad would be eligible to appear when a user searches for the specific phrase *tennis shoes*, in this order, and without any other words in the search term.

Bing's approach to exact match is somewhat similar, though it does differ in some subtle ways:

> [It] triggers the display of your ad only when the exact word or words in your keyword, in *exactly* the same order, appear in a customer's query. Your keyword *red flower* would *only* match searches for *red flower*, with no spelling variations. With exact match you might see fewer impressions but a higher click-through rate, because your ad is shown to people who might be more interested in your product.

Further, Bing seems to ignore words like "the", "a", "an", etc. Table 4-6 provides a comparison of how exact match is handled by Google and Bing.

Table 4-6. Black Cat on exact match

Search query	Google	Bing
Cat	no	no
Black	no	no
Black Cat	yes	yes
Black Cats	no	no
Free Black Cats	no	no
Cats that are Black	no	no
the Black Cat	no	yes

Negative Keywords

Suppose you only had a cat to sell and wanted to make sure you were not showing up on searches for "Black Kittens". You would want to make that a negative keyword.

Google allows for different match types on negative keywords (*http://adwords.google.com/support/aw/bin/answer.py?hl=en&answer=67991*):

> I. *Negative Keywords*
> You can add negative keywords at both the ad group level and the campaign level. Adding a negative keyword at the ad group level means that the term will only affect the ads in the ad group. A campaign-level negative keyword will apply to all ads in all ad groups in that campaign. [...]
>
> For example, adding *free trial* as a negative keyword to your account would prevent your ads from showing on any search queries containing the terms *free* and *trial*. It wouldn't prevent your ads from showing on variations of these terms, however. It also wouldn't prevent your ads from showing on search queries that only contain one of the terms.
>
> For example, the search queries *one-day trial* and *free test* could trigger your ads, while *free one-day trial* could not.
>
> II. *Negative Phrase-Matched Keywords*
> You can create a negative phrase-matched keyword by surrounding the term with quotation marks. Here's an example:
>
> > "free trial"
>
> If you were to add "free trial" as a negative keyword to your account, the system wouldn't let any search query containing the phrase *free trial* trigger your ads. The search query *free trial lesson* would not trigger your ads, for instance. The rules of phrase match still apply, however, so your ads could possibly show on the search query *trial* or *free one-day trial*.
>
> III. *Negative Exact-Matched Keywords*
> You can create a exact-matched keyword by surrounding the term with brackets. For example:
>
> > [free trial]
>
> Adding this as a negative keyword would prevent your ads from showing on the search query *free trial* only. Search queries such as *free trials*, *free*, and *one-day free trial* could still trigger your ads.
>
> It's a good idea to add relevant variations of your negative keywords, including both the singular and plural forms. [...]
>
> Note: When adding keywords directly in the negative keywords section, there's no need to include a negative sign (-) before each keyword.

Bing only has one match type for negative keywords, which is phrase match (*http://community.microsoftadvertising.com/blogs/advertiser/archive/2010/10/25/feature-comparison-series-match-types-and-negative-keywords.aspx*). However, you can apply negative keywords at different levels, with different results depending on the level, as outlined in Bing's documentation:

- **Campaigns.** Campaign-level keywords apply to all keywords in a campaign, unless you also associate negative keywords with an ad group or a specific keyword. Each campaign can contain thousands of negative keywords.
- **Ad groups.** If you associate negative keywords with an ad group, campaign-level negative keywords will not be applied to that ad group. Each ad group can contain thousands of negative keywords.
- **Specific keywords.** If you associate negative keywords with a specific keyword, campaign-level and ad group-level negative keywords will not be applied to that keyword. Each keyword can have a list of negative keywords of up to 1024 characters, including commas.

Table 4-7 compares how "black kittens" is handled as a negative keyword in the two search engines.

Table 4-7. Black Kittens as a negative keyword

Search query	Google negative broad match Black Kittens	Google negative phrase match "Black Kittens"	Google negative exact match [Black Kittens]	Bing negative match Black Kittens
Cat	yes	yes	yes	yes
Black	yes	yes	yes	yes
Black Cat	yes	yes	yes	yes
Black Kitten	yes	yes	yes	yes
Black Kittens	no	no	no	no
Free Black Kittens	no	no	yes	no
Kittens that are Black	no	yes	yes	yes

Tracking Broad Match Words

Broad matching in paid search is a very useful way to build up new word pairings to help improve your impressions across a variety of words. Broad match is defined by Google (*http://adwords.google.com/support/aw/bin/answer.py?hl=en&answer=6136*) as follows:

> With broad match, the Google AdWords system automatically runs your ads on relevant variations of your keywords, even if these terms aren't in your keyword lists. Keyword variations can include synonyms, singular/plural forms, relevant variants of your keywords, and phrases containing your keywords.

> For example, if you're currently running ads on the broad-matched keyword *web hosting,* your ads may show for the search queries *web hosting company* or *webhost.* The keyword variations that are allowed to trigger your ads will change over time, as the AdWords system continually monitors your keyword quality and performance factors. Your ads will only continue showing on the highest-performing and most relevant keyword variations.

When you bid on a set of words on broad match, you can also generate a report of what words your ads ran on. To get this report, simply follow these steps:

1. Sign in to your AdWords account.
2. Click the Campaigns tab.
3. Click the Keywords tab.
4. Check the boxes of the specific terms you want to see that drove traffic, or leave all unchecked to see all words that drove traffic.
5. Click the "See search queries" button above your statistics table.
6. Select "All" from the menu to analyze the search queries for all your listed keywords.

Running this report will help you understand what actual words are driving the clicks through your AdWord campaigns. You can use this information to create lists of positive and negative keywords. Say, for example, you're a cat breeder and you're selling cats. Suppose the current litter of kittens is orange. When you're starting out, you may run a broad match campaign on "cats" to learn about what words people are using to find cats. Suppose you discover that "grey cats" and "tan cats" are driving most of the traffic. Since you don't have any grey cats, you'll want to put "grey" on your negative keyword list. This will guarantee that any searches with "cats" and "grey" in them will not display your ad.

To this list, you'll add all the terms you do not want to show up on, effectively saving you money by ensuring you don't rank on nonrelevant terms. "Tan cats" is a relevant description for your "orange cats," so you may want to capture people looking for "tan cats." You don't have to do anything to make sure your ad shows up on these searches, but you may want to consider creating a new ad specific to this term to run on exact or phrase match. By creating a more relevant ad with relevant copy, perhaps better describing your tan cats, you may be able to capitalize on conversions.

The negative keyword list will be important for filtering out words you do not want to spend money on, but you will want to continue to run the original keyword on broad match if you want to keep learning other terms that are used to find cats—essentially, data mining the results that trigger clicks to your site. We can see an example of setting up a negative list in Figure 4-5. We can apply negative keywords both at the campaign level and the ad group level in a variety of ways that we will not get into here, as we are focusing on analytics and not list setup.

Figure 4-5. Building a negative keyword list

Based on the data you get from your search queries list, you should be able to quickly build up a negative list of words that you don't want to show up on. The sooner you build up this list, the sooner you can stop spending money on clicks that have little to no value to you.

The other source of negative keywords is your clickstream data. If you are tracking the volumes of traffic and conversion rates from your search terms (and if you aren't, what are you doing?), you should be able to use the clickstream data to identify words that are not performing in terms of creating conversions or that have poor or negative ROI.

These are words you may want to add to your negative list. By weeding out underperforming words and irrelevant terms, you will increase the likelihood that your remaining keywords will rank well on broad matches, driving traffic to your site and creating positive ROI for you.

You will also need to make some decisions about the words you keep in your keyword list. For example, you will want to consider what words should be set to [exact] match or "phrase" match so you can keep better track of these terms and how they perform. You can create more targeted ad groups specific to these sets of words, and once you have an understanding of which words you want to show up on for exact or phrase matches, you may even decide to turn off your broad match words.

If you decide to go from broad to exact match, the effect is essentially turning everything that you are not matching as an exact phrase into a negative list. Your keyword list will also likely have a higher CTR as you become more precise in your ad messaging and start to display more relevantly on more controlled sets of words, and you should start to see higher conversion rates.

Running on broad match, though, is a good way to identify words that have the potential to drive or influence your paid search campaigns in the long term. You may discover words you hadn't thought of that turn into top-performing words, which is ultimately what you are striving to develop. Your goal should be to build up a set of top-performing words while removing any words that underperform by placing them on your negative list.

Tracking Top-Performing Words and Underperforming Words

To track top-performing paid search words, much like we did on the SEO side, we will need to develop a dashboard, spreadsheet, or matrix that tracks our words along with some KPIs that are important to each of those words. We want to track our average visitor value, cost per acquisition, and ROI. All of this data is available either through your clickstream data or through your keyword management tool, if you've set it up to capture conversions. By comparing our cost per acquisition and our average customer value, we will be able to determine if we are running a negative or positive ROI. Table 4-8 shows the kind of table you will want to build up.

When we look at our ROI, we can see that some words are performing better than other words. You will likely discover that 80% of your revenue comes from 20% of your keywords. When looking at your keyword list, you should work down from highest ROI to lowest ROI, ensuring that your top-performing words have full coverage. This will help us plan our budget. If you do not have full coverage on one of your terms that has a high ROI, you may consider pausing a lower-ROI term to maximize exposure of the stronger ROI terms.

 When a campaign first starts, purchases from early clicks will result in an extremely high ROI. You should wait until you have enough statistical data to make an informed decision before you start making changes—usually three to four weeks of data is enough, though if they are low-volume terms, you may need to wait longer.

Table 4-8. *Paid search top-performing and underperforming words*

Keyword	Cost per click	Visits	Conversions	Average visitor value	Cost per acquisition	ROI
Black Cat	$1.34	28	8	$125.36	$4.69	$120.67
White Cat	$1.23	23	3	$190.25	$9.43	$180.82
Grey Cat	$1.54	29	6	$175.23	$7.44	$167.79
Tan Cat	$1.23	98	9	$183.25	$13.50	$169.75
Orange Cat	$1.65	21	1	$250.36	$34.65	$215.71

The top-performing words should be rewarded with further investment, while the underperforming words should be paused and reviewed. There may be reasons why these words are not converting well. For example, the words may be more costly due to poor Quality Scores, or they may have poor bid strategies or high competition. This is not to say you should give up on these words; what you should do is investigate if there is something incorrect in the ad copy or something related to the landing page of the lower-ROI words that may be reducing the volume of sales and thus bringing down the average visitor value. You may also have an instance where the word cannot be paused, as it sells a critical product that has a higher lifetime average value than it does an average customer value. In these cases, the revenue is not in the first sale, but all the resulting sales.

Tracking Paid Search Quality Score

Quality Score (QS) is a very important factor to track in your paid search campaigns, as it impacts the position and price you pay per click. Quality Score is determined by the engines dynamically at every search. However, Google provides some general feedback to Quality Score within AdWords as well. It is basically made up of the following elements, as listed at *http://adwords.google.com/support/aw/bin/answer.py?hl=en&answer=10215*:

- The historical CTR of the keyword and the matched ad on Google
- Your account history, which is measured by the CTR of all the ads and keywords in your account
- The historical CTR of the display URLs in the ad group
- The quality of your landing page
- The relevance of the keyword to the ads in its ad group
- The relevance of the keyword and the matched ad to the search query
- Your account's performance in the geographical region where the ad will be shown
- Other relevance factors

If you are uncertain of the importance of this metric, consider the results of a detailed study run by ClickEquations on the impact of Quality Score (*http://www.clickequations.com/blog/2009/03/the-economics-of-quality-score/*). Table 4-9 shows how they found it impacted bids.

Table 4-9. Quality Score impact on cost per click for Google AdWords

Quality Score	Discount or increase in CPC
10	Discount of about 30%
9	Discount of about 22.2%
8	Discount of about 12.5%
7	Break even
6	Increased by about 16.77%
5	Increased by about 40%
4	Increased by about 75%
3	Increased by about 133.3%
2	Increased by about 250%
1	Increased by about 600%

By having an understanding of what you can expect in terms of discount or increase, you get an idea of how important Quality Score is to you now. It can be the difference between paying less than a dollar per click to more than six dollars per click. Monitoring your Quality Score and being cognizant of the factors Google lists will ultimately help you further drive down costs and improve your ROI by reducing the average cost per acquisition.

You can find your Quality Scores by navigating to your campaigns and then your keyword lists (Figure 4-6). In the "Status" column, you will see what looks like a word balloon; moving your mouse over this will show you the QS for each keyword set up in your campaign. Take note of the keywords that have a low QS, and consider pausing or modifying them to improve their QS.

Quality Score can be improved by targeting pages that are more relevant—try including the keyword in the page title, in the URL, or in H1 tags. Quality Score can also be improved by altering your bid strategy and improving the click-through rate of the words. Quality Score will also improve with historical trust. Over time, if you run campaigns with high CTRs targeting relevant pages, your QS can also improve.

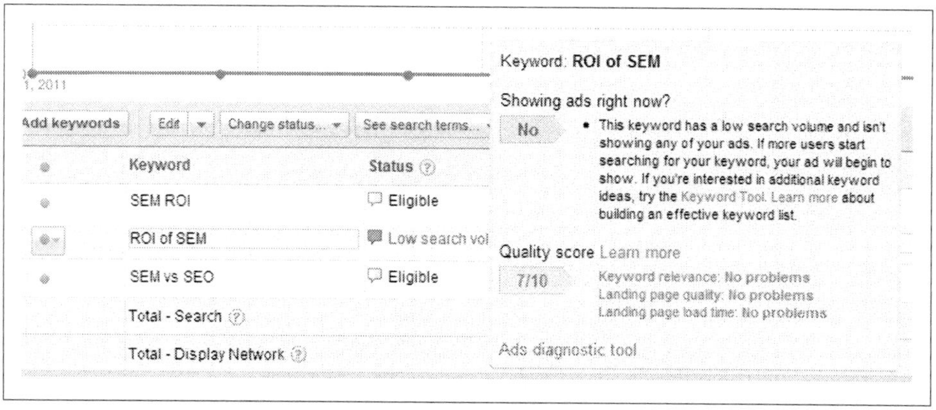

Figure 4-6. Quality Score showing for a word

Seasonality and Words

The last topic to cover is seasonality and words. In both SEO and paid search, you may see some unusual spikes in certain terms during the year. This phenomenon is referred to as *seasonality*. It may be influenced by weather, holidays, events, or other annual occurrences. Seasonality is something that should be fairly predictable for your campaigns, as it is something that occurs annually. Do you have an annual announcement that goes out? If so, you may expect a spike after that announcement. Do you see sales increases around Valentine's Day or some other holiday? Again, that sort of seasonality is predictable. To identify susceptible keywords, you can test your words in the Google Keyword Tool. Figure 4-7 is an example of a seasonality effect. Searches on the term "valentines" spike in February, with some occurring in January but virtually nothing through the rest of the year. We can also look at the term "engagement," which you might expect to show some seasonality relating to Valentine's Day. We see some increases on this term in March, April, August, and October, but there doesn't appear to be any sort of pattern between "engagement" and "valentines" in terms of seasonality. If we ran a jewelry store, we might therefore decide it is not important to be aggressive on the term "engagement" in January and February, when many of our competitors may be out trying to get more traffic. However, if our sales tell us differently, we might decide we need to compete in that market regardless of what the search volumes tells us.

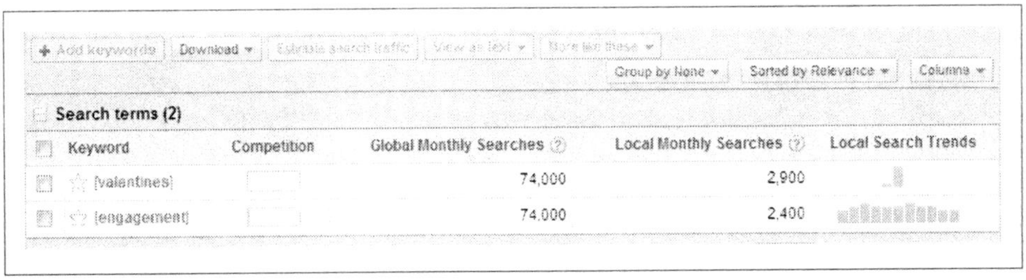

Figure 4-7. Seasonality in the Google Keyword Tool

Being aware of seasonality can help you prepare campaign budgets, ads, and bids, possibly getting them to a point where you can turn them on and off. For your SEO campaigns, it allows you to plan in advance what terms you will need to have on your pages at different times of the year if you want to rank on some of those seasonal keywords. If you plan to rank on "valentines" in your SEO campaigns, you should start to work on building your ranking in late December, to ensure you have plenty of time to get indexed, and start to build links to the page through link-building campaigns. There should be no excuse for annual occurrences catching you by surprise. Being prepared for seasonal business spikes will mean you can spend more time optimizing and less time worrying about implementing.

Concluding Thoughts

Looking back at this chapter on words, we see how important it is to both understand and track how we perform on different keywords, as well as the impact tying the wrong words to the wrong page may have on our conversion rates. Poorly set-up ad groups can result in low Quality Scores, which means increases in your cost per click. SEO pages with many words clustered around them that are not tightly related to the goal of the content may also result in low conversions. Segmenting and refining your keywords will help you increase ROI. Although this may feel like a lot of work, it is a short-term pain for a long-term gain. We will come back to some more keyword issues when we get into tracking competitors. We will learn how to compare how our competitors performed on those words and how we can use analytics to figure out what is needed for us to surpass them in the results page.

CHAPTER 5

Coordinating SEO and Paid Search

*Your SEO and paid search campaigns can provide
you with a more holistic model of what is
happening on your site related to search.*

In the grand scheme of things, some users who click paid search ads may not even realize they have done so. The fact that we refer to them as different topics does not mean that an end user distinguishes between them. Further, we can use the tactics discussed in this book to test both types of campaigns and apply what we learn across the board.

 I find it interesting that most companies continue to separate their SEO and paid search efforts, and even more interesting that companies continue to let the agencies that spend their paid search budgets own these strategies. The biggest value I ever saw was when we decided to separate "church and state," if you will—meaning that we did not give the agency total control over the spend, and instead put a secondary team in place to perform auditing.

This meant that we did not get "good news" stories every week, and instead we had conversations about improving, optimizing, and driving more value. The catch-22 I think many agencies that control their own spends find themselves in is the expectation that there will be a positive ROI, when the reality is that not every hit is a home run.

The moment the agency spending our budget stopped having control over the investment was when we saw our biggest leaps. By bringing the strategy in-house and placing it under the control of impartial parties, we gained much greater control over our search programs and enabled coordination between the SEO and paid search teams. Part of success is enabling open and honest conversations.

Thinking of your users from SEO and paid search globally as search users can help you figure out how to block holes and build up defenses against competitors. A frequently pushed paid search strategy is to pursue the long tail. In some cases, though, this may not be the right course of action. Some companies, such as industry leaders or companies looking to break into a segment, must be visible on non-long-tail words. In these cases, paid search may end up being a loss leader. That is, a negative ROI may be acceptable as part of a long-term plan to establish or maintain leadership in a specific segment. From a simple perspective, think of paid search as pursuing a strategy of instant gratification and control, and SEO as "slow and steady wins the race." You can turn paid search on and off swiftly and strategically, while with SEO it takes time and effort to gain and sustain rankings.

Tools you will need in this chapter:

- Clickstream tracking package (Google Analytics, Adobe SiteCatalyst, etc.)
- Spreadsheet program (Excel or something similar)
- AdWords or some other paid search tool
- A/B or multivariate testing tool (Google Website Optimizer, Test & Target, etc.)

Monitoring CTR from Paid Search and Applying Your Findings to SEO

By monitoring your high-CTR paid search words, you may be able to identify some places where you can alleviate some of those clicks through SEO. Audits of your highest-CTR terms can provide you with some ideas as to which terms and words you need to be thinking about for SEO.

Remember that every click on a paid ad is money spent. Some paid search professionals cite the high CTR they get on terms, but the savvy person will recognize that terms with high click-through rates may also represent the greatest aggregated cost. To figure out which paid search terms would make good SEO subjects, you want to evaluate both search volume and ROI. Focusing on terms with only 20 or 30 searches per month might not be a good use of your time, but terms with 1,000 impressions and an ROI of 80% could be worth the work.

Use SEO as a long-term strategy to try to alleviate pressure on areas where you are spending a significant amount on paid search. If you are planning to spend the time required to boost your SEO efforts, you will probably want to be looking at key tactical words that are critical to your business, and you will need to determine your ability to rank on these terms, based on on-site and off-site ranking factors as well as an analysis of your competition. Building top rankings from an SEO perspective may yield the same results and CTR you see in your paid search campaign. In fact, a strong position in this ranking may result in even more traffic for you. Given that more people click on the organic links as opposed to the paid links, targeting high-CTR terms can have some quick traffic benefits for your site.

Further, if you keep track of paid search terms that have a high CTR (as well as other KPIs), as we've done in Table 5-1, you may notice that you already have SEO rankings on some of these terms. Are these SEO terms seeing a similar CTR? If not, why aren't they? What is different about your paid search result versus your SEO result? There may be some other key learnings in your paid search results that can be applied to your SEO results. We'll look at these later in this chapter; for now, however, be aware that tracking words in SEO and paid search and noting performance differences may indicate issues with one or the other of your campaigns.

Table 5-1. Tracking SEO versus paid search results for a word

Search type	Average ranking	CTR	Volume of traffic	Conversion rate	Average order value
Paid search	1	4.6%	345	3.6%	$387.12
SEO	6	3.8%	285	3.4%	$345.24

Setting up tracking like we see in Table 5-1 can indicate where there may be room for improvement. Seeing that our first-position ranking is slightly outperforming our sixth-position ranking in SEO, we may infer simply that there is value in a first-position ranking, or that there is something we are doing better with that landing page compared to the SEO landing page. While the SEO results may seem to be trending well compared to the paid search results, this is not necessarily the case. We can see that we have more room to grow our SEO results. What would be the impact of improving our current SEO position to 4? With what we already know, we can make projections as to what improving our position will mean for traffic—but what if we also look at some of the other factors in our paid search campaign?

Slightly higher conversion rates for paid search indicate that we are identifying and targeting our purchase audience more efficiently in paid search. Are both terms driving to the same page? If not, what are the differences between the landing pages? It's important to look at paid search (as that's where we learn), and then apply that to our SEO landing page. We also see higher average order values for paid search traffic. Do we have different products featured on the paid search page? What happens if we move these to the SEO page? It's not simply about position, but what happens after the click.

A/B and Multivariate Testing—Applying Insights from the Paid Search Page to SEO

In Chapter 3, we covered A/B and multivariate testing. Moving beyond CTR is a major leap, as you go from being someone who knows how to generate traffic to someone who knows how to do something with that traffic. Paid search allows for some quick tests of users coming from search traffic. That is perhaps the greatest advantage paid search has over SEO.

Testing words and page layouts for users coming from search can yield significant improvements in your conversion rates, and in site stickiness. Testing your landing pages with paid search traffic can help you get bounce rates down, which will improve your overall site engagement. You can track the results of your experiments to see which variations of pages perform better.

You can also use tools like Adobe Test & Target or Google Website Optimizer to help facilitate quick testing of pages. You can do A/B testing, which is when you run one variation of a page or element against another, or multivariate testing, which is when you run multiple tests at the same time to find out which combinations yield the best results. Both forms of testing can be effective ways to improve user conversion rates and reduce page bounces from your site.

Page testing is key for traffic from search, as people coming from search have an expectation of the kind of information that will be delivered to them. A keyword entered is the first indicator of what a person is looking for; your page should reflect this expectation. The satisfaction of this expectation is measured by the bounce rate of visitors to your page and your conversion rates.

Testing Titles and Descriptions in Paid Search

You can set headlines and provide descriptions of keywords in your paid search campaigns (Figure 5-1). This correlates to page titles and meta descriptions in SEO. While meta descriptions are not always used, when they are pulled by the search engines they can be very powerful. Many people ignore the title tag and description in SEO as an opportunity to draw people in, focusing instead on making their pages keyword rich to try to improve rankings. In the paid search space, however, there is a whole world of focus put on the writing of headlines and descriptions. It has been shown that headlines and descriptions can improve CTR as well as conversions if they resonate with and project the expectations of the users.

The challenge with SEO is that sometimes your page title directly impacts your ranking, so adjusting this may be scary. Others may be more willing to take the chance if it may mean driving more traffic to the site. The page title is one element that engines always use in calculating SERP positions, and it can be a highly valuable tool for driving traffic to your site if you find you cannot get above a certain ranking position.

Testing out headlines in paid search enables you to quickly see what resonates with people; you can then apply these findings to your SEO campaign and monitor results there. Sometimes you won't see the same trends in your SEO results as in your paid search campaign, but in other instances you will see direct correlations. Unfortunately, there is no way to predict exactly what will happen, but you may see some rising patterns in words and terminology that drive traffic.

Identifying terminology patterns in your paid search descriptions and applying them to your pages that target organic search may result in significant improvements to your

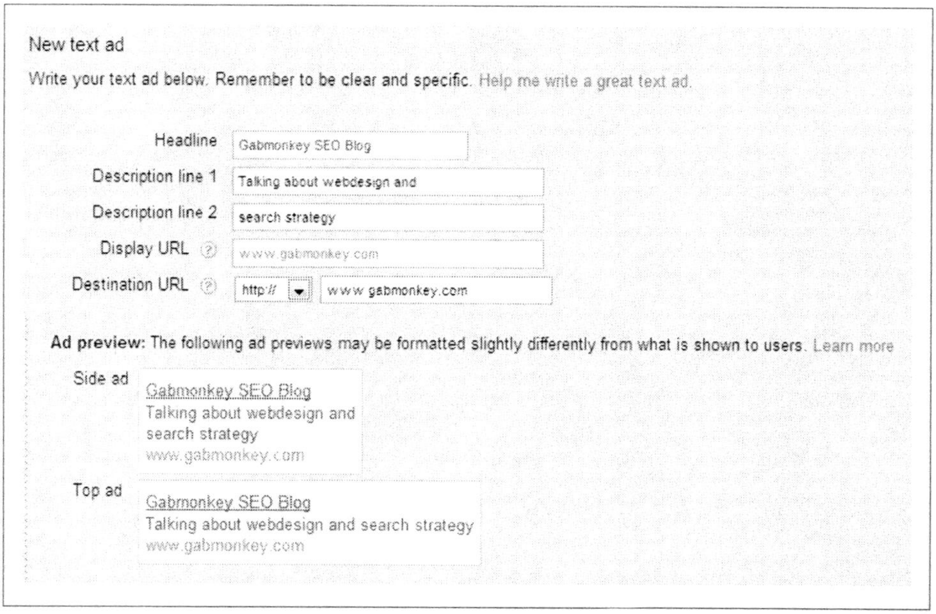

Figure 5-1. Setting page titles for your paid pearch campaigns

SEO campaigns. For instance, you may find that word position is important: leading with your key term rather than having the key term in the second position of a sentence may alter your CTR. Again, these are things we can quickly test with low spends in paid search; we can then apply what we learn to our SEO campaigns across larger sections of our website.

Finding Your Gaps and Plugging Them with SEO or Paid Search

When doing competitive analysis, you may realize that there are certain terms, words, or segments you are not ranking for that you feel you should. Or perhaps you're launching a new product and you want to create awareness about it. Understanding the gaps in your search strategy will help you understand where and how to focus your SEO and paid search efforts.

While ROI may drive some decisions, you may also consider how to take market share away from competitors. This may be costly, but in some markets—typically, developed markets or markets in very specific segments with limited competitors—it's a necessary evil.

Further, if you run a small site, your SEO strategy may be limited due to the reduced volume of content. In this case, paid search may be able to pick up the slack from not having enough content to develop your SEO long-tail strategy. There are times where paid search is far more advantageous than SEO. Paid search can be far more nimble than SEO; it can be more precise and can be wielded like a surgeon's scalpel.

Evaluate in your SEO strategy where you are ranking poorly but feel you must have a presence, and establish a beachhead for those terms with your paid search strategy first. If you are targeting competitors, you may want to consider what are referred to as *conquesting campaigns*, where you bid on their branded terms. You may never be able to rank on the SEO terms, but you can buy some presence in the paid search space to ensure brand visibility.

Conquesting can be an expensive effort and it may yield low or poor traffic, but if your hope is simply to get some visibility, it may fit into your strategy. Again this may be a loss leader for you, and it's relevant to very few search strategies, but if you find a competitor running a campaign against you that targets your brand, you may see paid search as an opportunity to rank on competitor terms to ensure you have a voice or presence in that campaign.

You may also find that there are new pages you are launching where it is critical to your business to show up on certain terms. While SEO will likely get them to rank, it may not be a certainty. Paid search, on the other hand, guarantees that you can turn on or off the visibility of these pages in the search results almost immediately. Once you start to see your pages rank in the organic listing, you can turn off your paid search campaign and divert your budget somewhere else.

Lastly, you may see an opportunity to run concurrent SEO and paid search campaigns to dominate a results page. There are some great advantages to having a paid search campaign run synchronously with your SEO campaign. You may see more traffic, improved engagement, and uplift in sales. You may, for example, dominate a non-branded term that is critical to your business organically, but if it's highly competitive you may choose to run a paid search campaign at the same time, to eliminate one more spot where your competitors may be able to compete against you. The more space you own on the results page, the less visibility your competitors will get, and the more visibility you will get. Further, you may not pay much for the paid search bids, as more users may click on your organic listing; however, only testing will prove this to be true.

Running SEO and Paid Search Together

When you combine your SEO and paid search strategies, you have an opportunity to dominate the search results. At this point, it is about maximizing exposure while trying to minimize costs. To run a paid search ad concurrent with your organic results you need to look at several KPIs, the first of which is whether your SEO efforts are offsetting any of your paid search efforts. When running concurrent strategies, you should monitor your KPIs to understand if you are maximizing your coverage and spend, or if you are throwing away money on your paid search campaign or not delivering solid leads through your SEO efforts.

To establish whether our SEO and paid search strategy is generating positive revenue, we first need to establish a baseline. Regardless of whether it is SEO or paid search you are going to focus on to get a dual listing, the KPIs we want to track are the same. For our example, we'll assume we already have an SEO ranking and are now planning to bid on the terms from a paid search perspective. When looking to bid on a term that already has an established ranking, there are six KPIs we want to track. These KPIs are:

- Traffic from search term
- Cost per acquisition
- Average order value
- Conversion rate
- Bounce rate
- Average value per visitor

With these six KPIs, we can set a baseline that will tell us if the traffic we get increases or decreases as whole, as well as the impact on our current rankings (if we see a decrease in SEO traffic, that means we may have moved traffic from one bucket to another, which isn't so good if we don't see higher conversions and average order values). We also want to monitor bounce rates. If we see deeper clicks into our site, we may be able to infer that our combined efforts are driving traffic that is more engaged. The downside to this is that it's only an inference; there is no confirmation that this traffic is better traffic, unless we are running multiclick tracking or monitoring the assists from our terms in the purchase funnel. In that case, we can actually tell if these changes are impacting our total sales.

Knowing the average value per visitor and cost per acquisition will also help us establish if we are seeing an improvement in ROI. We can use our ROI equations to evaluate our combined SEO and paid search effort, as well as running the equations separately on SEO and paid search effort, to better understand how each program is influencing the other. If we see a total cost per acquisition increase for either SEO or paid search, but a decrease for the opposite program, we then need to know if the overall program is bringing our cost per acquisition up or down, as well as what our average value per visitor is doing. For example, suppose our paid search campaign has a CPA of $1.45, and our SEO campaign had a CPA of $1.35 before we started our paid search campaign, but now has a CPA of $1.02. The average is then $1.24, so our total CPA is 11 cents less than it was before we combined our programs—which is great news if our average value per visit stays the same or increases.

The second part of that equation is understanding what our average value per visitor is. If our cost per acquisition goes down but our average value per visitor also decreases, we may be hurting ourselves in the long run if we look at our net profit. Assume our CPA was $1.35 and is now $1.02, and our average value per visitor was $3.40 and is now $2.02. While our CPA has improved, our visitors are now spending less. More acquisitions but less money spent by each customer can result in a net loss. Be aware of the impacts your changes have not just on acquisition cost, but on revenue generated also.

When 1 + 1 = 3, and When It Doesn't

One other comment you will often hear is that by running SEO and paid search together you will see an increase in traffic, conversion rate, average order value, or something else. I do not want to completely discount these claims, but again I urge caution and suggest that you confirm these findings for yourself. In the world of science, results should be easily repeatable. In the world of search, the same should apply. You may find that while you are getting more traffic, it's not good traffic. It may not be resulting in more conversions or sales, or it may end up abandoning at a higher rate. Just because there are case studies that indicate a certain result does not mean that the theory holds true for everything.

Test and retest, then audit your campaigns to figure out where you can maximize value. Ensure that you are not just basing your strategy on a study you read about. Studies can provide ideas of campaigns to run, but until you have qualified the results, monitor and test. You may find out that running SEO and paid search words concurrently generates an increased cost per acquisition, but that the average value per visitor also increases. You may see higher spends, or more conversions through your site. Higher CPAs do not always equal a higher average value per visitors, though. Remember, our goal is to decrease cost per acquisition while increasing average value per visitor, as well as growing the number of visitors to the site. You should now have the tools to begin testing your theories by tracking average cost per acquisition, average order value, conversion rates, and value per visitor. These will be the metrics you want to track to determine whether running SEO and paid search together will benefit you or not.

Concluding Thoughts

You should be leaving this chapter knowing that SEO and paid search campaigns can impact each other when they are run together. You may see positive or negative impacts; in either case, it is not a bad idea to experiment with the influence your SEO campaigns have over your paid search campaigns and vice versa. Establish some baselines for your ranking campaign before introducing a second factor so that you can measure what sort of influence your changes have. Further, before giving up on a campaign, you may want to test other factors, such as ad copy, page titles, or other search result page factors that you can influence. You may find that changes in the search results can further impact your campaigns in a variety of ways. Your selection of words for your page titles may be influential to getting more traffic to your site, or a small change to your ad copy may see conversions increase. There are both on-site and off-site factors that can influence what a user does from the click to the conversion.

CHAPTER 6

Site Search Analytics

*Site search can provide deeper insights into
what your customers are looking for.*

Site search can be a form of navigation for people on your site. It may actually be a very common form of navigation. Sites such as Amazon put a great deal of emphasis on their search bar by placing it front and center. Understanding who is using your site search and where, why, and how can provide critical insight into both your SEO and paid search programs, in addition to improving your site's conversion rates. Site search is also unique in that you have control over the results it returns. Site search comes in many different flavors, from free options from Google to paid options from Microsoft to custom-built options such as Amazon's search. Whichever option you use, what is happening with your site search will be a key analytic to track and measure, allowing you to improve your overall site findability and the user experience.

By the end of this chapter, you should have some ideas of what you can track through site search, as well as how to implement some of these tracking programs. For our examples, we will use Google site search as our assumed site search engine, though I will also call out some ideas that may help improve more sophisticated engines if you have the option. If you can afford it, a fully customizable site search is better than a free noncustomizable site search. Before we begin, I should also point out that while I will cover some elements of what you can track on site search, this is by no means an exhaustive look at the power of site search and all the features that can be tweaked and refined. The goal of this chapter is to get you thinking about site search, how important it is to your customers, and how to measure some relevant data points to see if it's working for you or against you.

One of the biggest opportunities for increasing sales that I have ever seen was through site search. Just based on the sheer volume of traffic most sites see through their site search, it is almost a no-brainer that effort should be put into creating incremental revenue based on traffic volume. Yet still, it has consistently been one of the most neglected parts of a website.

There are few companies that I have seen that have realized the value of site search and moved beyond thinking of it as just a means to find another page on a website. Amazon is one of them. In the next few years, I think site search will become bigger and more important, but I don't think the change is happening as fast as it should be.

Many companies fail to realize that site search is an opportunity to market and connect with people and to really change the perception they have of a website. The results page and how it is displayed (and, more importantly, what information it contains and how it is categorized) is a big opportunity to really bring people deeper into the website.

As quick as marketeers have been to jump on SEO and paid search, I think they've really missed the boat with site search, particularly when you have a highly engaged, highly motivated customer at your doorstep.

Tools you will need in this chapter:

- Clickstream tracking package (Google Analytics, Adobe SiteCatalyst, etc.)
- Spreadsheet program (Excel or something similar).
- Access to your site search admin console if available
- A/B or multivariate testing tool (Google Website Optimizer, Test & Target, etc.)

Site Search as Navigation

You should think of site search as another navigation option people have to get around your site. While it is fantastic to have a well-formatted taxonomy of links and navigation that creates your site information architecture, it is even better if users can tell you what they're looking for and be directed to what they need right away. Think of your site search like a door greeter that asks customers, "What are you looking for today?" The better your door greeter is at directing customers to the correct location in your store (or website, in this case), the easier it will be for them to find what they are looking for, and the happier they well be. Now think of your search engine as a recommendation engine as well. Not only does your door greeter direct customers to where they are going, but he will also suggest some products that may be of relevance based on the items they are searching for.

Site search should not be relegated to the back of your website, for people to use only if they can't navigate your site. But if people are using it only because they've run into difficulties navigating your site, it may be even more important that your site search works well. Site search may be a customer's last-ditch effort to find what she's looking for before going off to a competitor's site. Do you really think you can afford to offer your customers a mediocre site search experience? As part of your semi-monthly or monthly metric reviews, you should include a section on site search, so you can understand its usability and any problems it may have.

Considering site search as a navigational element also means you will be able to leverage what terms people use in your search box. Do you call widget A one thing while customers call it something different? While the meaning may be the same, changing the name used in your navigational element to match the term customers usually use when searching for that product may improve clicks on that element. While you may want to develop your own lexicon for your product lines, if you do not have the necessary marketing dollars, you will likely be better off ceding to the users and changing some links on your site to fit with user behavior patterns.

Once you begin to think of site search as a navigation element, you will start to get more ideas as to how to track site search, and how to make improvements to it. Site search should be a focus of constant testing. If you have the capability to modify the appearance and results, you should not be afraid to regularly devise new tests that you can run on your site search engine and results, even testing how and where you display your search box.

Some people are of the mind that if a user does a site search on a page, it takes away from the opportunity to convert from that page. This is a silly notion for people who only see the smaller picture. There are many people who may come to a page and require more information before deciding if they want to commit to your product, or they may have any number of other questions that can be answered through your search box. The danger of reduced conversions is only a problem if your search results are so poor as to be useless to a customer, as this could result in high abandonments. Establishing some site search KPIs will help you figure out if you have a site search problem.

Establishing Your Site Search KPIs

Your site search KPIs can start out basic and develop as your site search grows in sophistication. A few KPIs we will look at are capturing terms with high bounces, tracking search terms with no results, capturing pages arrived at through site search with high exits and with high success rates or conversions, tracking search patterns across your site (including which pages generate high volumes of searches and which searches lead to secondary searches), tracking the number of pages spidered, and creating and tracking special campaigns. By the end of the chapter, you should have a basis for developing your site search strategy and making informed, data-driven decisions about what needs to be improved.

Capturing Terms with High Exits

The first site search problem you will want to address is exit rate. Exits are usually bad; they indicate a failure to serve a user's need. In the case of site search, an exit should be defined as when a user searches for something and then immediately exits your site without clicking on any links. This may indicate a failure of the search engine to return any (or any useful) results. Typically we approach this by looking at the volume of searches for a term and its exit rate.

When a user leaves the site, it is a lost opportunity, and there's nothing worse than losing an opportunity. We also need to take into account that we cannot fix all the problems for all search terms. To enable an approach that will make this task manageable, we need to set up tracking and analytics. Google Analytics fortunately offers a decent site search section. We'll take a quick look here, but if you want to learn more about how to set up site search tracking, read *Google Analytics* by Justin Cutroni (O'Reilly). Google Analytics reports are detailed enough that you should be able to find all the information you need in them. As you can see in Figure 6-1, there are many different ways to look at your site search metrics; this will be the focus of most of the rest of this chapter.

To capture terms that result in multiple follow-up searches, navigate to Content→"Site Search"→"Search Terms." The value in the "% Search Exits" column tells us how many people exited the site after performing a search. Because these are percentages, we may want to use a weighted sort. Click on the "% Search Exits" column and then check the "Weighted Sort" box (Figure 6-2). This returns items sorted based on a combination of the percentage and the number of users affected, so we can focus on the most actionable results first. That is, even if the top results have a lower % of exits than some of the others, we know that by fixing these issues we will impact more users.

Once you have done the weighted sort, you can start working with the data. You may want to start by taking the top terms that people are exiting on and running them through your site search box to see if they return zero results. Alternatively, if you are lucky and your search reporting software already covers results with zero results returned, you can run that first to see what is not being indexed or found, and ideally you can map some XML to those results to improve the searches on those terms.

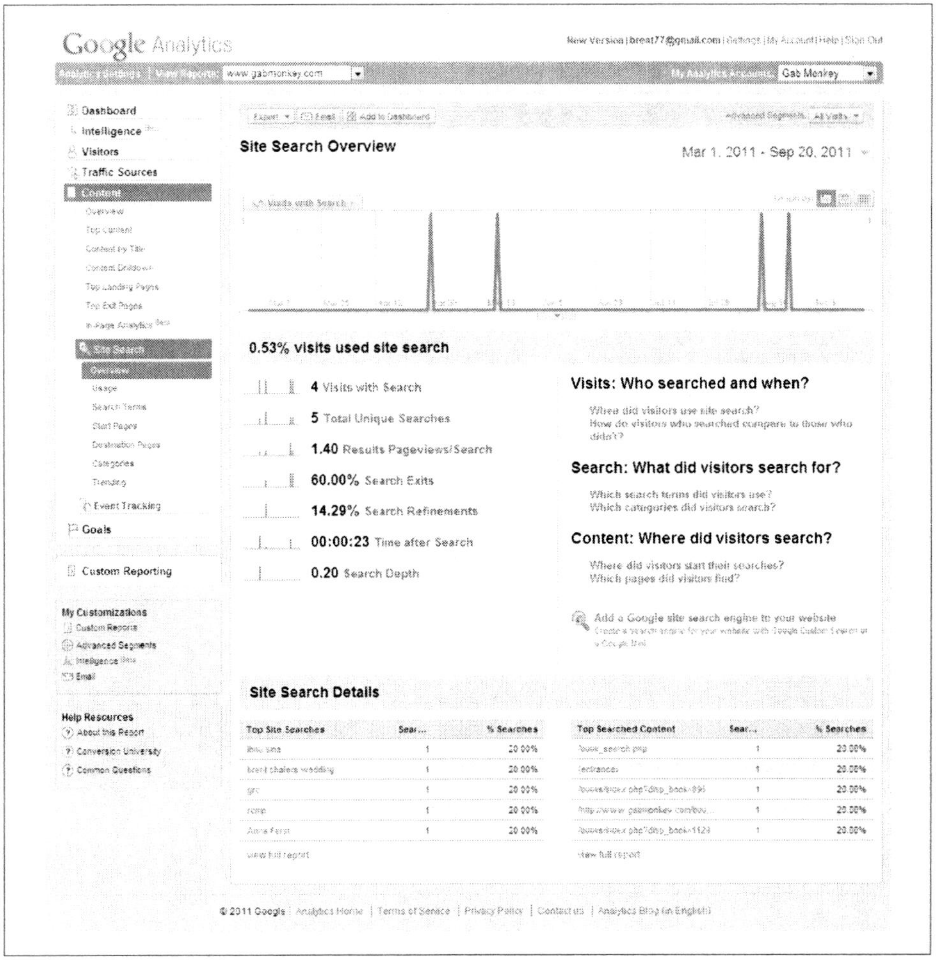

Figure 6-1. Site search overview in Google Analytics

The data in Figure 6-2 shows us that the query "search," while it is run often, results in a high bounce rate. The query "GUI bloopers" also has a high search rate, but it appears further down the list, as its exits are not as high as some of the other search terms. Applying the weighted sort filter gives us a good idea of which terms we should address first, based on number of unique searches and % search exits.

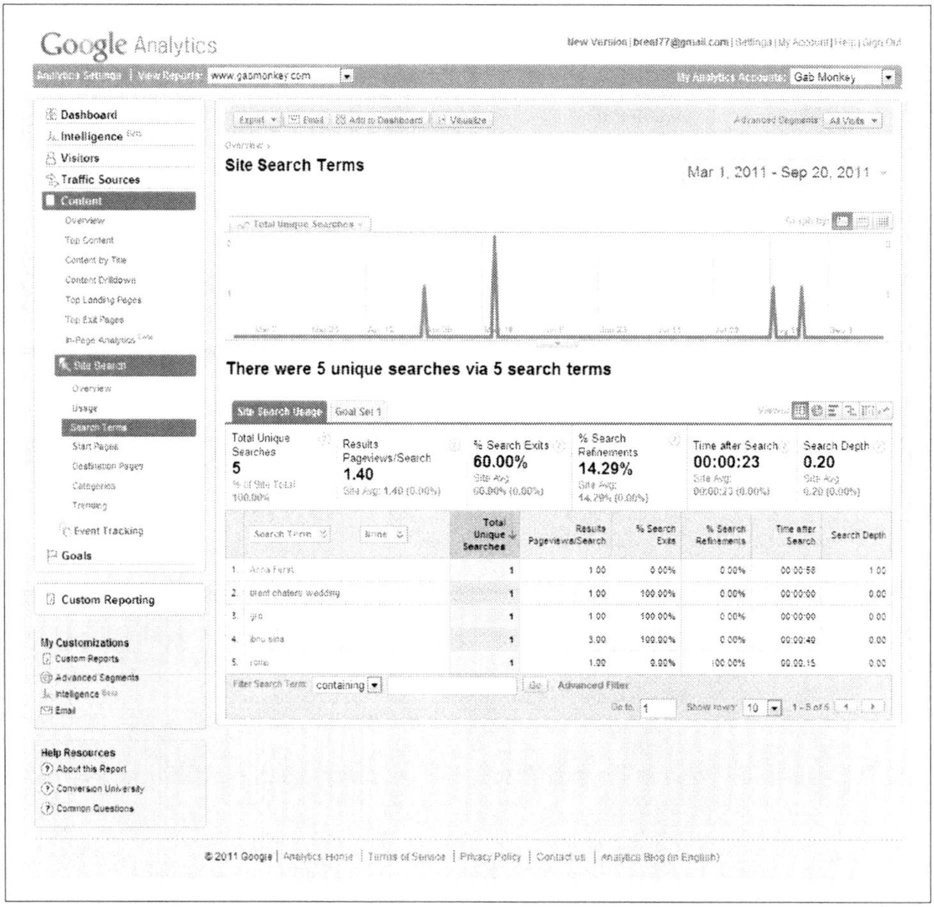

Figure 6-2. Site search terms in Google Analytics

Because of the high volume of searches on "search" that result in abandonment, we need to do some further research as to what results are coming up in the site search results for this term. We can also look at whether any users refined their query further. In Figure 6-3, we can see that this result was sometimes followed up with the query "test." This pattern might result from the IT group applying tests, which we can validate with that group, or from users who are searching for "search test." In the latter case, we should look at including any content we have around search testing in the results for "search."

The only real way to get an understanding of the bigger searches that seem to result in high exit rates is to run them yourself and see what comes up. You may see that the links are not very relevant, perhaps creating such a lack of trust in your search engine that users are immediately leaving your site. You may also find that there is a mismatch

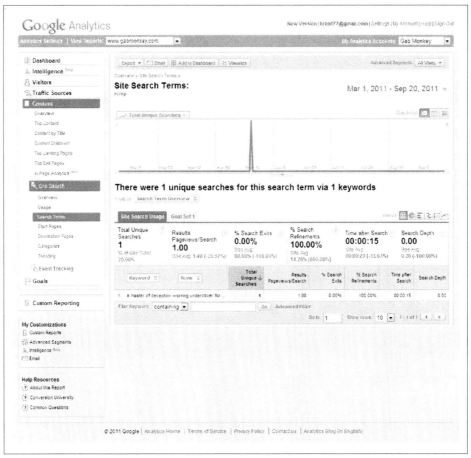

Figure 6-3. Site search terms in Google Analytics

between the terms users are searching for and what you call your products. In this case, you may need to reconsider the naming conventions you use in your navigation.

Capturing Secondary Searches

You may see that some searches often result in secondary searches. Ideally, your analytics tools can also enable coverage of these types of searches. Google Analytics does an OK job of giving us an idea of what sorts of patterns occur. We can find this information under "% Search Refinements" in the Site Search report. This measurement indicates the percentage of times that a follow-up search was performed after the intial search for each term.

To find out what those follow-up terms were, click on the word you want to investigate. You will see a drop-down list above the search terms that says "Analyze" next to it. If you want to see what other terms people searched on after the initial search for the selected term, select "Search Term Refinement." You will be provided with a list of words (Figure 6-4). By exploring these secondary search terms, you may see that people who look for one item also have an interest in another item, and this information can help you refine your site. For example, knowing that people who search for "cars" frequently go on to search for "fuel economy" may influence you to include fuel economy information on the pages you have about cars. You may also realize you have a categorization issue. If you have a complicated product taxonomy, you may have grouped together products you thought were similar, but search patterns may reveal different product associations on the part of your customers.

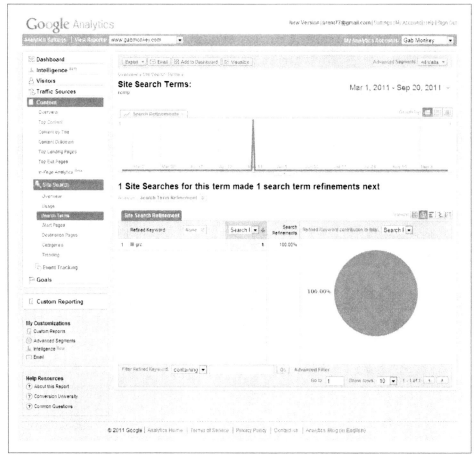

Figure 6-4. Site search terms and associated follow-up terms in Google Analytics

Capturing Pages with High Searches

Pages with high search volumes may be a good or bad thing. The good thing is that the page is piquing enough interest to get people to search for more content or information. The bad thing is that they haven't found what they're looking for on that page. Your web analytics package should be able to identify pages with high search volumes; in Google Analytics, this data is found under Content→"Site Search"→"Start Pages." Targeting pages with high search volumes will help you get an understanding of what pages may be lacking in content or cross-linking. By understanding what terms are driving significant volumes on a particular page, you should get an idea of where you need to improve cross-linkages (either adding them or making existing links more prominent within the page design). You may need to try several versions of the page to find something that works. Running A/B or multivariate tests using a tool like Google Website Optimizer or Adobe Test & Target will help you better identify where a link gets more clicks and ideally decrease searches for a particular term by improving the page's usability.

Capturing Pages with High or Low Success Rates

Aside from understanding which pages trigger a search, we want to understand which pages users come to through site search are providing good or bad results. Once we have understood searches that result in instant exits and searches whose results trigger secondary searches, we need to know which results people are engaging with but finding unsatisfactory. We can identify a bad page as any page that results in one of two sequences of events: a search, then a click to a page, then an exit; or a search, a click to a page, and a new search.

Tracking a search that leads to a page and then to another search is a fairly sophisticated site search analytic. In packages like Adobe SiteCatalyst, you can track this by creating custom pathing reports with your search page set as the starting and end point of the path, and any page in the middle. This is actually one of the places where Google Analytics will let you down: although you can do it with some hacking, there is no easy way to track a search, a click to a page, and then a second search. If you can capture this data, however, you will be able to identify pages that are not serving the end user well. You may want to try to find out what terms are driving people to these pages from your site search so you can get a better understanding of what people expect to find on these pages.

Likewise, if we look at a search that leads to a click and then to a site exit, we need to understand what is on that page that is driving people away. Do we have content that is actually driving clicks outside the site? Or are people simply leaving by choice? If we can track on-page links with high clicks and they are external links, we should have our answer; if we don't see this, we must assume people are changing the URL in the browser's address bar. Again, finding out which terms drove people from your site search to these pages will help improve your site's usability.

Tracking Special Campaigns

Special campaigns are essentially the equivalent to paid search for site search. These are results you control and for which you can determine certain trigger points. These will likely be associated with keywords or terms you have outlined, and you will have a specific end goal in mind for clicks on these results. When you're setting this up, ensure that you also set up tracking on these links so that you can track a click to a sale, or some other action that has an ROI attached to it. Further, you may want to monitor how frequently these campaigns are triggered and how many clicks they drive, as well as the click-through rate. You may also want to consider doing some A/B or multivariate testing to refine the way you format these links. You may try running images versus no images with the results, or changing the terminology in the results. Running tests to see which people are clicking through and attempting to drive better sales will further improve the ROI you see from site search.

Tracking Spider Volume

Knowing what your spider is doing on your site is important. How many pages are indexed? How frequently is the spider re-crawling your site? Can you find out what is in the index? These are all questions that likely can be answered only through your search spider backend. You will need to log in to your search account to discover the answers to these questions. If you don't have access to this, or are not reporting on some of these baseline analytics to understand the health of your site search, you should probably go get that enabled now. Endeca, Fast, Autonomy, and Siderean all have backend interfaces that allow you to monitor activity and indexing of your site.

The health of your site search is critical to its usability. If the spider is not able to effectively crawl your pages, you can expect a poor set of search results. If your spider cannot understand your content, again expect poor results. In some cases, spiders can also accept XML feeds to parse rich media such as videos, images, and audio formats. Your XML files will indicate what your content is about, possibly through transcripts of the video or audio, or descriptive text about the image. This metadata should be supplied to the engine, and you should track how much of this supplied data is or is not being indexed by your spider as another point for your site health analytics.

One last point on spidering: some solutions use XML files exclusively to provide metadata and information about pages on your site. In this case, you will not be looking at how well-spidered your site is, but how well-represented your site is in the XML. Using metadata that describes what a page is about without having access to the specific content on the page allows for some sophisticated relationships to be built that can be utilized in faceted navigation and other elements of your site. Ensuring that your XML files are populated with the most robust and descriptive content possible is the most important thing when dealing with site search that does not use spidering as its primary source of data.

At this point, you should have some ideas of what to include in your site search KPI dashboard. Most of these KPIs are great for auditing purposes, but what about capturing the monetization of your website?

What Is the Value of Your Site Search?

ROI and value are again the core of what we want to know about our site search programs. How do we track the value of site search to our customers? The easiest and simplest answer is to see how many people who used your site search went on to purchase a product. While this may be a great high-level analytic, and is certainly something you may want to track in an executive dashboard to illustrate how important (or not) site search is to generating revenue, it is not the only metric we should be considering.

We already know we may run our own custom campaigns on site search. Each of these should be set up to capture monetization data. Managing campaigns takes time, time is money, and time poorly spent is money wasted. Tracking the average value per visitor through your site search can help you understand if the time and effort you are investing on site search is worthwhile, and where your time will best be spent when setting up your custom campaigns. Further, just as you would with any paid search campaign, you should be tracking at the campaign level to understand what levels of traffic and conversion they are driving (Table 6-1).

Table 6-1. Sample data to track for site search programs

Campaign	Spend	Impressions	Clicks	CTR	Conversion rate	Revenue generated	Avg. value per visitor	Cost per acquisition
Red Bikes	$546	3,526	965	27%	3%	$689	$20.67	$18.86
Green Bikes	$986	3,896	456	11%	2%	$968	$19.36	$12.65
Blue Bikes	$2,536	10,256	4125	40%	5%	$15,509	$775.45	$12.29

Remember that cost per acquisition is based on clicks that convert, so in this case we must multiply the number of clicks by the conversion rate to get the number of actual purchases. Knowing the average value per visitor and cost per acquisition, we can now see that we are getting the best ROI from the Blue Bikes program, and the worst from Red Bikes. Breaking this data down into simple, understandable values helps us to understand where our high-value and low-value opportunities exist. We can clearly see that the work on Blue Bikes is paying off; the other campaigns, on the other hand, are not generating nearly as much revenue as we'd like, and may want to think about some conversion rate optimization. For example, we may want to look at the landing pages we are driving people to and investigate whether they are fulfilling their purpose or if they have high abandonment rates. Conversion rate optimization is key to improving your campaigns.

CRO for Site Search

Conversion rate optimization in the realm of site search can be greatly enhanced by the various data points provided through site search that you may not be able to get from a traditional search engine. Remember that the people using your site search have also likely used another search engine. This simple fact can provide you with great insights into your users' psyches. We can try building out a model of our users based on what we can see and track in site search. What follows may be a bit more theory than practice, but it should provide you with some ideas in terms of what your users are thinking when searching. Some pieces of data we will want to look at are:

- Search and refinement
- Language use
- Depth of search (viewing multiple pages versus single pages)
- Repetition of search
- Average ranking clicked on

These five elements can provide some profiling of what our users are like when engaged with search. While not a model that will predict exactly how users engage with Google, Bing, or any other external search engines, this modeling will give you a much better idea as to how important rank, position, and relevancy are to a user of search. Ultimately, these insights should help you improve the usability of your own site search.

Search and Refinement

By understanding what terms are refined, we can get a better idea of how a search moves down a search funnel. You may see very broad terms leading to more multiterm keywords, or you may see very tightly associated words. The nice thing about this is that you can apply what you learn directly to your site, to improve the user experience and to build up a list of related words that your pages should be ranking on.

Further, to improve your conversion rates, you may want to have some of the words you see frequently associated appear on your landing page together. This gives users a visual cue about the specificity of the page and its content. You create an early association to what may be the next search term early on, like you are predicting what the user is thinking. You can also apply this thinking to faceted navigation.

Faceted navigation is an example of search refinement (Figure 6-5) where you provide your users with a larger taxonomy and allow them to narrow it down based on features, classifications, categories, or other refinements. Dell and Amazon first popularized this type of navigation, allowing users to refine searches by checking boxes or clicking links to narrow down search results. You can apply how users refine terms in natural language search to faceted navigation, by looking at how users move from broader search terms to more specific terms. Looking for language patterns that can be applied to faceted elements can help you improve the user experience by bringing search elements further into the navigation of your site.

Figure 6-5. *An example of faceted navigation to refine search results*

Language Use

How do people describe your products? Look at the branded and product/service-type searches users do on your site search. If you have filters that can be applied against searches, see if you can have these modified to categories to see what sorts of searches happen in these categories. Can you easily distinguish search terms for support from product terms? Are there terms that are vague? You may realize that you have been promoting a product, when many people were looking for support.

You should now know that you can segment and filter data in your clickstream package. By setting up site search filters, you can see if there are more searches for particular terms in the support bucket or the product bucket. You can use this information to determine whether campaigns you create around those terms should be support campaigns or product purchase campaigns.

Language use can also provide you with insight into new trends. If you or a competitor is launching a product, you may see early trends where people who know the brand well and follow it are searching for that product. You may want to see what terms trend during these new launches to help you build a list of keywords to track and target for both your site search and SEO campaigns.

Depth of Search

Depth of search has to do with whether, when people search on a term, the page they go to serves their purpose. Do they click through to a page and quickly go back to the search engine to try a new search, or are they clicking further into your site from that page? For pages that create deeper clicks, what about those pages is it that draws people further into the site? Are the pages more relevant to the search terms? Are there certain design patterns that are drawing people in? For example, do you have images or buttons that drive lots of clicks? Are the links phrased in such a way that they draw people in? There is a difference between "Follow me on Twitter" and "You should follow me on Twitter."

A/B and multivariate testing of landing pages is not just for paid search and SEO—you can apply the same principles to your site search campaigns as well. This kind of testing can really help push the bar on your conversion rates. Circling back to differences in the text, you may be able to make improvements in areas that seem insignificant, such as changing the color of a background or the simple wording of a sentence. Testing the little things can sometimes yield big results.

Repetition of Search

Studying how searches evolve can provide us with insights into how people narrow down their thoughts. They may start broadly searching for "car," and then search for "red car," then "red Corvette." You can get a better idea of how searches are refined on external sites by looking at how people use your own search engine.

Our discussion of first-click, last-click, and multiclick tracking applies here as well. Multiclick tracking will give you a better idea about certain keyword funnels. You will be able to see which words are "enabling" words that spawn many further variations of searches, and which words create a very poor set of further search terms. If you think of this as a word pyramid, some word pyramids will be larger than others, as shown in Figure 6-6.

```
         CAR                                MOTOR
     MOTOR ENGINE                     ENGINE, CAR ENGINE
CAR REPAIRS, ENGINE REPAIRS, REPAIRS    CAR ENGINE SERVICING, ENGINE LIGHT
REPLACE AN ENGINE, OIL CHANGE, DIY OIL CHANGE
```

Figure 6-6. Word pyramid of related searches based on past searches

Learning about what drives other searches may give you insights into what to place on your landing pages. We can see that the term "car" is often associated with "motor engine" and, further on, "oil change." This may be content we should either link to or, if relevant, discuss on the landing page in an attempt to cut our customers off at the pass. When building your pyramid, you will want to look at what terms have the highest search volumes. For example, if there are more searches for "oil change," that should be the first topic to address. Consider it like a voting system for popular content.

Average Ranking Clicked

As mentioned in "Capturing Traffic Volume Based on Positioning" on page 103, search engines are starting to pass on information about the SERP positions of referring search results. You may be able to capture this data through your website analytics program. Likewise, you may want to track the positions of the results from your own search engine that people are clicking on to get to your content. Understanding what percentage of your users are first-pagers versus deep clickers can help you understand the patience of your customers.

Tracking the rank clicked also can provide insight into the relevancy of your pages. If the most relevant page is being ranked number 1 but is not receiving the bulk of clicks for a term, you should ask why this is. Is there an issue with the page title or the page description that results in a lower-ranking page appearing to be more relevant? Usually a lower-ranking page getting more clicks indicates an issue with the optimization of the content presented in the site SERP. If the wrong page is getting most of the traffic, you may need to change strategies and look at how to optimize a page that you may not have felt was relevant, but that the clicks are telling you is. To improve conversion rates, look at adjusting how your site search is presenting results to your users. If possible, experiment with video and image results as well. CRO starts at the result page.

Tracking Trends

Knowing which searches are trending on your site can provide you with some great insight into what is hot in your space or market and drive some of the biggest CRO improvements. Amazon is perhaps one of the best at implementing trends based on search. Amazon's "people who viewed this item, also viewed this item" engine is largely powered based on people searching for a product, then searching again and clicking on another product. As I pointed out earlier, Amazon uses site search as a navigation element.

Tracking trends and top queries can provide users with click fodder—essentially, content that they may click through simply to see what everyone else is looking for. Twitter is an excellent example of this: the top trending tweets are searched out based on hash tags, a common nomenclature people use to classify their tweet topics, and these are positioned prominently on the site as top trending topics.

What you learn by observing trends and habits can be applied to the navigation and improvement of your site. By tracking search patterns, you can also help your customers refine their searches. On your product pages, you could include a box that indicates that people who searched for this product also searched for another product. Providing a link that indicates "People who searched for 'X' also searched for 'Y'" may improve the usability of your site search. You could even include in the search results a small preview of some results from a similar search, so that from the customers' perspective, they are basically getting two searches for the price of one. Leading your customers through their search queries effectively can dramatically increase the usability of your site and the likelihood of sales conversions and more page impressions. As unique as people are, there are times where collectively we are not as unique as we think. Think about how you can apply group data from your site search results to improve user engagement and the overall user experience.

Follow the trends of your site search; automate tracking if you can, and at the very least ensure you are reviewing the top 10 or 20 results monthly to see what people are looking for. Is there anything you can do to make finding these items quicker? By improving the user experience bit by bit, you will ultimately end up improving the overall experience.

Site Search Seasonality

Like SEO and paid search, site search can see seasonality effects. When we talk about trends, we also want to consider seasonality. Being able to predict seasonal trends in site search can help you make sure you have content prepared in advance.

If you are in the flower business, you will likely be ramping up your external search programs around Valentine's Day. But what are you doing on your site search? If you don't have a search engine that enables you to run special campaigns, consider placing a Valentine's Day message that is persistent on your search results page.

Work with what you have, and analyze the site search data you are able to collect so that you can see patterns that indicate rising trends as well as seasonality trends. When you're looking at rising trends, you need to consider the impacts of seasonality on those trends. Your search program should get to a level where you can map out trends on a calendar and predict with a certain degree of certainty what will be searched on when.

Concluding Thoughts

While we have covered several KPIs, you may find there are others that you can use to further improve your site search. For example, you might want to monitor the average speed at which results are returned, or try testing out icons to indicate content types such as PDF versus HTML documents. Site search can be the most powerful tool on your website that you have access to for learning about what your customers are looking for.

As I've pointed out several times now, Amazon has built a business around massive amounts of content and a very well-honed site search. It has applied faceted navigation elements to its search results, as well as recognizing trends and similar search patterns in order to recommend further products. The amount of refinement that has been done on Amazon's search is perhaps paralleled only by Google and Bing. Do not let this deter you, though. You do not have to be an Amazon; what you do need to do is look at how you can capitalize on your site search results to improve your overall customer experience.

CHAPTER 7

Correlating SEO/Paid Search and Site Search

*Looking across all your search data points can
provide you with perhaps the biggest insight into
what customers are looking for from you.*

SEO, paid search, and site search each offer a unique opportunity to understand the mind-set and the interconnected thoughts of the people who are looking for your content. The one downside to this data is that it is drawn from people who have already found you, not from people who have not found you yet. That is, in some way or another, these people have had at least one interaction with your brand.

SEO provides insights into the relevancy of your content to a specific set of terms. There really shouldn't be many surprises when looking at what words drive people to your website if you are in a clear and defined field or if your site has a clear and defined focus. If your website is about cars, you should expect to see a great deal of car-related terms driving traffic to the site. In this case, what you are looking for is not so much themes as language and use of words, and pairings between search terms. Looking at two- or three-word search terms can give you a better idea of associations people make when looking for your type of content. This can give you insight into language use, and you may discover geographical variations as well. If your site is an exception to the rule of one thematic element—for example, if your business is involved in many disciplines or your site hosts blogs that cover a variety of topics—there may not be a simple theme that you can expect to see driving traffic to your site. In this case, you will need to look at theme clustering, or thematic grouping. You can figure out how to do this through your analytics program.

Paid search provides a testing ground for terms whose relevancy to your market or segment you are uncertain of. Perhaps they are terms that you think are thematically relevant, but you don't have any traffic to validate this. You can use paid search to test terms and thematic elements and to validate the quality and type of traffic you get. You can also get a sampling of interaction data based on the words and terms that drive people to your site. Looking at this, you will be able to formulate more informed strategies for both your SEO and site search campaigns.

Site search allows you to see what people are looking for on your site. They know your brand, but do they have their own terms for describing your products? Looking at the terms people search for is a good way of determining whether your product naming conventions are in sync with how your customers think about your products. Site search is a rich source of data to gather and analyze in order to further improve your SEO and paid search campaigns. Conversely, SEO can give you some ideas of where your Site Search is lacking, based on empty site search results. The three search sources can all provide feedback to each other, in both directions (Figure 7-1).

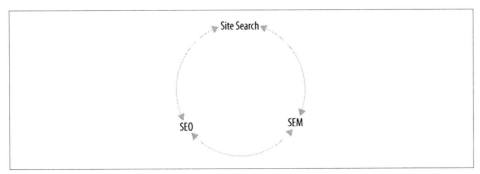

Figure 7-1. Search source cycle

Tools you will need in this chapter:

- Clickstream tracking package (Google Analytics, Adobe SiteCatalyst, etc.)
- Spreadsheet program (Excel or something similar)
- AdWords or some other paid search tool
- A/B or multivariate testing tool (Google Website Optimizer, Test & Target, etc.)

Pulling Terms from Site Search for SEO/Paid Search

Site search can provide a wealth of information, potentially providing more insight into the users' search patterns and behavior than any other of your search touch points. Site search, when tracked, can return any and all variations of search patterns people utilize on your site. Granted, you are dealing with a specific segment of users who are likely familiar with your products, services, or offerings, but still, you have access to valuable raw search data.

Depending on the volume of traffic your site gets, you may or may not be able to glean useful insights from site search patterns. However, if you can establish some patterns of site search, you may be able to figure out where in the search path you have gaps.

Search leads from SEO only deliver traffic that the search engines feel is relevant to your site, while paid search only provides traffic through words you think are relevant to your site. Site search allows you to see what your customers are actually entering as search terms without the search engine or your assumptions interfering in the query to be tracked. Enabling the management of site search should be a top priority, not just to help you improve your other search campaigns but also to improve the usefulness of your website. You should not be surprised if your site search is one of the most-used sections of your website, especially if you have a very large site.

Utilizing site search to build keyword lists to sample for both SEO and paid search may prove very fruitful. Once you've identified the most frequently searched terms on your site, you can compare those terms against the terms that drive traffic to your site via organic and paid search. Begin with your SEO keywords. Terms that are highly searched via site search should be cross-referenced against terms that appear in your SEO list. Any terms that do not appear in your SEO list should be added to a list of terms that should be tested for relevancy. For any terms that do appear in your site search list, look at the volume of traffic generated as well as the rankings of those terms in the search engine result pages. Any term that ranks poorly is also a candidate for testing.

You should end up with a list of potentially relevant words. You may need to further filter this list to eliminate completely irrelevant terms. Once you have your short list, validate that these words are not in your paid search campaigns. What you are left with should be prime candidates for some paid search testing. Set up campaigns for each of these terms to validate keyword volumes as well as the quality of traffic from these search terms.

You should be tracking what has become your standard dashboard of raw traffic volumes, exit rates, conversion rates, sales assists (if trackable), and average value per visitor. You will also want to track and log who else is competing on these terms. Are they highly competitive terms, or are they low-competition terms? You may find that there is a set of terms that it never occurred to you to target with your paid search or SEO campaigns. Testing the terms in paid search allows you to perform quick evaluations with minimal spends to determine how much traffic they generate and the relevancy of that traffic. You may want to test these terms against several existing landing pages, or develop a new landing page with content you think may be relevant to searchers on these terms. To get an idea of what may work, look at the sites with the top SEO rankings on these terms.

While you can use tools such as Google Website Optimizer for A/B and multivariate testing, you can also run these tests manually. It is important to understand how each variation differs, and what impact these changes have on your results. Build up a test case for these keywords and log how the terms perform against different landing pages. You may end up with a test case like the one in Table 7-1, using paid search to deliver traffic.

Landing pages and entry points can and do impact revenue. Beyond landing pages, users may hit other pages, all of which can be tracked in your clickstream data. Looking at Table 7-1, we can see that page-1 has the highest average value per visitor and the highest conversion rate. As this appears to be the most successful landing page, I would focus on this page for capturing elements to improve conversions and maximize revenue.

Table 7-1. Example of testing one term against different landing pages.

Web page	Raw traffic	Bounce rate	Conversion rate	Sales assists	Average value per visitor
http://www.site/page-1	123,323	38%	3.8%	12.2%	$234.56
http://www.site/page-2	143,443	38%	3.3%	12.6%	$231.45
http://www.site/page-3	125,432	23%	2.5%	14.4%	$215.43
http://www.site/page-4	189,485	27%	2.9%	14.1%	$227.89

Building out a new page for a second set of paid search tests would be beneficial before investing heavily in SEO activity. Test this page against your new baseline metrics and validate how it compares against the current pages. I would set this page up as a no-index page for the search spiders, as it will eventually replace an existing page on the site.

You will want to maintain that old page's inbound links, and page rank, while you're testing out a new page to capitalize on improving conversions and assists. When you do launch your new page, replace the old page. If your paid search campaign was showing positive results, you may want to continue to run that concurrently with your SEO efforts and monitor revenue from both the SEO and paid search traffic.

Using site search to expand your SEO and paid search campaigns can be a very cost-effective way to build a keyword list, using terms that your customers are telling you are relevant to them. The first rule in understanding your search campaigns is to exhaust all data you have access to that provides insights directly from your customers before expanding out. The only time you would want to break this rule is if you are new to the market or if you are introducing a new product and have no footprint from which to leverage data (in which case, you may look for third-party case studies or other sources of data).

Applying Site Search Patterns to SEO/Paid Search

Site search can also provide a better understanding of *search funnels*, or keyword pathing. Search funnels are when you get a search followed by a second search. To get any sort of insights, though, we need to look at the data in aggregate.

A typical search looks like Figure 7-2, where we see a keyword followed by several related searches. This investigation may also prove valuable in discovering where your site search is breaking down. Searches followed by further searches usually indicate two things: the first is an unsuccessful search result, where refinement occurs because of irrelevant content, and the second is a successful result delivering content that requires further investigation. How can you distinguish the two? You can't, really. This will require some good old-fashioned investigation by clicking and following the paths of your users. Then you will need to make some assumptions about what the users were looking for or saw.

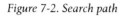

keyword 1 --> related keyword 2 --> related keyword 3 --> related keyword 4

Figure 7-2. Search path

Looking at site search patterns gives us a very unique insight into how users string words and terms together. As we saw in Chapter 6, you can capture searches in Google Analytics along with the other related terms that were searched. More advanced analytics tools can be adjusted to allow for tracking the search path or entire paths through a site. In analyzing your pathing reports, you should look for reports with multiple interactions with site search.

You should be able to track the original search term, the page clicked to, the following search term, and the following page clicked to. As you start to see these patterns, you can look for multiple instances of the same patterns occurring, and for any evolution in these patterns. This can help you identify pages that could be improved with the addition of cross-linkages, as well as potential problems with your content. People who search for a term and then repeat a search for a very similar term are very easily categorized as having gotten unsatisfactory search results.

Folks who do a broad search and then a more narrow version of that search give you a better idea of how search refinement may work. One trick you can use with Google Analytics to capture data on search refinement is to include a refinement option for users to select. For example, you can include a category drop-down in your site search, allowing users to select whether they're looking for pages related to products, news, support, and so on. Google Analytics can capture that selection as well as the search term.

Capturing these refinements in site search can help you improve your landing pages for your site search users, but you may also be able to apply this data to your SEO or paid search campaigns. The caveat here is that site search users who are familiar with your products and are searching for a specific product may lean toward support, as they are already users (as opposed to people new to your products who may be looking to purchase). There is no easy answer here; your analytics tools will provide you with insights into the areas to target, but you will need to do some A/B or multivariate testing to validate what works for SEO/paid search traffic as opposed to site search users. There will always be some differences in usage, but there is still data that can correlate and provide indications as to what areas you should be focusing on. Utilize this data and apply where and when you can both what the analytics tell you and what your own investigations into the data and the user experience reveal.

Site Search—Capturing and Using the Second Term

Your site search provides a rich idea of what your website encompasses. It can be thought of as a navigational tool, providing an index of all the pages on your site and how they are related. Further, as we have seen, you can track referring search terms and follow-up site search terms to get a better idea of what visitors to your site are really looking for. Knowing this, you can get into more sophisticated uses of your data. If you can track what terms brought a person to your site, you can apply a secondary search against your site search engine and return the results dynamically in your web page, to further aid your user in navigating your site (as well as correlating this data against the other related searches people have performed on your site). That is, you can basically create a section on a page that shows what other users thought was relevant or related to the landing page. You can also use site search data to refine faceted navigation elements on your site. Amazon and Google are very effective examples of this: both provide a spot where correlated or related searches are presented to the user (Figure 7-3).

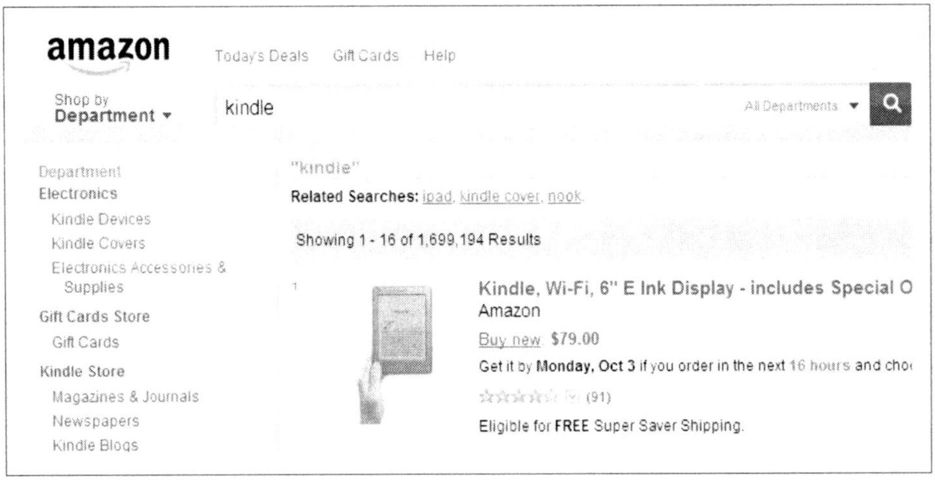

Figure 7-3. Related searches

Offering up related searches can provide a more predictive path through your site. Providing refinements (facets) based on data you have already collected can also help you retain users, by ensuring that you return results you know to be relevant. While developing these sorts of real-time applications that utilize your site statistics is beyond the scope of this book, this example illustrates how you can move from using data from search in a reactionary manner to providing a real-time service to your end users. All the user engagement information you need is already available based on site search and SEO traffic and terms.

If you can track what terms brought a person to your site, you can apply a secondary search against your site search engine and return the results dynamically in your web page, to further aid your user in navigating your site (as well as correlating this data against the other related searches people have performed on your site). That is, you can basically create a section on a page that shows what other users thought was relevant or related to the landing page.

Establishing real-time applications that draw upon your search analytics data unleashes the power of the information you have been collecting. You can use this data everywhere from your home page, through to articles, to products. Integrating search data into your site to provide navigation points dynamically uses the voice of your customer to build data elements and can provide relevant links between your content that you may never have thought of.

Revisiting Site Search, Capturing the Second Term

In further refining our search knowledge to understand how users are interacting with our site, we may want to track the initial referring search from SEO or paid search, and the following site search query (if any). Tracking the secondary search terms provides further insight into how users refine their searches: users may be coming to the site on a very general term, then refining their search on the entry page.

You can use the data you collect to help reduce bounce rates. For every user that refines her search through your site upon entry, there are plenty of users who do not. By applying what you learn from the more determined users to the less determined users, you may be able to lower bounce rates for that segment of traffic. For example, suppose you find that large volumes of traffic come to a page on your site from the term "red cars," and that many of these users go on to do secondary searches on your site for "sports cars."

Assess the landing page, and determine if there is any content on the page relevant to "sports cars" (or links to such content elsewhere on your site). If there is, is it prominently displayed on the page? If not, move the content around on the page (or provide cross-links to help the user find her way to the content). Again, I cannot stress enough how effective A/B testing is for improving the usability of your site, not just from a search perspective but from a user perspective, too. You can run A/B or multivariate tests to try out different wordings of section titles, different imagery, or alternate positionings of content on a page.

Tracking on-site follow-up searches to referring search terms can also provide you with insight into what your users see as relevant content. You may discover that you have the wrong page organically ranking for a certain term, and you may need to focus on getting a different page to rank organically for that same term. Understanding the traffic you are getting and the language your visitors use will help you ensure that you are presenting them with relevant content earlier in their experience with your site as

---

opposed to forcing them to find the content through their own clicking and determination.

You will not be able to satisfy all people all of the time, and you will have to learn where and when to draw the line. Otherwise, you will find that you are constantly trying to optimize your content to other sets of terms. To make sure you don't get stuck in this cycle, use the data you have access to in order to determine which changes will likely improve revenue the most.

You should consider setting two statistical bars. The first will determine what percentage of people arriving at your site from external search go on to use your site search. This may range from 3% to 30%, or more or less; it depends on the content and the users. The second bar to set is the volume of secondary searches you may see on a term before you decide to incorporate content related to that term into your landing page. Where you set this bar will depend on the page itself, your ability to modify the content, and whether you feel the secondary search term is highly relevant to the topic of the page.

You will begin to see that everything we have been tracking through SEO and paid search can provide data points to apply to your site search. You can even take SEO and paid search queries and track their pathing through your site to further aid in optimizing your site search algorithm. Providing a set of related searches, as well as a set of results that show that people who looked at page "A" also looked at page "B," may further improve the usability of your site. These are again all features that will require A/B or multivariate testing on your end, but they are also features that can be enabled through the data you have collected.

Testing Paid Search Pages on Site Search First

Site search can be a great testing ground for paid search, before you roll out a new campaign. If your site search allows for custom search results, like the paid results of the big search engines like Google and Bing, you can leverage your own traffic to test titles and descriptions without spending a dime. Running tests on your own site can be a very quick and cost-effective way to validate users' CTR. Like anything else with site search, it's important to remember that this is an audience that is more familiar with your products than typical users of a search engine, but your CTR ratios should be similar to what you would see on an external search engine.

If you do choose to test your paid search campaigns on site search first, you will need to establish some baseline numbers. Run a few paid search campaigns in sync with your site search variations to validate that you are in fact seeing similar behavior on your site search as you do on your paid search campaigns. If there is a big difference, you may not be able to run these sorts of test on your own site. There can be a number of reasons for this. For instance, you may be in such a specific product segment that the specificity of your user base significantly skews the data. You may also find that your site users are more highly engaged with your content and prone to clicking through weaker ads than an external user.

The other missing component will be the lack of competing ads running on your site. You may find that something that tests very well on your site does not perform as well on search engines, due to the higher volume of competition. For this reason, I suggest only testing words that have low competition, and that you expect to find some usefulness for.

The last thing to remember is that when dealing with CPC paid search campaigns, you only have to pay per click, and you determine how much you are willing to pay. So, depending on your market, segment, and competition, you should be able to run some tests quickly without incurring big costs. This is one of those times where it becomes very dependent on your market, segment, and competition.

Pulling Terms from SEO/Paid Search to Improve Site Search

While tracking your SEO/paid search traffic volumes, you will also want to apply some of what you learn to your site search. If you see large volumes of traffic coming from SEO or paid search from specific queries and then using your site search, you will want to validate whether these users are searching for the same thing again on your site. If they are, do you return them to the same page they entered on? If this is the behavior of your site search engine, this is likely a very unsatisfactory experience for your users. A quick way to ensure this doesn't happen is to modify your site search to capture the referring page and blacklist it from the following results. You can also capture the frequency with which this happens, and look at the pages it's happening on. Think about what other content you have on your site that is closely related, and ensure it's cross-linked and prominently featured in your site search results.

Testing the Effects of Optimization on Site Search and SEO

As you optimize your entry pages to reduce bounce rates, you will find that you may have a juggling act to perform between external SEO and site search SEO. Depending on your site search platform, and specifically whether it uses spiders to interpret your site content, you may find you have to think about your SEO pages in two different ways when looking at on-page ranking factors.

Site search may utilize meta descriptions and keyword tags heavily, while these play little to no role in rankings for external SEO. If you are not fortunate enough to have total control over your site search results and your site search utilizes different mechanisms from external SEO, you will need to utilize your analytics to determine which pages should be optimized for external search and which ones should be optimized for site search.

As you optimize these pages, you will need to think about not only SEO ranking factors, but your own site search ranking factors as well. The challenge you may face is deciding what to do about elements that may improve site search ranking but negatively impact SEO ranking. For example, some site search tools require very specific formatting of title tags to determine the ranking of a page. Page titles can impact your organic rankings as well, though. To decide whether you should focus on improving page signals for site search or SEO, you can use the data you have on revenue and traffic source to decide which is the better option.

Concluding Thoughts

Site search can provide a wealth of information that you can apply to both your SEO and paid search programs. Site search can be utilized as a testing ground, as well as a way to provide users coming from external search with a quick and easy way to find other related content dynamically as your website grows. Site search can be an easy-to-leverage option to allow for scalability by simply applying some of what you know about the traffic coming to your site and utilizing your site's features.

Capturing and sharing data from search in real time can greatly improve the user experience, and can be a first step toward creating a customized experience based on user data and interaction throughout your web pages.

CHAPTER 8

Competitor Research and Competitor Tracking

Search is a competitive landscape.

Both SEO and paid search are about driving profitability by improving position, relevancy, and popularity. A well-executed search campaign, be it SEO or paid search, can significantly influence the volumes of traffic you get, as well as your conversion rates and ROI. Your competitors in search may not even be competitors you face in the offline world. Online you may find yourself competing with Wikipedia, Amazon, news and magazine sites, and more.

In the world of search, you compete not on products, but on words. Fortunately, today we have more sophisticated tools than ever before to track how competitors rank, and why they may be ranking as they do. SEOmoz has a very useful set of tools that you can use to research why your site and your competitors' sites rank as they do. You can also use Majestic SEO and AdGooRoo to further track competition for your SEO and paid search campaigns. Monitoring your competitors will come down to three basic tactics: monitoring those ahead of you, those behind you, and your overall search footprint compared to your direct competitors.

Tools you will need in this chapter:

- Clickstream tracking package (Google Analytics, Adobe SiteCatalyst, etc.)
- Spreadsheet program (Excel or something similar)
- AdWords or some other paid search tool
- Keyword tracking program (e.g., WebPosition)
- Competitor tracking tools (AdGooRoo, SpyFu, etc.)
- Voice-of-the-customer survey data (Survey Monkey, etc.)

Tracking Share of Voice

Share of voice is a traditional marketing analytic that measures your advertising weight as a percentage. This same analytic can apply to search. This is a large aggregate number, and while not exact, it should provide you with an idea of how much market share you have on your large set of keywords compared to your competition. The most important thing to remember here is that you should be tracking nonbranded terms. If you rank on competitor terms, you may track those as well, but tracking against your own terms will significantly skew the results. The intent should be to understand how you compare with your competitors on competitive terms. You can use KeywordSpy (*http://www.keywordspy.com*) or WebPosition (*http://www.webposition.com/*) to track your share of voice against competitors, or search for other similar tools. WebPosition tracks not just who you think are your competitors but also other sites that frequently show up on your terms.

Setting up the report is pretty straightforward. Create a WebPosition account and populate the form as shown in Figure 8-1, adding your domain, a report name, any subdomains you may have, a list of competitor sites, keywords or phrases you feel you should rank on, and which search engines to check or monitor, as well as how deep to run the report. I would not bother going beyond 20 results, as most traffic will come from the top 10 results, but anything in the top 20 may be close to moving into a top 10 position.

Running the report will tell you how you currently rank for your targeted set of words, as well as how your competition ranks on these words. The report returned is pretty minimal and basic, and could certainly use some improvements to extract share of voice. However, by extracting the data out from the keyword report (Figure 8-2), you can filter this out yourself in Excel or another spreadsheet tool of your choice. Alternatively, you can import this data into your own database and format it as you see fit.

Pulling the data into a spreadsheet (Figure 8-3) allows you to manipulate the data fairly easily. The quickest way to get a share of voice is to filter by URL type. Filtering by primary URLs will show your own site's URLs. You should know how many keywords you are tracking in total. In this report, we are tracking six keywords, but our site or competitor sites only show up on two of these words.

You also have the option of filtering across one or several search engines. When looking at share of voice across multiple engines, you need to multiply the number of words you're trying to rank on by the number of search engines—so, six words across two search engines is twelve.

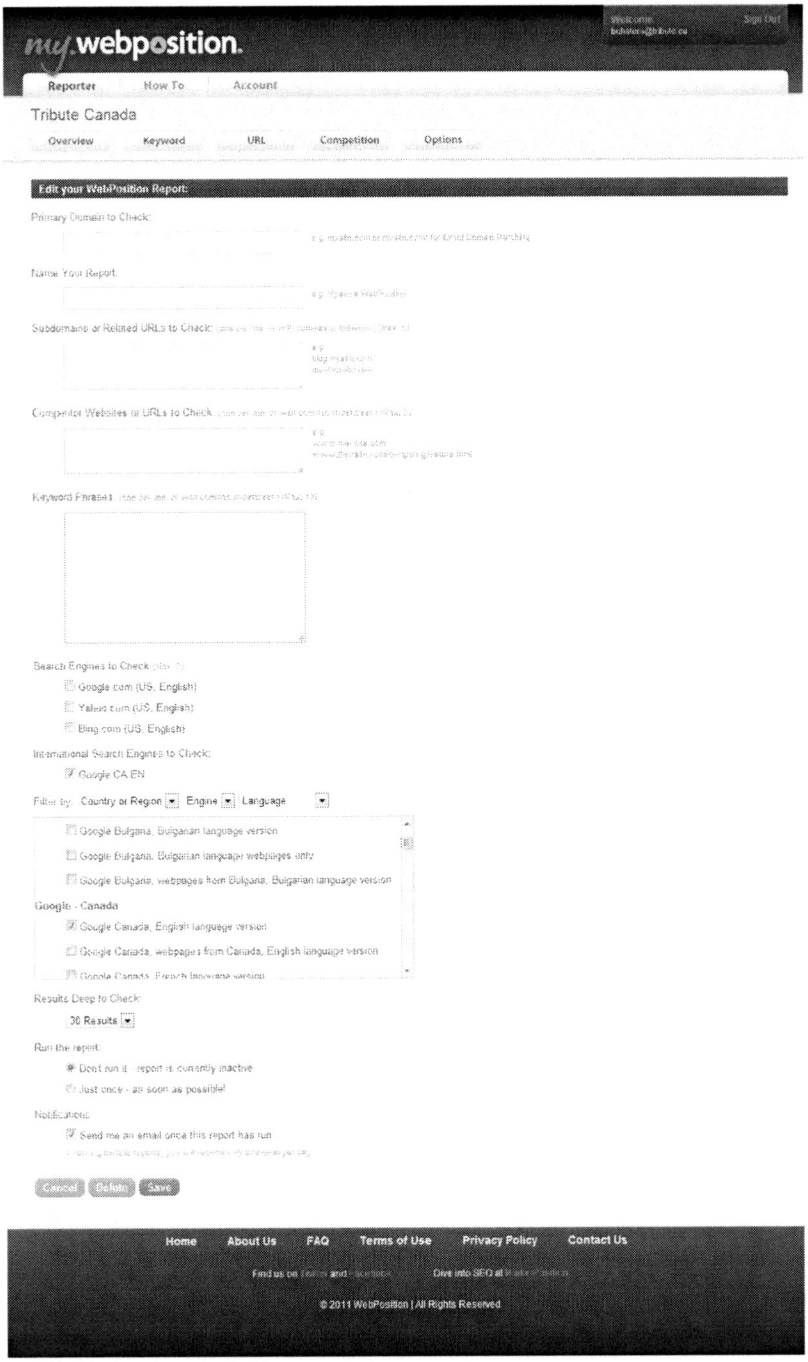

Figure 8-1. WebPosition report configuration screen

To figure out your share of voice across those two engines, you divide the number of words you rank on by the number of words you're trying to rank on. In this case, we end up with 1/12 or an 8.3% share of voice. This is a very basic share-of-voice calculation, and it has some flaws that we can fix with a bit of refinement. The first flaw is that you can have multiple pages rank on a term, so realistically you could end up with 24/12, which is 200% share of voice. This is OK if you also look at all your competitors the same way. The second, more complicated problem is that different rankings can have different CTR values and therefore greater or lesser importance.

Say, for example, you discover that you and a competitor both have six pages that rank on six terms each. However, you know your competitor is getting more traffic. This is most likely because your competitor is consistently ranking on a higher position than you. When looking at share of voice, it's important to take these issues into account.

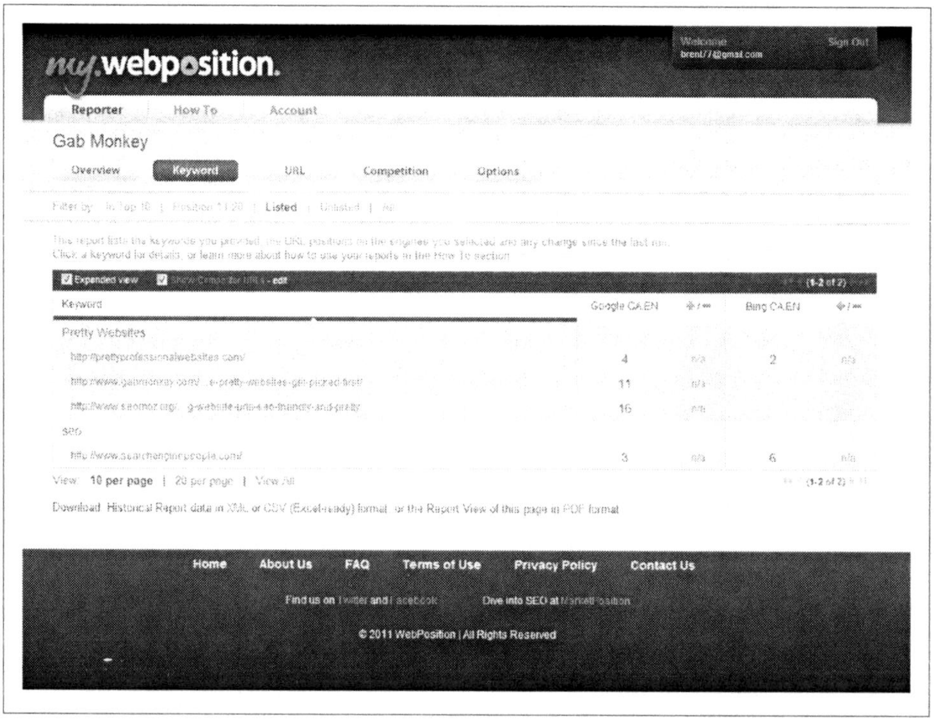

Figure 8-2. WebPosition keyword report

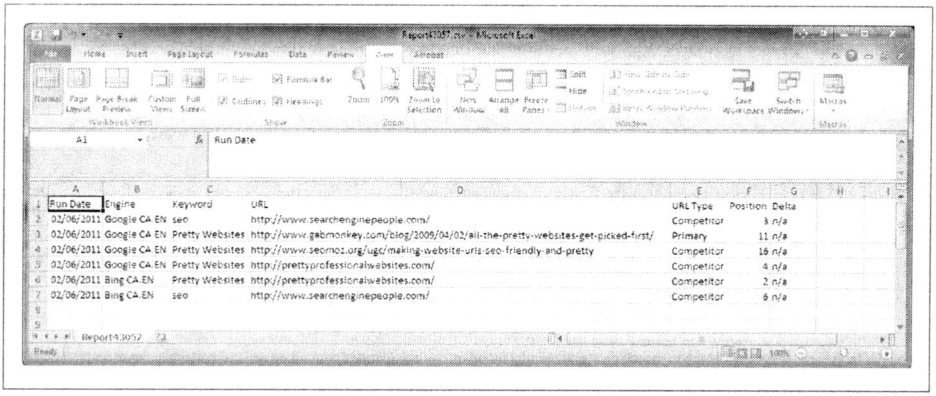

Figure 8-3. WebPosition keyword extracted data

Refining Share of Voice

To refine our share-of-voice calculation, we need to account for duplicate entries and their positional rankings. Fortunately, we don't actually have to remove duplicate rankings; we only need to account for how valuable they are. When we looked at the average CTR of rankings and postions in Chapter 2, we saw a general trend based on search ranking and click volume. Table 8-1 repurposes this data for us to estimate the value of each position in the search results. Using this as our baseline, we now have enough data to build a formula to provide a reasonable approximation of share of voice.

Table 8-1. Search results CTR from Chapter 2

SERP position	SEO results—no universal search
1	42.3%
2	11.92%
3	8.44%
4	6.03%
5	4.86%
6	3.99%
7	3.37%
8	2.98%
9	2.83%
10	2.97%
11 and beyond	0.66%

Let's assume that we have both a number 2 and a number 8 ranking for a particular term. We could then say that we anticipate getting about 14.9% of the search volume on that keyword, or in other words, that we have about a 14.9% of the share of voice on that term. To expand this out to multiple keywords, we need to total our share of voice per keyword and then use a weighted average to figure out the overall value. You will need to map the SERP position to the weighted average CTR in your spreadsheet (by doing a find and replace, creating a macro, or creating a formula in a secondary cell). You can then add up all the values in the column that is representative of CTR, and divide that number by the number of keywords you are tracking to get your share-of-voice value.

 Share of Voice = ((Total Expected CTR for 1st Position Ranking × Number of 1st Position Rankings) + (Total Expected CTR for 2nd Position Ranking × Number of 2nd Position Rankings) ...) / Total Terms

The code in Example 8-1 can be used as a macro in Excel to translate all your positional rankings into CTR values. Once you have set up the macro, you can simply hit Ctrl-R to run the macro and translate any cells you have highlighted into the corresponding CTR values. Typically, I copy the entire column and make a new column so I can see both positions and CTR values more easily. This macro will also convert anything that is text into a 0.66%. It is not perfect code, but for most needs it will make your conversions much more efficient as you calculate the weighted average.

Example 8-1. Macro to translate SERP positions to average CTRs

```
Sub position()
'
' position Macro
'
' Keyboard Shortcut: Ctrl-R
'
 Dim rngCell As Range

   For Each rngCell In Selection.Cells
       If rngCell.Value >= 11 Then
       rngCell.Value = "0.66%"
       End If
   Next rngCell

   Selection.Replace What:="1", Replacement:="42.3%", LookAt:=xlWhole, _
       SearchOrder:=xlByRows, MatchCase:=False, SearchFormat:=False, _
       ReplaceFormat:=False

   Selection.Replace What:="2", Replacement:="11.92%", LookAt:=xlWhole, _
       SearchOrder:=xlByRows, MatchCase:=False, SearchFormat:=False, _
       ReplaceFormat:=False

   Selection.Replace What:="3", Replacement:="8.44%", LookAt:=xlWhole, _
       SearchOrder:=xlByRows, MatchCase:=False, SearchFormat:=False, _
       ReplaceFormat:=False
```

```
Selection.Replace What:="4", Replacement:="6.03%", LookAt:=xlWhole, _
    SearchOrder:=xlByRows, MatchCase:=False, SearchFormat:=False, _
    ReplaceFormat:=False

Selection.Replace What:="5", Replacement:="4.86%", LookAt:=xlWhole, _
    SearchOrder:=xlByRows, MatchCase:=False, SearchFormat:=False, _
    ReplaceFormat:=False

Selection.Replace What:="6", Replacement:="3.99%", LookAt:=xlWhole, _
    SearchOrder:=xlByRows, MatchCase:=False, SearchFormat:=False, _
    ReplaceFormat:=False

Selection.Replace What:="7", Replacement:="3.37%", LookAt:=xlWhole, _
    SearchOrder:=xlByRows, MatchCase:=False, SearchFormat:=False, _
    ReplaceFormat:=False

Selection.Replace What:="8", Replacement:="2.98%", LookAt:=xlWhole, _
    SearchOrder:=xlByRows, MatchCase:=False, SearchFormat:=False, _
    ReplaceFormat:=False

Selection.Replace What:="9", Replacement:="2.83%", LookAt:=xlWhole, _
    SearchOrder:=xlByRows, MatchCase:=False, SearchFormat:=False, _
    ReplaceFormat:=False

Selection.Replace What:="10", Replacement:="2.97%", LookAt:=xlWhole, _
    SearchOrder:=xlByRows, MatchCase:=False, SearchFormat:=False, _
    ReplaceFormat:=False

End Sub
```

 A weighted average is used here because each ranking will carry a different weight. You will need to know how many pages you have in each ranking position, and multiply the total number of rankings by the average CTR. In Excel, if you know the total number of rankings for each position, you can place them in a table like so:

Position	Average CTR by position	Total pages ranking in position
1	42.3%	52
2	11.92%	26
3	8.44%	30
4	6.03%	45

You can then use the following formula to get your total (assuming the first column is "A"):

=SUMPRODUCT(B2:B5,C2:C5)/SUM(C2:C5)*100

In this case, you should get 19.83% as your total.

Establishing your own share of voice should now be a very simple task based on the data and reports at your disposal. You may also choose to run the same share-of-voice calculation against your competitors. You can filter on your competitors based on URL and extrapolate their share of voice to establish exactly how you stack up against the competition.

A share-of-voice report can be a very enlightening data point. You may discover that your competitors are not driving as much traffic from search as you thought they were compared to your site. Let's run through an example. Suppose you think that ACME company focuses highly on SEO, and you suspect they are getting more traffic than you are (as we'll see shortly, you can get an idea of this by looking at ComScore or Compete data).

By generating a share-of-voice report, you can determine if your competitor is getting as much traffic from your SEO keywords as you are or if they are getting more. You may learn that they only have a 4% share of voice while you have a 30% share of voice on those keywords, meaning you should be seeing larger segments of traffic. There are several possible explanations if you know that your competitor is getting more traffic than you. One is that they are getting large volumes of traffic from other words that you are not monitoring or measuring, or words that are not relevant to your business. They may be pulling traffic from paid search, or through banner advertising, social media, email, or other campaigns (not to mention vistors who type their URL directly into a browser). What you can rest assured of is that your SEO keywords and share of voice is not where you are losing ground.

Given that we are looking at share of voice for search, you would then want to deduce how much traffic your competitors are deriving from paid search. Paid search share of voice is no different from SEO share of voice; we simply need to utilize a different tool set to get at the data. The best tool set I have come across to date is AdGooRoo. Share of voice for paid search differs slightly from share of voice for SEO in that you need to look at both position and *coverage*. Coverage is how frequently your ad copy shows up over time. If your budget is spread thin, you may only see your ads showing up for part of a day, or you may use day parting to display your ad during certain periods of time.

You will want to predict the number of clicks you get versus your competition on the keywords you overlap on. AdGooRoo's reports provide a very simple and easy to interpret set of charts where you can track competitors versus your-self to understand both spend volume and estimated number of clicks (Figure 8-4). This saves us a great deal of effort, as we don't need to clean the data; we simply need to pull the report and review it.

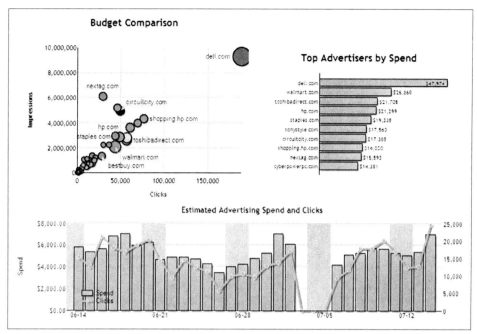

Figure 8-4. AdGooRoo competitor tracking

Tracking Against Competitors

Tracking share of voice is a good way to monitor how you are performing in relation to your competitors, and also to identify the emergence of new competitors. If your share of voice increases, it may mean you are moving up the rankings, but you may also want to keep an eye on what's happening with your competitors. Be aware of *keyword overlap*, or the set of words that you and a competitor are both targeting. You will probably have some words that do overlap, and some that do not. Knowing which words your competitor is targeting that you are not can give you some ideas about directions to pursue. This is known as *keyword mining*.

KeywordSpy offers a report that tracks the overlap of sites and keywords. Another fantastic option is SpyFu (*http://www.spyfu.com*). The stronger the overlap (Figure 8-5), the more competitive you may be over a set of terms. SpyFu also shows the variance in volume of terms. You can track on both organic and paid search, which can be useful depending on the types of campaigns you are running.

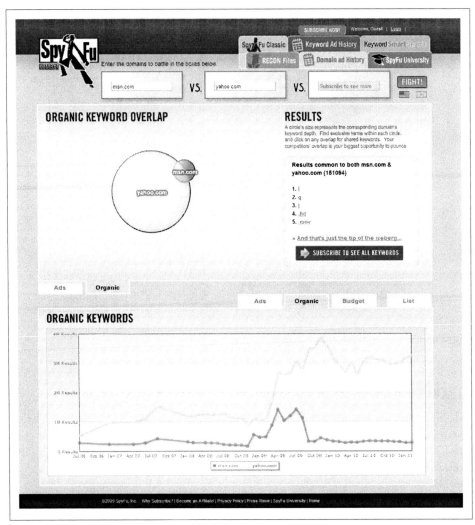

Figure 8-5. SpyFu keyword overlap

Selecting the middle of the Venn diagram will display the words you are competing on. To get the full list of your competitors' keywords, you will need to subscribe to SpyFu's services. Monitoring this list and reviewing it every month or two can provide you with insight into how your competitors are growing their lists of keywords and their sites. KeywordSpy also offers tracking of your terms based on rank, which is useful because both rank and volume are important. You may discover that you have a larger set of keywords than a competitor but rank very poorly on them in comparison. There are two ways of approaching rankings: you can try to rank well on a few key terms, or rank OK on many key terms. Some sites are fortunate enough to rank well on many key terms, but this is typically an exception to the rule. This is an area you will want to focus on if you are a search strategist.

To improve your rankings, you may look at what other terms your competitors are ranking on. Looking at the terms that are in their part of the Venn diagram and doing a bit of keyword research can help you see what your competitors are doing well on. Are they targeting a variety of other related keywords that you are not competing on? Do you see a heavy favoring of their own branded terms? Do they have a larger site and therefore more pages than you, and most likely a larger assortment of keywords? Some sites may outperform you simply because of their sheer size. Conversely, by doing this kind of research, you may find that sites you thought were beating you at the SEO game or the paid search game are in actuality not as competitive as you thought.

Capturing Competitors' Keywords

Your competitors may have specific SEO strategies in place for specific sets of words. Surprisingly, it's often easy to identify these sets of words. These terms can be discovered through metadata, links, and footers. Each of these can be scraped, or you can go out and manually view this data yourself. Running audits may not be the most glorious of jobs, and it may require some low-tech work, such as trolling your competitors' pages looking for hints of what they may be doing. However, the effort you put in can be well worth it.

Mining Metadata

Large sites may embed metadata, including keywords and page descriptions, within the HTML of the pages themselves. While this data is not useful to optimize a page for organic search, it is still used by site searches because of the high degree of trust that the site search algorithm can place on the terms in these meta tags. Further, meta descriptions may be used by search engines to display descriptions of pages, which can improve the CTR of pages in the SERPs.

Viewing this information can give you an indication of what your competitor thinks is important about or relevant to specific pages. You may also find that there are custom meta tags in their headers that provide some insight into how they segment pages internally and how the content is evolving (e.g., pages may be labeled "sales" or "pre-sales"). It is worth doing at least a top-level audit of some of your competitors' key pages to learn more about the keywords they're targeting and the language they use to describe their products.

Mining Links

Links are another well-known factor for ranking well in SEO. Looking at the links on a page, as well as the links that appear as part of the standard navigation, can give you another idea of how your competitors view their sites and their products. Websites are designed with taxonomies in mind, often referred to as the *information architecture.* Understanding the architecture of your competitors' sites can tell you how they think about and categorize their products.

The most important product categories will be structured as parents or emphasized in some way on their sites. If you think your competitor is focused on product A, but product B is really more dominant on their site, it is likely that this is the focus they have online. Regardless of any external campaigns they may be running for product A (TV, print, radio), their site architecture will be one factor that determines the importance of their pages to a search engine, and this can be indicative of where their long-term priorities and commitments lie. Clicking through and getting to know your competitor's site can be very advantageous.

 To really understand how pages have built up links organically on your competitor's site, you can use a spider to crawl the site and identify pages with large numbers of inbound links. The best tool for this is Majestic SEO (see the Appendix for details).

Mining Footers

Footers have recently become a very popular navigation as well as SEO utility on many websites. Some sites have what are called "fat footers," which are populated heavily with links. Sites that are part of a network may include cross-links to other domains in their footers. Footers, like links, can be very keyword-rich areas that provide insight into your competitors' thoughts. Some footers may even be blatantly stuffed with keywords or terms that do not fit in with the text on the page but work well for building up keyword associations for other pages on the site. Fat footers can carry negative SEO weight, depending on how they are set up. Fortunately for us, we are not looking to mirror design decisions; we merely want to mine the footers for keywords and other information.

Again, you may have to look at multiple pages, as there may be several variations of the footer for different site sections depending on how the site is designed. Building up a list of the words you find and the pages they link to can help you better understand the information architecture of your competitor's site. This, combined with the data you have pulled from metadata and observations about general site navigation and home page organization, will provide you with a useful set of data that can be applied to comparing terms you rank on and that your competitor may be trying to rank on. These may be special terms you monitor much more closely in your share-of-voice reports.

You can set up mini share-of-voice reports, to track how you perform on 30 or 40 highly competitive terms that both you and other sites are attempting to rank on. These may be terms that can generate thousand or tens of thousands of visits in a week. These should also be terms that you review on a much more frequent basis (say, biweekly) to understand the exact impact your search strategy is having. These may also be terms you develop highly aggressive paid search campaigns around, to further improve your revenue and bottom line.

Capitalizing on User Behavior

You may also be able to use your users to "spy" on the competition. You can glean information from them through quick surveys that you run on your site. You can ask simple questions such as, "If you are considering purchasing our product, who else are you considering purchasing from? Why?" It's a simple question, and the responses you get can be very useful.

For example, if your customers tell you they are considering another company because they cannot find support on your site, you will know you need to improve the findability of online support for your products. Websites that see search as their primary source of traffic need to move away from the front-door model that assumes people will come in from the home page. Instead, they need to recognize that people may come to their site through the back door, through windows, down the chimney, and any other way they can get in. People who enter your site via search and land on a page selling one of your products but who really want support should be able to find the support section easily. Based on survey feedback, you might want to make the support information about that product much more prominent on the page.

You may also want to focus on what I refer to as *keyword conversion*—converting people to use your own branded terms over those of a competitor. For example, if you sell widgets and your top product is called Company A Widget, there is a high likelihood that people who came to your site on the term "widget" will return to it if you can get them to search for "Company A Widget" the next time they're looking for information on the kind of product you sell. Your copywriters will need to become highly skilled at developing copy that can lead from common language to company-specific language without distancing the copy from the user. Apple is a company that does an excellent job of this.

Ideally, the new term that you influence users to search on will be a term that you fully dominate—for example, "apple computers" as oppposed to just "computers." These subsequent searches on terms that are more tightly aligned to your brand tend to allow for multiple links related to your brand to show up, and increase the likelihood of return visitors. The more brand-specific the term is, the more likely you are to dominate the results.

Imagery can help in building your brand, as can repeating your company name as part of the product name instead of the industry name. Many companies have been very successful at building up strong brand terms that allow for term domination; again, Apple is perhaps the biggest brand to do this successfully, labeling laptops as MacBooks and cell phones as iPhones. You may not be able to achieve this kind of success, especially in an area with a lot of competition. However, if you are in a niche market, you may be able to get your brand name highly associated with an obscure product. If you can develop the industry language toward your brand terms, you can lead both through search and as the industry standard.

Tracking Competitors' Branded Keywords

Understanding your competitors' terms—both the keywords they are bidding on and the terminology they use to describe their own products—can help you identify areas of opportunity and spaces in which they may be looking to grow. You can track this kind of language very easily, by watching for the appearance of the company's name in press releases and other publicly released documents online. There are two goals here: one is to understand what your competitor is doing, and the other is to understand how the search engines interpret your competitor's name. Tracking what your competitor does online with its terminology can be done by looking at press releases and other news items. You can set up Google Alerts (*http://www.google.com/alerts*) to alert you via email or RSS when it finds new pages on terms you specify. Following the alerts can provide you with an idea of how Google perceives your competitor in the online space, as well as keeping you abreast of announcements and other timely updates. The downside is that if your search parameters are too broad, you may need to wade through a lot of noise.

The other way to spy on your competitors is to launch paid search campaigns on their branded terms on broad match (see "Tracking Broad Match Words" on page 127). You will likely identify a variety of terms that might drive traffic to your site from clicks. The downside to this is that it can become rather expensive to maintain and monitor. You may also find that you don't get much traffic, or that the traffic you get converts poorly. The other option is to use tools such as SpyFu (*http://www.spyfu.com/*) or KeywordSpy, as discussed in "Tracking Against Competitors" on page 179. Both of these allow you to see what terms and words your competitors are tracking or trending on, and they are a much more cost-effective way to spy; also, this approach does not tip off your competitors that you are looking to play in their space.

Unique terminology should be easy to monitor, but slowly rising trends may indicate a slow launch of a product to keep an eye on. Look for terms that are moving through the rankings at a steady pace, toward a top page result. You will likely find that terms that move up through the rankings will have had a steady increase of back links being built as well. You can use Majestic SEO (*http://www.majesticseo.com/*) to track the back link base to specific pages. Look at how and what people are linking to on your competitors' sites. Knowing what pages are linked to will allow you to build competing pages before your competitors secure the dominant SERP positions.

Capitalizing on Competitor Spikes and Marketing

As you build up your competitor-monitoring resources, you will want to start to capitalize on your competitors' marketing. You may be able to piggy-back on their terms and rising trends by being savvy and monitoring when they are making press announcements. Press releases can drive quick bursts of searches for specific terms—for example, every Apple announcement puts fanboys in a crazy state looking for more information. Monitoring your competitors' press releases will allow you to pull out terms that may be relevant and that you can plug into your programs to ride the wave.

For this strategy to be effective, it will require the ability to turn your paid search campaigns on and off very rapidly. You will also want to monitor these campaigns very closely when they are deployed. Tracking ROI on these words will be almost futile, as this strategy is much more targeted toward raising awareness. If anything, these clicks may be high-funnel activities, to build brand awareness in an emerging market. Track CTR, cost per click, and bounce rates very closely. The paid search campaigns should be targeted at pages that can speak to your competitors' announcements. Perhaps you may run rebuttals to claim they have made, or you may elevate a similar product you already have.

You will also want to ensure that these campaigns are set up in separate accounts from your other campaigns, so as not to impact your Quality Scores or the relevancy factors of your existing paid search campaigns. The other reason to run these separately is that you will want to be able to build up your keyword lists, and move over terms that may surprise you as high-performing words to one of your core campaigns.

The analytics you measure through your campaign will focus on the awareness phase, so be prepared to see low conversions. Your goal should be to engage your users, to get them to click and dive deeper into your website. Your KPIs for these sorts of campaigns should include the following:

- CTR
- Bounce rate
- Average number of page views
- Average time on page
- Engagement with any social media widgets or emailing the page to a friend
- Any other indicators of a person engaging with your content

Tracking these points will give you a very clear view of your ability to beat your competitor to market on search terms. The earlier you are to market, the more likely it is that others are not yet aware of your competitor's new product. You may be able to turn this defensive strategy into an offensive strategy by cutting your competitor off at the pass and ensuring that you remain at the forefront of the mind of anyone in that market segment looking for that type of product.

Tracking the Effectiveness of Your Competitors' Marketing Through Metrics

As you move your keywords into position to cut off your competitor, you will want to measure how effective their marketing strategy is. You may find that they outperform you simply due to a well-funded marketing push. If you are outfunded, there may be little you can do. However, you might be surprised at what can be accomplished through some grassroots tactics.

One of the most interesting side effects I've seen of a social media response was in regard to a competitor's claim against one of our products. The claim was pretty bold, and our social media team quickly jumped into action to provide our company's point of view.

In literally days, the social media channels (Twitter and blogs) began pointing back to our site's rebuttal, using the competitor's own marketing terms. Through monitoring, we were able to see where the competitor originally ranked, and then use our appearance in the rankings as a counterpoint to their very specific marketing slogan.

The social media chatter, along with the search rankings, had a measurable impact on our competitor's campaign. We went from a zero share of voice to a much heavier and visible share of voice, negating a portion of their campaign and providing us with new customers and improved awareness of our products.

In addition to deploying paid search strategies, blogging and creating some of your own noise in the social sphere can further reduce the impact of your competitor's message. What you will want to know is what sort of impact all of this work will have on your ultimate goal, which is to take away some of your competitor's share of voice. We can track this the same way we did earlier, but on a smaller scale.

Develop a list of keywords that you want to go after, and then measure both your ranking and your competitor's ranking. Taking a snapshot of the environment before the campaigns are launched can prove to be very helpful. This is not always possible, but it's good to have this data if you can get it. Once the campaigns begin, start to monitor share of voice right away.

Track what percentage you are able to capture, as well as your competitor's share of voice. As you do this, keep in mind the principles of ROI. What is the value of this space to yourself, and to your competitor? You should be tracking your ability to either minimize the impact they have on a space you already own, or maximize your voice in a new space you are both competing on.

Your ROI measurements will likely be low, as you will be tracking people who are just getting acquainted with the products. You will also likely see a slower uptake in purchases. While there will be some early adopters who like to be the first to get in on something new, they are a small group; most people are more cautious. If you run multiclick tracking, you may want to extend the time between a browse and a buy. There may be longer delays—up to double or more—before a purchase happens.

Tracking the user base through your site, as well as tracking follow-up searches or repeat visits to your site, should also provide insight into how effective you are at driving people to more relevant content. The more repeat customers you have, the better your campaign is running. So beyond the metrics we were looking at when exploring capitalizing on our competitor's marketing, we will also want to track the number of new versus returning customers. This KPI can help you understand if this space is targeting people who may be new to your brand, or people who are familiar with your brand and may already be customers. Both analytics can have positive spins. In the one corner you have acquisition, and in the other corner you have retention. Both are good metrics to have, but understanding the split may help you modify the message you present.

Existing customers need to be told why they should remain with you, while new customers will likely need a deeper introduction to what your products are and what services you offer. You may find that you need more high-level and deeper introductory content depending on the group of users your campaigns target and draw in.

Brand Conquesting

The last competitor strategy to look at and track is referred to as *conquesting*. A conquesting campaign is when you go after established terms and keywords that your competitor has a clear foothold on. These are typically also their highly branded terms. The best example of a conquesting campaign is the soft drink wars. Both Coke and Pepsi have very set customer bases, with a small fraction that is undecided and could go either way any day of the week. To try to get these middle-ground customers who may be in the consideration stage, Coke bids on Pepsi's brand and Pepsi on Coke's.

In this case, the spend likely has a negative ROI, but gaining any of these middle-ground users could mean an improved overall lifetime value for either company. I have only seen conquesting used in very select cases, and it is usually very targeted, with a highly specific message about why their brand is better than the competitor's or why the competitor's brand may not be very good.

If you're in a position where you need to fight for middle-ground users, you may consider launching a conquesting campaign to attempt to lure some undecided users away from your competitor. The easiest way to do this is through paid search, but this can also be very costly. If you're considering going down this route, remember that you can define what the landing or entry page is as well as your copy. If you can construct a very concise and relevant landing page, you may find that your conquesting campaign is surprisingly beneficial and results in some wins.

You may also find a conquesting campaign is relevant in highly competitive markets where a single user may result in a large deal. When tracking these campaigns, you will need to provide very clear and concise metrics to whoever is sponsoring this effort. There should be very clearly stated targets and objectives. The principle should not be to "get customers"; instead, it should be something more specific, like "to acquire customers looking for product A and feature B." Targeting specific niches will make your campaigns much more successful than if you blindly targeted all competitor terms.

Look to win your battles on the small fronts, not on the larger front. Take away small pieces of your competitor's market share to grow your own in ways that allow you to generate a positive ROI, and look at the overall lifetime value of a customer. Every single acquisition may have a high lifetime value that you now own. Establish what the life-time values are for customers you acquire, and you will find it much easier to justify the spend, as well as getting a better picture of the big-picture ROI.

Tracking brand conquests requires a different set of KPIs. Conquesting is typically low in ROI, so you need to really focus on the lifetime value of a customer. You may need to take a "try and buy" approach, giving something away to get a customer to consider your brand.

To measure the success of such a campaign, you can use 30-day trial periods, coupons, or shipping out free sample products. Success can then be measured by the number of products you send to users who have never before used your products. This requires more than just capturing clickstream data, though. Before giving a user the opportunity to try your products, you will have to ask "have you ever tried product XXX before?" with a yes or no option. Anyone who answers "no" and goes on to try your product counts as a success.

Concluding Thoughts

Competition in SEO and paid search will come in many forms, including both your traditional competitors and surprise competition. You may even find you are competing against partners. When looking at your search campaigns, quickly outline who are your friends, who are your enemies, and who is neutral. You may find that by working with your partners you can more effectively limit your enemies' rankings and positions. "Neutral" competitors are not really a threat, and should only be of interest if they rank higher than you or if you think they are taking some of your share of the traffic.

Your primary objective should be to get yourself into a dominating position, where you block your competition or push their pages down the rankings. Competing in search can involve a lot of strategic thinking, and it requires even the best search strategists to have a variety of data points ready at their fingertips. You may even want to build into your monthly dashboard a competitive section, to report on where potential threats may be coming from. Being able to target and isolate threats before they emerge is the best asset you can have when looking to defend against a competitor's change in position.

If you are highly effective at cutting off competitive threats before they arise, you may find yourself in a position where it is questioned if what you're really doing is cutting off the competition. This is where your analytics will be the most handy. Providing the data that you used to identify the rising threat, as well as the tactics used to neutralize it, will help you paint a better picture of what exactly you have done to maintain market share and limit the growth of your competitor.

CHAPTER 9

Tracking Off-Site Trends

A good portion of search takes place
outside of your website.

Tracking off-site trends for both SEO and paid search is critical to understanding and running successful campaigns, as well as being able to explain exactly why or how a ranking or traffic volume has changed. SEO requires an understanding of links, neighborhoods, social media, and more, while both paid search and SEO require you to understand what other marketing activities are happening off-site. Do you have any print, TV, or radio spots running that may drive more search volumes and therefore more clicks on your paid search campaigns? Do you have specific terminology in these campaigns that should be incorporated into your paid search campaigns to maximize your findability from other marketing sources? Further, knowledge of off-site trends that may affect your overall campaigns may help you resolve questions that arise about any spikes or dips.

Tools you will need in this chapter:

- Clickstream tracking package (Google Analytics, Adobe SiteCatalyst, etc.)
- Spreadsheet program (Excel or something similar)
- Link measurement tool (SEOmoz Open Site Explorer, Majestic SEO, etc.)
- Link authority and page trust measurement tool (SEOmoz Open Site Explorer)
- Google Webmaster Tools
- Social media tracking tools (Radian 6, SocialAnalytics, etc.)

Analyze: Explaining the Bumps and Spikes

Data analysis is part storytelling, and part detective work. The storytelling part is where you need to explain the data. Where you as the analyst see numbers, you must now weave this into a story that both describes the issue and presents solutions or actions that must be taken. Being able to explain your data to others is just as important as being able to dig through it.

You will at some point end up with hills and valleys in your analytics reports. Some of these may be attributed to seasonality, but usually there are other driving factors. The example in Figure 9-1 shows a sudden drop on day 3. Any astute manager will immediately ask what happened on that day. The rest of the graph seems to trend in a very gradual pattern, so what was going on day 3? In this hypothetical example, the dip could have been caused by any number of factors.

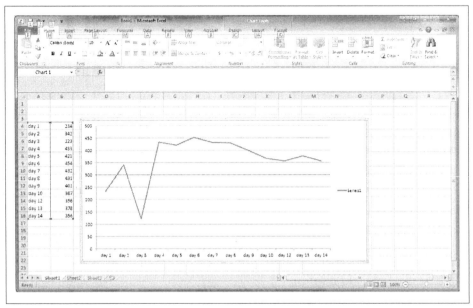

Figure 9-1. The hills and valleys of traffic data

To eliminate potential factors, work from the inside out. That is, start with what you know about the site. Were your campaigns put on hold? Did you exhaust your budget on the second day? Can you segment your traffic to see where traffic stopped coming from on that day? These are all factors that should be very closely tied to what you do, or at least within your realm of knowledge. Then move to the next set of questions, looking at the hosting platform. Was the server down? Were there networking issues?

Next, move from technical issues to external influences. From hosting questions you may move to marketing questions. When the program launched, what was done? Was an email sent out? Was there any additional advertising? Did a radio spot begin to air, or did a print magazine go out with an ad in it? You may find that on launch day there was an email blast that was sent out, resulting in a high open rate, and then nothing further was done until the fourth day, when a print or TV campaign was launched. Then over time that advertising campaign started to fizzle out.

Beyond your own marketing activity for SEO, consider algorithm changes, acquisitions, PR (both good and bad), development updates from your IT department, site section changes, and navigation changes as potential impacts to your organic rankings.

Your data is only as good as the explanation you have to go with it. Data alone cannot always tell a full story. Sometimes you may have to craft a bigger picture to make sure that the full story is understood. Analytics is not simply about looking at numbers, but interpreting those numbers. You may need to be able to explain when there are reporting issues, such as a tracking beacon being removed, or marketing plan changes. Good analytics come not from the tools, but the people who use them. Again, keep the 90/10 rule in mind! The people are the ones who will be able to interpret and understand the data that the tools provide. There will never be one tool that magically tells you exactly what is happening. And the more complex your business is, the more important data analysis will become.

Explaining bumps and spikes or hills and valleys will be the core responsibility of most analysts. Analysts should be looking for what is causing the spikes and marketers should already have an idea of when programs went into market. If your company runs offline programs, all the marketing programs should be tracked through a calendar that is shared with the search and web teams. This calendar will prove invaluable to digital teams, and particularly the analysts who must interpret the data points. A line chart with spikes and valleys suddenly has a story to go along with it. It may even help in refining the marketing strategy, by pointing out marketing activities that have little to no effect on online activities. Tracking data against a story ultimately makes your data more presentable.

Auditing General Trends

As part of your overall SEO tracking, you should be monitoring general trends. What are these general trends?

- Off-site link diversity
- Traffic fluctuation based on segments and sources
- Development rate of competitors' links
- Social influences and discussions
- SERP rankings
- Share of voice
- Conversion rate changes
- Engagement rate changes
- Search engine indexation

These are the key analytics you should be monitoring on a fairly regular basis with regard to what is happening off your site. Some of this you already know how to track, and those metrics should be built into your search dashboard review. We'll be looking at how to track the rest of them throughout the remainder of this chapter. These metrics will also help you tell your analytics' story and provide more data points to pull from.

Developing a dashboard of general trends will help you to identify quickly when issues may arise. Depending on the nature of your site, the trends you need to track may differ from this list. If you don't have paid conversions, you may be looking at impressions delivered, time on site, use of site search, clicks to other websites or other parts of your site, or any number of other key indicators. You may want to track coverage for paid search campaigns, or some other metric that is important to the success of your business. However, this list should provide you with a starting point for thinking about which trends to track.

Measuring Off-Site Link Diversity

If you are tracking SEO rankings, you may find yourself suddenly wondering where some of your traffic has gone. While your marketing department's efforts may influence traffic volumes, there are other factors that can play a role. One of the biggest may be your SEO strategy. Suppose you have built up rankings on some very prominent keywords that are responsible for a good portion of your business traffic. Suddenly, this traffic starts to decrease. You quickly segment your traffic and see that the big drop is in the organic search segment, so you filter this down to keywords and you see that some of your high-value words are not driving as much traffic as they used to. You validate your SERP rank and see that you have slipped from a number 1 position to a number 2 or 3 position. Why have you suddenly slipped in the rankings? And who has taken over the number 1 position? You may find that they are a new entity in your space and that they have received a lot of great PR, as well as fully utilizing their social networks.

One of the reasons sites rank well is back links. This is a core principle of the PageRank algorithm defined by Google. It is about increasing the number of links from a diverse group of high-quality, topically relevant domains. If you have the choice between 10 links from one site or one link from each of 10 sites highly related to your own, the second option is better. Link and domain diversity can influence ranking position significantly. While not the only reason for changes in position and rankings, it can be an important factor.

Understanding how your back links are built up and how to create more of these links can help you understand where you are weak against a competing site. Majestic SEO can provide a great deal of insight about back links, as shown in Figure 9-2. It allows you to filter the back links by domains and to see if the links are in frame sets, if they are nofollow links, if they are in images, and what the *alt* text is. Further, you can zero in on specific terms by searching for text in the URL or anchor text. By filtering on ACRank, you can get a very general idea of the value of links from different pages. This is not a PageRank number, but a value that Majestic SEO has developed for its own

Figure 9-2. Majestic SEO showing back links to a website

use. It should not be used exclusively to determine the importance of a page, but it can give you a very general idea.

You can filter by domains, URLs, and subdomains to get an idea of the variety and volume of back links your site has developed. You can also look at a high-level view of your site as well as other competing sites to understand back link strategies, and see when back links suddenly started to develop. Finding patterns in this data can be made easier by using the back link history tool to view how you compare to your competitors. In Figure 9-3, we can see how *msn.com* and *yahoo.com* vary, with Yahoo! developing both more back links in total and more back links from different domains. The second chart, showing the number of domains, is the more valuable, as it shows domain diversity and growth. While large amounts of back links are great, they can only stretch so far. Domain diversity is where you will see the greatest uplift in back links to a site.

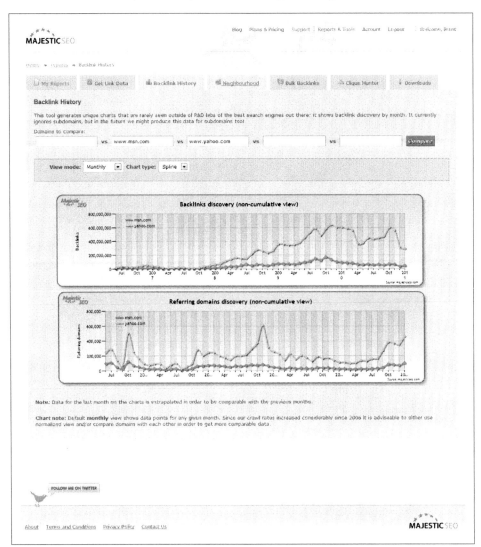

Figure 9-3. Majestic SEO showing the overall trends of back links and links from domains

The diversity and quality of back links can be used to track rising trends on your site, and your competitors' sites, in two ways: using the text in the back links and monitoring how rapidly back links are appearing. Sudden bursts can indicate hot topics, or aggressive link building or buying campaigns.

The terms used in the back links can provide an idea of rising topics, as well as which pages are hot or generating solid link baiting. Looking at inbound links from other sites will help you to understand the overall domain rank and authority of your site compared to other sites. The flow of link building over time can also give you some insight into when your competitors get aggressive in the market, or potentially launch new products.

Beyond link diversity is the issue of link quality. If you run a website about movies, a link from *IMDB.com* may be worth more than a link from *joesmovieblog.com*. The authority and quality of links can be measured with PageRank and by considering topicality—meaning that to be a quality link, it should come from a high-quality site with a similar focus to your own. You can find the PageRank of a page on the Google Toolbar (Figure 9-4). Monitoring link diversity can help you understand not only how your site is performing from a health perspective but also how your competitors are trending.

 PageRank is only relevant to Google. It can be an indicator for other engines, but no other search engine besides Google has access to this data. Further, PageRank is only updated a few times a year, so as an indicator, it's sort of like horseshoes and hand grenades; it's close but not always exact.

Page Rank Indicator

Google

Figure 9-4. Google Toolbar showing PageRank

Webmaster Tools—What It Can Tell You

To dive deeper into your back link audit, you can utilize Google Webmaster Tools. This tool set will provide you with details as to how your site is indexed and perceived by the engine as well. While not exhaustive, the data returned can indicate a great deal about what is happening with the pattern of links to your site. There are three key reports you can use to understand how and where people are linking to your site.

The Site Keyword Report

The first report is the keyword report (Figure 9-5), which can be found under the "Your site on the web" section: click on "Links to your site" and then click on the "More" link under "How your data is linked." This report shows how your data is linked from sites, including your own, and lets you see which keywords appear in these links. Coupled with the "Keywords" report (also found under "Your site on the web"), which shows "the most common keywords Google found when crawling your site," it can give you a great deal of insight into what words your site is identified with.

You should review the keyword report under the "Links to your site" on a semi-regular basis, and validate if this is an accurate depiction of how your site should be represented. The words and terms that appear here should be generally reflective of your overall topics and content. If they aren't, your only course of action is to improve your own site linking architecture and look at link-building campaigns targeted around specific words or terms that you feel are relevant to your business.

The Links to Your Site Report

The second important report is the links to your site report, located in the same area as the site keyword report. This report (Figure 9-6) shows who is linking to your site and points out the most prominent linkers. This can give you an idea of who Google sees as providing the most relevant links to your site. As with Majestic SEO, what we are looking for here is links from a wide variety of domains.

The larger the variety, the healthier your site SEO score is. The data from Webmaster Tools can also tell you how many links you get from each domain, as well as how many pages are linked from that domain. This is valuable as you may be looking for many links from some key domains, not just for SEO purposes but to grow traffic referrals from those sites as well.

 This data can also work as a flag for your webmaster of black hat tactics being deployed by your site. A sudden influx of links from many sites that all appear to be the same text is an indication that someone may be buying links. As important as link building is, link buying can significantly impact a site's rankings.

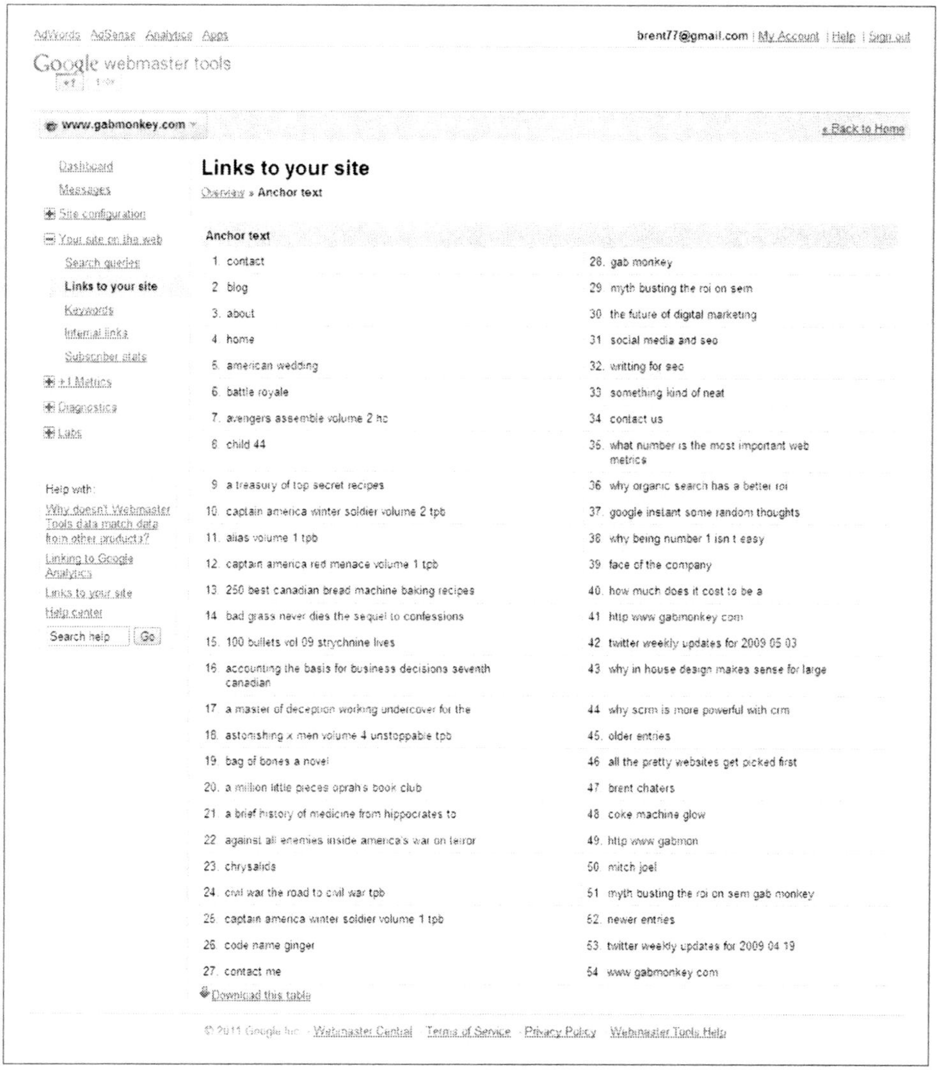
AdWords AdSense Analytics Apps
brent77@gmail.com | My Account | Help | Sign out
Google webmaster tools
www.gabmonkey.com
« Back to Home
Dashboard
Messages
Site configuration
Your site on the web
Search queries
Links to your site
Keywords
Internal links
Subscriber stats
+1 Metrics
Diagnostics
Labs
Help with:
Why doesn't Webmaster Tools data match data from other products?
Linking to Google Analytics
Links to your site
Help center
Search help
Go
Links to your site
Overview » Anchor text
Anchor text
1. contact
2. blog
3. about
4. home
5. american wedding
6. battle royale
7. avengers assemble volume 2 hc
8. child 44
9. a treasury of top secret recipes
10. captain america winter soldier volume 2 tpb
11. alias volume 1 tpb
12. captain america red menace volume 1 tpb
13. 250 best canadian bread machine baking recipes
14. bad grass never dies the sequel to confessions
15. 100 bullets vol 09 strychnine lives
16. accounting the basis for business decisions seventh canadian
17. a master of deception working undercover for the
18. astonishing x men volume 4 unstoppable tpb
19. bag of bones a novel
20. a million little pieces oprah s book club
21. a brief history of medicine from hippocrates to
22. against all enemies inside america's war on terror
23. chrysalids
24. civil war the road to civil war tpb
25. captain america winter soldier volume 1 tpb
26. code name ginger
27. contact me
28. gab monkey
29. myth busting the roi on sem
30. the future of digital marketing
31. social media and seo
32. writting for seo
33. something kind of neat
34. contact us
35. what number is the most important web metrics
36. why organic search has a better roi
37. google instant some random thoughts
38. why being number 1 isn t easy
39. face of the company
40. how much does it cost to be a
41. http www gabmonkey com
42. twitter weekly updates for 2009 05 03
43. why in house design makes sense for large
44. why scrm is more powerful with crm
45. older entries
46. all the pretty websites get picked first
47. brent chaters
48. coke machine glow
49. http www gabmon
50. mitch joel
51. myth busting the roi on sem gab monkey
52. newer entries
53. twitter weekly updates for 2009 04 19
54. www gabmonkey com
Download this table
© 2011 Google Inc. - Webmaster Central - Terms of Service - Privacy Policy - Webmaster Tools Help

Figure 9-5. The Webmaster Tools links to your site keyword report

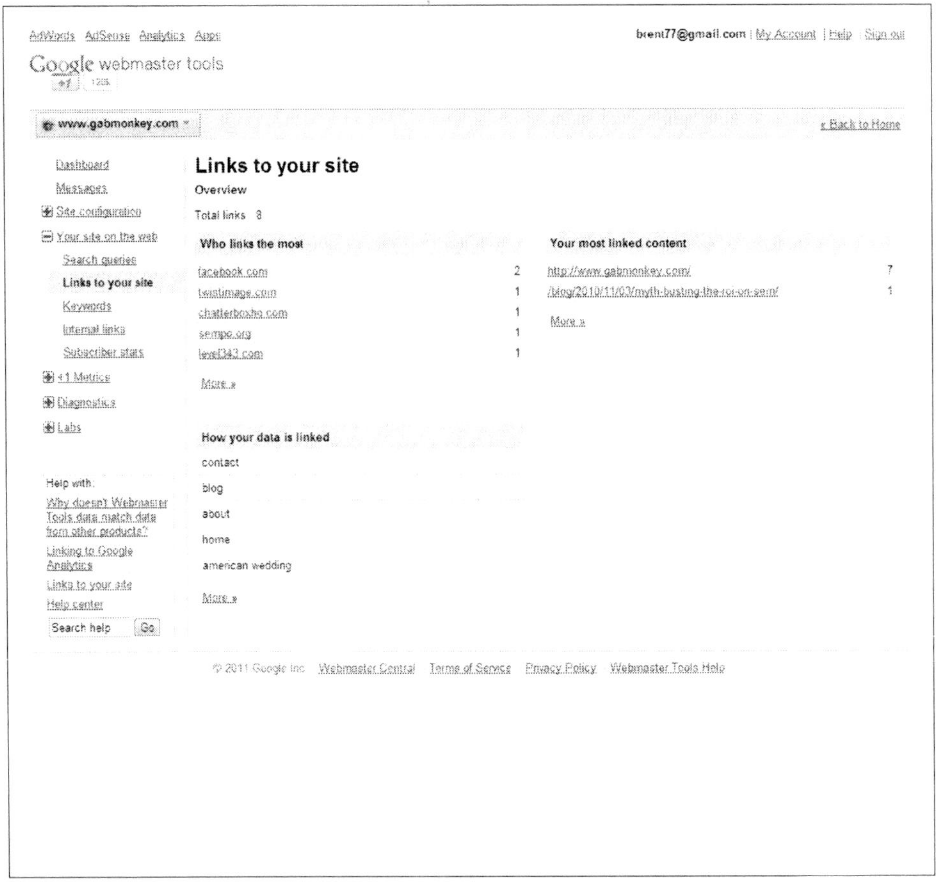

Figure 9-6. Webmaster Tools links to your site report

Expanding each domain will provide you with details on which pages on your site are being linked to. You can export this data as a CSV file to further manipulate in a spreadsheet or import into another custom program you may have developed. You may also want to save these reports to maintain historical data, as Webmaster Tools does not allow you to track back historically. Saving these reports every quarter will provide you with some historical insight, should you ever need it.

You may use these lists of links to conduct further research into the value of the links in Majestic SEO, or to understand if there are other linking opportunities to develop with one of these sites. You may want to reach out to sites you know are linking to you and let them know you appreciate the traffic and the links, and would like them to be placed more prominently on those sites if possible. Link building should not just be about SEO improvements; there should be an additional uplift of some incremental traffic from the links you build up.

Suppose you log in to Webmaster Tools one day and pull up your links to your site report. You want to look at all your linked pages to see the number of links to them and the source domains (Table 9-1). To access this information, you would click "Your site on the Web"→"Links to your site," then click "more" under "Your most linked content."

Table 9-1. Sample links to your site report data

Your pages	Links	Source domains
/folder/page1.html	10,720	8
/folder/page3.html	1,541	2
/folder/page2.html	63	1
/folder/page5.html	1	2
/folder/page4.html	1	2
/folder/page7.html	1	1

There seems to be a major anomaly with *page1.html* compared to the rest of the pages. Over 10,000 links from only eight domains is rather suspect, and should certainly raise questions. Clicking on the suspect page should provide an indicator of which site(s) are providing all these links. Looking through the list, you should be on the look out for either suspect domains that do not relate to your site or domains you don't recognize with high inbound links.

Experience has shown me that some sites may link to your site as part of their standard navigation—particularly blogs. If another site includes you on its blog roll, you may see a significant amount of inbound links from that site. Typically, I don't worry about this, but you may find an opportunity to reach out to the blogger and suggest that she link to some of your other relevant content as well. If she's a big enough fan, you might even offer to provide notifications of new content. This may result in improved link quality, if the blogger posts a topic similar to yours or a response to your new content.

The Most Linked Pages Report

The most linked pages report should correlate to the more popular sections of your site. This report (Figure 9-7) can give you insights into which pages on your site are good link baiting pages. You may be able to use this information to optimize referral traffic from these sites and improve your conversions. Segmenting traffic from key SEO referral sites can provide you with a better idea of the types of customers you are getting. If, for example, you run a website that sells bathroom fixtures and you find that mostly construction-related sites link to you, this may indicate that you have a much heavier imprint with contractors as opposed to home owners looking to do renovations. Again, segmenting your users will help you to further understand which customers you truly have.

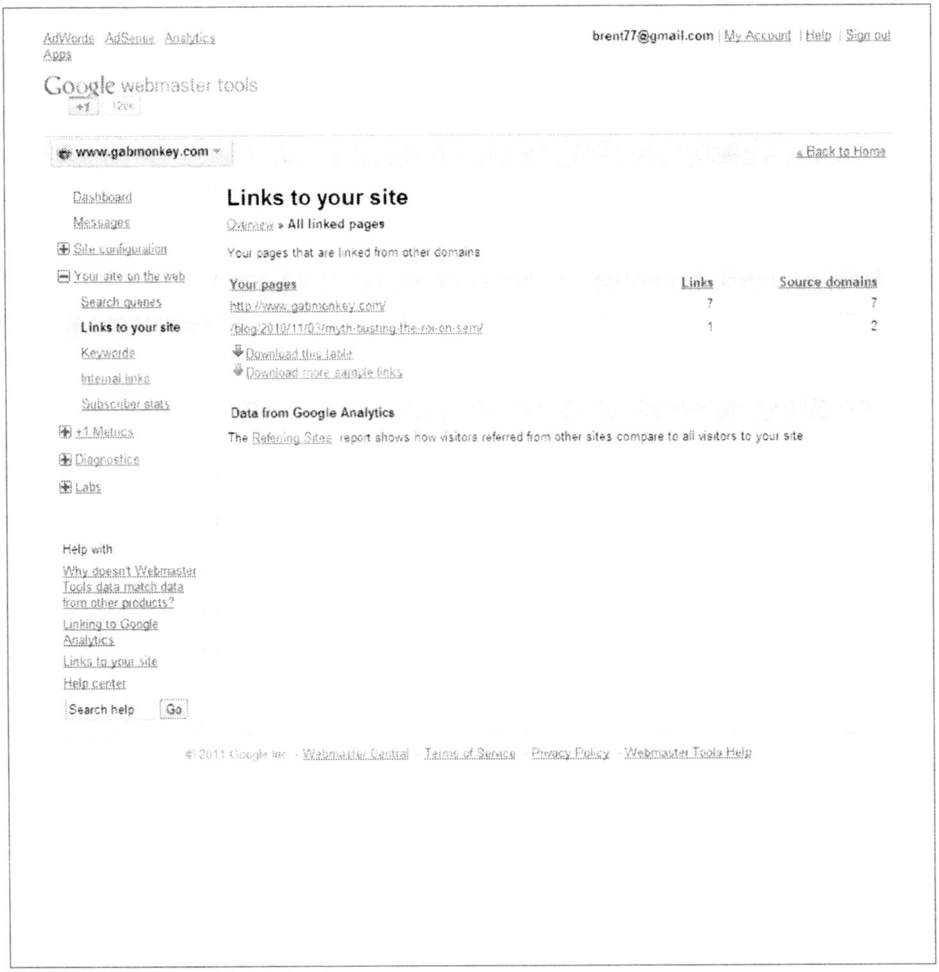

Figure 9-7. Webmaster Tools most linked pages report

By crafting your web page in such a way as to clearly indicate a contractor section and as opposed to a home do-it-yourself section, you can segment your traffic while serving all customers' needs. Monitor how many clicks the contractor section gets, and track how much engagement your "do-it-yourself" section gets. Without your customers recognizing it, you have quickly segmented traffic on that page into two groups. This bit of information can help you further improve the design and content of the page. If you find that 80% of your users are contractors who know what they are doing, adjust the page to address their needs more than the DIY segment. Monitor, measure, adjust, and repeat until you see the improvements in traffic flow you are looking for. These off-site measurements relate to both your SEO and site usability. Build up data points to improve your site as a whole and focus on CRO, LPO, SEO, and paid search to maximize your customer conversions and site usability.

Tracking Neighborhoods

If you're looking to run a link-building campaign, you will want to investigate the types of sites and links? you can expect to generate. In SEO, there are what are called "good neighborhoods" and "bad neighborhoods." The concept is pretty simple: some websites have good reputations, while others have bad reputations for selling links and being generally untrustworthy. Links from good neighborhoods can benefit you greatly, while links from bad neighborhoods have little value or impact.

Bad neighborhoods should be weeded out, and your focus in link building should be on the good neighborhoods. To discover some of these good neighborhoods, you can run reports in Majestic SEO to find out where links to other known good sites come from (Figure 9-8). By running the Clique Hunter report, you can find out who links to both you and your competitors. By adding in other competing sites, you can look for who links to some of your other competitors but not yourself. To get the full value of the report you will need to subscribe, but in terms of link building it is a great resource to start with.

In larger corporate environments you may also want to track bad neighborhoods if you have multiple groups responsible for your search programs. Some groups may stumble upon what they think are great link-building techniques, only to fall prey to a link-buying scheme that could result in your pages or site being blacklisted by the search engines. Search analytics is not just about reporting on the performance of your campaigns, but also about auditing and controlling your content, site, and brand. There are no defined lists of neighborhoods that could get you blacklisted; it is more a case of repeated patterns.

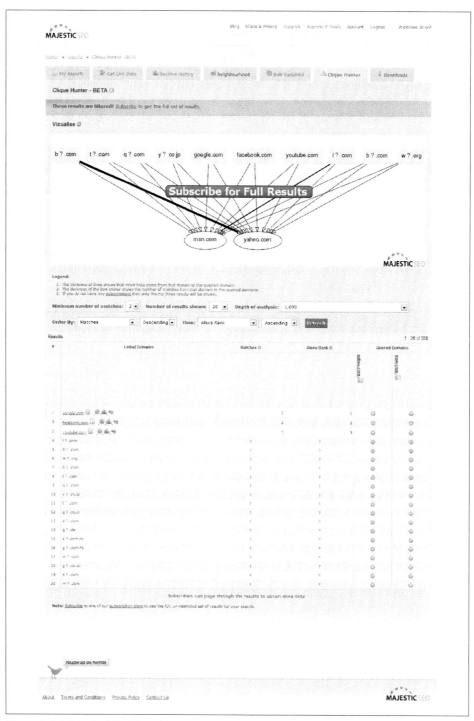

Figure 9-8. Majestic SEO Clique Hunter report

Utilizing your inbound link tracking tools, you can spot when patterns arise. Going back to our monitoring of competitors, we can turn that same model around and use it on our own sites, looking for large numbers of inbound links and then investigating where those links are coming from. If you see many links, and if when you start to look at the referring pages you find that the links either come from cloaked content that is not visible to you or are contained in the footers of the various sites, you may be dealing with link-buying issues. It's best to find out about this sooner rather then later and address the practice and your policies with the members of your organization that may be deploying these link-building campaigns.

Tracking Diversity of Links

Improving link diversity is one of the best ways to improve your rankings organically. A page with high link diversity receives a variety of links from many domains, through a variety of keywords. If you're targeting a specific term, you may want to see some synonyms for the term you hope to rank on. Tracking link diversity can be beneficial to understanding your true potential to rank on a term. Understanding the link diversity of those ranking ahead of you also helps to paint this picture.

Sites that have a high level of link diversity may be difficult to overtake, or you may find the gap is just too big. At this point, though, you should realize that ranking on a term organically is not just about one factor, but a combination of factors. Link diversity it is yet one more data point you can use to analyze the realistic opportunities you have specific to a keyword. Further, knowing how the overall domain performs based on bulk back links will be another factor to consider in determining site authority.

Running Majestic SEO's Bulk Backlink Checker on a specific URL will show you how many links you have compared to a competitor on a specific page. Looking at a page-to-page comparison can provide greater insight at the micro level than looking at overall back links to a site. While the domain authority is important, so too is the page-specific data. Establishing both the volume of links and the anchor text will help you evaluate whether you have a chance of beating a competitor out of a search spot. Filter out all the nofollow links to get a better idea of how the search engines will interpret the data. If you find that you are close in links on a site, expand to the domain authority and look at how many inbound links you have from all the sites by running a Bulk Backlinks report. Then look at the domain and page ranks to get an idea of the value of these links.

Tracking Domain Rank and Page Rank

Domain rank and page rank capture the value, authority, and trustworthiness of a site or page. These metrics play a key role in determining how you will rank in the search results. Domain rank looks at the entire site and how authoritative it is, while page rank looks at a specific page. Google only provides PageRank data, and this data is usually updated only a few times a year. To get at this data we need to use third-party tools that approximate how Google and Bing perceive the weight and importance of a page. The more authoritative a page is perceived to be, the more weight it has to redistribute its authority.

Think of page rank as a cup that can be filled up. Once it's filled, it can then fill up several other cups (or in this case, other websites). It does this through linking to other pages. Every link on a page can fill up another page a little bit, but no cup can be empty, so it retains a bit of its rank as well. The result is that the further a page is from an authoritative site in links, the less on that site's value will trickle down to that page.

When page rank is passed, it is split evenly across all links, including nofollow links— so, a page with 10 links, two of which are nofollow links, would still pass only one-tenth of its authority to each of the other eight pages. This means that adding nofollow links to third-party sites does not help you retain page rank in your site. The only advantage a nofollow may have is to deter spammers from posting many links in a public forum by limiting the nofollows off-site.

To track page rank data, SEOmoz provides two tools: Domain mozRank and mozRank. The values these tools return are not numbers provided by any search engine; instead these are numbers that SEOmoz has developed that can be used to estimate the value of pages. This data is found in the Open Site Explorer report (Figure 9-9), which provides details about inbound links, number of linking root domains, and more.

This data becomes very useful when trying to understand how and why certain pages rank in the positions in which they do. These are yet more analytics you can put into a keyword research diagram to figure out exactly what your chances of a page ranking on a specific term are. Pagerank can be a very important factor, but domain rank is also important. For example, even if your site has the exact same content as Wikipedia, it is likely that Wikipedia will outrank you, simply because of the authority of its parent domain. To move past this top-ranking site, you would need to grow your page rank significantly beyond that of Wikipedia, to compensate for your less authoritative domain.

Tracking both your and your competitors' page and domain ranks over time will also help you anticipate if a competitor may overtake you on specific key terms that are important to your overall search strategy. Anticipating issues before they arise will allow you to become proactive and ensure that you retain the ground you have gained, as well as understanding what ground you are close to gaining.

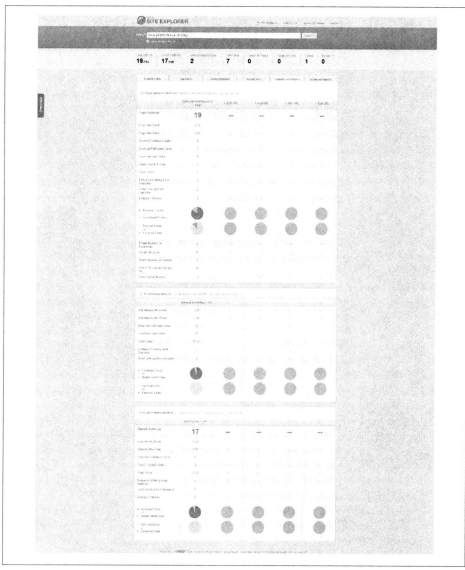

Figure 9-9. Open Site Explorer report

Tracking External Campaigns (TV, Radio, Print)

When we looked at telling stories about the hills and valleys in your analytics, we talked about the impact offline activities such as TV, radio, and print campaigns. You should be able to measure the effectiveness of any such offline campaigns. To track how much traffic these campaigns drive to your site through search, you will need the copy of the TV, radio, or print ads. As I've mentioned several times in this book, search is about findability. Be it people finding you directly or through search engines, the plan should be to always have a way to be found easily and quickly. It's important to include your web address in any external campaigns. Perhaps surprisingly, many people will type URLs into a search box to find you. These are easy-to-track searches that you can capture through simple keyword filters.

To track more accurately the influence your off-site campaigns have, extract all the keywords and keyword variations from the ad copy, plug these words into a spreadsheet, and track the search volumes that come to your website based on these terms. By now, you should also have a marketing deployment calendar that you look at to help predict and explain sudden rises or dips in the search volumes you're seeing. The challenge is that with search there can be other unknowns, such as something else going viral that was not expected, or a conflicting marketing program that your company is running at the same time.

For your paid search terms, try running A/B tests using words and ad copy that is very closely associated to your external campaigns, and words and terms that have historically performed well. You may discover that during marketing campaigns paid search terms specific to that campaign outperform your usual strong variations. This is where aligning your content is important. By ensuring that your page contains the same terminology as that used in your off-site campaigns, you reassure the customer that he is in the right place to investigate your product or whatever was being promoted.

By understanding the influence offline marketing has on search, you can start to look at ways to use other mediums to drive searches relevant to your site, and terms that you know you will rank well on. The feeding of data from SEO/Paid search to marketing and back should be a two-way street to allow you to maximize traffic and generate relevant clicks to your landing pages.

Years ago, when the company I was working for first began running paid search campaigns, everything was running nice and smoothly until one day we saw an insane increase on clicks for a specific product model. It instantly became one of the most-clicked terms in one of our campaigns.

As the web marketing and offline marketing teams were separate at the time, nobody in the online team could figure out what was going on—until some water cooler chat revealed that an offline radio campaign was running in major markets. The radio campaign specifically called out that product model. The radio run tied back to when we saw the increase in searches and clicks. The missed opportunity was that the ad did not link to the landing page that was tied to the promotion. This could have been capitalized on much more efficiently. We learned our lesson, however, and from then on we always included search as a line item during the planning and building stage of our marketing campaigns.

Another lesson here was that this particular product had a very friendly, easy to remember name, and it was part of the jingle in the commercial. Other products featured in the campaign that had less customer-friendly names did not see the same spike. We drew the conclusion that "easy to remember" + "catchy jingle" = "users remembering and searching for the product later."

I have seen the same impact around product hype and announcements as well. When offline activity generates excitement, it can drive online activity and demand.

Tracking Social Volume and Social Media

Social media, specifically Twitter and Facebook, has been confirmed as an SEO influencer (see the blog post at *http://www.seomoz.org/blog/google-bing-confirm-twitter -facebook-influence-seo*). Bing uses Facebook data directly as part of a partnership (*http: //www.seroundtable.com/bing-facebook-personalization-13416.html*). Google is also deploying +1 (*http://www.google.com/+1/button/*) as a way for users to send social signals on the relevancy of links.

Data from Twitter is pulled by the search engines and used to find more relevant real-time results or pages that may be trending as hot in the social space. We won't get into a full social media strategy here, but this should be a consideration for SEO. The more discussions and back links to your site from social media there are, the more likely you are to show up in the SERPs. This is especially true for new pages or content that you may launch. Tests have also shown that links from Twitter can help a page move up in the rankings (*http://www.seomoz.org/blog/the-tweet-effect-how-twitter-affects -rankings-12781* and *http://www.seomoz.org/blog/facebook-twitters-influence-google -search-rankings*).

There are some advantages to exploiting social channels beyond SEO. A presence on Twitter can result in many followers, although it may generate little actual traffic;

Facebook may be a source of significantly more traffic (if fewer followers). Digg can also provide large volumes of traffic, should you make it to a top page in one of its categories. Of these sites, Facebook provides the most feature-rich interface for analytics (Figure 9-10). You can track number of fans, impressions, likes, shares, and more, by adding tags to your site using Facebook's Open Graph. Further, through the API export, Webtrends and some other analytics packages are beginning to utilize this data to tie into your clickstream data.

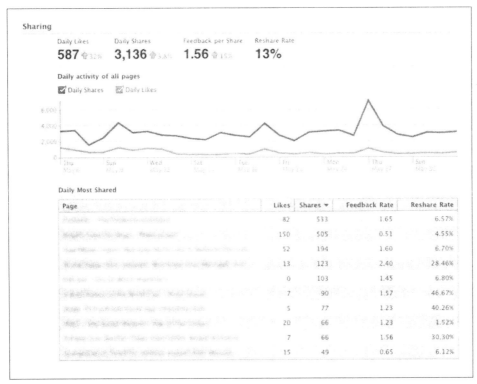

Figure 9-10. Facebook analytics page

Facebook may have the lowest impact on your overall SEO efforts for sites such as Google and Bing, due to the closed nature of the Facebook community, where content is captured and stored behind pages. You may question whether it's worth investing into adding Facebook content, but considering that Facebook has beaten Google several times in terms of traffic, and considering that Facebook also has its own search engine, being findable on Facebook can be a very important way to drive traffic to your site. You can consider it as an alternate search engine, and capitalize on having your company's profile page indexed and optimized for Facebook search.

There are several options for tracking the volume of noise generated about your company through social media. Some of the bigger and more expensive options are Radian6 (recently acquired by Salesforce) and Attensity360. On the more affordable side (read: free) you have Addict-o-matic (Figure 9-11), which can provide a top-level overview of terms people are searching for on Twitter, FriendFeed, Flickr, blogs, and other social media sites. The data is useful for seeing how you are perceived in the social media outlets, but it is by no means as actionable as the data you may get from one of the paid solutions. Your other option is to build and save custom searches on Twitter, and then utilize that as a way to monitor your social mentions. You can also use Yoono or another aggregator to allow you to connect across several social media platforms.

The biggest challenge in tracking social media is the volume of content and background noise you will have to deal with. Refining your targets and improving your tracking will help you to manage uplift in SEO as well as your online brand. As with any other analytic, you may want to look at segmenting to make tracking more manageable. Setting up alerts or tracking for your company name plus the term "sucks" could be used as part of an early warning system to help you identify problems you need to deal with, while your brand plus the term "rocks" may be a positive response you want to further highlight on your website. Social media is something companies can no longer afford to ignore: it can alert us to rising and falling trends, it is monitored by search engines to figure out what topics are rising the fastest, and it has made quick responses to customer concerns all the more important.

Tracking Changes in the SERP to Improve Clicks

Search results for both SEO and paid search include a title, and some copy. Both of these can have a surprising influence on what number of people click on your link. A relevant and engaging title and description can significantly improve your click-through rates. While being number 2 may mean that you get less clicks statistically than the number 1 result, this does not have to be the case—that's why tracking actual results is just as important as tracking your position. Building a page title and description that are more engaging or desirable to be clicked on than those of the page ranking above you can be a very smart and simple strategy to deploy. In fact, this strategy may be so simple that your competitors deploy it too.

Depending on the man-hours and time you have, you can use KeywordSpy to monitor the titles and descriptions used in paid search ads for certain words, or you can perform this manually. Changes in titles or body copy can indicate that a competitor is working on the presentation of their page, changing their keyword focus, or getting more aggressive on a term. By reading through the changes, you should be able to identify what sort of impact your competitor is trying to have. This is, unfortunately, a very labor-intensive activity, and there are very few quick, out-of-the-box solutions to help improve this sort of tracking organically. Ironically, because paid search is so focused on ad copy, paid search teams often spend a great deal of time A/B testing titles and descriptions to improve CTR, as well as monitoring competitors' ad copy. In contrast, SEO teams seldom look at this level of data, and instead work at improving their own

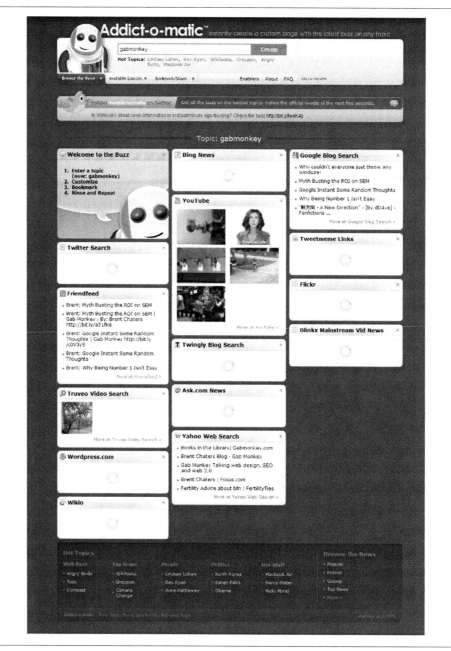

Figure 9-11. Addict-o-matic

titles based on what they think will rank well. A simple look at ranking pages for a search term can provide a great deal of insight as to what sort of content you might want to include in your title and description.

Concluding Thoughts

Tracking off-site influences on everything from page rank to search results can help improve your positioning and CTR, as well as helping with CRO and LPO. Search is strongly influenced by what happens off your site as well as what happens on your site. Some off-site ranking factors, such as page rank, are stored in the search engines, while others are influenced through inbound links. Monitoring the web of links between pages can provide you with a host of macro- and micro-level metrics that can help you improve your SEO and paid search campaigns significantly. Because each of these factors is just one piece of the puzzle, it can be helpful to dashboard out some of our KPIs when tracking specific terms and considering why and how they rank the way they do. Simple dashboards can provide great insights into why a page is ranking so much higher than your own.

Table 9-2 is an example of how you may track data on websites and what you may see. The top-ranking site for a specific keyword has a higher page rank and domain rank, as well as more unique links from many domains. These results may actually fluctuate significantly depending on the term, as other factors (such as overall relevance of the site to a term) play a role in ranking as well. While you can use this example as a starting point, you may want to add additional columns to paint a fuller picture; we will get further into this in Chapter 14, where we look at creating dashboards to bring all of our metrics together.

Table 9-2. Tracking results for a specific keyword

Position	Website	Page rank	Domain rank	Unique linking domains	Total inbound links	Social media links
1	www.site1.com	65	78	368,698	1,236,698	159
2	www.site2.com	59	62	259,952	958,958	369
3	www.site3.com	61	61	63,125	1,154,589	693

CHAPTER 10

Tracking Mobile Search

Mobile search is a rapidly emerging market.

From 2008 to 2010, mobile traffic on Google increased by a factor of five (*http://search engineland.com/google-mobile-query-growth-dramatically-higher-than-pc-38203*), and it is being predicted that mobile searches will account for 20% of total searches by 2012 (*http://techcrunch.com/2010/06/16/mobile-search-20-percent/*). Further, mobile data traffic volumes are expected to rise 40-fold over the next five years (*http://techcrunch .com/2010/03/30/mobile-data-traffic-rise-40-fold/*).

Without a doubt, mobile search will continue to grow.

This growth will also mean changes to search patterns. Note here that I say "search patterns," not "search algorithms." For the most part, the mobile search algorithms in use today are very similar to the desktop search algorithms. The biggest changes will be in user behavior, with a trend toward highly local and personal searches by users looking for instant fulfillment of their needs and desires. Optimizing for mobile devices is not so much about creating different pages as it is about understanding the needs of these users and the type of content they are looking for. For example, we know that local search is much more important to a mobile user. Do you have location-specific content on your site? Do you have a local search strategy?

A web browser designed for use on a mobile device is unlike any traditional web browser you would find on a PC or laptop. Mobile devices are typically not shared by multiple users; they tend to be always-connected devices that their owners can't leave home without. Mobile devices have very different displays and screen resolutions than what we are accustomed to on PCs or laptops, and they require different ways of engaging with content and inputting responses. This input may be through touchscreens, joysticks, small keyboards, or voice commands; many devices also include built-in cameras and GPS receivers. All of these factors impact website engagement. All of these factors mean we have a lot more questions to ask.

Tools you will need in this chapter:

- Web analytics package that separates mobile users from regular users (Google Analytics should fit the bill)
- Google Keyword Tool or some other keyword research tool
- Web page speed measurement tool (e.g., *http://www.selfseo.com/website_speed_test.php* or *http://webwait.com/*)

Do Desktop and Mobile Users Search the Same Way?

Do mobile users search the same way as users on a desktop or laptop? Do we see patterns where keyword length or number of words per search drops? Do people type differently on a mobile device, perhaps using short forms of words? Do search volumes on certain keywords differ between mobile and desktop users? 20% of searches are mobile (*https://sites.google.com/a/pressatgoogle.com/googleplaces/metrics*), while 1 in 3 (33%) from smartphones are about where the user is (*http://www.screenwerk.com/2010/09/08/google-33-of-smartphone-queries-local/*). Clearly, we need to look at our own user bases and find out if we're missing an opportunity by not targeting or optimizing for this segment of search traffic.

Due to the limited interface on a mobile device, it may be cumbersome to type detailed searches. Also, assuming that most people will use a mobile device much more spontaneously than they would a computer, we may expect to see different search patterns and terms coming from these two types of devices.

Why Is This Important?

For both your paid search and SEO campaigns, you will want to ask this question. As we have learned, competition decreases as search complexity increases. How does this rule hold for mobile devices? If we are going to bid on PPC paid search terms, we don't want to bid on terms so complex that they don't drive any clicks. And for SEO, we want to understand how competitive this new space will be. If we want to target more mobile users, will we need to adjust our strategy of going for *long-tail* terms and focus more on midtail terms? Will a lack of complexity in search terms (i.e., one-word rather than two- or three-word searches) impact our mobile traffic rates? Do we see as many searches for our branded terms on mobile devices?

Answering the Questions

To explore the differences we may see in keyword volumes, let's go back to our bike shop example. The Google Keyword Tool should answer a lot of our questions.

First, we want to look at exact and phrase matches. How often are users searching for exact terms, and how much opportunity is there for longer-tail terms? Keep in mind that these are *estimates*, not exact volumes; still, they should be close enough to give us an idea of user behavior based on device type.

We will use the search "red bikes" as our comparison point. First we'll look at the search volumes on desktops and laptops, by going to "Advanced options"→"show ideas for", and selecting "Desktop and laptop devices." Our sample results are shown in Figure 10-1.

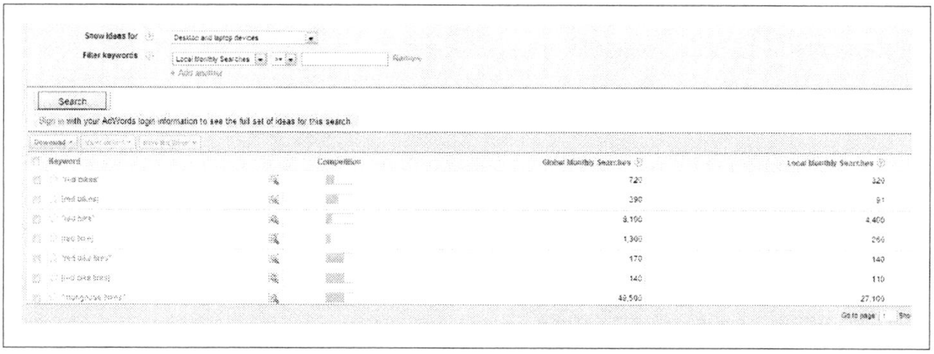

Figure 10-1. Keyword research on desktop and laptop devices

Percent of Coverage of [Exact] Term = [Exact Match] / Phrase Match × 100

The first thing to notice is that there are 320 monthly searches for "red bikes," while [red bikes] only accounts for 91 searches. This means that exact match searches account for 28.43% of searches around this term (91/320 × 100 = 28.43). 71.57% of searches, then, must include that term plus some variation. We also see a little bit of seasonality in the trends graph, with rises in spring and fall for these search terms. We also should probably take note that [red bike] gets more searches than the plural version [red bikes] (almost three times the volume, in fact).

Next, we look at the number of mobile searches (Figure 10-2). All you need to do to view this data is change your selection under "show ideas for" from "Desktop and laptop devices" to "All mobile devices."

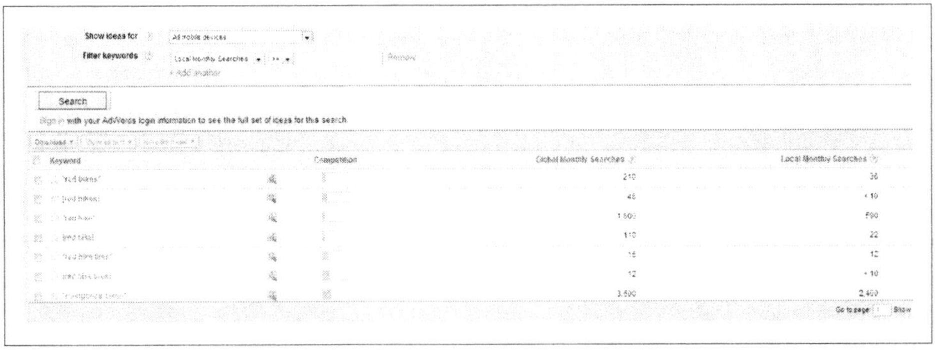

Figure 10-2. Keyword research on mobile devices

Looking at the data returned, we see there are some big drop-offs for the term [red bikes]. There are less than 10 searches a month on this term, and only 36 phrase match searches for "red bikes," meaning that *long tail* search volumes are also diminished. If we assume there are 10 exact-match searches per month, we can plug in our numbers again to get the percentage of exact versus phrase matches. This works out to 27.7%—basically the same proprotion we saw on desktops. However, because we don't know the precise number of exact match searches for this term, we should verify our findings by looking at the number of searches for "red bike" and [red bike].

If we plug the numbers for this term from the desktop and laptop searches into our formula, we see that searches for [red bike] account for only 5.9% of the total volume, leaving 94.1% of searches as *long tail* searches incorporating this term.

Looking at "red bike" and [red bike] searches on mobile devices, crunching our numbers reveals that 3.7% of searches were exact-match searches, meaning 96.3% of searches were for *long tail* variations. Next, we have to consider whether the difference in numbers from desktop to mobile devices is big enough to warrant further investigation. In this case, I don't think it does. However, we can't draw too many conclusions from just one example. The next step is to look at the list of mobile search keywords and identify other words or terms with high search volumes. We can then research those terms using the desktop and laptop filter to see whether the search volumes are comparable, or if mobile users are looking at different words and terms.

Let's look at another example. For the term [bike shops], we see that on mobile devices 8.5% of searches are on the exact phrase (Figure 10-4), whereas on desktops the number of exact searches is 4% (Figure 10-3). This is a difference that might be worth investigating. We may guess that because mobile devices have GPS awareness, mobile users are conditioned to search for locations in simple terms and without including geographic data in the search term (e.g., "bike shops" rather than "bike shops in

Manhattan"). To validate this for your geography, you might go back and search for terms like "bike shops in…" that include the names of local cities, states, or provinces. You might also want to expand out to broad match searches, to see if you can identify other anomalous terms or patterns. You may find that some niche markets are more susceptible to certain search styles, too. For example, people on bikes may be more prone to using mobile search, as they are on the go already.

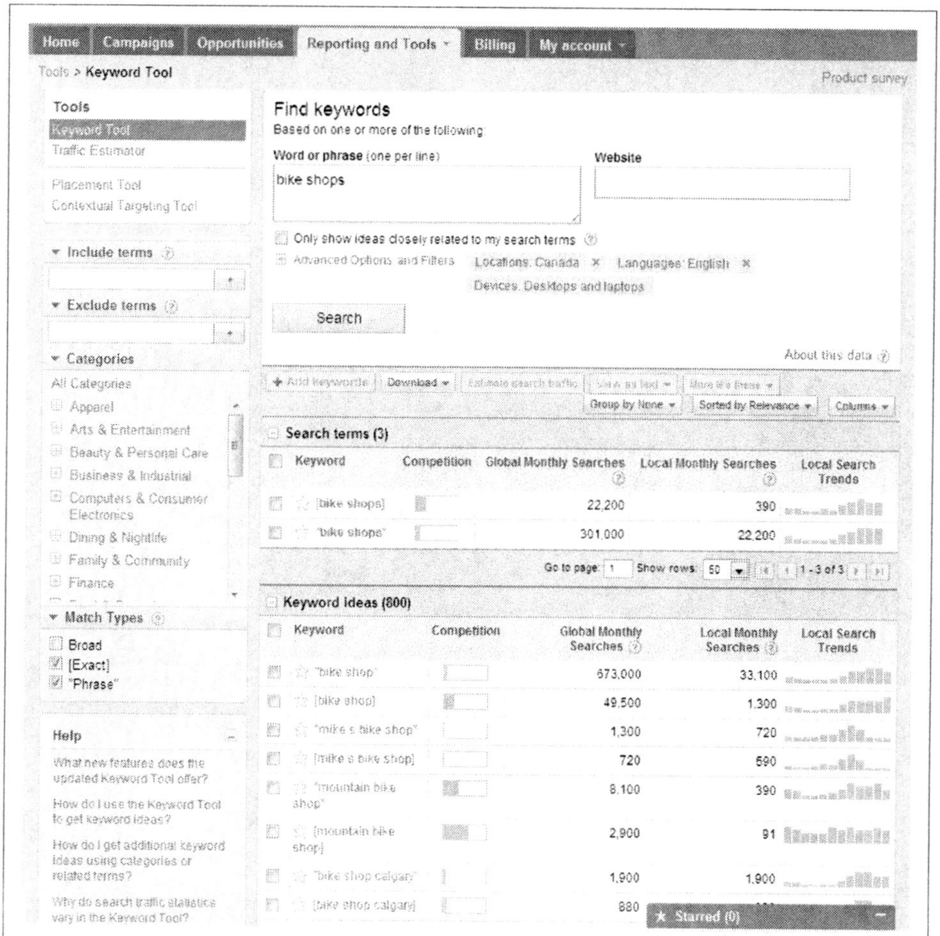

Figure 10-3. Search volume on "bike shops" on a desktop

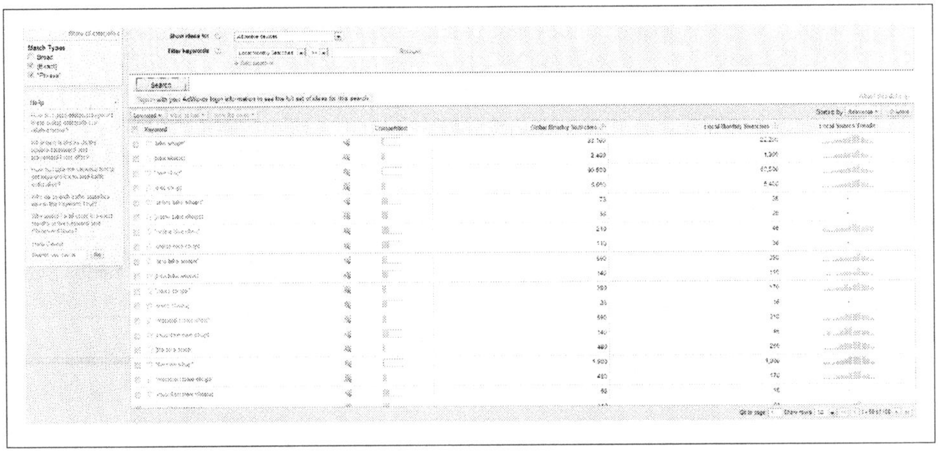

Figure 10-4. Search volume on "bike shops" on mobile devices

You will also want to look for terms in the mobile list that do not show up on the desktop list and vice versa. Ask yourself why that might be. Look for large discrepancies in exact versus broad match terms as well. This will help tell you if mobile searchers are being lazier on *lon-tail* terms than desktop users, or if they are being more precise.

If you find more precision on mobile devices than desktop devices, or vice versa, you will have to decide if you want to target those more precise terms on that type of device. You may decide you need to create an entirely separate mobile site to address search patterns if they impact your niche or market significantly enough.

How Important Is Geography for Mobile Searchers?

The Google Keyword Tool allows us to segment search volumes by geography and language because it understands how important location can be. When considering user intent, it's important to think about the specifics of a user's search. Geography can affect behavior—for example, someone in Colorado is more likely to search for information on skiing conditions than someone in Florida. There are also seasonality effects to local search patterns, as this example demonstrates. When you then introduce mobile devices into the mix, we have to wonder how much more of an impact geography has on search terms.

Let's take another look at our "red bikes" example. In Figure 10-5, we can see that on desktop and laptop devices local searches accounted for about 44% of global searches on this term (320/720 × 100). In contrast, looking at Figure 10-6, we can see that on mobile devices local searches accounted for only 17% of global searches (36/210 × 100). So, we can surmise that users in our current geography, "United States," are not using mobile devices nearly as much as users elsewhere in the world when looking for information on "red bikes."

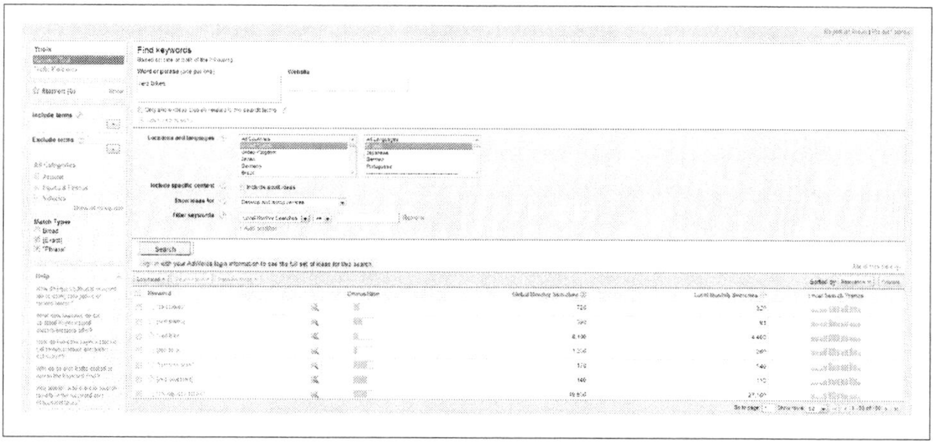

Figure 10-5. *Keyword research on desktop and laptop devices for local monthly searches*

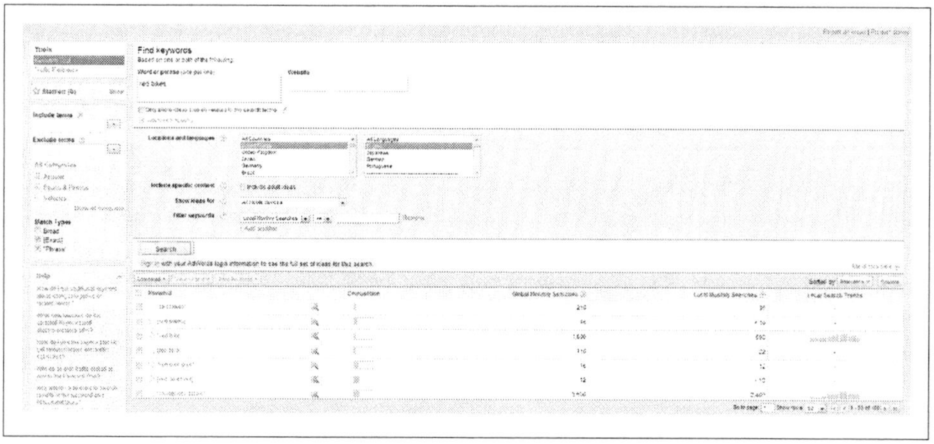

Figure 10-6. *Keyword research on all mobile devices for local monthly searches*

Percent of Local Searches as Part of Global = Local Monthly Searches / Global Monthly Searches × 100

Now let's go back and look at "bike shops." We see that on desktops, "bike shops" gets 135,000 local searches compared to 301,000 globally. On mobile devices, locally we see 22,200 searches compared to 33,100 global searches. Thus, the United States accounts for about 44% of all searches on "bike shops" on desktops, while on mobile devices the United States accounts for 67% of searches on this term. This tells us right away that people in the United States are much more actively searching for "bike shops" than anywhere else on the planet.

If you were the owners of a large bike shop chain in the United States, it might be worthwhile to consider how to target these mobile users. We know that people in the United States are less likely to search for "red bikes" on their mobile devices, and more inclined to search for "bike shops" on those devices. We also can see that the term "red bike" in general is searched less than "bike shops." We can make some guesses about the users' behavior in general based on this data. People looking for "red bikes" are most likely looking to buy a bike, and are likely still in the early stages of investigating types of bikes. In the United States, it would seem that people prefer to do this on their desktops. However, searching for the term "bike shop" indicates that the user is looking for a specific location. He may be looking to purchase a bike from a bike shop, or to get a bike fixed. Either way, people in the United States who search for "bike shop" are likely looking for a location, and they are more likely to do this on their mobiles than people elsewhere in the world. We could also assume they are looking to go to the bike shop fairly soon. At this point, you would want to test and see if you rank well for that term locally on mobile devices.

Go to your targeted search engine (in this case, Google) and put in that search query to see who is listed. You can then start to build up your strategy based on the analytics techniques you've learned, and decide if it's a reasonable target to go after. If you are a national chain in the United States, then the answer may very well be "yes." If, however, you are a regional chain, then the answer may be "no."

Now let's dive deeper into local search: suppose you are not the owner of a large chain store but of a local shop in, say, Austin, Texas. In the Google Keyword Tool, try pairing up "bike shops" with "Austin." Entering "bike shops Austin" will give us an idea of some of the variations of this phrase people have been searching for (Figure 10-7). At this point, because we're looking at such an exact geography, we don't need to worry about global versus local search volumes, though we may do a sanity check just to see if there is something very askew.

If you are dealing with a geographic location where there is another similarly named city on the planet, you may want to see if people in your country are searching on that term widely or not. If there is a big gap, you may need to make some strategy decisions.

You can geo-target paid search, and if you haven't done so, you should get on that now. As you've just discovered, you may be getting lots of clicks on your terms from people in other countries, wasting money for no reason.

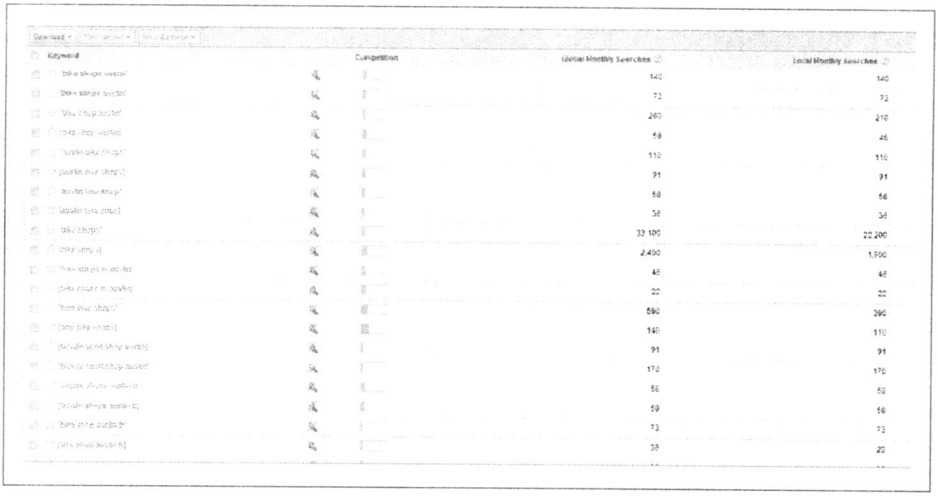

Figure 10-7. Keyword list for mobile searches related to "bike shops Austin"

Running "bike shops Austin" through the Keyword Tool with Match Type set to "Phrase" turns up many variations, including "bike shop Austin," "Austin bike shop," "bike shop in Austin," and more. These results can start to give us an idea of word positioning for these mid- to *long-tail* terms. At this point, you may want to put together a list like the one in Table 10-1, where we look at the phrase match searches. The reason we are looking at phrase matches is because we want to know the order of the words, but also account for *long tail* opportunities. We also want to know what total search volume is for each variation.

Table 10-1. Keyword list

Keyword "phrase" match	Keyword "phrase" match	Volume of desktop searches
Austin bike	590	4,400
Bikes Austin	390	1,900
Bike Austin	260	1,600
Bike shop Austin	210	880
Bike sport shop Austin	170	46
Bike shops Austin	140	880
Austin bicycle	110	1,300

Looking at our list of keywords and comparing mobile searches to desktop searches, we see a few anomalies. Sorting the list by volume of desktop searches, we see that "Austin bicycle" trends toward a larger search volume than "bike shop Austin," "bike sport shop Austin," and "Bike shops Austin." However, on mobile devices, this is not the case; in fact, "Austin bicycle" ranks lowest (probably because mobile users are more inclined to use the short form "bike" than the longer "bicycle" when searching).

You can take findings like this into account when putting together your mobile strategy. In our case, we might make a conscious decision not to focus on that word pairing. Further, there is a greater search volume on the term "bike sport shop Austin" on mobile devices than on desktop devices. This may be a very specific niche market we can target for the mobile market.

Looking through this data, it is clear that there are trends that differ on mobile and desktop devices, from a geographical and a keyword standpoint. It appears that mobile users are engaging with search slightly different than desktop users.

Some folks may look at some of the mobile numbers and say those numbers are so small right now as to be insignificant. I certainly wouldn't argue that point. What I would argue, however, is that we know mobile usage is growing, and rapidly. While mobile numbers are relatively small today, they may eventually come to surpass desktop numbers. Further, many companies feel that because the search volumes are so small, it's not yet worth focusing on this segment. This means you have time to experiment and make mistakes in a less competitive market. It's easier to recover when there is less competition.

It's also important to keep in mind that the algorithms don't change too much from desktop to mobile search (although I suspect we may start to see more disparity over time, as mobile devices also provide GPS data to further aid searches in the background, and more weight will be given to websites designed for mobile devices). What we already do see, however, are changes in user behavior with search engines. With this knowledge, we can start to cherry-pick some terms that may do well with mobile but not desktop users. This kind of thinking also opens up another set of questions we want to answer. How likely are we to get repeat traffic from mobile visitors? And do mobile users from search convert better than desktop users?

Do Mobile Searchers Return More or Less Frequently?

This is a more important question to ask on mobile devices than desktops because the technology and the use of it is still so new. Are people who use mobile devices looking for "hit-and-run" content, or are they looking to be frequent engagers? An example of a highly engaged website would be Facebook. People go to and use that site frequently. A "hit-and-run" visitor may be someone who has a question, such as "what movie won the Oscar for Best Picture in 1983?" The likelihood of the website that delivers that answer being revisited in the near future is slim.

How often are you seeing repeat visitors to your site on mobile devices? Do they come and then never return, or do you see customer loyalty from people who find your site through search? Device type can impact frequency of visits and type of use for any website, and with the mobile sphere being new, it's important to explore how these users are looking for your content and what kind of content they are seeking.

Due to the limited screen space on mobile devices, you don't have the luxury to populate a page with navigation and links. You need to think about how you can lead these users deeper into your site, or you need to get very, very good at returning the correct content (that is, exactly what the person is searching for). Looking at your content, do you expect mobile users to have a higher bounce rate? Meaning, do you expect them to look at one page only and then leave, or to look at more than one page? A high bounce rate isn't necessarily an indicator of a bad site; it may be an indicator that you do a very good job of providing the information your users need rapidly.

We need to build out test cases that will answer the questions, "Are mobile users as site-loyal as desktop users?" and "Do mobile users click through content at the same rate as desktop users?"

Both of these questions can be answered with any standard web analytics tool that tracks visitor return frequency (Adobe SiteCatalyst and Google Analytics are some options). We'll use Google Analytics for this.

Navigate to "Traffic Sources" on the left, and make sure "Search Engines" is selected.

Click on "Advanced Segments" and select "All Visits" and "Mobile Traffic," as shown in Figures 10-8 and 10-9.

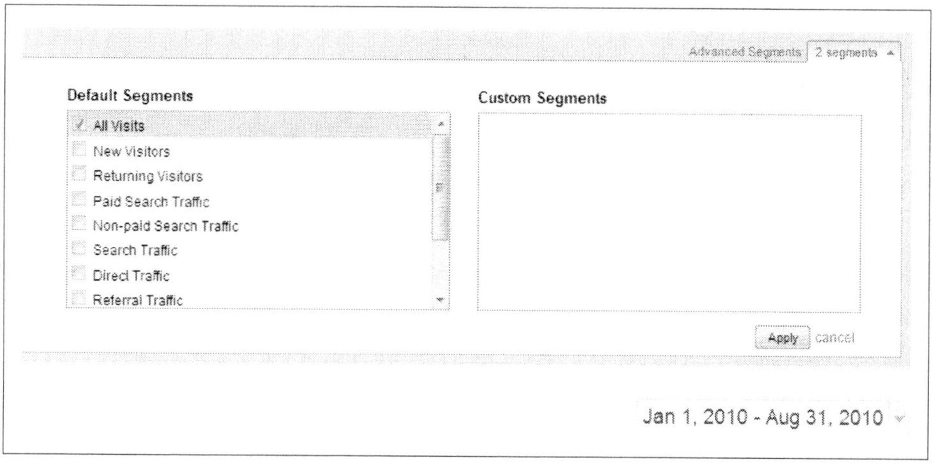

Figure 10-8. Google Analytics "All Visits" filter selected

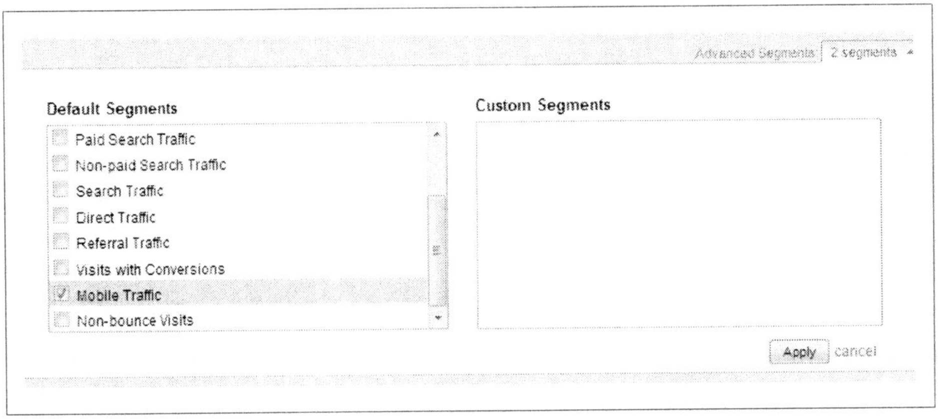

Figure 10-9. Google Analytics "Mobile Traffic" filter selected

You should end up with filters that provide an overview of general traffic as well as mobile traffic (Figure 10-10).

What this data is telling us is that from January 1, 2010 through August 31, 2010, a very small portion of traffic to this site was mobile traffic. Only eight visitors were mobile users. This data set, while too small to provide real statistical significance, will work for the purposes of our example.

Table 10-2 summarizes the site interaction statistics for both categories of users. Comparing our mobile users to our baseline of all users (which includes mobile users), we can make the following observations:

- They view 0.05 pages less per visit on average.
- They spend about 2 seconds more on the site.
- They have a lower bounce rate than the average user (0.53% versus 0%).
- They account for a lower number of new visitors, meaning that more mobile users are repeat users than regular users (though not by much).

Table 10-2. Summary of PC versus mobile site interaction

Metric	PC users	Mobile users
Average Page Views per Visit	2.30	2.25
Average Time on Site	00:00:12	00:00:14
% New Visits	95.49%	87.50%
Bounce Rate	0.53%	0.00%

Based on this data, we can start to build up a profile of what our current visitors from mobile devices versus desktop devices are like. These numbers also provide the answers to our two questions.

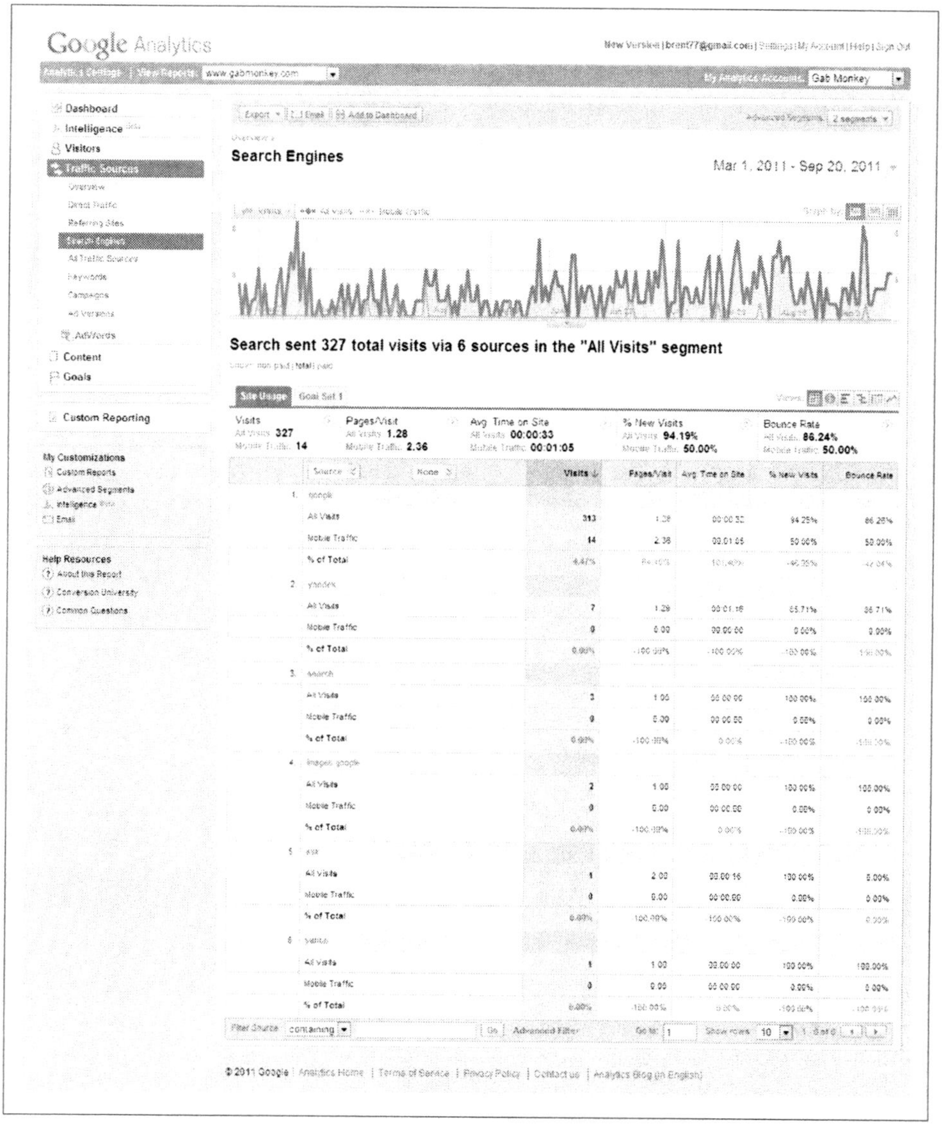

Figure 10-10. Traffic overview with "all visits" and "Mobile Traffic" filters applied

Are Mobile Users as Site-Loyal as Desktop Users?

For this site, mobile users are more likely to return than desktop users. This means that for mobile users, we see slightly stronger loyalty to our site. This may be because we provide easier ways to access our site on a mobile device, or it may be that our content is more geared toward people on the go. To get at the reasons, we could provide a questionnaire on the site, asking questions like "Why did you come to our site?," "Did you find what you were looking for easily?," "Do you prefer using a PC or a phone to access our website?," and any other questions you may have.

Do Mobile Users Click Through Content at the Same Rate as Desktop Users?

In this instance, the answer is that mobile and desktop users seem to click through content at about the same rates. Differences in average number of pages viewed per visit, time on site, and bounce rate are minimal. This indicates that our users from search are engaging with our content in very similar ways, regardless of device type. This is no judgment on the numbers themselves, of course. You may actually want very few clicks on your site, or you may want many clicks on your site. You may want to decrease the time spent on your site or increase it, depending on what your site does. What is important is that we see similar user behavior patterns right now. This is something we will want to monitor over time as the number of mobile users grows, to verify whether the numbers for our mobile site remain close to the numbers we see on the desktop site. This will provide us with a baseline of engagement levels between the two sites, and it will alert us to any sudden drops or increases in one or the other that we might need to investigate.

Tracking Paid Search on Mobile Devices

Paid search campaigns on mobile devices are slightly different from traditional PPC campaigns. The primary difference is the advent of *click-to-call* technology, where you set up a phone number in your ad that smartphone users can click to place a call. For AdWords, you can read more on this at *http://adwords.google.com/support/aw/bin/topic.py?hl=en&topic=27504*. There are an assortment of ways you can set up your click-to-call campaigns, which we won't deal with here as we are looking at how to track and measure this as opposed to how to set it up.

The really nice thing about Google AdWords is that it provides a way to track inbound calls from your click-to-call campaigns right in the tool itself *(http://www.google.com/ads/innovations/* and *http://adwords.blogspot.com/2010/11/measure-phone-calls-you-get-from.html)*.

If this isn't an option for you due to some company policy, the only other solution is to go out and get multiple phone numbers you can use and get tracking set up for inbound calls. This becomes a bit more complicated, as you will need to look for a solution that allows you to integrate phone calls into your CRM or sales system (or some other monitoring system) for tracking. You may or may not need to correlate the phone numbers back to the campaigns manually as well.

Depending on the complexity of the software available to you, you may need to use one phone number for many campaigns. This provides a more general overview of the success of multiple campaigns in aggregate. The upside to this is that this solution will work for other PPC options, such as the Bing and Yahoo! networks. One option would be to use a service such as Dial800; you will need to contact them for pricing, but they offer 1-800 toll-free numbers, call tracking, and call routing, so you can still manage calls on your end, as well as calls recorded and having call volumes provided back to you.

Aside from the click-to-call option, tracking paid search or PPC on a mobile device should be the same as on any other device. It will also help if you set up a spreadsheet or database to track your search data. An example of some data you may track is in Table 10-3.

The advantage of click-to-call is that it offers instant access to a human through an already connected device.

Table 10-3. Example of what to track for mobile campaigns

Campaign name	Phone number used	Avg. cost/ click	Mobile URL	PC URL	Clicks-to-call	PPC clicks to mobile pages	PPC clicks to desktop pages
Campaign #1	555-252-3355	$1.52	m.site .com/url1	www.site .com/url1	12	255	182
Campaign #2	555-252-3356	$1.52	m.site .com/url1	www.site .com/url2	55	82	38

You may also wish to expand out the table to include capturing conversions or deals closed by each campaign, so you can see which is the most efficient at closing deals. Keep in mind that high volumes with low conversions can be just as effective as high conversions with low volumes. If you have the data, you may also want to capture the average order value. This will give you a truer picture of which format generates the highest revenue for you.

Does Device Type Matter?

Mobile devices have brought us back to the early days of the Internet. There are so many devices, screen sizes, and web browsers that device type may impact the usability of your website for both SEO and paid search traffic.

There are mobile devices that provide a full browser experience; there are others that only provide a text experience. There are some that provide JavaScript support, while others do not.

If you cannot cater to all the device types, try to figure out what most of your users are using to connect to your site. Google Analytics can provide you with data on what devices people are accessing your site with. Why is this important? If you know the devices people are finding your site with, you can try to improve that experience.

In Google Analytics, go to "Visitors"→"Mobile"→"Mobile Devices." You will see a list of all devices used to access your site (Figure 10-11).

Figure 10-11. Google Analytics showing mobile device types

Once you know which device types are most common, you can target your mobile users with pages that are designed to be as easily accessible as possible for them.

With this report, you can also get a better idea of how many pages your mobile visitors are viewing, how much time they are spending on your site, and what the bounce rates are like. Remember, it's not all about the number of visitors; you should always be looking for potential issues. Here, we would look for devices with poor bounce rates. Given the variety of devices on the market today, different devices may be better suited to your website than others.

You may want to apply a second filter as well: for example, filtering on operating system and applying the "source" dimension or "keyword" dimension (Figure 10-12) to dive deeper into the data and get an understanding of what words or search engines are being driven by certain phone types. You may notice a pattern of words or referrers having issues with your site. You can also apply a filter if you need to zero in on a keyword or referring source.

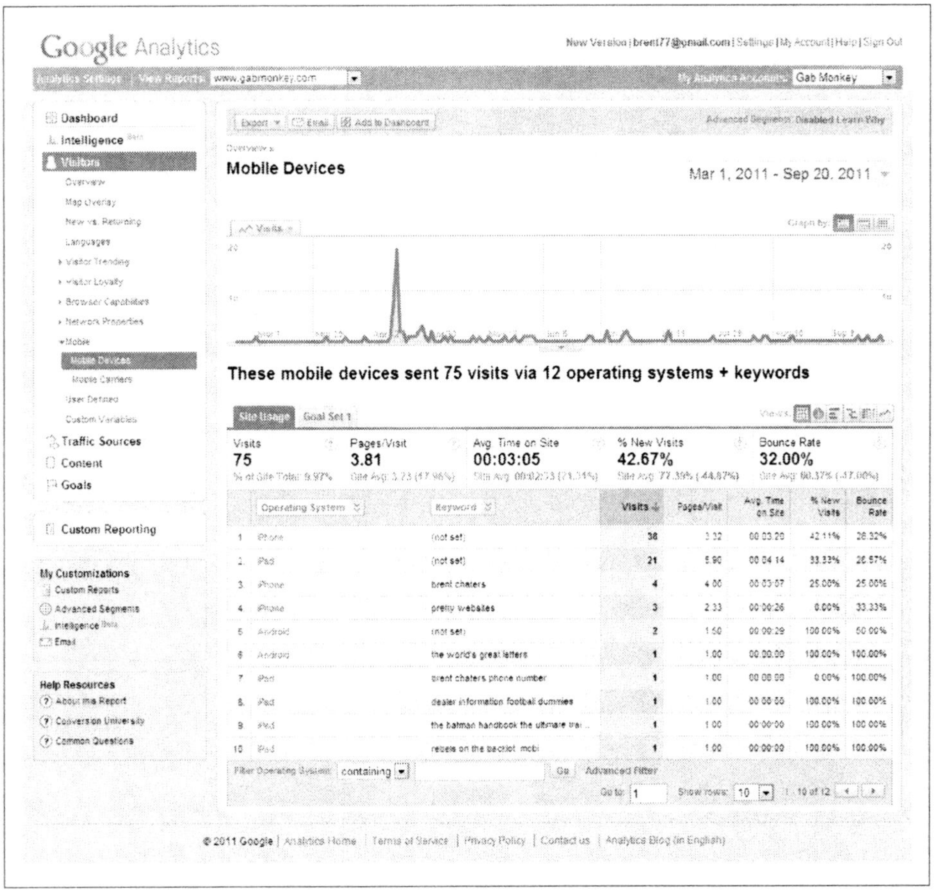

Figure 10-12. Operating system and keyword dimensions applied

Dimensions and filters can become your best friends as you look to learn more about what is happening on your site. Usually, we will move from a macro metric to a micro metric to learn more about what is going on. Start out with a big picture and apply filters and dimensions until you are able to see the smaller issues (Figure 10-13).

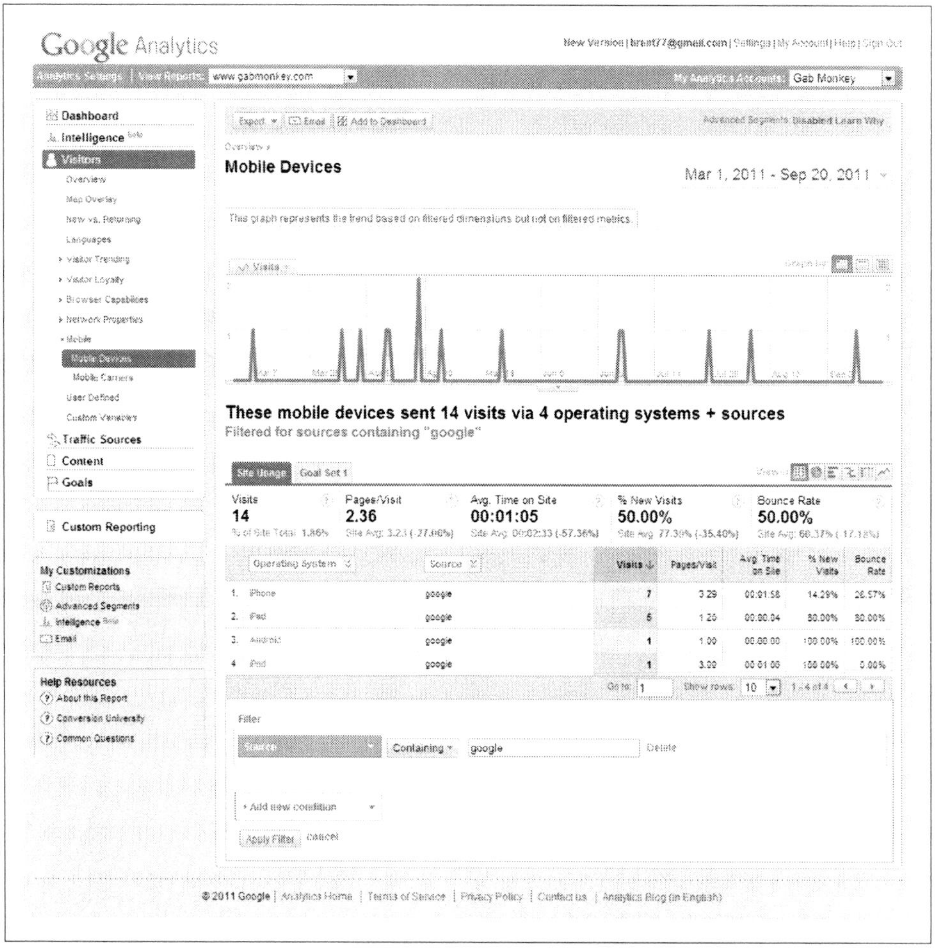

Figure 10-13. Operating system and keyword dimensions applied along with a filter on source set to "Google"

Do Mobile Users Convert Better than Desktop Users?

This is the biggest question we want to answer. Looking at ROI is no different on mobile devices than it is on desktop devices. In this case, we will want to run all the same scenarios we did before, but filtered out to mobile users. You can refer to Table 10-3 as an example of what we track differently for mobile users. Mobile users may be much more prone to calling. When capturing call leads, also have your sales reps capture closes and volumes. You can apply that data to Table 10-3, as we've done in Table 10-4, to measure the revenue generated by these calls.

Table 10-4. Example of what to track for mobile campaigns

Campaign name	Phone number used	Avg. cost/click	Mobile URL	PC URL	Clicks-to-call	PPC clicks to mobile pages	PPC clicks to desktop pages	Average order value
Campaign #1	555-252-3355	$1.52	m.site.com/url1	www.site.com/url1	12	255	182	$560.32
Campaign #2	555-252-3356	$1.52	m.site.com/url1	www.site.com/url2	55	82	38	$456.76

With your mobile campaigns, you may find that slightly different goals are set depending on whether your mobile site serves a different purpose from your desktop site, or carries a more limited set of products to purchase or tasks to complete. You may also want to get mobile users to provide cell phone numbers to text instead of email addresses to contact. Make sure when setting up your ROI spreadsheets and formulas to capture the unique events that may only occur with your mobile users. Have you created an ROI for mobile app downloads? The ROI may be equivalent to an email opt-in, or it may be more valuable. Whatever the actions may be, establish your ROI values per action as outlined in Chapter 2.

At this point, you should have the skills to capture any ROI values you need, and if you're using Google Analytics or a similar web analytics package that allows for mobile tracking, such as Adobe SiteCatalyst, you should be able to apply the mobile dimensions and filters to your site analytics to filter out mobile interactions.

Concluding Thoughts

At this point, you should have a good basis for some tests you can run to learn about the behavior of your mobile and desktop users when it comes to search. Further, you should have an idea of how the algorithms may change in the future, and where they stand now. Most of the differences we see between our mobile and desktop users are due to differences in user behavior and intent, not in the search algorithms themselves. Understanding the user, not the algorithm, is the key to success in mobile search marketing.

CHAPTER 11

Social Media and Search

*Social media's impact on search is perhaps the biggest
shift in search since Google launched.*

As people become connected online, and connect to others, their social profiles grow. At the time of writing, Facebook had over 750 million active users, and Twitter over 200 million registered users. Google has also recently announced Google +1 and Plus (*https://plus.google.com/*), services that will bring social interaction and engagement to the search giant.

Further, Google and Bing have both confirmed they use Twitter as a search ranking signal, and Bing receives data from Facebook to rank pages for users who are logged into their Facebook profiles. Google will likely continue this trend and build upon its Plus project.

It is not a question any more of "if" social signals will play a role in search rankings— they *are* playing a role. The upside to this is that some of the most likely influential signals are also already highly trackable. From a search measurement standpoint, the key things to measure are:

- Facebook likes
- Tweets and retweets on Twitter
- +1s on Google

These three social signals are perhaps the strongest and most important from the perspective of influence over search results. Due to the newness of social media and its impact on search, however, measuring these signals is still a relatively new space.

Tools you will need in this chapter:

- Tweet trackers (backtweets.com, tweetreach.com, etc.)
- Facebook dashboard
- Spreadsheet program (Excel or something similar)

Social Media's Impact

In late 2010, Danny Sullivan of Search Engine Land asked both Bing and Google several questions about their use of social signals in ranking search results (*http://searchengineland.com/what-social-signals-do-google-bing-really-count-55389*). The interview confirmed that social media is indeed influencing rankings; what was unclear was the extent of its impact. Fast-forward several months, and the influence began to become all the more clear. Tweets could help move a page up the results, impacting rankings almost faster than link-building campaigns.

The challenge of using social signals is that there are many ways to consider their influence over a search result. A tweet from one user may be more valuable than many tweets from other users, and a tweet that is retweeted may have a stronger influence than it did when its author wrote it. But what impact do several tweets all linking to the same page have versus a single retweet of the same topic? As these signals develop, the measurement of them will also likely become more sophisticated.

Much as PageRank was developed as a measure of a page's relevancy and authority, the same will likely happen in the social space, with stronger social voices carrying more weight than weaker voices. A strong voice may be defined as someone who is repeated a lot (i.e., someone who is often retweeted). It may also be someone who has many followers, but who does not follow a large number of people. The Klout Score (*http://www.klout.com*) is one metric that is already in use (though it is not currently a factor in search rankings): it measures influence based on data collected from sites such as Twitter and Facebook regarding the size of a person's network, the content that person creates, and how others interact with that content (likes, retweets, etc.).

As discussed in "Tracking Social Volume and Social Media" on page 209, there are also tools that can help you monitor what is being said about your company in the social space. These include commercial options, such as Radian6 and Attensity360, and free tools like Addict-o-matic.

This chapter will cover a top-line way of capturing a general idea of the social signals that are occurring around your pages or your site. Social analytics and measurement is already a strong field that will only continue to get more and more sophisticated. Since our focus is specific to search, we will want to focus on the impact social signals have on our rankings, and potentially those of our competitors as well.

Social Personalization

Social signals have begun to change the face of the search results, and the rankings for individuals. What I call *social personalization* recognizes people in your social circle and provides results that these people have shared and the sources from which they shared them.

Bing has partnered directly with Facebook to tap into Facebook data to provide personalized results (Figure 11-1), which you can read more about at *http://www.bing .com/community/site_blogs/b/search/archive/2011/02/24/bing-expands-facebook-liked -results.aspx*. These personalized results are slowly popping up and will be influenced by how many of your friends are active on social media. The same happens with Google and Twitter, with Google giving emphasis to results that friends of yours have retweeted (Figure 11-2).

Figure 11-1. Personalized results in Bing from Facebook

The fascinating thing is that these results are based not on *your* past experience, but the experiences and actions of your friends or people you follow. Essentially, you are getting personalized results based on the activities of other people in your social circle and the influence people in that circle may have over you.

With personalized results becoming more and more prevalent, you may be able to affect your rankings not only through your optimization efforts, but also through your social influence and impact. It may not be surprising to see rankings change dramatically from one person to another, based on differences in their social circles and the different influences social sharing has on results.

As a result of this, to gauge whether you can overtake a competitor on a search term, you may need to consider your social strength, as well as all the other factors we have explored, through measurement of common social signals.

Figure 11-2. Personalized result in Google featuring tweets

Measuring Facebook

Facebook currently influences Bing results directly, though with limited impact, and some studies have shown a correlation between Facebook likes and Google's search rankings (*http://www.seomoz.org/blog/facebook-twitters-influence-google-search-rankings*). However, correlation does not equal causation. Google has said that Facebook likes are not a factor, but likes may indicate a higher propensity to link to content, and as we know, link building is a good way to boost rankings.

Further, we do know that Facebook plays a role in Bing results. As such, measuring the number of likes is still helpful when trying to ascertain the success of a page in Bing results, and may be useful if this data is opened up for other engines to utilize as well.

Fortunately, Facebook has made this very easy. By enabling the Open Graph protocol (*http://developers.facebook.com/docs/opengraph/*) on your website, you can capture likes and shares directly in Facebook (Figure 11-3). The protocol itself is not as daunting as it may at first appear, and Facebook provides good detail about what needs to be included in your site. There are four main properties you must include:

og:title
: The title of your object as it should appear in the graph.

og:type
: The type of object, corresponding to a set list (*http://developers.facebook.com/docs/opengraph/#types*). Mostly you will want "website", "article", or "blog" for online properties, but others may be applicable as well.

og:image
: An image URL that represents your object in the graph. Size and formatting restrictions apply.

og:url
: The canonical URL of your object. This will be used as the permanent ID in the graph.

Once you have Open Graph set up, you will be able to track interactions of users through Facebook's analytics. You can also export this data through an API into an analytics package such as Webtrends, which can integrate it with your clickstream data and data from other sources to provide more insights to your digital ecosystem as a whole.

Figure 11-3. Viewing the number of Facebook likes

Measuring Twitter

There are many options for measuring Twitter tweets and retweets. Perhaps the easiest way to measure your own retweets is directly in the Twitter interface (Figure 11-4). You can see how many times your original tweet has been retweeted, and by whom. This is beneficial if you are very good at promoting your own content. However, in most cases, you want to enable the users of your site to be your advocates themselves. For this, you need to look beyond your own Twitter account.

Third-party solutions such as TweetReach can show how far your brand reaches, while BackTweets provides information on tweets that link back to your site. The back links are the more important measurement and the better source of data. The information that BackTweets provides can show you both impressions and the number of page views as a result of tweets. In Figure 11-5, you can see that 19 tweets resulted in 131,000 impressions and 218 page views. This shows firstly how a few tweets can go a long way, and secondly the impact social media has directly on your traffic. Lastly, from a search analytics standpoint, the number of tweets has value to us, as we can quantify this with our other ranking signals, which we can capture in a table format (see Table 11-1).

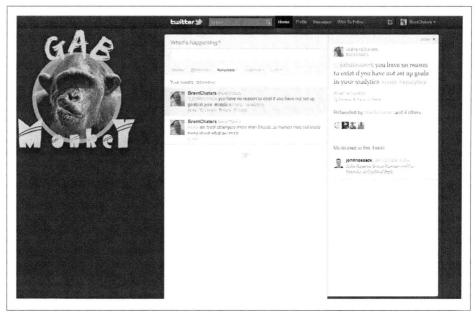

Figure 11-4. Viewing the number of retweets on Twitter

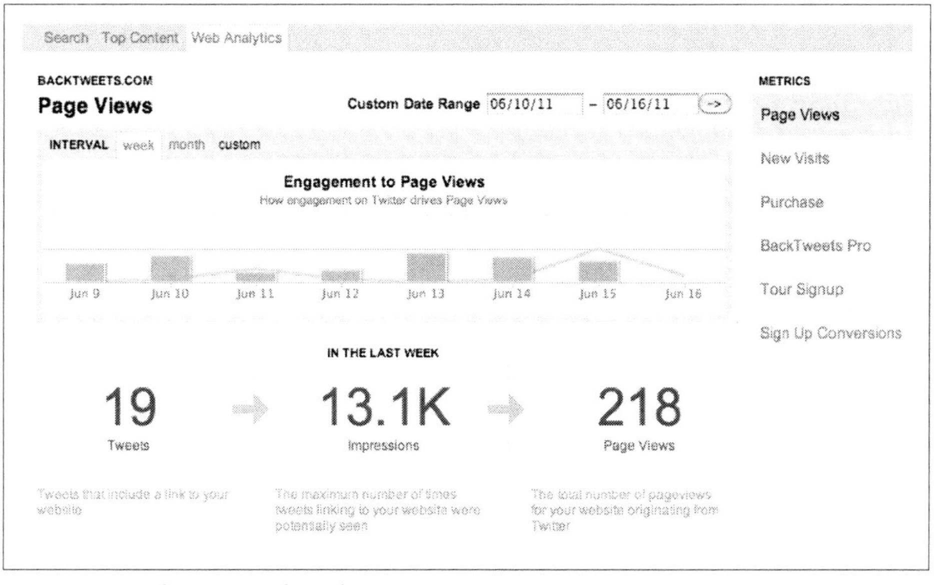

Figure 11-5. BackTweets results and measuring impression to page views

Table 11-1. Ranking signals including social signals

URL	On-site back links	Off-site back links	Linking root domains	PageRank	Tweets	Facebook likes	Google+1
www.somesite.com /page1.html	23,450	13,006	452	6	43	64	23
www.competitorsite .com/a-different-page.html	14,643	1,452	123	4	633	346	56
www.somesite.com /yet-another-page.html	34,562	21,653	742	7	21	62	23

Capturing data in this table format can provide greater insight into why a page is ranking as it does. We can examine this data for our own pages and compare it to data on our competitors' pages. This can be particularly helpful when trying to understand why a competitor may rank higher than we do. Looking at the data in our table, we may discover that while our competitor has a low number of back links, they have an extremely strong social presence that may be influencing their rankings and results. By looking across these multiple data points, we may discover that we must push for more sharing of our own content in order to continue to be competitive and sustain or move up in the rankings.

Measuring +1

+1 data is directly available in Google Webmaster Tools. To access it, expand the "+1 Metrics" menu on the left (Figure 11-6).

Three reports are available. The search impact report (Figure 11-7) provides the CTR and number of impressions of pages with and without +1s. This will allow you to see how much of an impact social personalization is having on your users and their behavior. This kind of data encourages us to think not only about rankings, but also about the shareability and relevancy of our pages to our users. On the Activity page, you can monitor new +1s, all +1's, and whether the +1s have occurred on your site or within the search results or ad network. This provides an idea of which pages are building +1's rapidly; you may see a correlation between these pages and where you are in the rankings. Finally, the Audience report gives you anonymized data on the people who have +1'd your pages.

Figure 11-6. +1 metrics in Google Webmaster Tools

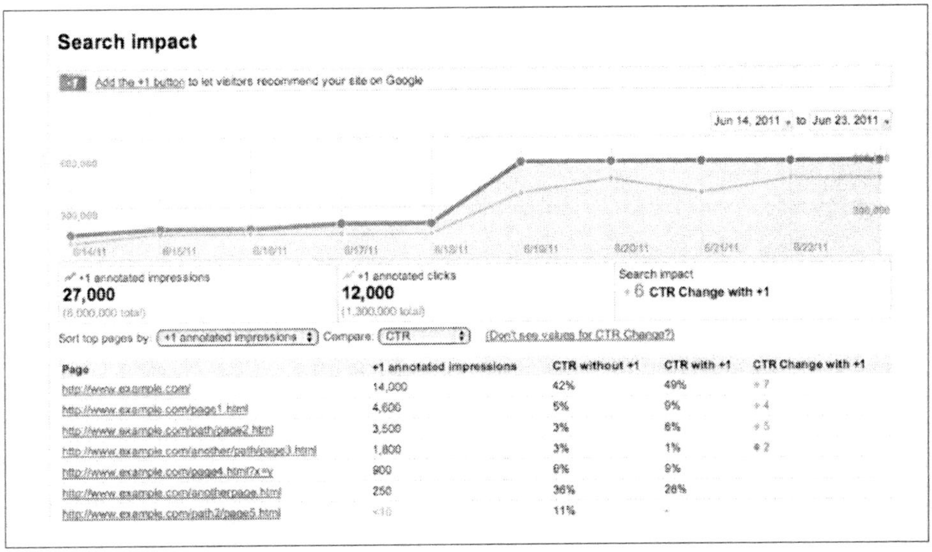

Figure 11-7. The search impact report

Because it captures the +1 data and shows you its impact on your results, this is perhaps the most accurate view of all as to the impact socialization has on your site in terms of rankings and traffic. Examining this data can show you how search and social media campaigns combined can influence not just your rank but the CTR and traffic from the engines. Google's data set is perhaps the most useful in terms of understanding early behavior and influence in the social space.

Concluding Thoughts

Social media can no longer be considered a fad. What we have begun to witness is our connected networks and relationships coming together online to provide improved information and data based upon who we know. I think over time this relationship will get even more sophisticated, as the importance of users will become relevant as well. For example, someone who you follow on Twitter, friend on Facebook, and +1 on Plus is likely a closer friend than someone you only follow on Twitter. The more locations you associate with a person, the more valued that relationship is likely to be, and therefore the more likely that person is to have greater influence over your likes and dislikes.

The challenge that the social space will face is more likely to do with privacy and the implications the sharing of this data has across major networks. The limit to sharing of data will likely come through court rulings and outcry from users. We have already seen some indications of this: for example, Facebook had to deal with end users voicing concerns over its privacy policy update in February of 2009: users complained about the amendments, which resulted in Facebook taking the stance that any future amendments would require a vote by users.

Whichever way the privacy rules change, I suspect social media and search will be intertwined in one way or another for a very long time to come. In pursuing their goal of providing the most relevant pages to users, the search engines will likely continue to use these signals—all the more so because they are more difficult to spam against, and they use sources trusted by the users to provide a more pertinent result (i.e., a result that has been voted as relevant by another person). This vote further indicates that the content of the page is less likely to be spam and more likely to be useful information that the person will want to see.

CHAPTER 12

Webmaster Tools—Data Direct from the Engines

SEO requires a great deal of site auditing and reviewing.

SEO ranking factors can be broken into on-site and off-site factors. Perhaps the least glamorous part of the SEO job is auditing and maintenance. As important as it is to measure success events and ROI, measuring and monitoring site health is even more critical. If you don't know what the spiders are doing on your site, you may be completely blind to potential bottlenecks. The *long tail* of search is made up of search terms that are highly unpredictable. In fact, it is so unpredictable that the best way to cover it is to ensure that every inch of your content is indexed. To do this, you need to be able to track the spiders. This chapter is an overview of Webmaster Tools, which is your interface to the spiders.

Tools you will need in this chapter:

* Google and Bing Webmaster Tools

The Basics

Both Bing and Google provide webmaster accounts (as do some other search engines, such as Yandex). The webmaster account is the search engine's conduit to you. It is through this account that you can access the information and data the engines choose to share to help you improve your search relevancy.

If you have not yet set up a webmaster account, you should do so both for Google and for Bing and familiarize yourself with the content and data in it. Covering the big two engines will ensure that your site gets maximum exposure, and you'll find many great assets and tools in the webmaster accounts to draw data from. You can sign up for a Google Webmaster Tools account (Figure 12-1) at *http://www.google.com/webmas ters/* and for a Bing Webmaster Tools account (Figure 12-2) at *http://www.bing.com/*

toolbox/webmasters/. Both of these suites provide you with insight into not only what their respective spiders see, but also some of what is happening with the traffic related to your site in the engine's search results.

Once you have your accounts set up, the main dashboard of each webmaster suite provides an overview of what is happening on your site. Currently, Google's Webmaster Tools suite provides deeper insight into what is happening in your search results. We'll look at that first.

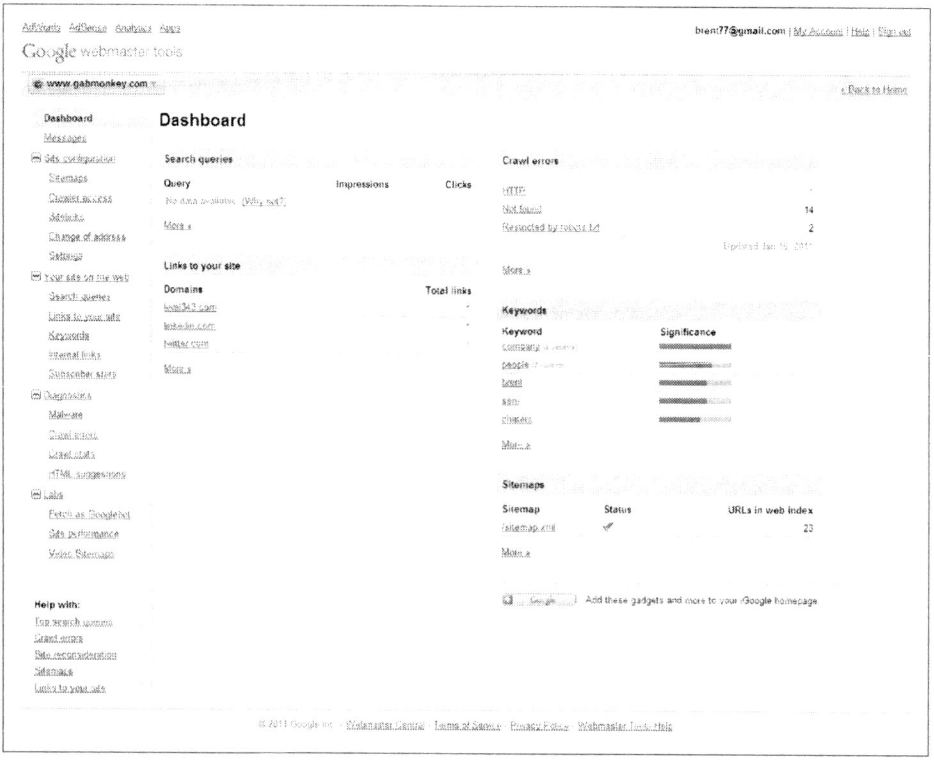

Figure 12-1. Google Webmaster Tools

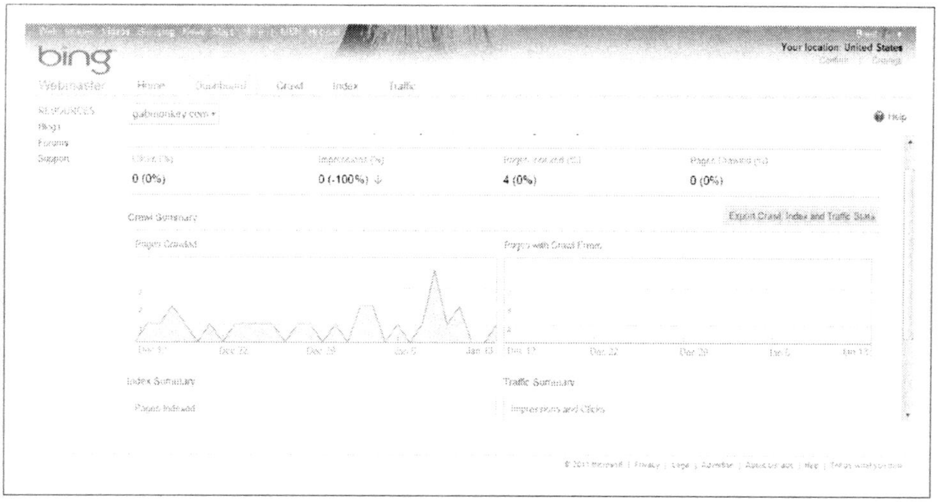

Figure 12-2. Bing Webmaster Tools

Google Webmaster Tools

Google's Webmaster Tools dashboard provides an overview of what the spider sees as sites linking to your site, pages it has crawl errors with, keywords it sees as highly relevant to your site, and any issues it has with the sitemaps you have submitted.

Messages

All of this data is highly valuable to understanding how the search spider interprets the content and data on your site. Further, Google will occasionally post messages to you through its messaging system: these may include alerts as to an abnormal volume of pages crawled, or updates regarding access of the site. You can find these under the "Messages" link on the left.

Sitemaps

The Sitemaps section (Figure 12-3) can be accessed under "Site Configuration." This is where you can submit sitemaps to be indexed, as well as seeing when your sitemap was last download and crawled, how many pages are in the sitemap, and how many of those pages are in the search index.

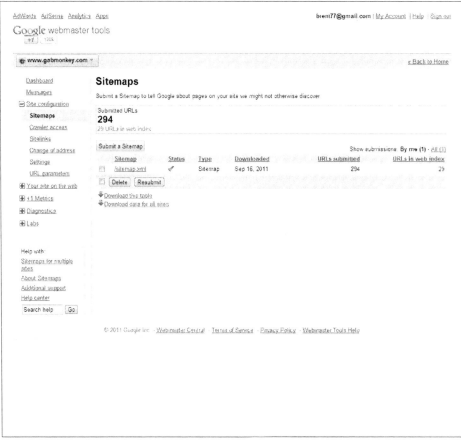

Figure 12-3. Google Webmaster Tools sitemaps

Keep an eye on the number of pages you have submitted and how many are in the index. In Figure 12-3, we can see that we've submitted 294 pages but only 29 pages are showing in the index. This may indicate that we have a lot of URLs that are not relevant, duplicate content, or (worst of all) pages that cannot be crawled or spidered. The first thing we should do is verify any crawl errors under Diagnostics. We will review this process in more detail shortly; for now, be aware of the ratio of pages submitted to pages indexed.

Crawler Access

Crawler Access (Figure 12-4), also under "Site Configuration," shows us how the Google spider interprets our site *robot.txt* file. The *robot.txt* file tells the spider which content to look at and which to ignore. Anything that is set up as "Disallow: /directory" will not be spidered (in this case, */directory* and anything in it will not be indexed by the spider). If you need to indicate to the spider not to crawl certain sections of your site but you are not comfortable or familiar with the syntax, there is also a tool to help you generate a *robot.txt* file. In the Crawler Access section, you can also remove URLs or sections of the site you do not want in the search index. This may come in handy if you accidentally left your staging server exposed to search spiders and it got crawled, or if you have content that should have been password-protected or not in the index.

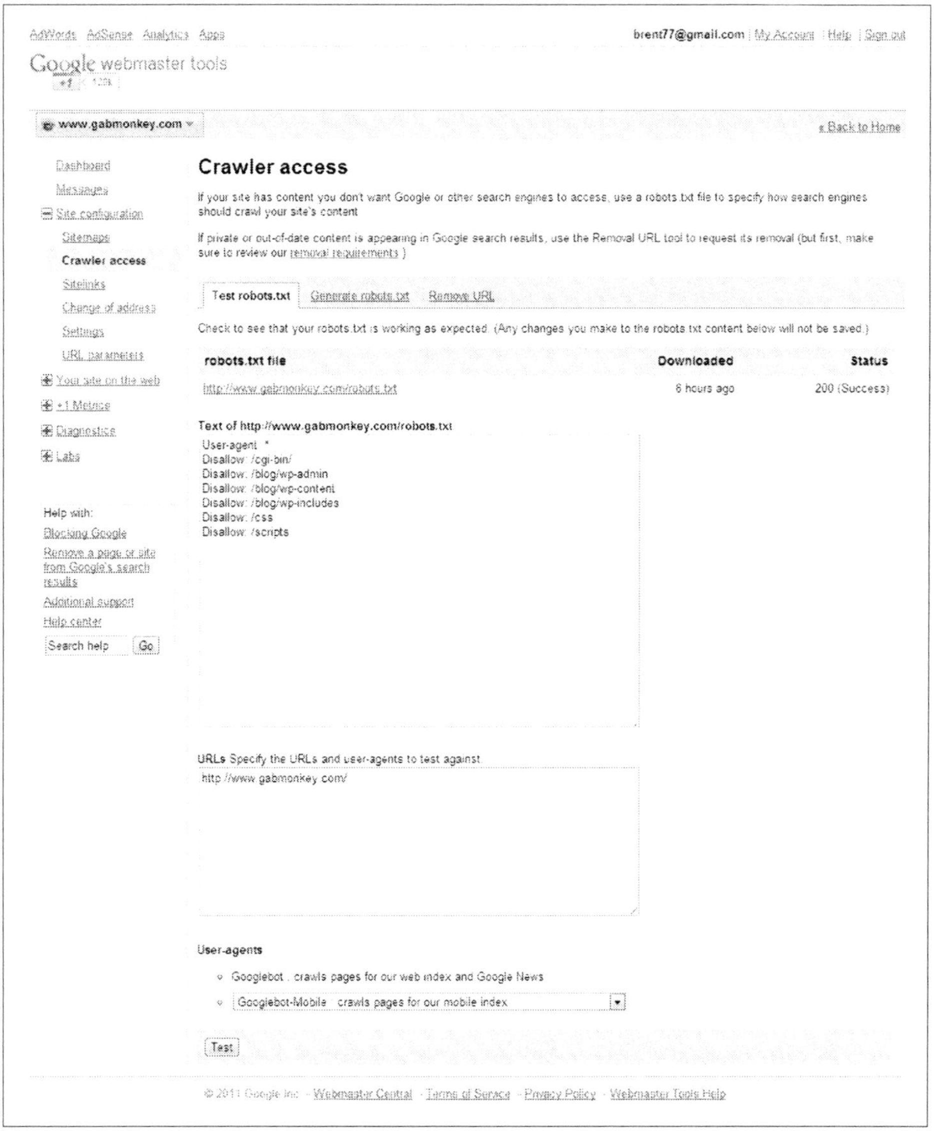

Figure 12-4. Google Webmaster Tools crawler access

Settings

The Settings section (Figure 12-5) under "Site Configuration" allows you to refine even further how the spider will interact with your site. If you run any campaign tracking using query string parameters you will want to be familiar with this section, as it enables you to inform Google which parameters can be ignored. The first tab, "General settings," provides the option to geo-target your audience. This is ideal if you run a large website that serves multiple countries and you have clearly defined sections for each country. You may also have different TLDs registered for each country. You can use this section to target countries, to ensure the right country pages show up in the right country searches. You may decide your *.com* domain is going to serve all countries, in which case you do not need to set a Geographic target for it. You can also set a preferred domain format, usually *www.website.com* or *website.com*, where you can let the engine know your preferred format for displaying your site content. The last section of this tab allows you to control crawl frequency. It's usually best to let the spider determine this; this reduces the risk of it under-crawling your server or crawling your server too heavily and potentially taking your website down.

The second tab, "Parameter handling," allows you to let the spider know how to handle parameters if you have dynamic content on your site. If you are using PHP, ASP, or some other server-side scripting language, you're likely using parameters in URLs to pass information amongst pages.

Further, you may use parameter handling for some of your site analytics tracking. Most site analytics packages that are set up through JavaScript-based software require parameters for campaign tracking. You can let the spider know that certain parameters (such as those used for campaign tracking) are always irrelevant and should be ignored in a URL. The other parameters in a URL may actually be relevant and required to ensure the proper or any new content is displayed. Ensuring that the parameters in use are set up correctly with regard to spidering is crucial to ensure that pages with dynamic content get indexed by the engine and show up in the search results in the appropriate format.

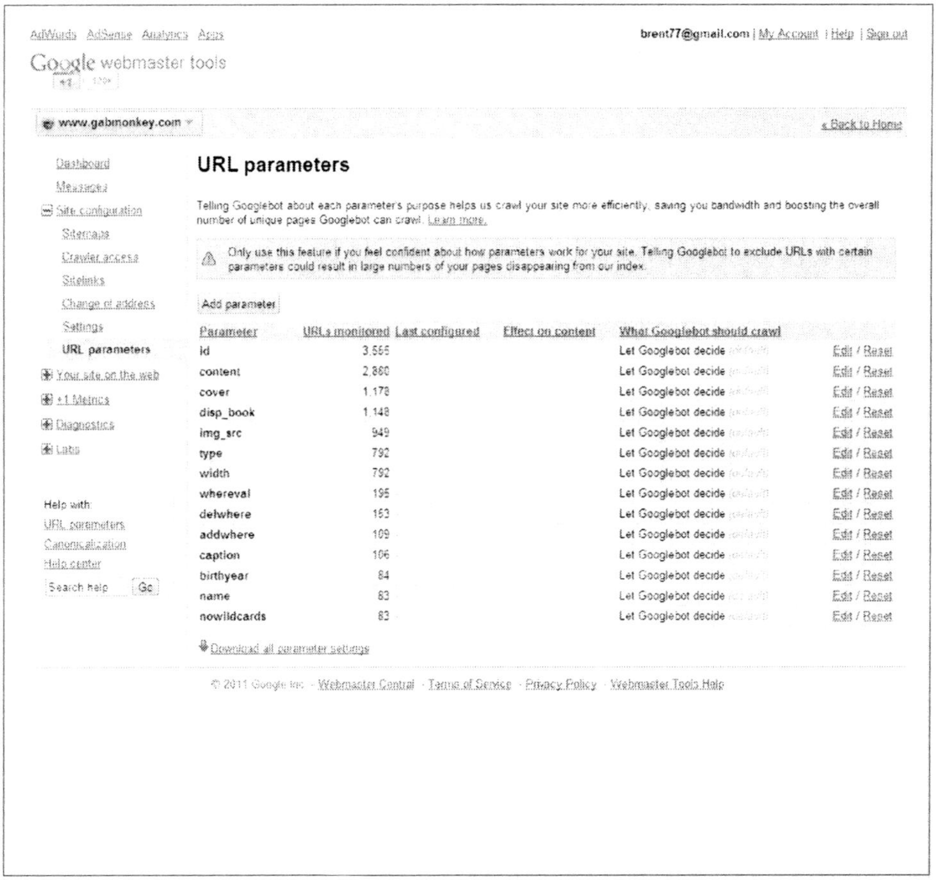

Figure 12-5. Google Webmaster Tools settings for treating URL parameters

Search Queries

Moving on to the next set of links, under "Your Site on the Web" we first see "Search Queries" (Figure 12-6). This section provides statistics on which words are driving traffic to your site, your average position for each of those words, as well as your top pages for impressions in the search results. You can use this data to determine if you have many important pages or one page that is driving most of your traffic.

Figure 12-6. Google Webmaster Tools search queries report

This data is fairly rich, but also not as exact as I would like. The data on impressions is only approximate, but it does allow you to perform some general benchmarking, including tracking of average SERP position and changes over time. You can also see the CTR for organic words, which is nice to know. A low CTR on an organic ranking may indicate that your title and descriptions are weak, and that you can expect to see your ranking begin to decline.

Further, by knowing which words are driving traffic to your site, you may get some insights into what users expect of your content. You can click on a word to see which pages on your site are being associated with it, and you can see if you have keyword conflicts across several words, or if one page is consistently driving the majority of traffic through a specific key term.

Links to Your Site

The "Links to Your Site" section (Figure 12-7) can help you identify which neighborhoods the search spider identifies you with. You can see what links to your site the spider sees, so if you are invested in link-building campaigns you can verify whether the links you build are indeed being indexed and captured by the engine. What you are not told is the quality of these links. This requires manual analysis and intervention.

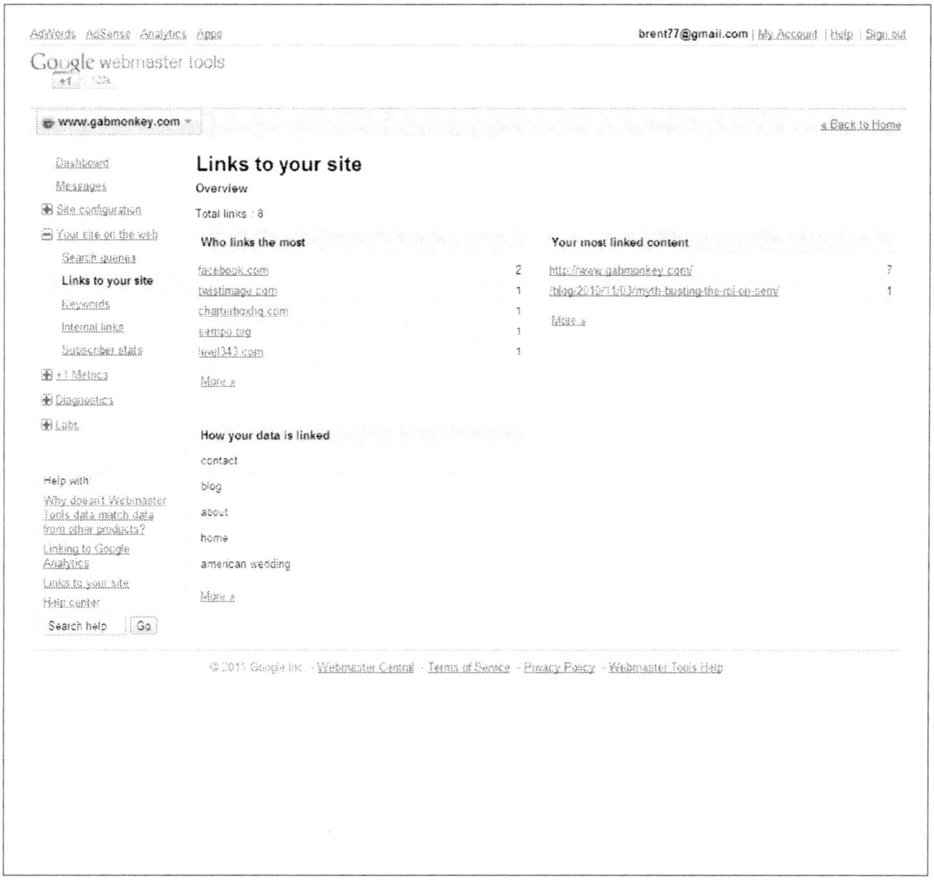

Figure 12-7. Google Webmaster Tools links to your site report

This section of Webmaster Tools also provides some insight into how your site is being linked through keyword terms. For a long time, link-building activities were based on the words used in the hyperlink to a page. While this is what is being reported here, it is a very old way of thinking about links. The search algorithm has gotten much more sophisticated: today it looks at the topical ideas on the linking page and compares them to those on the pages it links to, to identify how closely the pages are related.

In short, getting a link from a page with a keyword in it is not as good as getting a link from a page that is very topically relevant to your own page. For instance, a link from a page about "cars" to your page about "car engines" is much more topical than a link from a page about "flowers." In other words, this list of links to your site is only part of the picture regarding how the engine sees your data as being linked.

This section also provides insight into which pages are frequently linked to. In our example in Figure 12-7, we see that most inbound links are to our home page. This indicates that our deep content is not well linked to. Any link-building campaigns we run should therefore be focused on improving links to pages that are deeper in our site, to enhance our *long-tail* strategy.

Keywords

The Keywords section of Google Webmaster Tools provides you a list of keywords that occur frequently throughout your content. This is not to say these are the words driving traffic to your site; it's just a list of terms that appear often in your pages. It can also include variations of some terms, including different stemmed versions of these terms. To find out which pages a term occurs on most frequently and get a more detailed report on what variations of the term are in use, just click on it. This is a great way to quickly audit your site for topic relevancy.

Internal Links

There is a great focus by SEOs on external link building. What most fail to recognize is that your own on-site internal link strategy is just as important. With all the links in the world pointing to your site, if you have a poorly implemented information architecture you will have a hard time getting your pages to rank. Further, ensuring you have a relatively flat site architecture, where you can get to almost any page in two or three clicks, will make your site more spider-friendly. The Internal Links section of Google Webmaster Tools (Figure 12-8) provides a list of your top linked content based on your on-site linking strategy.

The top linked pages in this report should be those you perceive as your most important pages. If you consider a link as a vote for popularity, this list should also reflect what you perceive to be the most popular pages on your site. The internal linking strategy you develop should be an indicator of which pages you wish to see the most traffic flow through and to. This also helps the search engines understand what you perceive as the most important pages on your site.

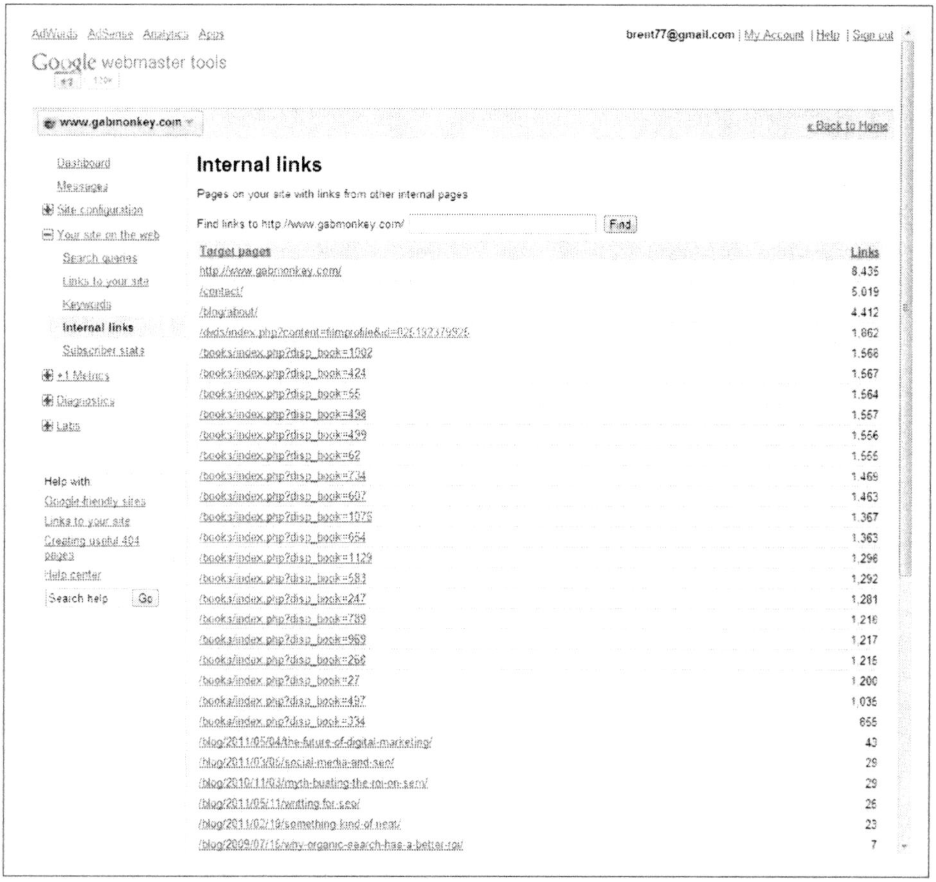

Figure 12-8. Google Webmaster Tools internal links report

Crawl Errors

When tracking the spiders, crawl errors is a key stat to look at. Are there sections of your website that are returning lots of 302, 403, 404, or 500 errors? Audit your list of error pages, and fix these once or twice a month in large groups. Not only will this improve the crawlability of your site, but it should improve customer satisfaction by ensuring your pages are rendering correctly and not throwing out errors. The crawl errors report is also a good way of seeing if there are sections of your site that are being blocked by your *robots.txt* file. If you see content under the *robots.txt* file section that should not be blocked, you may want to take another look at the settings in that file. You can also use this report to validate any crawl errors for your mobile pages.

Crawl Stats

The crawl stats (Figure 12-9) in Google Webmaster Tools provide some technical insights into what the Googlebot is doing on your site. You get three overviews: pages crawled, kilobytes downloaded, and time spent downloading pages. By knowing how many pages are crawled, as well as when crawl spikes occur, you can get an idea of how well-indexed your site is. While it doesn't give a specific number of exactly how many pages are in your index, the first report does provide a visualization of when and where crawl spikes occurred. This may help you identify when traffic increases due to a large volume of pages being crawled.

The other two metrics, kilobytes downloaded and time spent downloading, indicate how much effort the spider has to put into crawling your site. Getting page weight and time to download down will mean the spider can crawl more of your content.

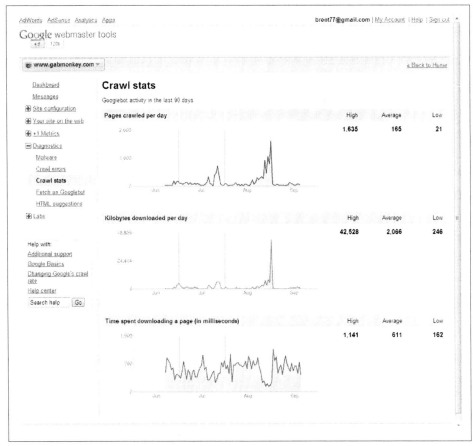

Figure 12-9. Google Webmaster Tools crawl stats

HTML Suggestions

The HTML suggestions (Figure 12-10) provided by Google are intended to help you identify potential issues with your site that may be impacting your rankings. Most of the focus of this report is around meta descriptions and page titles. While meta descriptions are not a factor in rankings, the search engine may use them to describe the content of your page in the SERPs. Page titles are another element that shows up in the SERPs. By having unique page titles, you ensure unique identifiers for each page. If something triggers an issue in the audit, you can click through the link provided to see which page or pages the issue occurred on.

You also get a report of nonindexable content. This may include content such as images, video, or other content that may be rich but cannot be interpreted by the search engine. Monitoring these reports can help you to improve click-throughs and drive more people to your website.

Figure 12-10. Google Webmaster Tools HTML suggestions report

Fetch as Googlebot

Ever wonder what the search engine sees on your page? This feature allows you to fetch a web page as the Googlebot spider. It will strip the page down to what it interprets, and you may be surprised at what is returned. The first thing you will notice is that no matter how pretty your website may look, Googlebot does not care; it strips all the nice-looking content away and looks only at the HTML elements that are returned.

Learning that it is not all about design when it comes to SEO is a big step for some people. Pages that may not be the nicest-looking can still rank very well on some very aggressive terms. Understanding what the spider sees is a good insight into the importance of content in getting ranked in the search results.

Site Performance

Google has already stated that page speed is becoming important. The site performance report (Figure 12-11) provides a list of pages on your site that are slow to load, and some suggestions as to how to improve these pages to decrease download times. This report also provides you with a benchmark in terms of where your site sits compared to the average performance of other websites across the board. There are two factors in improving these results: page design and the speed of your web server (that is, how quickly it returns pages to people making page requests). Google also provides a link to a tool that you can install into Firefox, if you're using that as your web browser, to quickly audit any page and get a list of recommended changes to make to improve page download times.

Video Sitemaps

The last section of Google Webmaster Tools is the Video Sitemaps section. Google allows you to provide a separate sitemap listing all the video content you have on your site, to improve the indexing of this rich format. Google uses this data to pull videos into universal search results for any video content that is not sitting on YouTube.

The report provided here will indicate any issues Google has processing your video sitemap, so you can address them. Video sitemaps help ensure your video content is indexed by the engines. This is important, as we know video content typically has a higher CTR than a regular link in the search results (see "Comparing CTRs across all types of search" on page 40).

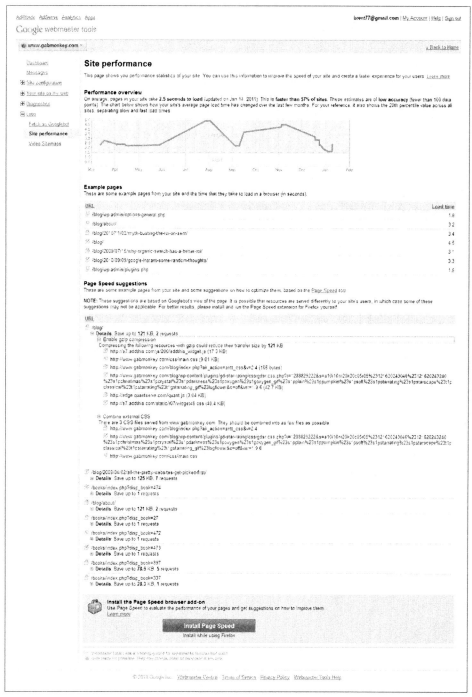

Figure 12-11. Google Webmaster Tools site performance report

Bing Webmaster Tools

Bing Webmaster Tools provides some similar services to Google Webmaster Tools, and it can give you some insight into what is happening with Bing's spider and the traffic Bing is sending you. It is worthwhile checking out how your site is performing in Bing, as you may find that Bing sends more qualified traffic than Google does. Bing has put a lot of effort into improving its Webmaster Tools recently, and continues to roll out new and helpful updates.

Dashboard

The Dashboard in Bing's Webmaster Tools (Figure 12-12), much like Google's, provides an overview and summary of what you'll find in each of the other sections. Pretty much any information you need from Bing is accessible from this dashboard. You can see how frequently you are crawled, how many pages are indexed, and the volume of traffic Bing is sending you. To learn more about any of these analytics reports, you can click the tab or the link above each report to dive deeper into them.

Figure 12-12. Bing Webmaster Tools dashboard

Crawl

The Crawl Summary report (Figure 12-13) tells you the rate at which your site is being crawled and lists any crawl errors the Bing bot has run into. Like Google's crawl errors report, this indicates any issues the bot may have; you should audit it regularly and react to ensure as much of your site is being crawled and spidered as possible. Further, the Crawl tab allows you to see details about what content is being crawled and how many URLs are submitted, and provides access to XML sitemaps that are detected. You can also determine the rate at which you want your site indexed, to ensure the Bing bot plays nicely.

Figure 12-13. Bing Webmaster Tools crawl summary report

Index

The Index Summary report (Figure 12-14) shows how many pages have been indexed by the Bing bot. This report displays pages indexed over time. In its current format, it's difficult to ascertain from this report how many pages sit in the Bing search directory. You will have to infer whether the number of pages indexed over time seems appropriate based on the size of your site and the frequency with which you publish content. If you know you are publishing 30 to 40 pages per day and you are seeing an index rate of only 5 to 10 pages a day, you can guess that the content you are publishing is not being indexed at the rate at which you publish.

Figure 12-14. Bing Webmaster Tools index summary report

Traffic

The Traffic tab (Figure 12-15) shows the volume of traffic Bing sends to your site. You get a report on the queries that drive people to your site as well as the number of impressions for your key terms, number of clicks, CTR, and more. This is a great report to look at if you want to understand how well you are doing at getting impressions and then driving clicks. What's missing is a listing of which pages were served for the search terms. All of this data can also be exported out to help you develop keyword-building strategies around specific pages and terms. Terms with low average positions may be terms worth improving on. The Traffic tab allows you to view your site by pages indexed and impressions, or by keywords. This dual view is very helpful for understanding not only which words are big drivers to your site, but also which pages are big drivers.

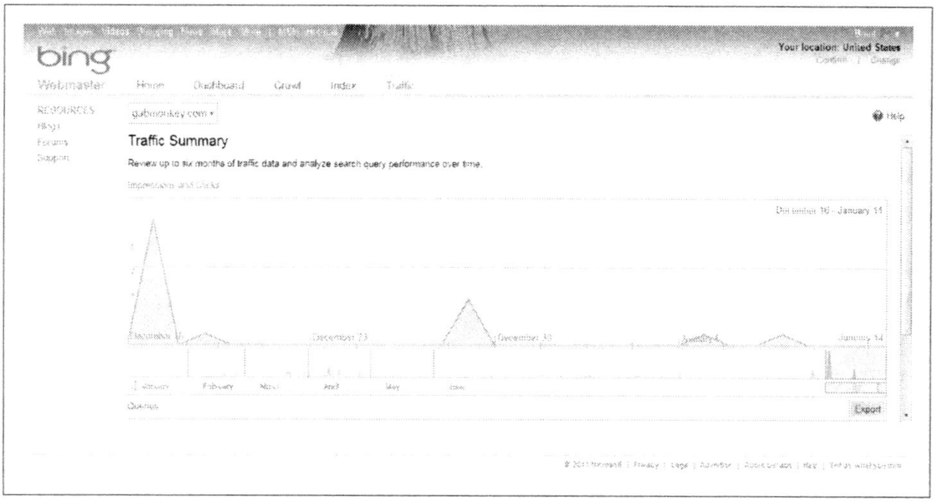

Figure 12-15. Bing Webmaster Tools traffic report

Index Explorer

The Index Explorer (Figure 12-16) provides detailed information on the pages within the Bing index. You can navigate to the pages through the directory structure the spider sees on your site. You can find out how many pages are in a directory and view details specific to each page, such as traffic volumes, number of inbound links, when the page was last crawled, and when the search engine first discovered it. You can also block the URL of a page or directory from being indexed and/or cached, and suggest a forced re-crawl of a URL.

The Index Explorer allows you to filter by date range, discovery range, HTTP codes, and pages infected with malware or excluded by *robots.txt*. To further audit the pages, you can click through the inbound links to get the list of external pages linking to a specific page (up to 20,000). You can even export this data, out to track your link-building campaigns and see if they are effective.

Clicking on the traffic details provides you with the queries that drive people to your pages as well as the number of impressions, number of clicks, average click position, and click-through rate. All of this data can also be exported out to help you develop keyword-building strategies around specific pages and terms. Terms with low average positions may be terms worth improving on.

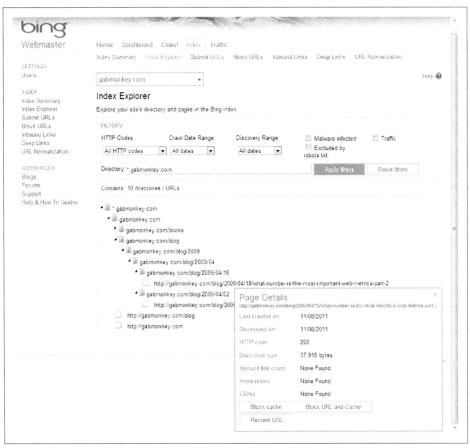

Figure 12-16. Bing Webmaster Tools Index Explorer

Comparing Bing and Google

After reviewing all the features of both Google and Bing Webmaster Tools, we can see that Google has a much fuller suite of tools that can provide deeper insights into what the spider is doing on your site, as well as how it interprets your content. Bing's biggest advantage over Google is the Index Explorer, which allows for drilling into some very specific user behavior data. The data from Bing, while highly useful for understanding your users, is not as robust when it comes to understanding issues that the spider may run into. Bing is, however, putting a great deal of work into improving these tools, and is always open to feedback and suggestions.

Each of these services can provide you with some insight into what the spiders are doing on your site. This is great data to have, as it's coming right from the source. What neither engine provides is information about other search engines and how frequently they are visiting your site. If you are an international company, you may want to look at how frequently Yandex, Baidu, or other large country-specific engines engage with your content. Some of these search engines provide a webmaster interface, while others do not.

To get a better idea of how your site as a whole is spidered, you may consider setting up log file readers to parse your web server logs, so you can see how frequently the spiders are visiting your site and at what rate they are downloading your content.

Concluding Thoughts

At this point you should be familiar with the Webmaster Tools suites of both the major engines, as well as what the spiders are doing. If the spider can't crawl your site, getting your site crawlable is the first major issue you have to deal with. Until a spider can index your content, you will never be able to rank on anything.

As part of your monthly or quarterly health check, you should validate that the spiders are not having any issues with your content, and that you are as accessible as possible. Sometimes changes can be applied to your server without your knowledge that may impact how spiders index your content. Staying on top of this can eliminate many headaches if you ever have to explain why traffic from search is down. It should be a quick check, but done on a regular basis.

CHAPTER 13

An SEO Audit (On-Page Factors)

*Site audits can fall under site health,
as well as site maintenance.*

Conducting audits of your KPIs should provide you with both a sanity check (do the numbers seem right?) and an opportunity to understand the whole of your site. Site audits should include 404s, 302s, multiple 301s, Flash, AJAX, and more. Much like you get an annual check-up at the doctor's, your website requires similar maintenance. Depending on your site's size you may run these audits weekly, monthly, quarterly, or at any interval you find appropriate. The point is to make the audits part of your habit, and to schedule them in. Monitoring site health is not a glamorous job, but it's well worth the reward in the long run. With well-run site audits, you will likely never see the results of your work, as everything will run smoothly. It is only when you don't run audits that you see the results of not maintaining site health, and this can quickly turn catastrophic.

Tools you will need in this chapter:

- Google Webmaster Tools
- Spreadsheet program (Excel or something similar)
- Web developer plug-in for Firefox
- YSlow for Firefox
- Site link checker (IIS toolkit)

Automating Issue Auditing

The more you automate, the quicker it will be to find the issues we'll cover here. In some cases it simply won't be possible to automate everything; in other cases there are very robust ways to automate tracking of issues. However, there should always be a human review of some sort to validate false positives and ensure appropriate checks and balances are put in place.

Running site audits should include looking at a number of elements, including broken links, on-page elements, and more. Fortunately, there are options to quickly find the very visible elements. Your first resource should be Google Webmaster Tools (*http://www.google.com/webmasters (http://www.google.com/webmasters)*). As we saw in the previous chapter, this suite includes a set of useful tools and reports that can alert you of problems with your site. The major alert is the malware alert: if you see this message, indicating that your site contains malware, the house is literally on fire. Stop whatever you are doing and investigate. Typically a malware alert indicates your site has been breached by a virus, or malicious code. Traffic to your site will likely plummet very quickly.

The issue itself will be captured by Webmaster Tools, but tracking it down will require good old-fashioned legwork. Typically you will be looking at some sort of injection attack, where data gets input into your database thanks to poor coding audits that allow SQL code to be passed in forms or URLs. Try looking in your database first, then following up with landing pages. You should engage with your IT team or your web hosting provider immediately, and have them scan your site for malware. Tracking this down and recovering can be a painful process, but is critical to react as quickly as possible.

Crawl errors (Figure 13-1) trapped by Webmaster Tools can give you an overview of the big issues the engine sees. Fixing the 404s can be tricky. The URLs listed may intentionally be broken as they lead to pages that have been removed, or you may find that a page reported missing is in fact still there. The challenge of tracking 404 errors in Webmaster Tools is that the 404 reporting can be a bit hit-or-miss.

The HTML Suggestions report in Google Webmaster Tools provides information on duplicate title tags, meta descriptions, or other on-page errors that may creep into the search index. Running through this list will provide you with some idea of the issues you have HTML-wise throughout your site. Again, this report is typically not all-encompassing, but it's a good start to finding what is potentially broken in your HTML.

Once you have gotten comfortable with Webmaster Tools, utilizing SEOmoz's Pro Dashboard (Figure 13-2) can provide you with a bit more insight into the errors in your site, and the pages with the highest volume of errors. The dashboard gives you a quick view of how many errors and warnings you have on your site. Depending on your subscription, you will find that your crawl limit to site size ratio impacts how many errors you find. Working through the SEOmoz report helps you find duplicate content, page titles, and more. The reports go deeper than what Webmaster Tools offers and provide much more detailed feedback.

Figure 13-1. Google Webmaster Tools crawl errors report

Another option is IIS SEO Toolkit. The Toolkit spiders your site and can capture what it finds to files for viewing after. For large sites, you may end up with hundreds of megabytes of data with this option turned on. For exceptionally large sites, you may end up with gigabytes of data. If you find your site has a large number of HTTP 500 errors, you may want to enable this feature to capture the pages to see where they are failing. The reports can be exported out into spreadsheets that can be easily sorted and ordered. Looking for duplicate title tags, long page titles, broken links, and more can help you evaluate how many errors you truly have site-wide.

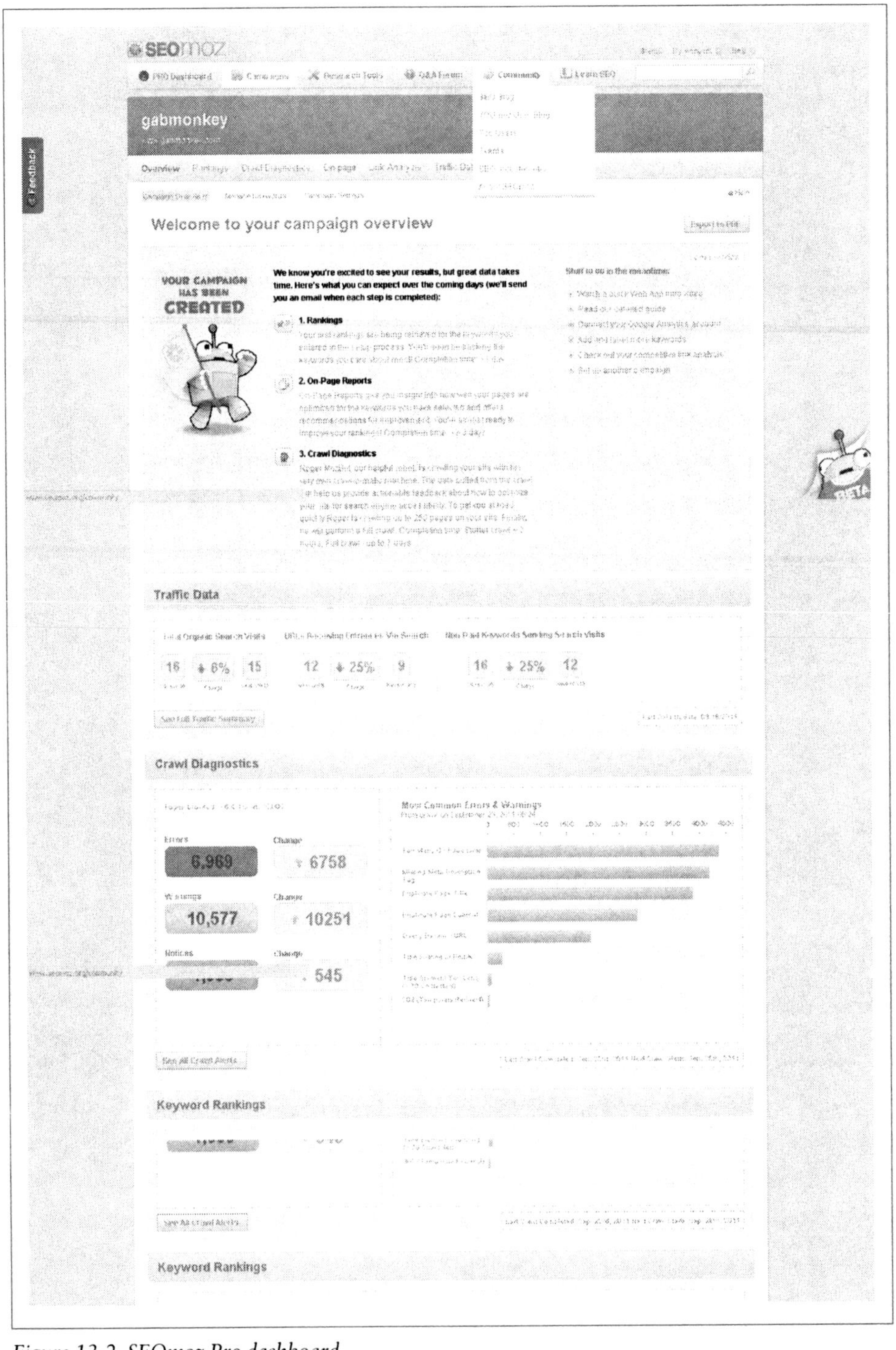

Figure 13-2. SEOmoz Pro dashboard

How to Audit a Page for SEO Elements

Looking at how and what you can automate is a great start, but the real meat of running audits comes from action. Once you get a feel for how to set up your audit, you will need to take action on the results. A spider or bot can offer suggestions. What you will want to do is develop an SEO checklist of items you feel are important. You may want to add other items particular to your website and needs, but here is a basic checklist to get you started:

- Page title is appropriate, with correct keywords.
- URL is appropriate.
- H1 tags are present and contain keywords.
- H2-H6 are utilized on the site.
- Content on the page is relevant to the targeted keywords.

The fifth item here is something a bot may never catch. Read your content to validate that it is relevant to expected search terms, and to ensure it is clean and free of typos. Content validation is one thing that cannot be fully automated; even with tools that can provide some measurement of the relevancy of your pages to LDA or LSI algorithms, you should still review your content to ensure that a human reading that content will be able to make sense of it.

Section 508, Applying to SEO Audits

Section 508 is an amendment to the Rehabilitation Act passed by the US Congress. It essentially makes it a law that all websites in the United States must be accessible to disabled citizens. Regardless of which country you are in this, this act has had a positive effect on the ability to audit pages from an SEO standpoint. The process of verifying that a site meets 508 accessibility guidelines fortunately overlaps significantly with the audits we need to perform on a page or website to ensure that a spider or bot can parse and interpret the page. You can find the full 508 standards on the 508 website, at *http://www.section508.gov/*.

There are several options for 508 auditing, including browser plug-ins and tools to automate checking. Doing a simple search for "section 508 validation" will turn up lots of results, as will going to the 508 website, and looking through the section on tools and resources. There are three things 508 auditing tools can do for you that are useful from a search standpoint: check images for *alt* attributes, verify that your document is semantically marked up, and check that your content is parseable by screen readers in an intelligent way.

If your company does have an accessibility team, you may be able to partner up with them to find out what may be broken from both an accessibility and a search standpoint. Working with your accessibility team can also allow you to remain focus on optimizing, while they focus on ensuring readability.

HTML to Look For

Your audit process should be easy to run through for anyone conducting the audit. A good HTML checklist should look something like Table 13-1. Completing the checklist may require a simple yes/no for compliancy, or you can provide rankings based on a score of 1–100, A–F, etc. You can also use this model for creating an overall audit of a website. For a detailed site audit plan, Danny Dover provides a comprehensive list of factors to consider in *Search Engine Optimization Secrets* (Wiley).

Table 13-1. Page checklist

Criteria	Compliant?
Is there a title tag?	
Is the title tag about 10 words or less?	
Do the keywords for the page appear through the body of the text?	
Is there a canonical link?	
Is the language specified in a content-language meta tag?	
Is there a robots.txt?	
Is there an H1 tag?	
Do any of the keywords appear in the H1 tag?	
Are there appropriate uses of <B>, <I>, <EM>, and <strong> tags throughout the page, depending on the version of HTML or XHTML in use?	
Do image tags have alt attributes?	
Do image tags have title attributes?	
Are abbreviations wrapped with the appropriate <abbr> tag?	
Are videos embedded correctly and is there supporting text?	
Is there Flash on the page? If so, is there alternate content?	
Are the files and folders named appropriately for where the files are stored?	

A simple checklist like this can be worth a lot when you need to have multiple people checking pages and validating whether or not they pass the audit or not. Requiring a paper trail including the page audited and a list of issues identified makes tracking problems much easier as well. As in all other forms of analytics, consistency is key when running site audit reports. Why would looking for an H1 tag on one page but not another be OK? Defining what your key on-page issues are and running this report consistently should result in not just an improvement in SEO traffic, but an improvement in conversions as well.

The reason I say you should see an improvement in conversions is that by looking at the page and the elements you will be verifying not just that all the right tags are there, but that the right content is there as well. By ensuring that your pages have the correct content for a relevant search, you should naturally see improvements in landing page conversion rates. If you do not, you need to figure out what the correct thing to have on that page is, because what you have is obviously not it.

Looking at your pages in HTML format can give you a good idea of how the engines see them—no graphics, no videos, just text content. Turning off CSS for a page can also help you to see how the document flows (so, something like Figure 13-3 becomes something like Figure 13-4). A good plug-in to use for this is the web developers plug-in for Firefox and Chrome.

Figure 13-3. CSS enabled

Figure 13-4. CSS disabled

Taking this a step further, we would also want to turn off JavaScript to verify that the page functions the way we expect it to. There should still be a usable page sitting under all of your styling code and scripting. If you yourself have a hard time using the page, a spider or bot will have a significantly harder time interpreting the data correctly. Determining usability for both man and machine is important as part of your site audit.

As you run through your HTML audit, you should be tracking content and visibility issues as well. For example, do your headers not seem to pop on a page? Perhaps this is an opportunity to try some A/B testing to see if making certain elements bolder will help call attention to content on the page. Using CSS means you can make any element look however you need it to look. There is no rule that says H1 tags must be visually bolder than H2 tags. Ideally the content in your H1 tag is the main focus of the page, but modifying styles can give very different visual cues to people looking at your site. As you run your HTML tests, keep a note of what else it may make sense to look at from a conversion standpoint.

Auditing a Page for Engagement Tracking

We've talked about engagement at a page level; however, there should be engagement across a site as well. Segmentation of your site is critical. You should know the different ways in which to slice your data, especially if you are responsible for measurement. Segmenting traffic is not simply about segmenting based on user features, but on-site features as well. Segments can be aligned to internal business goals, departments, product lines, or anything else that makes sense.

By segmenting your site, you can start to get a better idea of engagement as well. Different segments should have different engagement exceptions. Some of these engagements may be:

- Content consumption
- Product purchase
- Social engagement
- File download
- Push notification signup (email, RSS, Twitter, Facebook, etc.)
- Any part of the purchase cycle

Segmented users may have different engagements with your site. For example, users who are looking for product support may consume content, download a file, and sign up for email notifications about updates, while a user looking to purchase a product may download a coupon, ask for opinions or read reviews, and potentially purchase online as well.

Tracking each key interaction holistically can give you an idea of where your site excels and where it is weak. For example, how do you know if your lead generation is strong but your online sales are poor? To track this, you need to set up KPIs for these interactions and measure the engagement. Users coming from search can also be segmented based on the keywords they come through on. The difference of tracking a normal user from a search user is that you get one more data point, which is the word referral to the site. Segmenting by keyword can also help to define intent; for instance, we can look at segmenting users who are "purchasers" and those who are "information seekers."

The easiest way to start to pare down the keywords is to work backwards. Start with the action. So, if we're looking at purchasing, what are all the terms that drove people to make a purchase? There should be a top set of words; you can take the top half, top two-thirds, or whatever seems to make sense based on volumes that convert to a sale.

Now you do the same for people who came in looking for information and signed up for a newsletter. Again, establish what the top terms are. Once you have your two sets of words, you may need to look for duplicate terms (Figure 13-5). Is there anything that crosses over into both segments? These can be considered *cusp words,* meaning users could go either way on them. This third bucket can then be broken down based on volumes (bearing in mind that users may have come to the site for other reasons as well).

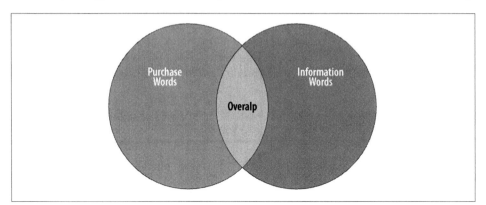

Figure 13-5. Keyword overlap by segment

Once you have built up your keyword lists, you can look at how many of the people who came to your site on each of these terms completed an action. Further, if you build up a set of keywords you expect to be associated with each of these actions, you can validate whether those words are in the other lists. As you process the data, you will want to look at CTR versus conversion rate. You know which words drive people to these pages, but how many people came to your site on those terms? We've been looking at the segment of our user population who came to the site and completed some key action. But what about other users who came to the site on those same terms but didn't complete an action? What we don't know is the conversion rate among all the people who came to the site on those keywords. Working back, we can look at how many people total entered the site on these terms, and then calculate the engagement rate by dividing the total number of conversions on these keywords by the total number of visits they generated across the site. You can look at this data as either a whole or word by word. What this provides you with is a baseline of what is already happening on your site, and how efficiently it's happening.

Many people get caught up in trying to measure what is *not* happening. Instead, in this example our goal is to look at something that *is* happening and figure out if it is happening as efficiently as possible. You may also find that your overlap words start to paint a different picture when you looking at those words by conversion rate for each of the key engagements. Knowing what is engaging and how successfully will help you understand the segments across your site, and may alert you when something is off; for example, if sales suddenly dip, you can look at your historical data to determine what is going wrong, and where.

Performance Monitoring: The Speed of Your Pages

Page load time is critical to both customers and search. The Aberdeen Group ran a study in 2008 that showed that a one-second delay in page load time can result in a 7% decrease in conversions (*http://www.aberdeen.com/Aberdeen-Library/5136/RA -performance-web-application.aspx*). Page speed is also a ranking factor utilized by Google—it's not a dominant ranking factor, but it is certainly a confirmed ranking factor.

Page speed is impacted by several things:

- Page weight
- HTTP requests
- Image sizes
- Database connections
- Complex table structures
- Uncompressed documents

Page weight is critical to maintaining good download speeds. Sites that are well-built using CSS and minimal images to reduce overall page weight will have significantly lower download times than sites with lots of big images. Ensure that all your framework images are as small as possible before even attempting to address any other issues. Reducing the overall size of your framework will be your first goal if you're looking to speed up your pages. Most web browsers will provide a page weight, and you can utilize plug-ins to benchmark page download times and page weights.

Beyond page weight, there are a variety of issues that may impact page speed. One quick way of assessing these issues is to use YSlow (Figure 13-6), which is a plug-in for Firefox from Yahoo!. It provides a report card–like result set that grades your page's performance on a number of measures you can take to improve your speed, and indicates what you can or need to do to improve the speed. The report is a very thorough analysis of all the elements that you need to consider.

Figure 13-6. YSlow analysis report

The following sections outline some best practices for improving your page speed. By following each of these steps and auditing your pages for these elements, you should be able to bring down page load speeds as much as possible. If you find you have a problem in one of these areas, you need to address the seriousness of it and determine whether the impact is to a single page or across the site. By improving page load times, you can improve both your SEO standing and the usability of your site.

Make Fewer HTTP Requests

Reducing HTTP requests can be done by combining files (such as JavaScript and CSS files) into single files, as well as creating image sprites (Figure 13-7). The term *sprite* refers to a collection of images placed in a single image file; instead of having to load a separate file for each image, you load the single file once and display only a section of it at a time to the user, using CSS. By combining all the images on a page into a single file you can reduce the number of HTTP requests for images significantly. This technique is typically applied for smaller images.

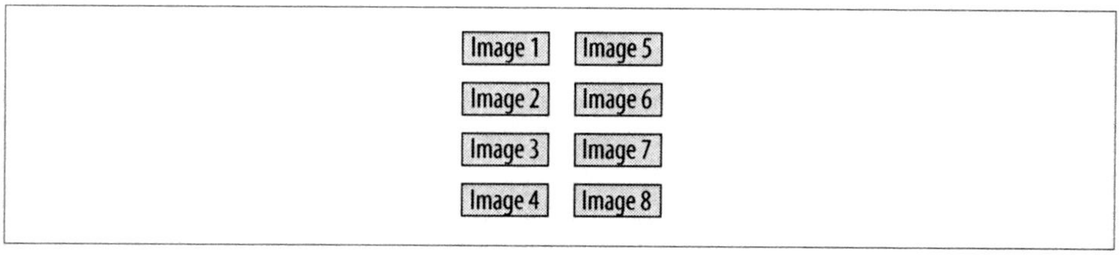

Figure 13-7. Image sprite example

Use a Content Delivery Network (CDN)

Content delivery networks, or CDNs, provide globally hosted servers that can serve up content based on proximity to a user. Akamai is perhaps the largest and most well-known provider of CDNs. CDNs are typically used by companies that are operating at a global level and have large customer bases, and your budget may not stretch to this. If you cannot afford a CDN service, don't worry too much about it.

Avoid Empty src or href

Removing the value of a *src* or *href* attribute and leaving it empty may seem like an OK way to remove content or links quickly—but in reality, some browsers may still make a request for an empty file to the directory the page is found in. Every HTTP request made translates into a slowdown in page speed. Needless requests can impact your page performance overall, and should be avoided.

Add Expires Headers

Expires headers tell web browsers how long they should cache a page for. The first time a user visits a site it may be slow to load, but components with an expires header will be cached and pulled from the cache instead of via a server request on the next page view. Expires headers can apply to images, JavaScript and CSS files, and any other content that may be static on your pages.

Put CSS at Top

CSS should be placed at the top of a page so the browser knows how to style the page as it is loaded; CSS acts as the guide for how everything should appear as the page unfolds during its download to the web browser. Well-formed and optimized CSS can be used to position sprites and reduce the number of HTTP requests the page makes.

Put JavaScript at Bottom

JavaScript should run at the bottom of the page. The challenge with JavaScript is that they do not run asynchronously—that is to say, they do not download alongside other files. Rather, pages may come to a pause as they have to parse JavaScript in the header, or inline. By placing the JavaScript code at the bottom, you allow most of the content to render before slowing the page down. You can also include a "defer" command in your JavaScript as follows:

```
<script type="text/JavaScript" src="http://www.domain.com/script.js" defer="defer">
</script>
```

The *defer* attribute in the tag lets the browser know that the script does not render any visual code, and it can be processed at the end of the page load.

Avoid CSS Expressions

CSS expressions are a way of dynamically setting CSS properties. It can be a very time-consuming process, as the expressions must be parsed every time a page is rendered, scrolled, or resized, and as the user moves the mouse. The need to re-parse the code can slow down a page immensely even after it has loaded, and can directly impact the user experience of your site. Removing all expressions will speed up the page performance overall.

Make JavaScript and CSS External

If you make your JavaScript and CSS files external to your web page, you can then enable these files to be cached so that repeated HTTP requests do not have to be made to your code base on every page load.

Reduce DNS Lookups

Every component on your page that is hosted on a different IP address requires a DNS lookup. The DNS acts like a telephone operator connecting a nice name to an IP address, and then connecting the server to the browser. Having multiple files spread across multiple domains or IP addresses can significantly impact page speed, as each request may involve not just providing the correct content, but looking up a new IP address.

Minify JavaScript and CSS

JavaScript and CSS can both be compressed using dynamic code compression tools such as Minify (*http://www.reneschmidt.de/tools/index.php/minify/*) and JSLint (*http://jslint.com/*). CSS files typically do not shrink as well as JavaScript files, and you have to be careful of rewriting code that may break something. If you use these tools, you'll have to do massive testing and quality assurance after running files through the minifying process.

Avoid URL Redirects

SEOs are always talking about 301 redirects, and looking for 302 redirects. It's easy to forget that redirects take a toll on the server: on each request a file must be parsed looking for redirects. Furthermore, each 301 redirect does not pass on the directs to another page; you can see little bits of PageRank slowly leak out. If there are too many redirects, the search bot may not bother indexing the redirect page at all and drop it from its directory. You can look for nested redirects through sites like *http://www.wheregoes.com/*, which show how and where redirects occur.

Remove Duplicate JavaScript and CSS

Duplication is bad, period. If the code is already on the page, or in a file, remove the duplicated content. Anything duplicated should be safe to remove; removing comments for production code can help reduce the file size as well.

Configure Entity Tags (ETags)

ETags are server-generated unique identifiers that provide a mechanism for browsers and servers to determine whether the version of a file that a browser has in its cache is up-to-date. When changes are made to a file on a server, the server updates the file's ETag. When requesting a file, the browser passes the ETag for its currently cached version of the file along to the server in an HTTP response header. The server compares this to the tag it has stored for that file and, if they are different, sends back a fresh copy of the file. If they are the same, it sends an HTTP 304 (Not Modified) message. Because this is a modification that needs to be made at the server level, it can be tricky to implement when you're working with a server cluster. Work with your server admin to get this set up correctly.

Make AJAX Cacheable

AJAX is a way of making asynchronous calls to the web server from a web page, without changing the state of a page—which is a fancy way of saying AJAX updates a page's content from the server without reloading the entire page through JavaScript. The same rules that apply to making other content cacheable apply to AJAX calls as well. Enabling caching of content pulled through AJAX will speed up the requests that are repeated for content already delivered. You may need to work with both your coders and your server admin team to perfect this.

Use GET for AJAX Requests

Using a GET instead of a POST when making AJAX calls can speed up the time between requests, as a GET requires only one call sensing both the headers and data, while a POST sends the headers, and then sends the data separately. Some web browsers limit URL length to 2 KB, though, so you may need to make a judgment call based on the AJAX request on the page.

Reduce the Number of DOM Elements

The Document Object Model (DOM) is a description of a web page at a code level. The more objects a document has in it, the more complex the page becomes. Every image, paragraph, and other HTML element on a page creates a new document object. A simplified DOM means an easier page to parse for both the web browser and your scripts.

Avoid HTTP 404 (Not Found) Errors

A 404 error is when a document is not found. A web page may render correctly but request a 404 as well. This can happen with broken images, or external JavaScript or CSS files that have been deleted or are missing. 404 requests can be slow, and as we know we should be working to reduce the total number of HTTP requests. Ensuring there are no broken elements on a page will quickly fix page-loading issues and will most likely make sure the page acts as intended. A working page is a page that makes the customer happy, and happy customers spend money and come back.

Reduce Cookie Size

Cookies are used to store variables from a user. Every time a cookie is requested or set it must be parsed, and the larger the cookie is, the longer it will take to read or write. Limit the use of cookies to only what is needed, to improve page performance and speed.

Use Cookie-Free Domains

Browser requests for static files such as images can sometimes be accompanied by cookies that are sent for no good reason and that slow down your web page. To keep your main domain cookie-free, you can create a separate domain for your images, or, if you have not set cookies on your root domain, you can create a subdomain to host your images from. For example, if you do not have cookies set for *domain.com*, you can use *images.domain.com* to serve your images. However, if you have set cookies for *domain.com*, you will have issues, and you will need to set up a different domain for image hosting.

Avoid AlphaImageLoader Filter

The AlphaImageLoader filter is an IE filter that tries to fix issues to do with showing alpha channels on PNG files. The problem with this filter is that it stops the browser while the image is being downloaded to render it correctly. This can result in a significant hit to your page load time, depending on the image size.

Do Not Scale Images in HTML

Images should be sized appropriately, and the size should be the same as what is used in the HTML of the page. Images should not be resized through HTML, as this can result in larger images being scaled down while the file size remains larger than needed. Resize all your images in an external photo editor and then place them in your HTML using the same width and height you specified in your image editing software.

Make Favicon Small and Cacheable

The Favicon is a small icon associated with your site that shows up in the browser bar, and sometimes in the favorites tool bar or bookmarks list. The icon is requested by the browser automatically, so even creating a blank icon can help speed up requests by avoiding a 404 error. The *favicon.ico* file resides in the website's root folder and should be small and cacheable.

Detecting Template Issues Versus Page Issues

If you are dealing with a content management system (CMS), or simply working with generic templates that utilize server-side includes, you will want to look for and be able to identify where search issues may arise. To audit for these issues you will need a working understanding of your site, but even without one you may be able to guess as to which issues are template-driven versus page-driven.

During your page audits to look at improving page speed, or on-page tags, you may start to see patterns. If every page has the exact same issue, this is typically a good indicator of a template-driven problem. The good thing is that fixes to template-driven problems are usually fairly easy to implement, and you may be able to fix all the pages at once. Working with your IT team, you should be able to get these sorts of issues fixed quickly.

The bigger challenge you are more likely to run into with templates is when the issue is not repetitive in the sense of every page having the same issue, but in the sense of every page having an issue that is not identical but that occurs in a specific location. Let's use title tags as an example. Every page has to have a title tag. However, you may find that the titles on the pages are poorly written. Some CMS systems may pull title tags from another element on the page, such as an H1 tag, or from an internal naming convention that is not very helpful. For example, you may see something like "2342pr ACME product," where the numbers are a product SKU and this is followed by the company name. This isn't very keyword-rich or beneficial from an SEO standpoint, but the real problem lies in the CMS.

Fixing these issues may be difficult, and in some cases they may be almost impossible to fix without major code rewriting. CMS selection is a critical decision any company must make. Ideally, the CMS should be flexible, and the search team lead should be able to give some input when the selection is made. However, the reality is that you may need to deal with any number of configurations, and when you do, it will require diligence and highly coordinated efforts with your IT teams.

Decide exactly what it is you need output in your content, and document the format and how the content should be positioned; also be prepared to create content that must use certain consistent parameters. To return to our page title issue, you may find that you have to create a set of rules such as "Keyword - Product name - Company Name", where the last two elements are autogenerated, and the first can be configurable but may default to a specific keyword if not defined. The rules you generate can then be applied by your IT team, once they understand the specifics of what you are looking for.

Auditing a Page for Keywords

As you audit your pages, you'll want to look at the keyword presence on each page. Keyword density is an old way of looking at the relevancy of a page to a specified word or term. Some still use this metric as it's easy to understand, and some use tools that take the keywords and apply a weight based on the HTML tags they are positioned in. For example, Kgen (*https://addons.mozilla.org/en-us/firefox/addon/kgen/*), a plug-in for Firefox, allows for capturing keyword clouds on a page. You can edit the configuration of Kgen to apply more weight to words that are in the title tag, or H1 or other tags throughout your document, and this will give you an idea of which words are more predominant on a page.

Today's search algorithms are much more sophisticated than this, though. There are theories on the use of LDA, LSI, pLDA, HTMM, and Google's pattern on Phrase Based Indexing and Retrieval (YaPaIR). There are a variety of ways to run information retrieval from a search database; the SEOs are always trying to break the code, while the engines are always trying to perfect it and reduce spam.

SEOs are constantly trying to figure out what algorithms may be in use, but these algorithms are constantly evolving: Google claims to change its more than once a day, or more than 400 times a year. Even if we could figure out what the base algorithm was, we know that it will have since been tweaked to improve results, reduce spam, and offer a better variety of choices and better interpretation of some results. From an SEO standpoint, this means we cannot rely fully on any keyword tool to tell us if this page should rank highly, as the algorithm used will be different from Google's and Bing's.

SEOmoz has created a tool (Figure 13-8) for measuring the relevancy of a page based on LDA that is currently in a labs format at *http://www.seomoz.org/labs/lda*. This tool provides an idea of relevancy based on sampling and the keyword selection you make, rather than doing a simple keyword density check. Further, the sophistication of the search engines is such that they are now recognizing variations of words and topical themes of words, so when looking at why a page ranks as it does we must consider not only keywords but inbound links, the relevancy of the pages that link to it, and their topical models as well, which is why it's important to have a solid site information architecture, to help define the hierarchy of pages and topics.

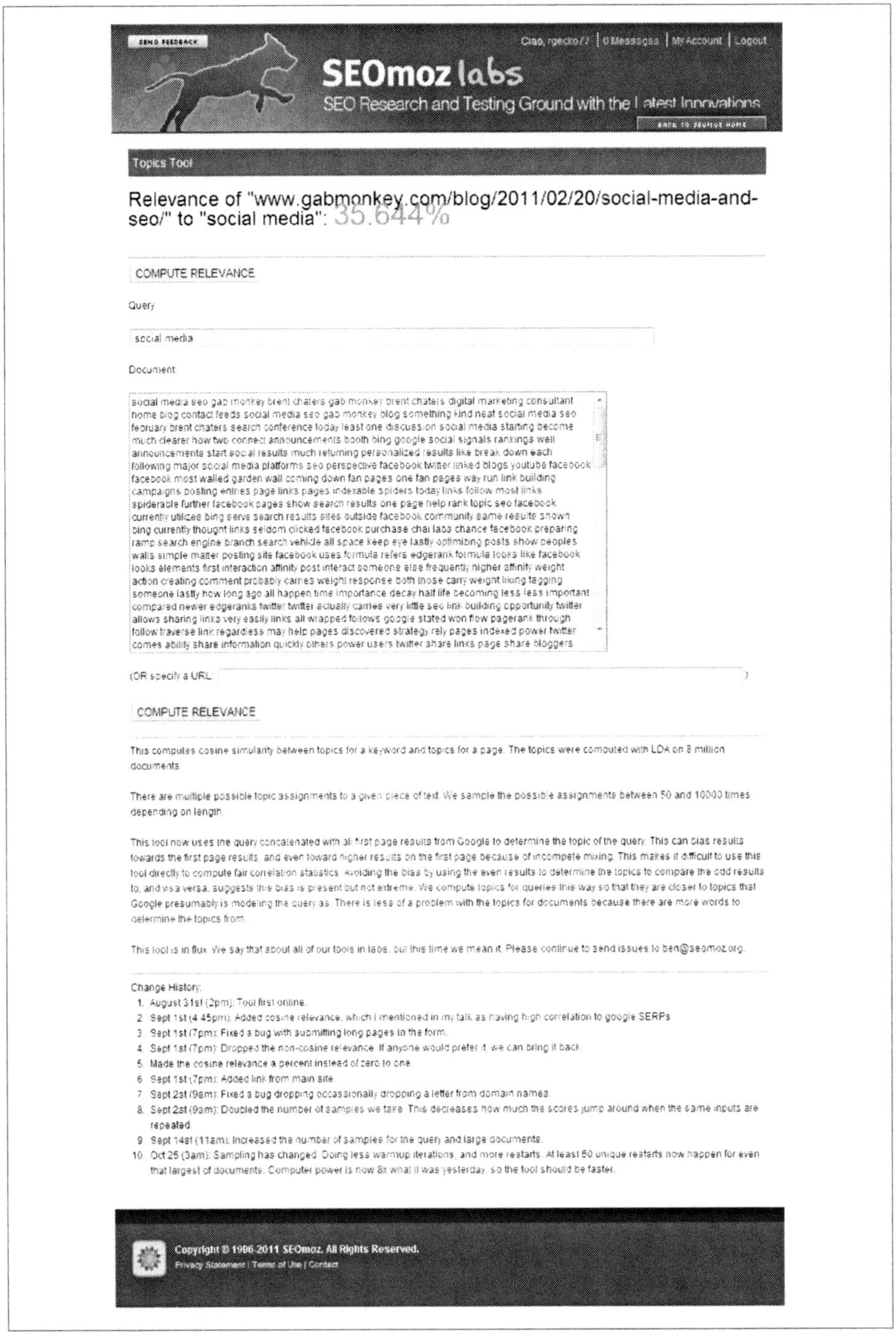

Figure 13-8. LDA topic tool

Auditing a Page for Placement in Your Site's Information Architecture

Information architecture has to do with the linking of pages and how they relate to each other, and with creating a defined categorization of pages and topics to improve the navigation and usability of your website. Information architecture also impacts your SEO, as top-level pages should rank better than deeper pages. The challenge most websites face is that the pages that you say are the most important are not necessarily defined based on site linkages as the most important. Figure 13-9 shows an example of how linkages, both on-site, and off-site, can show which pages are important. The home page, symbolized by the house, links to products, support, and services, while the deeper pages have many links from products, as well as back links to the product page. There are actually very few links to the home page in this site. From a search perspective, the only indicator that the home page is the home page may be that it sits in the root of the site and is named *index.html*.

The product page is likely to be perceived as the most important page, and therefore likely to rank better than other pages on the site. This may or may not be the desired outcome, as it may just be a listing of many different products that should be categorized and separated out further and that does not in itself offer much value. The links to and from other pages define the relevancy of each page. Google's original algorithm was based on the principle that each link to a page is like a vote: the more votes a page gets, the more weight it carries, and the more weight it carries, the stronger its votes are. The same applies to links within your site.

You may not be able to control external links to your site (although you can investigate them and engage in link-building campaigns, as we discussed in Chapter 9), but you certainly control the link structure within your site, and you should be able to validate that the link structure supports your view of which should be the top linked (most important) pages. You may be surprised to learn that some pages you think are top pages are in fact not. The home page typically carries the most weight, as it by default represents your website, so even if it does not have a large number of inbound links it will show up for searches that are topically related to your content, but where the engines cannot determine which page is the best fit.

The IIS SEO Toolkit allows for spidering of a site to find out which pages have the most inbound links (Figure 13-10). You can find the most linked pages under the Links tab. When you view this report you will get a much better overview of how your sitenu truly ranks from a numerical standpoint. Simple numbers will tell you which pages have the most inbound links in your site, and therefore are most likely seen as the most relevant pages on your site. It's a difficult task to sculpt link structure through a site, but if you're wondering why a specific page does not rank for a term, bear in mind that it may be because you are your own worst enemy and have defined a poor link structure throughout the site. In Figure 13-10, the contact page is the most linked-to page, along with the about page. This may or may not be a good thing, depending on the goal of the site. In this case I do want the about and contact pages to be the most relevant of all pages, and therefore the most findable through the site. Every page should have a link to those pages.

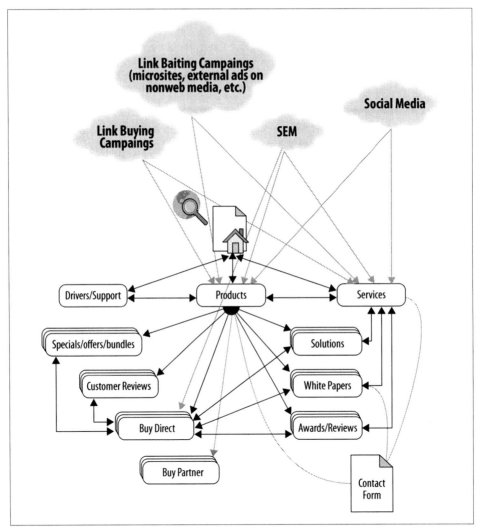

Figure 13-9. Information architecture

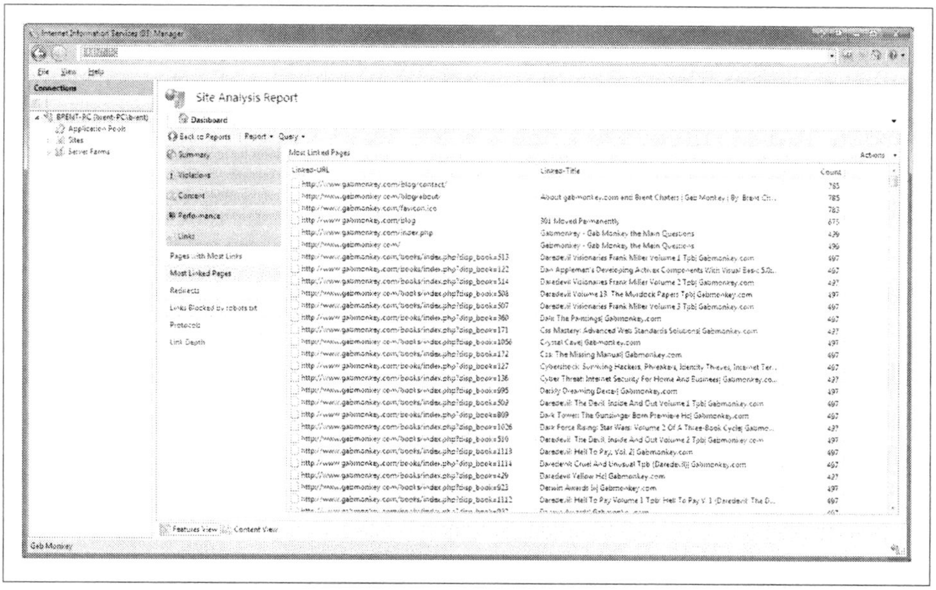

Figure 13-10. IIS SEO Toolkit most linked pages report

Finding the Bad Stuff—404s, 302s, Multiple 301s, and More

The last sitewide issue you will need to deal with is finding all the bad stuff on your site such as, 404s, 302s, and multiple 301s. The IIS SEO Toolkit (http://www.iis.net/download/SEOToolkit) can provide some insight into these issues as well. When you run your report you can look for broken links, 302s, and pages blocked by *robots.txt*. You can also scan for long titles, missing *alt* attributes, nonrelevant link text, invalid markup, and more. Running this scan can help you trap major errors, and it should become habit.

Once a month, set aside a day or two as site health days. These days will be fully dedicated to site-wide cleanup. You may not be able to fix everything, but by dedicating some time to these fixes every month, you can get your entire team to jump in and help minimize the errors throughout the site. If everyone sets out to fix a few pages, update a few titles, add some *alt* attributes, and so on, you will see improvements in your site, particularly through *long tail* searches. The issues you fix can help you send clearer signals to the engines about the relevancy of your page.

The IIS SEO Toolkit should become a common utility in your arsenal of search audit tools. Running site audits and tackling pages with the most breaks will pay dividends over the long run. You may also identify issues on some of your more important pages; you should be scanning for this on a regular basis to ensure your site does not have major breaks that can impact revenue generation.

Beyond the typical page issues, you are very likely to run into two major SEO issues: Flash and AJAX. If your site relies heavily on one of these technologies, it can quickly become the bane of your existence. The search engines are getting better at parsing and interpreting Flash and AJAX, but they still cause problems, for the following reasons:

- Deep linking is difficult.
- It can be difficult to interpret the content, depending on how it is generated.
- It's difficult to understand the information architecture.
- It's difficult to extract semantic information and relevancy from the documents.

Dealing with Flash

Flash as a technology has been around for a very long time. It became a favorite of many website designers because it allowed for rich media and animation to be easily brought to the presentation layer of a website. The challenge of Flash is that the files generated are compiled in a nonsemantic structure. Even if the Flash file uses XML to generate its content, the file may appear empty when parsed.

Search engines have been working with Adobe, the developer of Flash, to better index Flash content, but the results are spotty at best. Your site audits should include finding all Flash elements, and then making a decision about what content is in the Flash files and whether or not it potentially not being indexed will have an impact on your overall site content and semantics. If the content in the Flash file is relevant and rich content that would do wonders for your SEO programs, you may want to reconsider how you present this content.

There is now an alternative to Flash: HTML5. With HTML5 we can reproduce many of the techniques that Flash provided, with semantics that search engines can understand. The challenge of HTML5 is that it requires more work to ensure cross-browser functionality, something you don't have to worry about with Flash. All that matters with Flash is whether the plug-in to parse it is installed. This, however, does mean that on Apple mobile devices there is no way to view Flash content, as Apple has refused to support Flash on its iPhone and iPad products.

To give you a better understanding of how a search engine may interpret your Flash content, Adobe has created the Flash search engine SDK. Information on it can be found at *http://www.adobe.com/devnet/flashplayer/articles/swf_searchability.html*. The SDK will help engines better parse and interpret Flash content, but the engines' integration of this technology has been spotty at best. If in doubt, leave Flash out.

Dealing with AJAX

AJAX, like Flash, has issues with being parsed and interpreted. The upside to AJAX is that you can work around the limitations without impacting your AJAX application. Because with AJAX there will likely be some sort of server-side scripting present, you may have more options (e.g., using server-side scripting to maintain variables and information while changing page state, as opposed to having a page that is asynchronous). The only time you may not have an option is if your application is using XML or external RESTful systems to feed content. If, however, the code is on your site and you have a server scripting language at your disposal, you can create a site that allows for graceful degradation.

"Graceful degradation" means that the site will still be usable even if JavaScript is disabled. By building your scripts in such a way as to still create unique URLs, you can at least make for a spiderable site. Further, you can generate sitemaps to help the engines find your deeper content. The major issue you will run into is that most links to your pages will link to the main page, unless you also address this.

Google introduced a standard for making AJAX applications crawlable in 2009 (*http://code.google.com/web/ajaxcrawling/docs/getting-started.html*), and Bing has recently announced its support for this format *(http://searchengineland.com/bing-now-supports-googles-crawlable-ajax-standard-84149)*. The scheme uses specially formatted URLs, allowing for your AJAX application to have separate URLs for each section of the site, while still remaining a stateless page. This format is not applicable to other search engines yet, but larger sites such as Twitter have already started to adopt it. When running your site audits, look for AJAX and verify that the correct URL formats are used. As the URL formats are still developing, this process will likely require a manual audit, but you may be able to have a developer who knows the site well create a tool that will help you audit your site for AJAX code, to help speed up your audit times and boost your success rate for identifying pages.

Detecting Duplicate Content

There are some tools that will help you do this. One option (available only for Windows 7) is the IIS SEO Toolkit, which can be found at *http://www.iis.net/download/SEOToolkit*. There are a couple of quirks when setting it up:

1. To turn on IIS in Windows 7, go to "Control Panel"→"Programs"→"Turn Windows Features on or off."

2. Ensure that under "Internet Information Services"→"World Wide Web Services"→"Application Development Features," everything is selected (Figure 13-11).

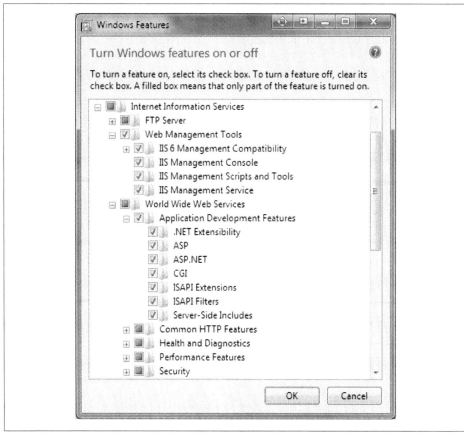

Figure 13-11. Setting up IIS for the SEO Toolkit (step 2)

3. Go to *http://www.iis.net/download/SEOToolkit* to install the toolkit.

4. To access the toolkit from your Start menu, choose "IIS 7.0 Extensions" → "Search Engine Optimization (SEO) Toolkit" (Figure 13-12).

5. Under "Management," locate "Search Engine Optimization."

6. You should now be able to click "create a new analysis" and run the spider.

After the spider has run, a report will be generated. Select "Content" (Figure 13-13) and you will see several options to track duplicate files, titles, descriptions, and keywords. The most important here will be files and titles. Duplicate files are identified using a hash sum check. If there has been even one minor change, the hash sums will not be identical and the pages will not be identified as duplicate. If you are still seeing duplicate file issues on your site after running this check, you may have to do some more digging, either manually or using a paid solution.

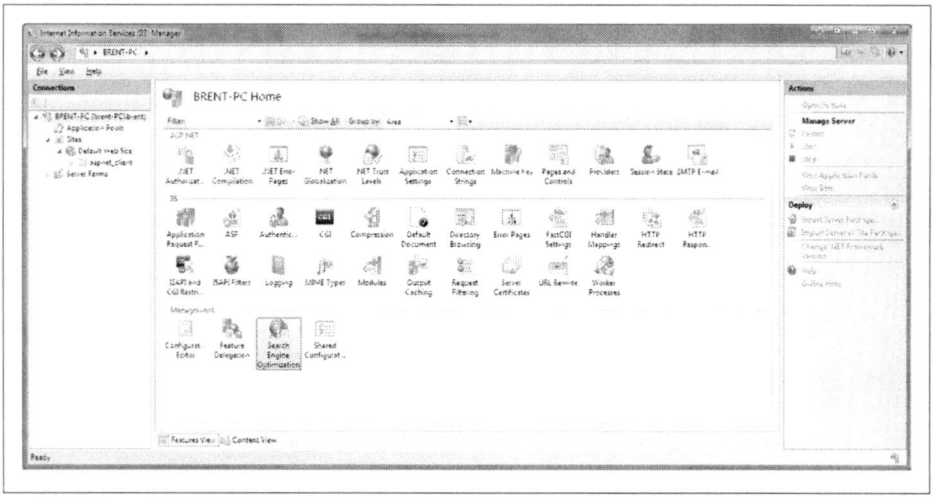

Figure 13-12. Launching the SEO Toolkit

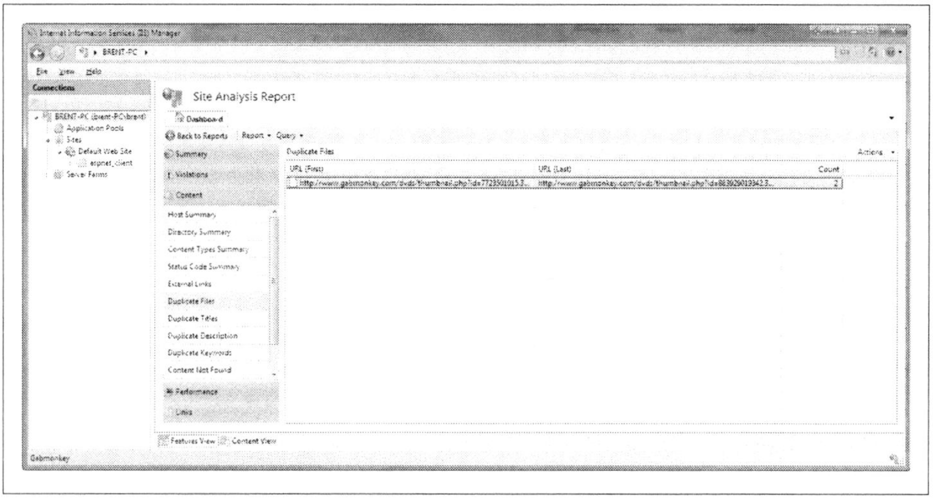

Figure 13-13. IIS SEO Toolkit report screen

Validate that all your pages that appear as duplicate content are set up with the correct canonical tags. You can also create a self-referencing canonical tag on the page you are going to optimize, to ensure that any variations of that URL for tracking purposes are also canonicalized back to the correct page. Just don't make a self-referencing URL for every variation of the same URL—for example, *www.domain.com/goodpage.html* and *www.domain.com/goodpage.html?tracking=campaign* should both get the same canonical tag that points to *www.domain.com/goodpage.html*. In addition, if anyone scrapes your site, and they are not savvy enough to remove the canonical tag, it will provide reference to your site as being the authoritative site (i.e., providing the engine with an indication of orginal authorship).

 A canonical tag is a way of strongly suggesting to a search engine how to deal with duplicate pages. For example, a search engine may recognize the URLs *www.some-url.com/webpage.html* and *www.some-url.com/webpage.html?cid=campaign-name* as different, while really the "cid" parameter is just code we've appended to the URL to track campaign data from other sites. The pages are for all intents and purposes the same page, but to a search engine the URLs appear to be different.

The issue here is that with organic rankings, the engine may split page rank and other ranking factors across the two pages, or it may choose to display the unfriendly URL rather than the more friendly URL, causing potentially inflated numbers for your campaign, as well as lower click-throughs if the URL appears untrustworthy due to the extra formatting it contains.

You can take back control by utilizing a canonical tag to suggest which page should be given preference over the other.

The tag, when implemented, is placed in the header of your HTML document and looks like this:

```
<link rel="canonical" href="http://www.example.com/product.php" />
```

This will help eliminate any page rank splitting or duplicate content issues you may have with your current site. This is the first step of cleaning up your pages and should be done regardless of any other optimizations.

 When using a canonical tag, make sure you are not setting it to point to the same URL. While the engines are supposed to take it as a suggestion and be able to determine duplicate content, there have been reports documented of this not being the case, and websites losing ranking on pages due to misuse of the canonical tag.

Concluding Thoughts

Site audits are a critical component of site optimization that any search person should be prepared to run. While some may argue this should be the webmaster's job, the reality is that with the impact these audits can have on SEO, the more often they are done, the better, and you will want to monitor the results. New pages being produced can help drive traffic for new terms, but in your existing content you may find some hidden gems that just need a little bit of love.

Further, because the search engines are constantly updating their algorithms (and especially after the Panda release from Google, which is all about quality, fresh, original, and relevant content), you should be constantly monitoring your site and pages for links and content that may be out of date or invalid. Keep an eye on developments in ranking signals that can help improve your position in the search results. As new signals emerge—like social signals, which were irrelevant a few years ago but are becoming increasingly important to monitor and watch for—you will need to look for new tools and new ways to audit for these signals through your site.

CHAPTER 14

Dashboards and Reports

Auditors look at the top-level overview; investigators
drill into the data and provide answers.

Dashboards are tools that can provide auditor-like insights, or investigator-like insights. Which one you use and how is completely up to you. Dashboards and reports are how we bring everything together to visualize our data. In the audits we have done so far we have focused on a single component or element, and to keep things simple I have tried to keep each element separate. But the real power of analytics comes when you begin to bring data points together.

Utilizing dashboards and reports should become second nature to you. They are not only a way to present data, but a way to create an impact. Dashboarding is an art, much like presenting or any other business practice. Your dashboards and reports will be the tools you employ most successfully, and presentability is a major factor to consider. You may find that your selection of auditing tools is affected by how presentably the data is provided to you. Some people are OK with raw data and numbers, but most people are visually stimulated and can recognize patterns more easily through charts and graphs, which also create a more dramatic impact.

Tools you will need in this chapter:

- Clickstream tracking package (Google Analytics, Adobe SiteCatalyst, etc.)
- Spreadsheet program (Excel or something similar)
- Presentation software (PowerPoint or something similar)

Know Your Audience

Different people prefer different visual styles. Further, when dealing with data, different people prefer different representations of that data. Know your audience and how they prefer to see data presented. Understanding and aligning your presentation to certain individual styles will help you push your goals much further than using generic data outputs that may be fine for you, but not to the taste of your audience.

Audience engagement is critical to ensuring action takes place. Many will argue that the numbers should speak for themselves, but unfortunately this is not usually the case. Too many times, I have seen well-founded and solid data discredited because the presentation of it was muddled or poorly laid out. I have seen data thrown away because the wrong PowerPoint template was used to display it. While this may not make sense, it's a reality and is one of the challenges we face.

Some key considerations when attempting to understand your audience should be:

- Are they high-level or low-level thinkers? That is, do they look at the larger picture, or are they micromanagers, looking at the littlest details?
- How many data points can these people easily digest? Are they comfortable looking at few or many?
- Are you dealing with an individual or a committee?
- How clear is the data? Data visualization is about presenting complex data in visual formats that are easy to interpret.
- Are they raw data or visual people?
- Are there certain brand colors that clearly identify their business? If so, utilize this for color coding.

Your understanding of your audience will be critical to your success, and these questions and others can help you build up a profile of the people you will be dealing with. The rest of this chapter will help you develop skills to create data presentations that are scalable to different targets and groups.

Understand Why Data Is Important to You

Before you consider your audience, you need to understand your data yourself. Why is the data you choose important to you? Frequently, reports will include data on the number of visits or page views. Ask yourself, is this data relevant? What does it mean to me? If you are presenting an increase or decrease in number of visits, you need to be prepared to explain why this is important and why it might have occurred. If you can't answer this question for yourself, then why is this data there? You may run into instances where someone insists a data point be present, and that's fine. It is your job to then understand why it is important to them, and what it means.

Relevancy of data is critical because it means that data is actionable. If the data you provide is telling your audience that sales are up, that's fantastic news, but what has caused the increase? Is there more traffic, and therefore more sales? If so, where is this traffic coming from? Is it search related? Driven by a social media program? Or something else? Did conversion rates improve? If so, which segment of traffic is converting better now? There are a number of questions that can be asked. If it helps you formalize the data, write these questions down on a piece of paper and lead with them as you present the data.

The flow of your presentation is also important. Consider the ordering of your data elements. For example, you may start with "sales are up," leading into "sales are up because of more conversions on high-margin products." You have now given value to the first metric with a second data point. You could then follow this up with "leads for these products came from organic search." Every journalist is taught the five Ws (and one H). These are:

- Who
- What
- When
- Where
- Why
- How

This is a perfectly fine approach to follow to get an understanding of your own data. These questions will help you have more knowledge about what you are talking about, and therefore make you more confident when it comes to presenting the data.

In 2010, BuySellAds commissioned Robin Richards to create an infographic (Figure 14-1) about its growth (*http://ripetungi.com/buysellads-com-celebrating-2-years/*). This infographic displays how data and interpretation can work hand in hand. Each section could be broken up into separate sections and represented as a set of slides, or it could be embedded in an email. The point is, this imagery tells a story. It also can serve as a perfect example of how we might go about answering most of our questions.

Who Is This Data About?

Tell your audience who this data is about. What segment of your user base is represented? People looking for support? Purchasers? A certain demographic? Create a persona or profile that represents the group of people your data relates to. This will help you and your audience interpret the data, and it may also allow you to make some assumptions about your user base that will help you dig into deeper elements. Knowing the *who* will allow you to better understand the answers to the other questions.

Robin's infographic tells us who the data is about right away by introducing BuySellAds and explaining who they are (Figure 14-2).

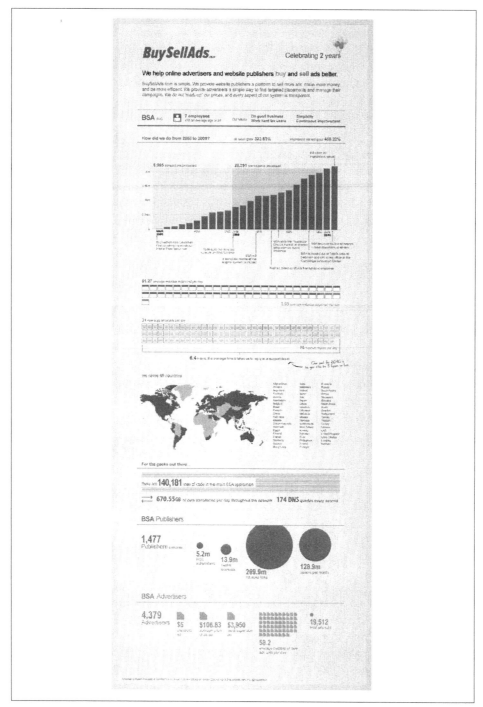

Figure 14-1. An infographic example

Figure 14-2. Who is this about? BuySellAds

What Does This Data Tell Us?

What does this data tell us? Does it tell us that something good or something bad is happening? When presenting your data points, it's important to be impartial and be prepared to present data that tells either a good story or a bad story. The *what* will usually be an indicator that the data is positive or negative. Both positive and negative data can create actionable insights. When things work well, you can look into duplicating that success in other segments of your site; when things are bad, you can identify what fixes need to be put in place immediately and learn from your failures. The saying "fail often but fail quickly" can apply to your data points. Running tests, be they A/B tests or some other form of testing, can show quickly what does or does not work, to allow you to make changes rapidly in the interests of LPO and CRO.

In some cases the *what* can be represented simply by green for good and red for bad; in other cases you may need to expand on the *what* more and provide some more detailed background. For example, if you ran an experiment on page design, you might need to present the whole experiment process, as that is what the data is about. In other instances you may simply need to show that social traffic is down and that this is now impacting SEO traffic.

Robin's infographic, as an example, uses color codes to identify how many new emails are received and how many are responded to per day (Figure 14-3). There is also a nice callout indicating what the current response time is and what the targeted time is going to be.

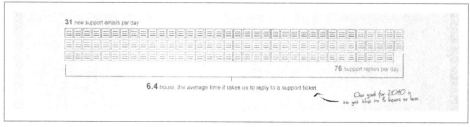

Figure 14-3. What does this tell us? It usually takes 6.4 hours to reply, and a goal is set to get this to 3 hours

When Did These Changes Occur?

Timelines are important to search traffic: as we've seen several times, seasonal factors may affect our data. The *when* may not just be the present; you may need to go back and look at historical data as well. If you have data that goes back years, you may want to look at year-over-year growth for the last 5 years. Is there a trend? Does growth occur at a rate of 5% every year? If so, 5% growth may be considered organic growth (e.g., keeping pace with natural growth in the volume of people searching), while a spike of 10% would be considered outside the norm. To identify seasonal trends you might want to break this data down further, looking at month-over-month results. For example, if you run a ski resort you will likely see a significant jump when the season opens. How does this jump compare to what you have seen in previous years, and what happens over the remainder of the season? Time frames allow you to put changes into perspective. Bear in mind, though, that these should always be specific to the question, and not necessarily to the way your business runs. For example, running reports from quarter to quarter may not be of benefit if your paid search programs do not track to the same fiscal calendar.

Robin's infographic shows a timeline with milestone callouts and volume of ad impressions shown over time (Figure 14-4). This version of a timeline with comments provides insights as to what was happening within the company over the period in question, allowing us to draw conclusions about potential causations or correlations between these changes and the growth in the number of impressions over this time period. This is a simple presentation of data that, while it may require input from other departments, tells a powerful visual story.

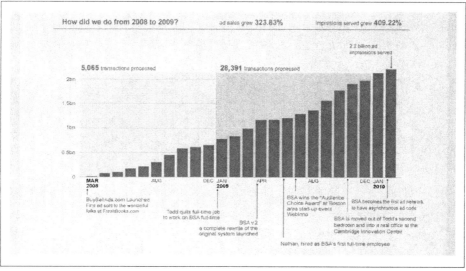

Figure 14-4. A timeline of changes

Where on Your Site Was the Impact Felt?

The analytic in question should focus around some segment of your site, be it a single page, a group of pages, or a set of desired actions. Where did you see the numbers spike? Unless it is an overall site health report or other top-level report, you need to identify the *where* of your data, making it clear which page or pages you are discussing. Even in a top-level report, you should make it clear whether the data relates to the website as a whole and, if not, identify the relevant section or sections of the site. Show what has happened in the last reporting period to those pages or segments, indicating clearly where the changes have occurred.

Robin's infographic using the timeline visualization to show where changes were made within the company (Figure 14-4) could just as easily map to changes within a website.

Why Did This Occur? Why Is This Important?

In answering the other questions, you began to construct a framework for interpreting the data you have collected. Why are we seeing this data? To answer this question, you may need to go beyond your website and investigate off-site factors (such as TV, print, or radio spots). Knowing the *why* is important as it helps people to interpret what they are seeing, understand if it's a one-time occurrence or a trend, and start to think about how they can apply what they've learned from the data.

Robin's infographic almost hides the *why*, but if you look closely you can see the company values (Figure 14-5). Why has there been success? Because of these two goals: simplicity and continuous improvement.

Figure 14-5. Mission statment and methodology behind the work

How Can We Learn from This?

How we can learn from our data is the most important question. How can the insights we gain be applied elsewhere? How can we expand on this success, or we minimize this problem? It's time to put aside your analytics hat and put on your investigator hat. You will need to be able to provide solid, concrete answers as to how to fix, expand upon, or modify the results you have presented, and this will require intimate familiarity not just with the numbers but with the background of all the elements that contributed to whatever issue it is you are covering.

The questions we've looked at should leave people with some ideas about learnings they can apply to other sections of the site, ways to make fixes or improvements, or tasks to perform. The analytics you interpret should be summed up in an actionable and understandable way. You may not have to go through each component with your audience, but as the analyst and investigator you need to be able to summarize or pull up this data to reinforce your points should questions arise.

The how is perhaps the hardest part to visualize in a presentation. It may be enough just to write down or speak to a list of points. In the case of Robin's infographic, the callouts with little arrows could be used to call out learning points and to make annotations to improve visualization of the hows.

Understand Why Data Is Important to Your Audience

Once you understand your data, you need to frame it for your audience. You may present data to your audience in any number of ways: in person, by email, over the phone, or through a webcast. Consider the medium through which you will present your data. Certain media lend themselves to brief displays with fewer points, while others enable or indeed require much more detailed briefs. If you will not be present to explain the data, you must ensure that all the fine points are covered, be it through appendixes or annotations.

If you will be presenting in person, you can adapt to your audience more naturally and engage in dialog, asking for questions and responding to individual points. However you are presenting your data, you will need to anticipate your audience. Different people may require different levels of detail. For example, an executive may simply want to know whether traffic is up or down as a whole, and why, or may be particularly interested in a single program. You may be able to consult your audience ahead of time to find out what their expectations are; this can help you create a framework for what you will be presenting.

Marketing teams may need feedback on data that justifies their budget spends; in this case, you should focus heavily on ROI. You'll want to show where ROI was maximized, which programs performed poorly and could potentially be cut, and most importantly, where you think would be a good opportunity to try something new, reinvesting savings from cuts or improvements in efficiency. Identify a couple of programs that have analytics showing some growth, but that have had little love. These may be ideal targets for investment.

You may also have to consider yourself as an audience—if you are responsible for the search programs, you may need to look at what is improving or worsening on a daily basis. Your report in this case may not have to be pretty and formalized, but it does need to be interpretable by you so that you can take action. You may look at your paid search programs daily to see which words on broad match are driving traffic to your site and which terms you might want to think about blacklisting.

Your audience and the presentation format will dictate how to present the data. In some cases you may use a full PowerPoint presentation, while in other cases you may use a Word document or an email to convey the message. How you present your data is critical to communicating your results effectively. Successful reports can provide you great satisfaction by being easy to interpret, but making a presentation can become frustrating if you have to explain your intent and what is being measured. Your ultimate goal should be creating clarity for your audience.

Segment! Segment! Segment!

Throughout this book we have looked at segmenting as a way of helping us to better understand the data we collect. The importance of segmenting cannot be stressed enough. Top-level numbers can be fantastic, but even those can be segmented out into total number of leads, total number of abandonments, and so on. As you create your dashboards, you will want to look at the parts as well as the whole picture.

Segmenting traffic is a very easy way to create actionable analytics. Segmented traffic can show which groups' needs are being met and which groups' needs are not being met. Let's say for example you have a conversion rate of 5%. Segmenting out this 5% can help us see what in these users' paths may have influenced their transactions. Are there specific pages they hit repeatedly before making a purchase? Now look at the other group, the 95% who are left. What do they not do that the 5% did do? You may need to segment in even more out-of-the-box ways. Do users on certain browsers convert more than others? You may find that people using the same browser as your developers convert at a much higher rate. If your developers only tested the site on Firefox but most of your users use a different browser (say, Internet Explorer), the poorer conversion rate for that segment of your traffic can have a serious negative impact on your sales.

This may seem like a common-sense thing that you would expect the site developers to consider, but these things often get overlooked. Segment your traffic repeatedly, and look at it in different ways. If you look at traffic that is part of your network of sites as opposed to traffic from other sites, you may find that your network traffic behaves differently from traffic from other referral sites.

Figure 14-6 shows a graph that segments out visitors who have come to the site more than five times by browser type. Most of these visitors are IE users, with some using Chrome or Opera. Our repeat visitors who are highly loyal are most likely, then, to be using IE or Chrome, and we can use this information when developing pages to ensure an optimal experience for these users, addressing any issues these browsers may have. Conversely, we may find that because our site works so well for these browsers, what we actually need to do is optimize our site for other web browsers to ensure that we aren't alienating other potential repeat customers.

The ways in which you segment your data can tell very different stories to those interpreting it. You may also find that the segments you define are open to varying interpretations, so when you do segment, make sure you are clear about it, defining exactly what the segment is and what it means. Simply saying "all SEO traffic" is not good enough; you may need to say "all SEO traffic from Google and Bing, over the last 30 days."

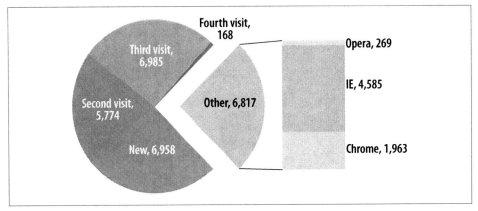

Figure 14-6. Segmenting your users

Dashboards for Executives

Executives usually require a different approach than others; they typically want to look at a top-down model to understand as much as possible at a glance. Executive dashboards present such a view. You do not have to be the CEO to see the value of an executive dashboard. Typically these dashboards are generated at a recurring interval and are circulated throughout the company. Think of it as your monthly statement of growth (or decline). Most analytics tools allow for the creation of simple executive dashboards that look pretty and offer some functionality. Google Analytics (Figure 14-7) presents an executive dashboard when you first log in, giving you a quick view of what's going on with your visitor numbers, traffic sources, goal completion, top pages, and more. This executive dashboard is a great introduction to other data points.

The executive dashboard should present at a glance enough data to spark some questions—and potentially answer some as well. In some cases the dashboard may present traffic-light indicators, where goals are red, yellow, or green. The hard numbers may be present, but at a glance, lots of green indicates everything is good, red indicates things that are bad, and yellow is designated for alerts. This formatting allows for a quick review of what is on track, what may be broken, and what should be looked at.

Color coding is such a simple way to create a dashboard that you should apply it even for your own purposes. During your own session audits, this can help you to quickly scan for anything that jumps out of the range of "good." This can be applied to conversion rates, bounce rates, traffic volumes from search, number of inbound links grown through a period of time, and many other metrics.

With executive-level data, it's also important that there is a way to drill further into the numbers. The Google Analytics format utilizes graphics to display information, without requiring a great deal of words or commentary.

Any one of these sections can be clicked on, and you may opt to include in your executive dashboard some deep dives into the data. You may want to talk about the fact that more than 70% of traffic is coming from search, while the rest is direct or from referrals. This may or may not be a good thing. There may be an opportunity to grow direct traffic, which in turn may impact organic traffic. Because this data is displayed as percentages of a pie chart, you may want to further explain that even though only 11% of traffic comes direct, that 11% accounts for over 30% of a target segment, which may be a very good thing for your company.

Executive-level data does not have to all be top-level data, but whatever you choose to include should be reported consistently on every report. You should not be making major modifications to your executive dashboard every month, or rebuilding it frequently. The goal is to create a common format for displaying what you want to convey, so you do not have to explain the general data and connections at each reporting period, but can get into the deeper segmented analysis that will enable actions to be taken.

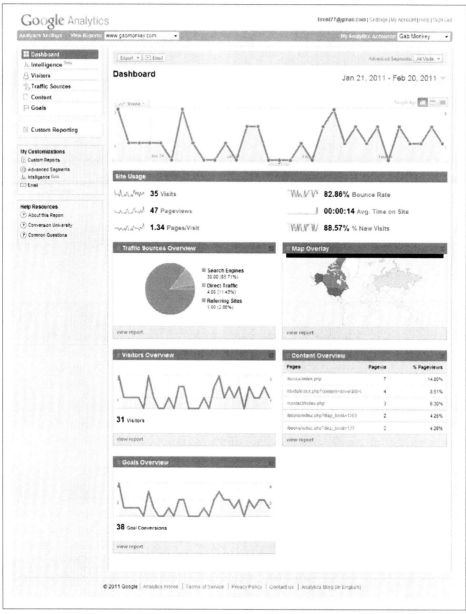

Figure 14-7. Google Analytics executive dashboard

Dashboards for Creating Action

Dashboards—even executive-level dashboards—should create action. Action is when someone sees the metrics and is able to apply them to something else, or when there is a clearly defined outcome. This may include improved funding, cutting of funds, reallocation of funds, applying practices that have proved effective to other sections of a website, and more. Your goal withanalytics is to get someone to do something.

It's a very simple concept, but all too often dashboards and reporting are so top-level or poorly explained that nobody is able to create or define an action to take. Your commentary and understanding of the numbers will be crucial to driving actions. If you cannot clearly articulate what is happening and why, you will have failed at your goal of creating useful reports.

Further, if you are creating reports that simply go into a black hole and nothing gets done, you have to ask yourself if there is any value in what you are doing. Some see sending reports that highlight key improvements as a way of self-promoting their worth; if this allows for positive investment, that alone counts as an actionable dashboard. Not getting a cut in funding may be the desired action or need, and in this case providing clear and understandable ROI metrics to reinforce the value you bring may be all that's required.

Not all actionable reports are overly complex, all-hands-on-deck-type reports; they can be simple illustrations of how to apply a lesson to multiple sections of a site. Some actions may only require the sign-off of a single manager and may be implemented in less than a day, while other analytics may bring everything to a halt and the required actions may take a great deal of time to implement. As the one creating the actionable dashboard, the onus of deciding what is important rests with you. You should be able to quickly flag both good and bad issues, and know when this data needs to be presented to other decision makers.

Actionable dashboards and reporting are not kept secret; they are open and shared. Any analytic that is kept secret will immediately become a focus of suspicion, as people question why it is dangerous for that information to get out. In some cases there may need to be control over who can see the data—for example, if it is critical to improving a major section of your site—but in most cases when the data is kept secret it is because the findings are not positive.

Reporting on poor performance is perhaps the hardest challenge you will ever face. It is easy to give positive feedback and good news, but delivering bad news often involves people checking and rechecking numbers to make sure the data is correct. Further, people often don't want to hear when things go wrong. There is a very good reason that Enron ran into the problems it did: nobody wants to give bad news.

Regardless of your role, you have an obligation to take bad news items and formulate plans around them. Bad news does not go away if you hide the reports from senior management; you won't help anyone by ignoring it. The most successful analysts will take the data and work with management to develop a plan on how to improve the situation, stemming the tide if possible and perhaps trying to see if the competition is also feeling the same pain.

You may discover that the bad news you are reporting on is an industry trend across the board: for example, all car sales are down by 34% and traffic to your site is down by 28%. Those two data points may have a very high correlation and impact on each other. If all car companies' sales are down, then most likely all car companies will also see decreases in overall site traffic. What might at first glance seem like a horrible anomaly may actually be part of a large ecosystem change.

Action plans and actionable analytics should accompany as much of your data as possible. End each analysis with some clear takeaway points, perhaps illustrating potential growth opportunities or calling out issues and suggesting how to respond to them. It will not always be you who is responsible for taking the action, but you will be responsible for putting thought into some options for what the action should be.

Dashboards Versus One-Off Reports

One-off reports are very common, especially in the search landscape. You will often find you are doing one-off reports when you are optimizing specific pages. However, this does not always have to be the case. You may be able to formalize your one-off report into a simple dashboard. You will find that there are certain numbers you look at repeatedly, regardless of how frequently you pull them. For example, throughout the course of this book we have looked at how to audit for keyword ranking and why certain pages rank the way they do. This is the kind of information you might want to include in your dashboard.

Formalizing your one-off reports into reusable dashboards or templates can save you a great deal of time for repetitive work. Ideally, your one-off reports should be limited to very special instances. For example, you may partner with another company and do something that is outside of the norm. In this case you may create a specific report that covers your company's KPIs, and a second to cover the other company's KPIs, that are then shared across companies.

One-off reporting may also come up after you run your standardized dashboards, if you discover something abnormal that needs explanation. Here, the one-off reports will be used to support or define the analytics in the overall dashboard. A dashboard should almost always have a few one-off reports to support specific insights. Reporting on the same insights every month is not beneficial to growth or learning; one-off reporting allows you to look, for example, at different segments, traffic types, and sources of traffic. Every one-off report you run can also be saved for later, to be rerun for another project or to validate that the changes you suggested had the expected positive effect on your programs.

Distributing Dashboards

The distribution of dashboards throughout your organization is critical to inciting action. Establish early on the frequency with which you will distribute your dashboards, as well as the content you will provide. The dashboards may be presenting executive-level content, or a very specific look at certain analytics. Establishing guidelines regarding the frequency and content of these reports will enable partners, supporting teams, and management to anticipate and plan around the metrics you will provide.

Further, establishing a set of dashboards for regular use will allow you to accurately track changes over time, and minimize your need to explain data points in each report. Every change to a dashboard will likely require you to explain why that change was made, what the new data represents, and, if old data was removed, why that data is no longer valid. Circulating the dashboards also gives better visibility to your work and efforts, and moves you from being a simple marketing tool to someone who drives sales and provides actionable insights that can grow your business online.

There are also services and tools that aggregate multiple data sources, such as Klipfolio (Figure 14-8). Klipfolio is nice because it can receive live data feeds and provide current and real-time data based on how frequently you update your Klips. Each dashboard can also be custom-configured for the relevant audience, so you may develop one dashboard for executives and another for a webmaster or marketing person.

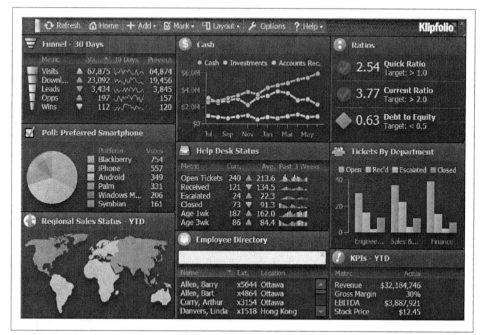

Figure 14-8. Example of Klipfolio dashboard

Building and Telling Stories with Dashboards

As you develop your distribution list, you should consider the audience and establish a model for telling a story with your numbers. Presenting plain numbers leaves too much open for interpretation. You are better off reaching out to other supporting teams to find out if anything they have done could have had an impact on what you are doing. You then want to weave that data into your story. For example, if you reach out to the accounting team, you may find that they recently saw a major increase in spending on server hardware. Following this up with the IT team may reveal that they upgraded the entire network feeding your servers, and that during this upgrade there was a day of down time. When you go to report on your analytics and the fourteenth of the month shows zero traffic, you can incorporate this data into your dashboard by calling out when the server upgrade happened. Further, you can pull marketing calendars to see when certain advertising goes into market to see if any of that may have had impacts on any of your key terms or driving forces.

Google Analytics allows for annotation of events along the timeline for pages. You can include data points as they happen, so if you ever have to go back historically you will be able to tell the proper story. For example, will you remember next year when your server underwent repairs, or when you migrated to a new hosting platform or rolled out a new section of your website? By adding the annotations directly in Google Analytics, you not only create reminders for yourself, but a method to maintain continuity. If you get promoted to a new job, whoever takes over for you will be able to go back to view all your annotations and quickly understand why and when something has happened.

The use of visuals can be critical in crafting your analytics story as well. The map example in Google Analytics provides a very clear story of where on the planet our users are coming from. The use of infographics has become popular in data reporting as well, because it utilizes numbers, graphics, and words to create compelling visuals.

The stories that your dashboards tell should also be clear and concise. If you find you are confused by the choice of words or what you are attempting to say, you need to revisit the formatting and message of the metric. Develop clear, simply worded messages that can be interpreted easily to save you the time and energy of reexplaining them. The larger your audience is, the more important clarity will become.

One Metric (Why Leading with One Stat Can Create Action)

The best way to create clarity is to highlight a single metric, or to target three key points. A single metric is something you can rally around and repeat over and over. Advertising works because it generates a simple message that is easily repeatable, and your goal should be the same with your analytics story. For instance, if you lead with "our website is up by 2 million visitors this month," you may repeat that again, explaining that "with over 2 million visitors to our site, we can attribute 30% of this increase to SEO and

15% to our paid search programs." By bringing the action back to the top-level metric, you create continuity in your story.

The approach of a single metric repeated is a very effective storytelling tool, and even if you find the metric you choose is not itself very actionable, you may be able to utilize its impressive scale to generate excitement. For example, knowing the number of visitors to the site is up by 2 million is great news that will generate a buzz. On its own that figure will make your boss happy and capture his attention, but how impressed will he be to see that your programs were responsible for 45% of that increase? Here, repeating the big number is to your advantage because the wow factor will make the news of your contribution resonate with him.

The other way to get your numbers to resonate is to keep your message on topic by clearly outlining three actions you expect to happen at the start of your message, reiterating them throughout, repeating them one last time at the end. Your message then will start with you talking about three actions that must take place for you to continue for you to see success, or to prevent poor results. You will follow up the summary of the three action items by describing each one in more detail and defining what must be done, in what time frame, and what the expected result will be if that action takes place. When you wrap up your presentation you will reiterate the three action items once more.

This repeating of three items three times makes the message resonate due to repetition. By limiting the message to three action items, you also reduce the chances of overwhelming your audience. Even if each action has many subactions, to get traction you need to group these into three big goals that must be accomplished. Without clear actions, you may end up with information paralysis.

Information Paralysis—When Too Much Info Creates Inaction

If you present your audience with too much data, you're likely to encounter a blank stare. Data can be a very powerful thing, but too much data can make for inaction. *Information* or *data paralysis* occurs when too much data is presented without enough background to interpret it. Analysts should be able to sift through data and pull out the core concepts and key figures. As a marketer, you may then need to explore these concepts and apply the data points to your marketing plans. As a salesperson, you may need to apply the data points to your sales forecasting. The analyst will have to work with others in the company to ensure that the data points in use are actionable, and not overwhelming.

A common mistake when we cannot make a decision as to what is helpful is to simply provide everything. Most people will not know what to make of a long list of web pages and the number of visits to each one. However, breaking these pages into sections or segments makes the data much more digestible. If the data is presented in an unfriendly fashion, most likely your documents will be opened and then discarded as there is no clear course of action.

Overloading people with data points can also turn into a deeper hole than you might have expected. Any data you present should be data you intend to talk about. Including data elements you are not going to talk about may lead to distractions. For example, if you have sub-segments in your segments but don't intend to talk about those sub-segments, you should remove them. Otherwise, you will end up fielding questions about them, which was not your goal, and you will waste your time on a topic that you may already know is not worth looking into. The data you include should support or benchmark your core message, and should not distract from the overall actions you want to see taken.

Concluding Thoughts

Presentation of data is critical to the success of reporting your analytics. You may want to consider taking a course on PowerPoint, or working with a graphic designer to develop an email template. The presentation of the data is just as important as the data itself. Clean, clear messages can resonate much more than tons and tons of data streams. Figuring out how to get these messages across is part art and part refinement.

I highly suggest looking at other reports and report formats, to see what works visually. Some analytics packages, such as Google Analytics with its dashboards and Adobe SiteCatalyst with its custom dashboarding features, make this simple. You may find that you need to do very little work to create simple, clear dashboards that communicate everything you need to say, or you may need to spend a few weeks developing a template that can be used over and over again. You may even find that a simple spreadsheet works for everyone and is a perfectly acceptable method for delivering the data. Your audience will determine the analytics you need to include and how best to present them, and you should work toward defining the optimal formats as early on in the reporting process as possible. Whatever approach you take, presentation of data should always be refined. This will ensure you get past the first hurdle—presentation—so you can get to looking at the numbers.

CHAPTER 15

Building Your Own Audit Tools and Enabling Others

The world of search analytics is still evolving today.
There is no one simple tool to perform all search audits.

In large organizations, you may need to enable others to perform quick pulls of data. Some of these data pulls may be complete time wasters, such as requests for how many words rank in a number 1 position. These data points, while great with other data, don't tell you a great deal on their own. In a well-defined space, you would ensure that everyone is educated as to what metrics are good definitions of success. If you define this as position ranking, expect to get lots of requests for position rankings; if it's ROI by keyword, expect lots of requests for this type of report.

Many of the tools in the search world provide APIs that allow you to mix and match data points and derive some very powerful insights. Further, there are many questions that cannot be answered by pulling from only one data point, but can be established by combining multiple reports. If you have the time to pull from each source, that's excellent; however, if your time is limited, I highly recommend that you get someone from your IT team to help build the tools you or others need to enable quick access to data that is not consolidated in one place.

Rubrics—How to Make Them

A very simple reporting tool you can use is a *rubric*. It provides a simple way of assessing issues, and grading them. This is a simple report card format that you can use to allow nontechnical people to grade the success of their own pages. A rubric should look like Table 15-1, where grades are assigned based on criteria that are described and can be met.

Table 15-1. SEO rubric

Expectation	Grade A	Grade B	Grade C	Grade D	Grade F
Title tag format and length	The title tag includes keywords as the first or second word, contains understandable language, and is no more than 60 characters long.	The title contains keywords and understandable language.	The title contains understandable language.	The title contains some keywords but is not relevant to the page.	There is no title tag, or the title tag repeats the keyword over and over.
Description meta tag use	The description meta tag is relevant to the content of the page, uses some keywords, and is no more than 150 characters long.	The description tag contains keywords and is relevant to the page.	The description tag is relevant to the page.	The description tag contains some keywords but is not relevant to the page.	There is no description tag, or the description tag just repeats keywords over and over.
URL format	The URL is short; contains keywords in the domain, page, or directory; and provides a clear understanding as to where you are in the site hierarchy.	The URL contains keywords in the domain, page, or directory, but also contains nonrelevant words, and provides clear understanding as to where you are in the site hierarchy.	The URL contains keywords in the domain, page, or directory, but also contains nonrelevant words as well as URL parameters and encoding.	The URL contains a keyword in the domain or page name, but there is also nonrelevant data and the URL contains parameters and encoding.	The URL uses special characters, does not contain any relevant keywords and is overly long and complex.

Rubrics provide a clean and easy way to present an auditing document for individuals with little or no experience in a specific field. The language should be common and clear, and the people in question should be able to quickly apply it to their pages to see how they rank for each element. SEO is not the only asset where this can be applied: you can use this tool for paid search or site search as well. As long as you have clearly defined objectives for each grade level, you can create a rubric for use.

The team at Google utilized a similar format to create their own SEO report card (*http://googlewebmastercentral.blogspot.com/2010/03/googles-seo-report-card.html*) to audit their own site. They looked at 100 pages, ranking each one according to whether it met the criteria and giving it a pass or fail. They then consolidated the total number of passes and fails to get an overall site score. This method is effective for looking at more than one page, and if you want to know how your site ranks, you can do random sampling to validate what your site's general score should be. The use of grading tools is a very simple practice to put in place.

All the data in the spreadsheet can be accessed through different APIs and could be easily modified to provide deeper insight into the pages and terms that rank, and what scores you would need to improve the most to get your own content to rank. This particular spreadsheet includes data from the SEOmoz API, Google data, and potentially parsing results from a Google search term.

Bringing together multiple data points can give you insights you might not ever find from one single source. Developing your own in-house tools will also allow you to get a leg up on the competition, as they will not have access to any of the tools you build or data you consolidate. In well-defined corporate structures there should be a separate analytics and reporting team that has the capability and depth of knowledge to link together multiple data points into usable content and formats, to support other business functions. You can take a stab at developing your own code, or have someone else develop it, or build off of someone else's efforts; any approach will be both a learning experience and an opportunity to improve your metrics and analytics reports.

At an enterprise level, data integration will be part of your maturity model and part of the evolution of your metrics strategy. To track off-site actions, you will need to look at data import. This is where clickstream tools like Google Analytics will fail you: Google allows for data out but not data in. Adobe SiteCatalyst, Webtrends, and other enterprise-level clickstream tools will allow for data import from third-party sources, allowing you to bring together a more complete view of customer interactions.

Creating Alerts and Triggers, Creating Response Plans

Beyond KPIs, you may develop some of your own alerts and triggers. You will want to create an action plan for each alert. Much like a server admin who carries a pager must respond to down-time alerts, as an analyst you may want or need to create alerts to notify you of big spikes or declines. Some tools, such as Google Analytics and Adobe SiteCatalyst, allow you to create triggers when there are significant changes that you define in the reports; you get an email updating you as to whatever the issue may be. You may define some key alerts such as:

- 404 limits, where a certain threshold means too many breaks in the site
- Large traffic increases or decreases
- Dramatic or decreases in inbound links
- Spikes in traffic from specific sources (such as Digg, or other large news sites)
- Major drops in conversion rates
- Anything else that may impact your search program rapidly

Alerts should be designed to be actionable and have a sense of urgency to them. Typically they will mean "drop everything and respond now to the issue." You should know who will need to be involved if an alert is triggered, how to contact them, how quickly the issue needs to be addressed, and what impacts it may have on the system. Once you have your action plan and team in place, you should immediately set to work assessing the situation and attempting to solve the problem(s) at hand, providing every person involved an action item to take away and perform.

Overriding Your Alerts: Why and When

On some occasions you will find that the alerts need to be overridden. For example, seasonality may impact the alert system significantly; in this case, you may choose to ignore or modify them for a set period of time. You may also choose to override an alert when there are known impacts coming, such as from a server migration or system shutdown.

A little bit of common sense should prevail, and you may still want to contact each of the stakeholders to notify them that there is an expected alert, or why there is no action needed. The one task that should not be ignored, however is a follow-up. Sometimes legitimate alerts happen during known system issues. For example, along with the servers being shut down for a day (resulting in a drop in traffic) a major change may be pushed out in the code that you are not warned about. Follow up with your sysadmins when the server comes back up and validate that all your numbers return back to an expected level. If something sits bellow the alert level, you will want to investigate to determine why it has not returned to its previous level.

Checklists of Items to Have for Setting Up an Analytics Plan

As you create your action plan for alerts, you will want to establish tasks, timelines, and roles. The first item to establish is a checklist. This checklist should be something simple such as the following:

1. Contact team members A, B, and C during alert.
2. Contact sysadmin to validate all systems are working.
3. Update team members of system status.
4. Contact coders to validate rollout or rollback of code.
5. Update team members of code status.

Establishing a set of rules like this ensures that there is a clear procedure and policy in place. You may notice that after each event there is a need to contact each team member. If this seems like overkill for your situation, this list could easily be modified to only contact each team member after multiple checks are performed. What is appropriate will depend on the issue and the severity of it, as well as the stakeholders' need to know. You may even have a more elaborate list that will include coordinating multiple groups and teams of people.

Building Out Timelines

Once you establish the contact protocol, you will also need to establish a timing protocol. Depending on the severity of the issue, you may send out hourly, bihourly, or daily updates to recap the issue and describe any progress made. Establishing a timeline will help maintain focus and minimize the danger of miscommunications or elements being overlooked as people work in separate silos on the issue.

The timeline should also allow people to better manage their expectations and the sense of urgency. It should not be used to make people feel inept or incapable of performing their jobs. Rather, the meeting times and process should be used to keep everyone motivated and positive, to isolate the issue, and reduce panic and stress among team members.

The greater the sense of panic or stress, the more likely issues are to get overlooked or passed by too quickly. The leader of each meeting should ensure that everyone feels comfortable with what they've been asked to do and able to complete the tasks they have been assigned in the allotted time. Anyone unable to make that commitment should not be scolded, or burdened with more work; instead, splitting out the tasks to enable people to fix the issues should be the primary goal. If other team members need to be brought in, they should be.

Establishing Roles

Your initial team should have clearly defined roles. There should be a single point of contact, as well as one person who is empowered to override decisions or to direct others to work outside their normal scopes. If for example you typically have to go through a three-week review process to release code, there may need to be someone who is capable of giving the OK to release fully untested code. These are judgment calls that must be made, and occasionally they may be made incorrectly. There is no right or wrong decision when people are under pressure, as long as the end goal is to improve the program and get things back on track. Problems further down the line can be dealt with, but you will want to log what did or did not work and have someone designated to take clear meeting minutes.

There should be people from each business or segment impacted represented within your group, even if some of those people only get updates. Communication and clearly defined roles will be critical to reacting to the alerts and data that comes in. The principle is to enable people to make decisions rapidly within the scope of their jobs, as quickly as possible.

As new people are brought into the team, you will need to define clearly their roles and responsibilities. You may find some people are only needed for short periods of time, while others will be required to be present throughout the entire process of investigating and solving issues. A successful action team will deploy quickly, locate the issue, and at least have an understanding of what is going on within the first day, if not the first few hours. They will then be able to quickly identify what must be done to improve the numbers and return to a positive threshold.

Being OK with Numbers Going Down

In some cases you will find that the numbers simply go down. They may even go below your threshold and trigger an alert. Part of your action team should be looking at external influences. If you find that the impact is a result of an external force such as an algorithm change by the search engines or an industry-wide downward trend, the team may have to accept the new numbers and establish a new baseline.

When dealing with falling numbers, threatening people who have no direct control over these numbers about not making their bonuses or losing their jobs will not help anyone. A solid analyst who can explain the external driving forces will have the data to back up her claims, and as a whole, the company will need to reevaluate its strategy. The search teams may be able to provide new insights or new strategies to modify the current trend, or it may be that a simple normalizing of data is needed.

It is important to recognize that managing SEO and paid search are difficult jobs, and there are many variables that are not 100% within the control of the individual. Massive updates from the search engines can impact some sites more than others. In some cases the search team should be able to predict these changes, but in others they are simply announced and the search community is forced to adjust. A perfect example of this was the launch of Google Instant Results, where there was a sudden frantic sense of urgency regarding what the changes might mean for search users. Ultimately, there wasn't much difference: the algorithm didn't change, only the rate at which the results were presented. Some user behavior patterns were impacted, but search results themselves were not modified, and very few sites saw any loss in traffic.

Concluding Thoughts

The most important thing anyone involved in the analytics side of search should take away from this chapter is that their ultimate goal is to create action. There are a variety of off-the-shelf tools as well as APIs that you can connect into to get deeper data points, but all the data in the world is irrelevant unless it leads to action. Everyone who is involved in online decisions should have some interest in search analytics, and everyone who has an online asset should have an interest in search analytics.

The Internet can be your greatest sales tool, serving more customers than your entire off-site sales team could ever manage. Taking the time to understand what is happening on your website, where the traffic is coming from, what the intent of the traffic is, and where it is going is key to a successful program. Search is of prime importance to your online business, as findability is crucial to driving traffic to and through your site. Search

Tool Listing

The following is a listing of the tools introduced throughout this book, and some alternatives you may want to consider. The list, while not exhaustive, should give you an idea of the variety of options out there, and a decent introduction to each tool. Some of these tools fall under a package set, such as those offered through Web CEO or SEOmoz subscriptions. Research each option, and try a few out to see what works best for you. The lowest-cost option is often used in this book's examples, to ensure maximum accessibility. The examples may call out specific features of some tools, though other tools may just as readily support the same features or require less effort.

Software Listings

Website Analytics

For an overview of this topic, see "Website Analytics" on page 11 in Chapter 1.

Google Analytics

URL: *http://www.google.com/analytics/*

Overview: Google Analytics (Figure A-1) is perhaps one of the fastest-growing website analytics tools on the market today. It requires that a JavaScript tag be placed on every page on which you want to enable tracking. It is a highly configurable, very robust website analytics suite. There are a great number of blogs and books to support Google Analytics, and a great number of hacks have been written to enable it to track metrics or analytics it may not track out of the box.

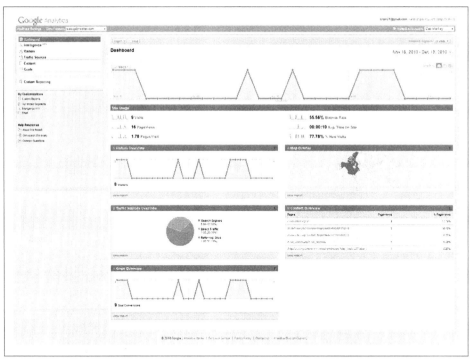

Figure A-1. Google Analytics dashboard

Google Analytics can quickly scale from a very simple and easy-to-implement website traffic monitoring tool to a very sophisticated tool tracking a complex set of data points. It is often the first choice for small businesses and personal websites, and many enterprise-level businesses install it as a secondary data source.

Google Analytics provides an API to extract data directly out of the report suite. The SEOMoz team has used this API to pull in data from Google Analytics to improve the SEO tool sets it offers. You can learn more about the API at *http://code.google.com/apis/analytics/*, as well as seeing examples of what others have built with it. Keep in mind while the API is open, some of the extended applications are not free.

Cost. Free.

Adobe SiteCatalyst

URL: *http://www.omniture.com*

Overview: Formerly known as Omniture SiteCatalyst, and now rebranded as Adobe SiteCatalyst (Figure A-2), this is the five-hundred-pound gorilla of commercial analytics tools. Adobe also offers tools such as SearchCenter, which helps track paid and organic search data, and Test & Target, which can be used for A/B and multivariate testing. All of these tools are integrated to work together seamlessly on both the setup side, when creating your page tags, and on the reporting side, offering reporting through a single portal. There are also many third-party tools that integrate with or can use data feeds from Adobe SiteCatalyst, through its API.

Unlike Google Analytics, SiteCatalyst can import data from multiple points, and you can also access data behind the scenes through the data warehouse, where all your data is stored. Enabling this in something like Google Analytics requires a great deal of setup and time.

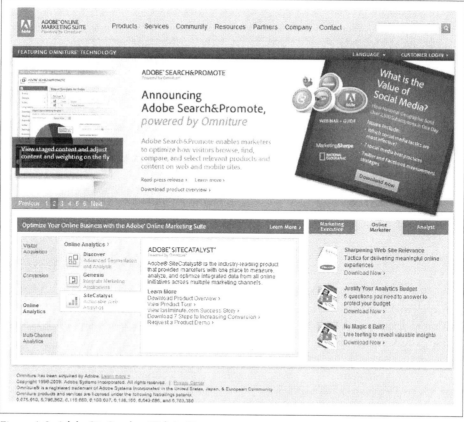

Figure A-2. Adobe SiteCatalyst Website Home page

Cost. Contact Adobe for pricing.

Other options

- Coremetrics, Inc: *http://www.coremetrics.com/*
- Webtrends: *http://www.webtrends.com/*

Link Tracking

For an overview of this topic, see "Link Tracking" on page 12 in Chapter 1.

Web CEO

URL: *http://www.webceo.com/*

Overview: Web CEO (Figure A-3) is more than just a back link checker; it's more like the multifunction Swiss Army knife of SEO. It allows for bulk submission to lots of smaller search engines, as well as monitoring uptime, responsiveness, and rankings and enabling auditing of some elements of your web pages.

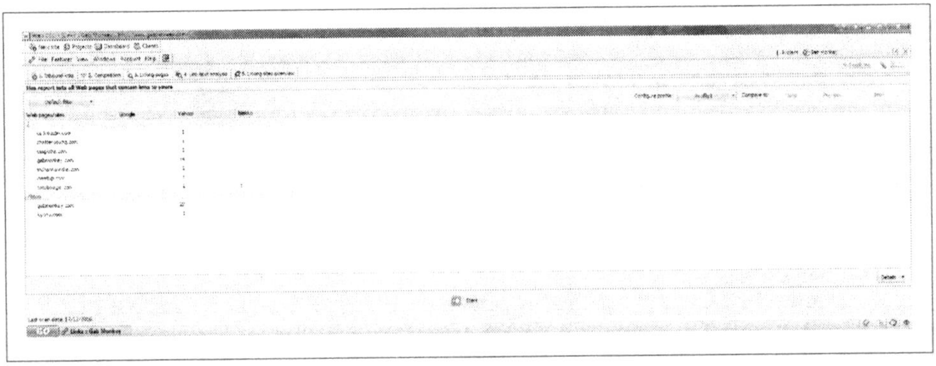

Figure A-3. Web CEO link report

As a back link checker, Web CEO provides high-level insight into the domains linking to your site, words used to link to your site, and other information such as whether the links are nofollows.

I strongly suggest that you try out this tool, and decide if it provides enough insights into what you are looking for. Watch for sales, as they do happen from time to time, making this software more affordable. Even the free edition is quite useful.

Cost. Free to $499 plus subscription fees.

Majestic SEO

URL: *http://www.majesticseo.com/*

Overview: Majestic SEO (Figure A-4) provides deep insights into sites linking to domains you control through its Backlink History tool and Bulk Backlink Checker. The Majestic Platinum plan also offers an API you can tap into, and subscription-based reports offer deep competitor analysis.

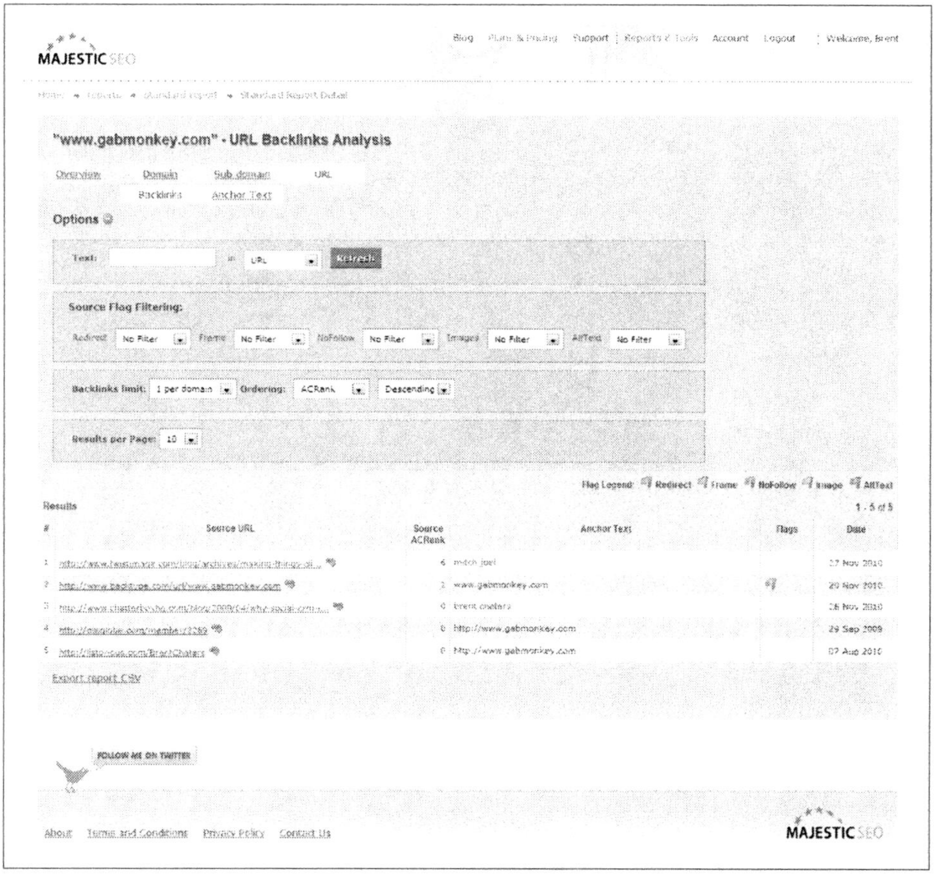

Figure A-4. Majestic SEO back link example

Majestic SEO's suite of tools includes a Neighborhood Checker that you can use to determine whether (if you host a domain on a shared platform), there is a chance that other hosted domains may burn that IP with poor SEO tactics. There is also a tool called Clique Hunter that offers a way to look for domains linking to other domains, a sort of "six degrees of separation" that is good for identifying link-building opportunities.

Cost. Free for some data; subscriptions range from £29.99/month to £250.00/month (or about $50.00 to $410.00).

SEOmoz Open Site Explorer (formerly Linkscape)

URL: *http://www.opensiteexplorer.org/*

Overview: Open Site Explorer (Figure A-5) is one of several powerful SEO tools from the SEOmoz team. Open Site Explorer gets its data by independently crawling the Web. The tool offers several filters allowing you to look at the data in different ways, including links that are nofollowed, links from images, image *alt* text, as well as regular links.

Digging deeper, filtering also enables reports on links from external pages only, internal pages only, and both internal and external pages. You can also target a single page, primary domain, or all subdomains to look at data at different levels. I strongly recommend that anyone serious about SEO sign up for a free account at least.

In addition to great tool sets, the SEOmoz community offers respected insights into SEO strategies, algorithm updates, and other industry news. Lastly, SEOmoz offers free and paid APIs at *http://www.seomoz.org/api* (*http://www.seomoz.org/api*).

Cost. Free to $99/month.

Other options

- SEMrush: *http://www.semrush.com*
- Advanced Link Manager: *http://www.advancedlinkmanager.com/*
- Yahoo! Site Explorer (this may become obsolete one day): *http://siteexplorer.search .yahoo.com/*

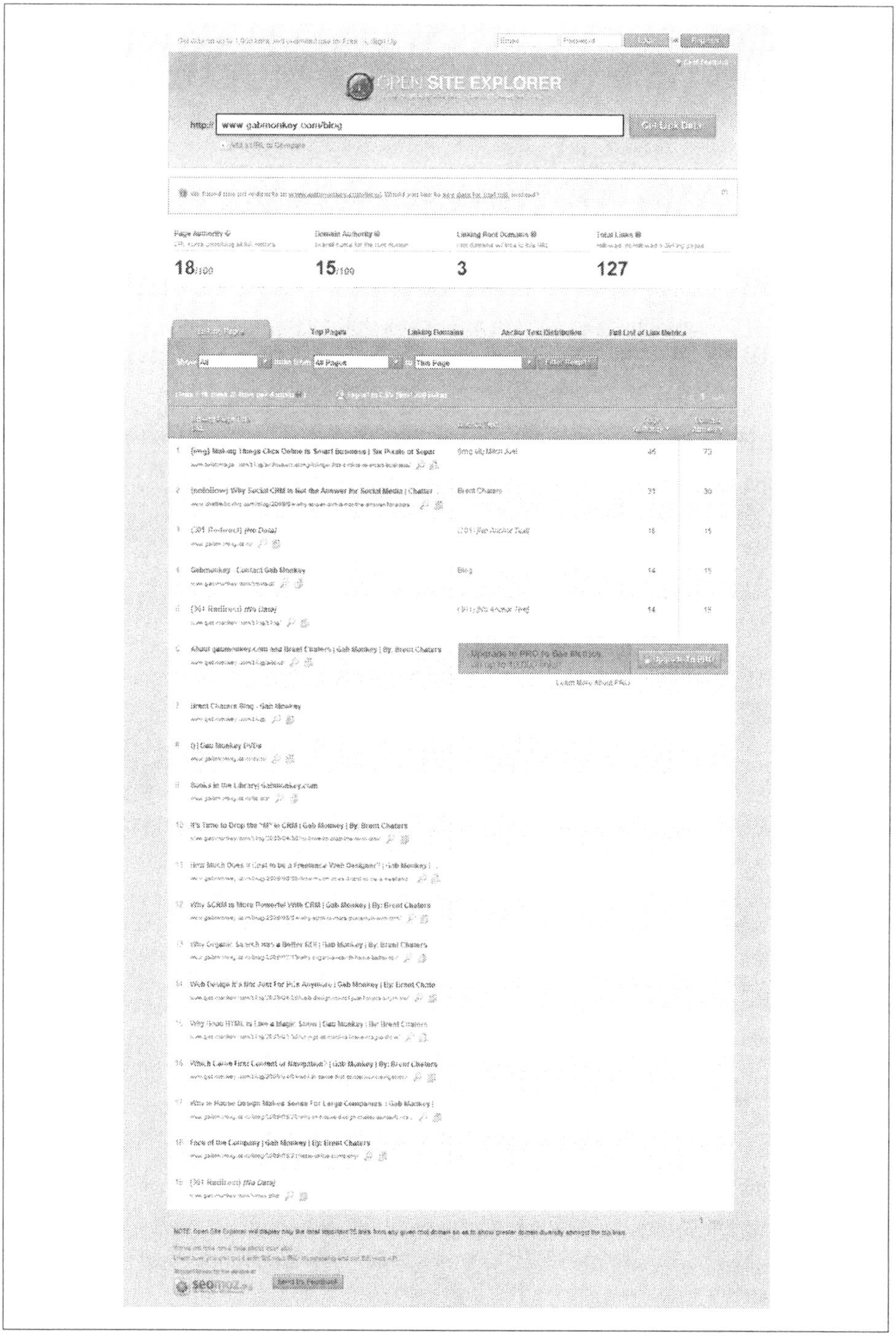

Figure A-5. SEOmoz Open Site Explorer example

Page Authority

For an overview of this topic, see "Page Authority" on page 12 in Chapter 1.

Google PageRank

URL: *http://www.google.com/toolbar*

Overview: Google Toolbar (Figure A-6) is a free download from Google for Firefox or Internet Explorer. You can find it at *http://www.google.com/toolbar*. It has several features, including quick links to other Google product offerings. On the toolbar you should see a green bar that, much like a fuel gauge, will show more green for pages with higher PageRanks. Moving your mouse over the icon will show you the PageRank for that page.

Figure A-6. Google Toolbar showing PageRank

The problem with the Toolbar is that its PageRank data is typically updated only twice a year, so the values it gives should only be viewed as approximations. Still, these approximate values should suit most needs. Google makes the following comment on PageRank on its website (*http://www.google.com/corporate/tech.html*):

> Relevance. As Larry said long ago, we want to give you back "exactly what you want." When Google was founded, one key innovation was PageRank, a technology that determined the "importance" of a web page by looking at what other pages link to it, as well as other data. Today we use more than 200 signals, including PageRank, to order websites, and we update these algorithms on a weekly basis. For example, we offer personalized search results based on your web history and location.

Cost. Free.

mozRank

URL: *http://www.seomoz.com/*

Overview: SEOmoz has a detailed explanation of mozRank (Figure A-7) at *http://www.seomoz.org/learn-seo/mozrank*. You can access the mozRank for a page for free through Open Site Explorer, under the "Full List of Link Metrics" tab, or you can extract it through the open API SEOmoz offers. You can also look at the Domain-level mozRank, which is tracked for both the domain you are looking at and the root domain.

mozRank can act as a sanity check against PageRank, as well as giving a better understanding of the popularity of the page based on the number of inbound links and the popularity of the pages that link to that page.

Cost. Free. But to access root domain information, you will need to subscribe to a pro membership for $99 per month.

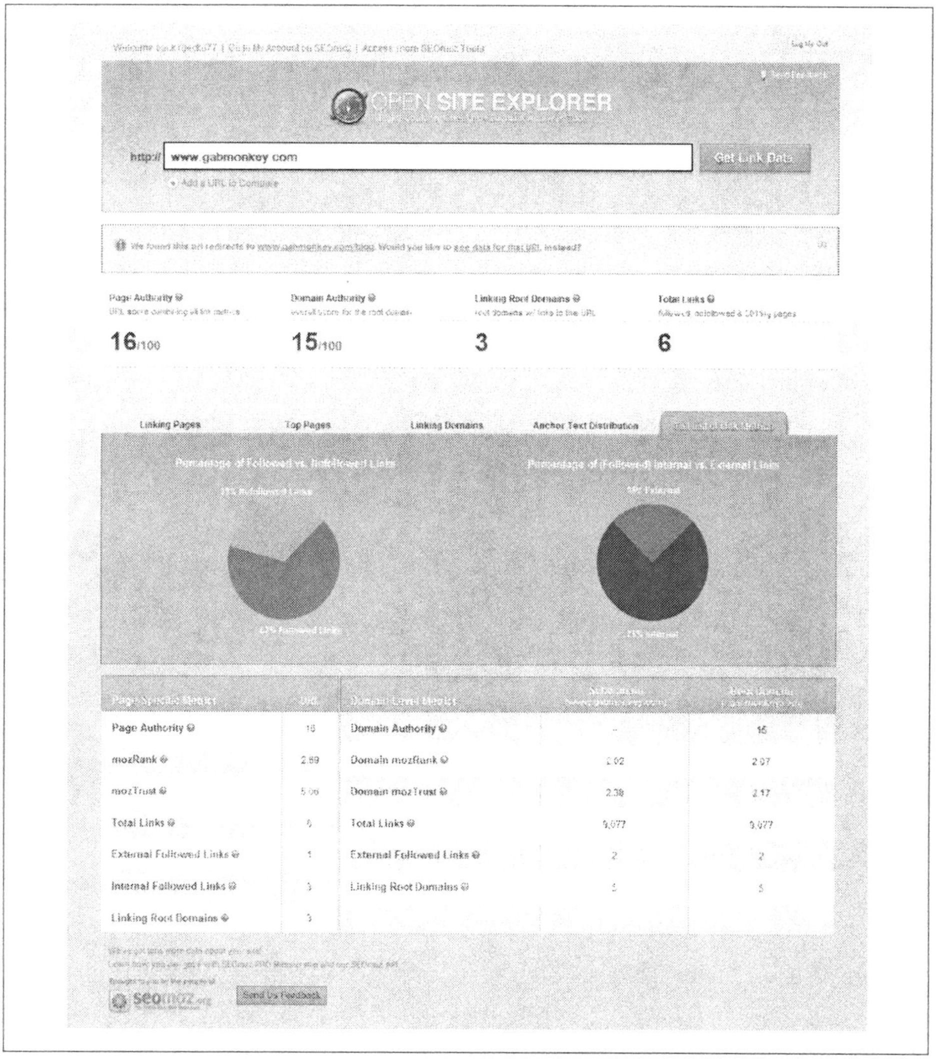

Figure A-7. Open Site Explorer showing mozRank and mozTrust

mozTrust

URL: *http://www.seomoz.com/*

Overview: SEOmoz has a detailed explanation of mozTrust (Figure A-7) at *http://www .seomoz.org/learn-seo/moztrust* that states:

> mozTrust quantifies the trustworthiness of a web page relative to all of the other web pages on the web. It is based off of an algorithm developed by Yahoo! search engineers that is likely similar to the trust algorithms used by Google and Bing search engineers. Just as links express global link popularity, they also express information about the trustworthiness of URLs. Receiving links from sources which have inherent trust, such as the homepage of major university websites or certain governmental web pages, is a strong trust endorsement. By measuring the occurrence and frequency of these endorsements, mozTrust can quantify trust on the web.

To access mozTrust, you will need to sign up for a SEOmoz account. This will also open up additional features in Open Site Explorer, as well as granting you access to lots of other SEOmoz tools.

Cost. $99/month.

Ranking Position

For an overview of this topic, see "Ranking Position" on page 12 in Chapter 1.

SEO Rank Monitor

URL: *http://www.seorankmonitor.com/*

Overview: SEO Rank Monitor (Figure A-8) allows you track positions in the search results. You can track competitors, and break down your keywords and stats. The tool shows you your top movers and losers in terms of position, as well as flagging words that are about to break into the number 1 position.

SEO Rank Monitor focuses on tracking SEO position in the SERPs.

Cost. Free for 30 days, then $19–$39/month

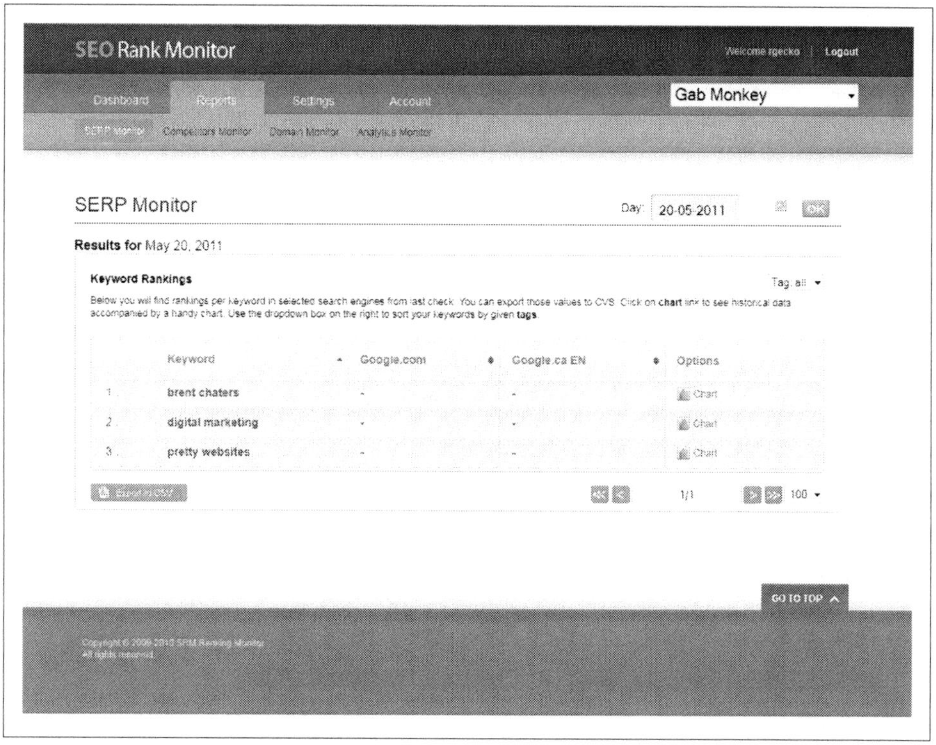

Figure A-8. SEO Rank Monitor homepage

WebPosition

URL: *http://www.webposition.com/*

Overview: WebPosition (Figure A-9) used to be known by the name WebPosition Gold, which operated as a desktop application. Due to the nature of how it pulled data from the search engines, it ran the risk of getting an IP address banned by the engines. WebPosition has since transitioned to an online service that can run similar queries without putting your IP address at risk.

WebPosition tracks international search engines as well, which can be helpful if you are looking to monitor some of the more obscure engines. WebPosition also offers a dashboard to show your top rising and falling terms. You can set up scheduling, and track your competitors.

WebPosition focuses on tracking SEO results in the SERPs.

Cost. Free 30-day trial, then subscriptions at $19/month, $49/month, or $19/month plus a fee per 1,000 SERPs.

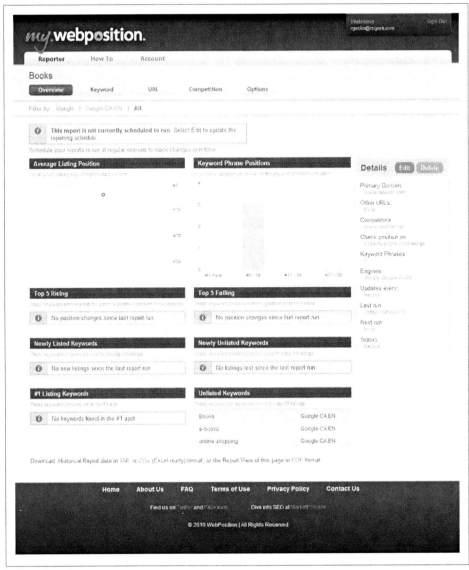

Figure A-9. WebPosition dashboard

AdGooroo Paid Search Insight

URL: *http://www.adgooroo.com/*

Overview: AdGooroo (Figure A-10) provides tracking of both SEO and paid search position and share of market. Several charts offer quick and easy to understand information on your competitors' campaigns. You can track competing ad copy and split tests, as well as tracking landing pages and estimating competitors' budgets.

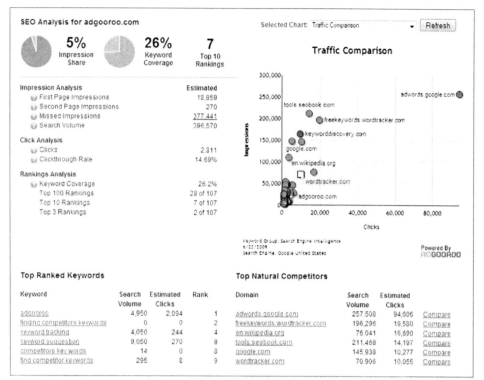

Figure A-10. AdGooroo dashboard

While the focus is primarily on paid search, AdGooroo also offers SEO tracking of SERP position and estimates for competitors' organic traffic. It looks at six search engines across 43 countries, as well as doing side-by-side domain comparisons.

Cost. Contact AdGooroo for pricing.

Google Webmaster Tools

URL: *www.google.com/webmasters*

Overview: Google Webmaster Tools (Figure A-11) provides a wealth of information. If you do not have an account set up, go set one up now. Webmaster Tools will be a frequently referenced tool. It provides a great deal of insight into what is happening on your site, direct from the source. Google provides notifications about issues on your site, and potentially links that explain what is broken, or best practices for fixing the issues. You can also track what words are driving traffic to your site and the average position of these words.

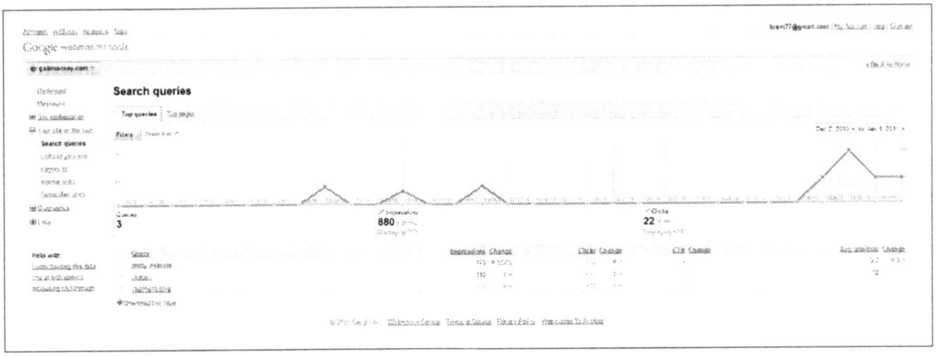

Figure A-11. Webmaster Tools dashboard

The downside to Webmaster Tools is that data is not retained for a very long period of time. You should set up biweekly or monthly reviews of Webmaster Tools as part of your auditing process and archive the reports externally.

Cost. Free.

Other options

- SEOmoz Rank Tracker: *http://www.seomoz.org/rank-tracker*
- Web CEO: *http://www.webceo.com/*
- Firefox Rank Checking Tool: *http://tools.seobook.com/firefox/rank-checker/*

Both SEOmoz and Web CEO offer tracking as part of the initial purchase of their software or subscriptions and provide similar features as the other software ranking solutions, with a focus on SEO.

Keyword Search Volume and Competition

For an overview of this topic, see the section "Keyword Search Volume and Competition" on page 13 in Chapter 1.

Google AdWords Keyword Tool

URL: *http://adwords.google.com/select/KeywordToolExternal*

Overview: The Google AdWords Keyword Tool (Figure A-12) provides insight and suggestions regarding terms you may be interested in targeting through paid search or SEO. It provides a competition density estimate for paid search, as well as the number of global and local monthly searches. The Keyword Tool also shows trends over time to help you understand if there is any seasonality.

While the tool is geared toward paid search, it can also be leveraged for SEO. You can use it for guestimating search volumes by making sure [Exact] is selected under "Match types" on the left. Exact matching will likely underreport the SEO volume as Google will also take into account misspellings and some other variations, but for SEO purposes this is the closest estimate you will get on a specific word or pairing, and the tool has recently undergone some changes to make the search volumes more relevant (*http://adwords.blogspot.com/2010/04/more-relevant-traffic-estimates-now-in.html*).

Cost. Free.

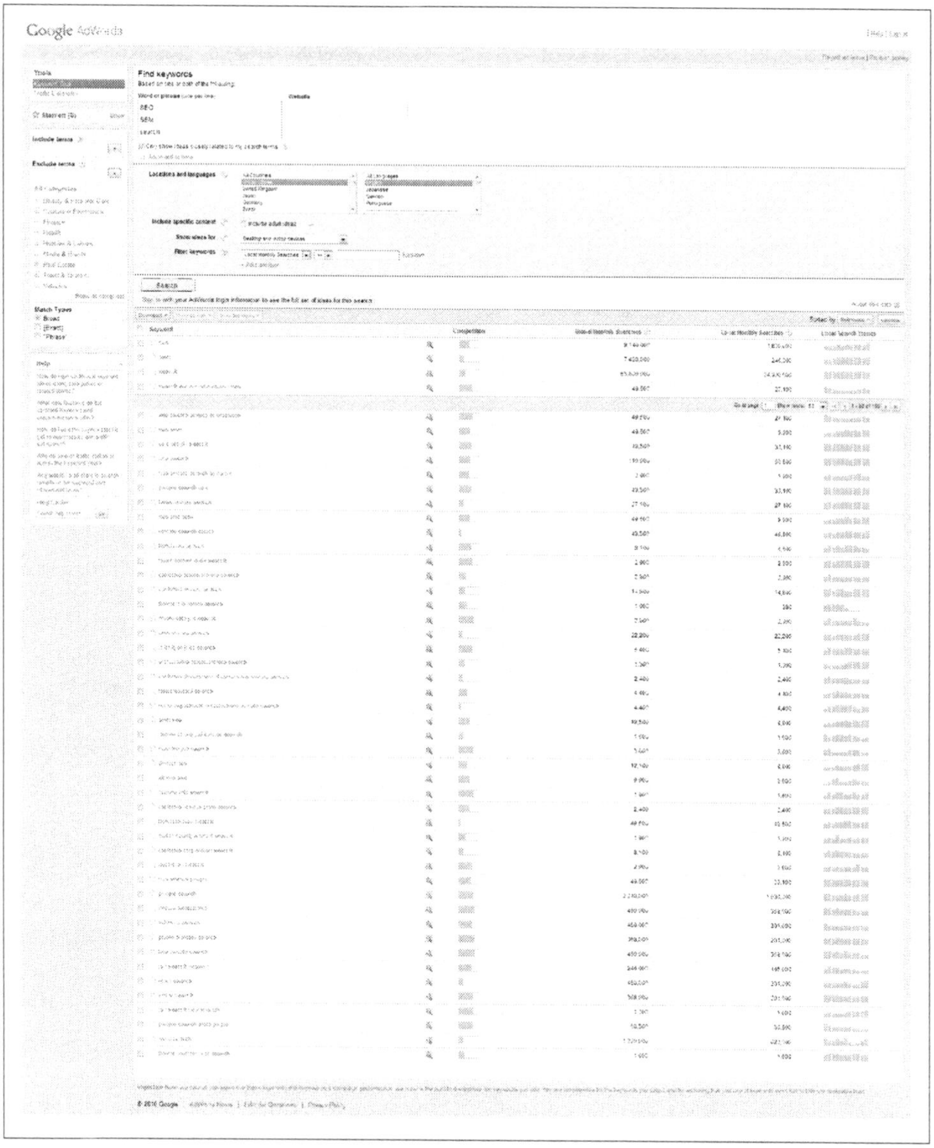

Figure A-12. Google AdWords Keyword Tool

Trellian Keyword Discovery

URL: *http://www.keyworddiscovery.com/*

Overview: Trellian Keyword Discovery (Figure A-13) is one of the older keyword research tools available. It offers insights into common spelling mistakes and seasonal search trends, as well as keyword density analysis and domain researcher tools.

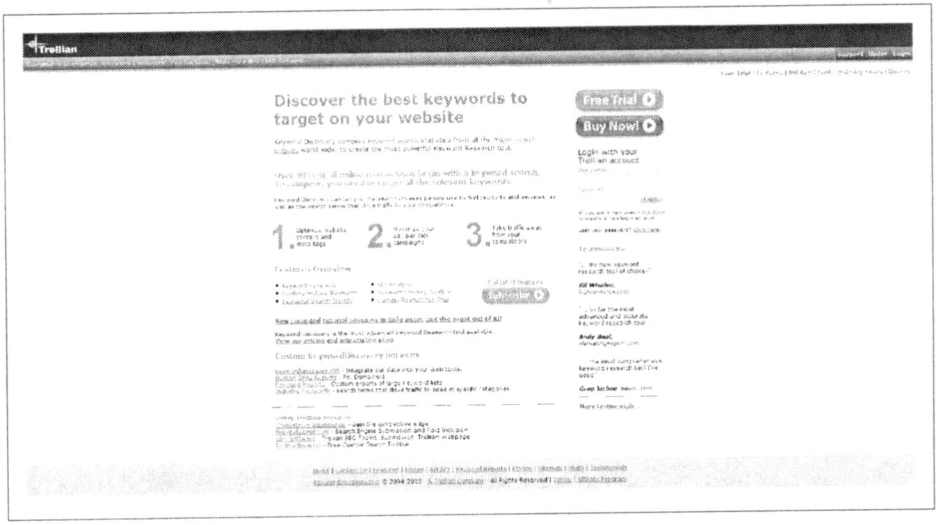

Figure A-13. Trellian Keyword Discovery homepage

Keyword Discovery also typically returns more keywords than the Google tools. When doing keyword investigation, it looks to provide you with more long-tail terms and it is targeted at helping you think of other related terms or words that may be relevant to your business.

Cost. Free to $199.95/month.

Wordtracker

URL: *http://www.wordtracker.com*

Overview: Wordtracker (Figure A-14) is actually a set of several tools, each with separate pricing: Wordtracker Keywords, Wordtracker Link Builder, and Wordtracker Strategizer. Wordtracker Keywords works very well with Wordtracker Strategizer and integrates with Google Analytics. Using both supplied information and information from your analytics, you can track words that work well for you as well as getting estimates of the traffic volumes and conversion rates you can expect.

Keyword Tracker also typically returns more keywords than the Google tools. Like Trellian Keyword Discovery, Wordtracker looks to provide more long-tail terms to help you dig deeper into alternative terms you may not have thought about.

Figure A-14. Wordtracker Keywords homepage

Wordtracker also offers an API with various pricing models depending on queries and number of calls.

Cost. $59/month, per tool.

Google Global Market Finder

URL: *http://translate.google.com/globalmarketfinder/index.html*

Overview: Google Global Market Finder (Figure A-15) is a fairly new offering from Google. It allows you to enter a set of keywords to be auto-translated and then provides an analysis of the global opportunities on these words based on country as well as language.

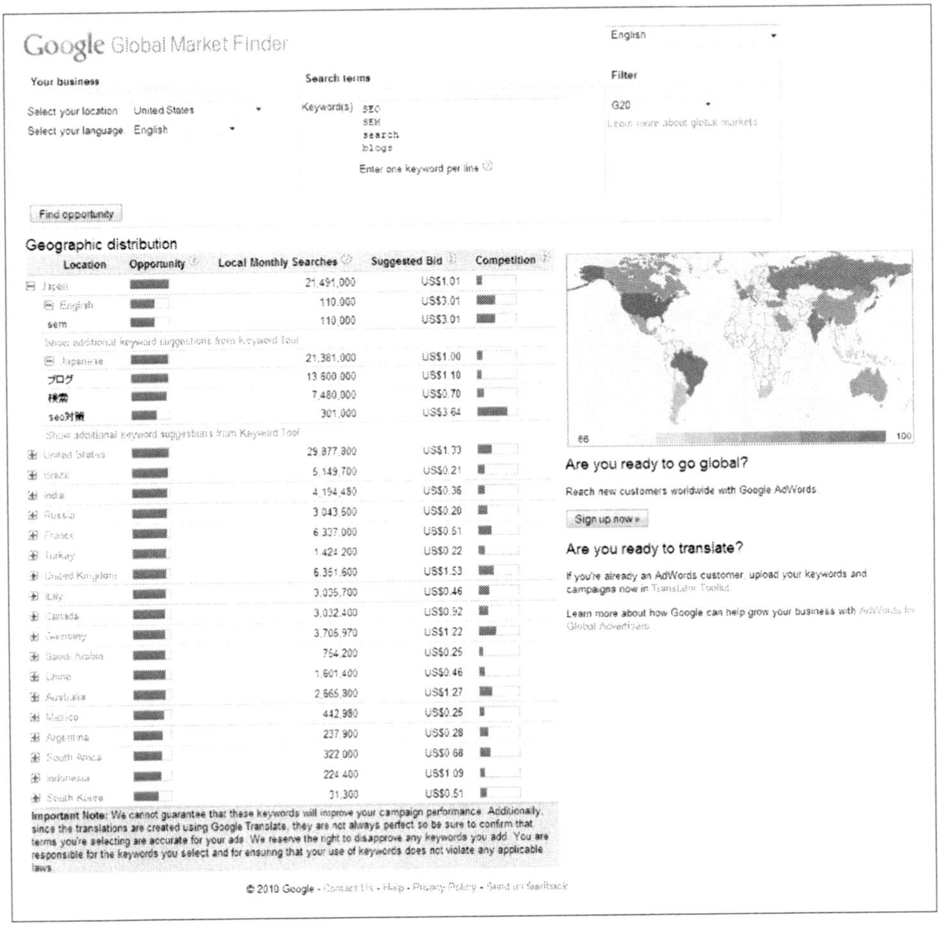

Figure A-15. Google Global Market Finder dashboard

While auto-translation is not always the best SEO or paid search strategy, it does provide some quick insights into markets you may not have thought of. It also provides the volume of English queries in each country. For anyone who is thinking of breaking into international search, this is certainly a tool worth looking into.

Cost. Free.

Other options

Lastly, you can go directly to the search engines and type. Auto-suggested words can provide some additional ideas of keyword pairings. This can be tedious, but it provides insight into strong word associations and pairings.

- Google: *http://www.google.com*
- Bing: *http://www.bing.com*

Social Links and Social Noise

See the section "Social Links and Social Noise" on page 13 in Chapter 1 for an overview of this topic.

SM2

URL: *http://socialmedia.alterian.com/*

Overview: Alterian SM2 (Figure A-16) scans across many different social sites to look for mentions of terms you may be interested in. You can also set up email alerts to be sent out as new mentions show up. You can limit which sites are scanned, or search them all. SM2 also provides a quick dashboard of mentions, retweets, and other pieces of information that may help you formulate some ideas as to how some of your terms are used.

As with most of the social media monitoring tools, you will also need to deal with a great deal of noise. Be prepared to filter out lots of data.

Cost. Free and fee-based versions available, contact Alterian for pricing.

Radian6

URL: *http://www.radian6.com/*

Overview: Radian6 (Figure A-17), which was recently acquired by Salesforce.com, is one of the larger enterprise-level brand management tools for social media. Radian6 provides very slick and clean dashboards and is focused on identifying trends and finding who your brand evangelists are. You also get a better support team than you would with some of the free options, to allow for some customization of your corporate needs. The support team should also be able to help guide you at filtering out a lot of the noise you may get in some of the free options.

Cost. Contact Raidan6 for pricing.

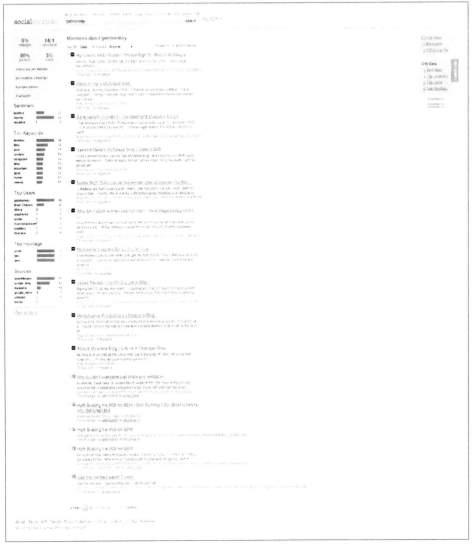

Figure A-16. Alterian SM2 dashboard

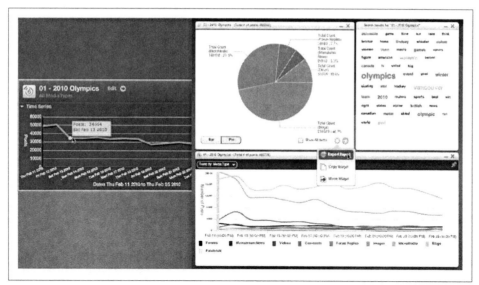

Figure A-17. Radian6

Addict-o-matic

URL: *http://addictomatic.com/*

Overview: Addict-o-matic (Figure A-18) is another free social media monitoring tool. Currently it is missing an alert functionality, but it does display information in a friendly interface, grouping content into similar bubbles based on source.

Addict-o-matic also tends to return a lot of noise within the results, but it should suffice for a cursory look when you need a high-level overview of what is happening around certain keywords.

Cost. Free.

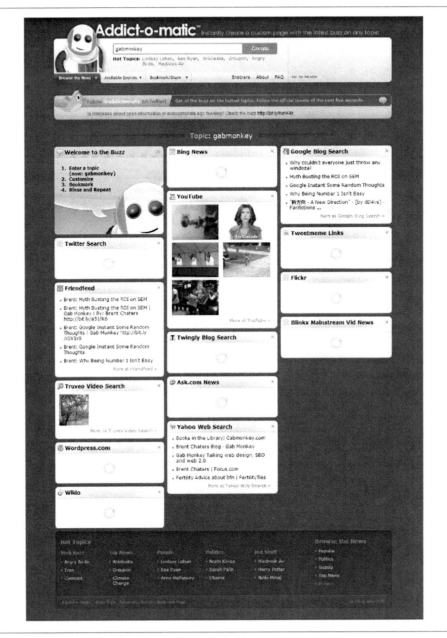

Figure A-18. Addict-o-matic dashboard

Other options

- Twazzup: *http://www.twazzup.com/*
- Buzzlogic: *http://www.buzzlogic.com/*
- Scoutlabs: *http://www.scoutlabs.com/*
- Reputation Defender: *http://www.reputationdefender.com/*
- Brandwatch: *http://www.brandwatch.net/*
- Socialmention *http://www.socialmention.com/*
- Attensity360: *http://www.attensity.com/*
- Argyle: *http://argylesocial.com/*
- TwentyFeet: *https://www.twentyfeet.com/*
- Sysomos: *http://www.sysomos.com/*
- Adobe SocialAnalytics: *http://www.omniture.com/*

Keyword Volume or Keyword Density on Page

For an overview of this topic, see the section "Keyword Volume or Keyword Density on Page" on page 13 in Chapter 1.

SEO Book Keyword Density Analyzer Tool

URL: *http://tools.seobook.com/general/keyword-density/*

Overview: SEO Book offers a variety of tools; one of them is the Keyword Density Analyzer (Figure A-19). You simply provide a URL, and it will go through and look at all the words on the page and group them by word, two-word phrases, and three-word phrases.

The tool gives you a good overview of the words and phrases on a page, and the frequency with which they appear. It doesn't give any indication as to what HTML tags surround the words, but it does allow for some configurability in terms of looking at meta tags and descriptions. You can also filter out stop words, and ignore words under a certain length and that occur with a frequency under a certain threshold.

Cost. Free.

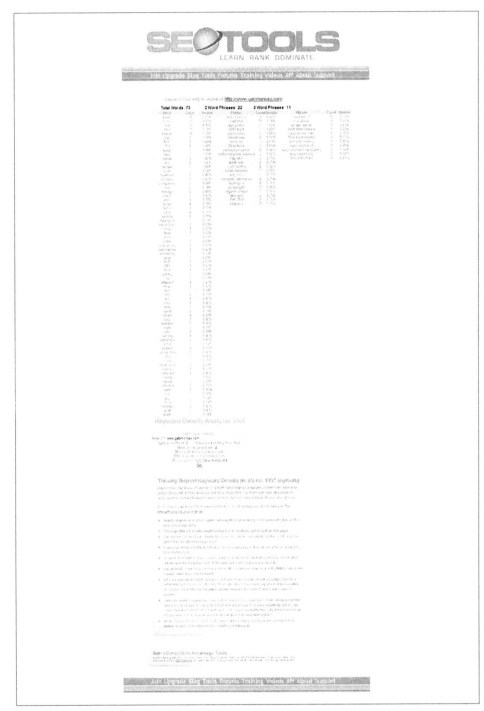

Figure A-19. SEO Book Keyword Density Analyzer Tool

SEOmoz Term Extractor

URL: *http://www.seomoz.org/term-extractor*

Overview: The SEOmoz Term Extractor (Figure A-20), much like the SEO Book Keyword Density Analyzer, looks at the words on a page, dividing them into one-, two-, and three-word sets. The Term Extractor also shows you what HTML elements the terms show up in, and how frequently. There is, however, no weight currently applied to what HTML surrounds the keyword.

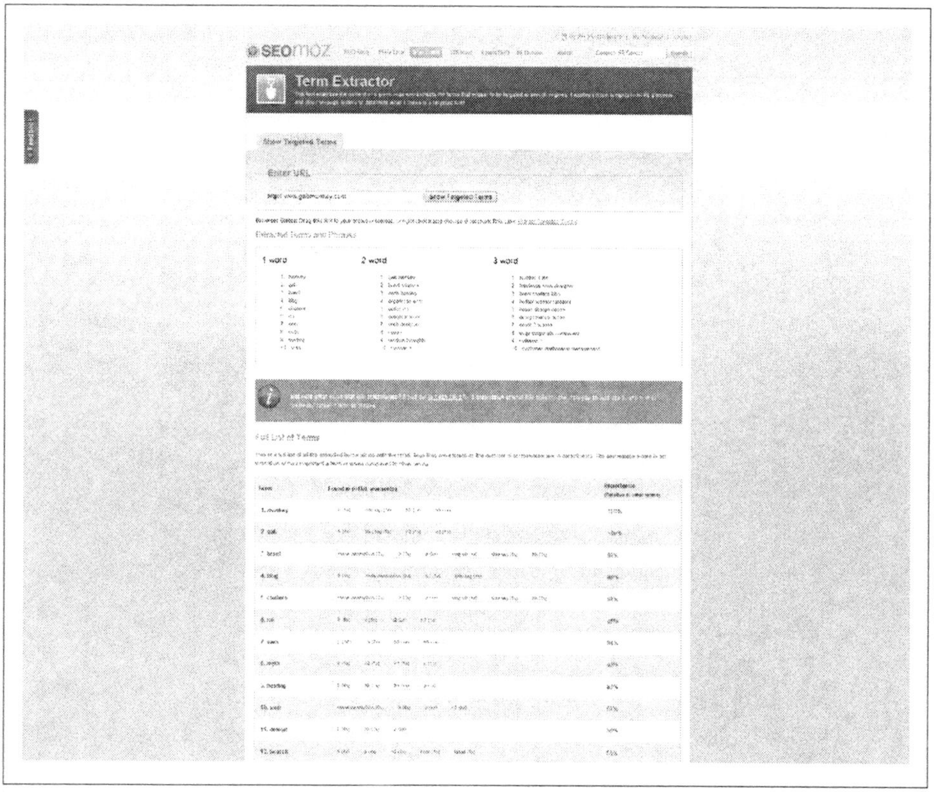

Figure A-20. SEOmoz Term Extractor

The Term Extractor also lists a relative "importance" for of all the words and phrases.

Cost. Free.

KGen for Firefox

URL: *https://addons.mozilla.org/en-US/firefox/addon/4788/*

Overview: KGen (Figure A-21) is a plug-in for Firefox that, once installed, you can find under View→Sidebar→"KGen: Keyword generator". KGen is a nice tool to have as it integrates directly into your web browser. It's configurable enough that you can create rules to not only measure keyword density but also apply some formulas to infer the importance of some words based on placement in HTML tags. Even better, you can create an ignore list to prevent some words being measured (such as of, to, it, and, etc.).

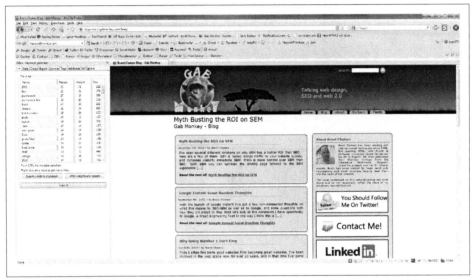

Figure A-21. KGen on the left side of a web browser

You can also look up synonyms for words to see if there are any alternatives out there. The tool can generate a fancy word cloud that shows which words have the most weight, which is also configurable. I strongly suggest building up your own set of rules that work for you, and saving them.

Cost. Free.

Other options

- Keyword Density Analyzer: *http://www.keyworddensity.com/*
- weBuildPages Keyword Density: *http://www.webuildpages.com/seo-tools/keyword-density/index.php*
- ranks.nl: *http://www.ranks.nl/*

Mobile and Geographic Traffic Estimations

For an overview of this topic, see the section "Mobile and Geographic Traffic Estimations" on page 14 in Chapter 1.

Google AdWords Keyword Tool

URL: *http://adwords.google.com/select/KeywordToolExternal*

Overview: Already discussed in "Keyword Search Volume and Competition" on page 340, this tool also allows you to set geographic targets, as well as tracking search volumes on desktop and laptop devices, all mobile devices, mobile WAP devices, and mobile devices with full Internet browsers, through the advanced options.

You can also use this tool to isolate keywords based on languages. The Keyword Tool will therefore not only give you usability insights based on device, but cultural and geographic insights as well.

Cost. Free.

Google Global Market Finder

URL: *http://translate.google.com/globalmarketfinder/index.html*

Overview: Google Global Market Finder doesn't provide mobile usage statistics, but it does provide geographic information as well as translations, as discussed in "Tracking International Searches and Linguistics" on page 107. The nice thing about this tool is how it breaks down the countries by language so you can get a feel for not just the geography, but also linguistic differences. As a paid search tool it also provides an estimated cost per click, so you can see what the costs are on terms in different regions based on language.

Cost. Free.

Competitor Insights

For an overview of this topic, see "Competitor Insights" on page 14 in Chapter 1.

Compete

URL: *http://www.compete.com/*

Overview: Compete (Figure A-22) offers some information for free, and deeper information for paid subscribers. You can compare up to three sites for free, getting data on number of unique visitors, top search terms, referring sites, categories, destination sites, top tags, and more. You can also look at current or historical data, going back two years.

Compete's data comes from over two million consumers across the United States; they use tracking technology in the web browsers of panelists who opt in to be part of their

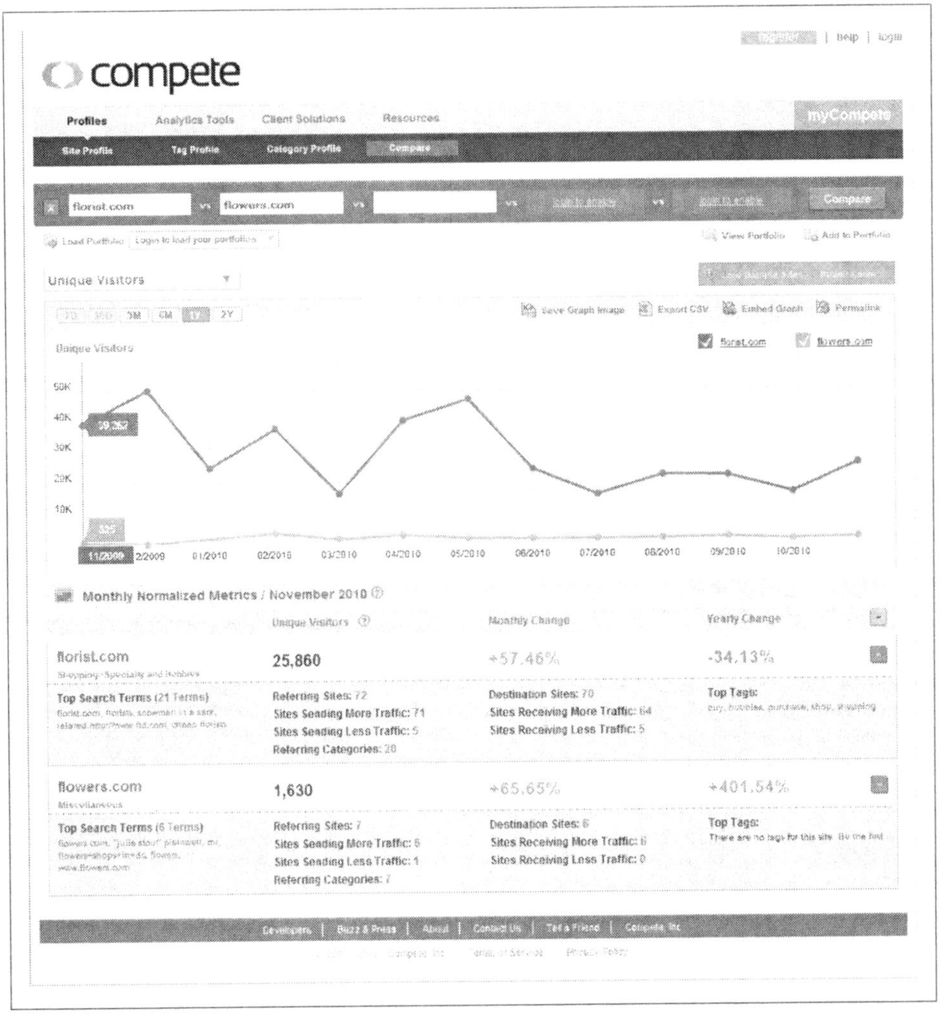

Figure A-22. Compete dashboard

data source. Compete also offers an API that can be accessed upon registration; you can also purchase deeper access to the API if it suits your business needs. Lastly, they offer a JavaScript that enables your site to provide you with further understanding of your traffic, based on Compete data.

Cost. Free to variable pricing based on plan; see website for more details.

Hitwise

URL: *http://www.hitwise.com/*

Overview: Hitwise, like Compete, uses browser plug-in technology to track people who opt into having their website viewing habits tracked. Hitwise offers a view into user behavior across many site data points and can provide deep insights for larger brands in terms of where they rank in industries, traffic volumes, who their immediate competitors are, and more.

Cost. Contact Hitwise for pricing.

Google Trends for websites

URL: *http://trends.google.com/websites*

Overview: Google Trends (Figure A-23) relies on sampled data from Google. This data is what it says it is: trending data. It is great for generating charts and visualizing over time how your branded terms compare to your competitors' branded terms. Google Trends provides a quick snapshot of patterns between two brands, but it does not provide the accuracy other data sources may offer.

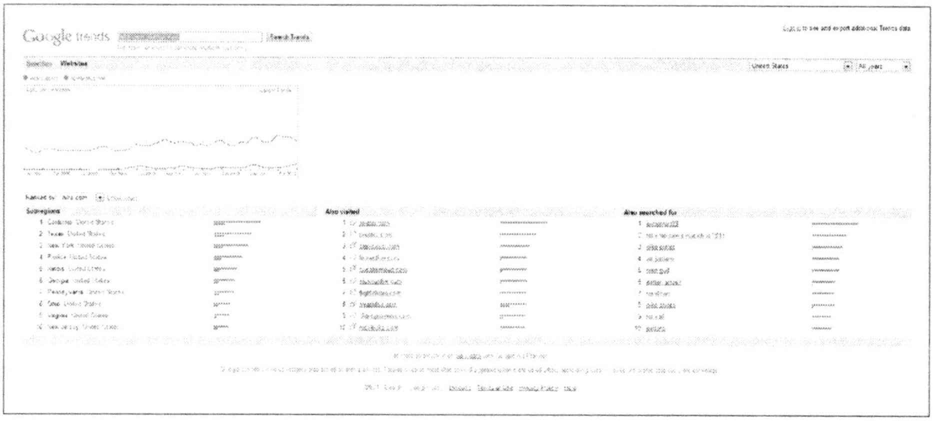

Figure A-23. Google Trends for Websites dashboard

As a tool for a quick overview, Google Trends provides some decent top-level competitor data. The Google Keyword Tool provides deeper data and search volumes, should you need to dive deeper into this data set. In addition, when you export data from the Keyword Tool, you can get month-over-month breakdowns to look for seasonality changes.

Cost. Free.

Other options

- comScore: *http://www.comscore.com/*
- Google AdWords Keyword Tool: *http://adwords.google.com/select/KeywordToo lExternal*
- Google/DoubleClick Ad Planner: *http://www.google.com/adplanner/*
- Web CEO: *http://www.webceo.com/*
- Woorank: *http://www.woorank.com/*
- SpyFu: *http://www.spyfu.com/*

Surveys—Qualitative Data

Surveys are a rich source of data and information. They move beyond following a user and allow you to understand sentiment—"why are you here?" and "what are you looking for?" questions. Survey data, when used well, can provide the insights that give you the "ah ha!" moment that allows you to understand what your customers need, and not what you think they need.

Survey Monkey

URL: *http://www.surveymonkey.com/*

Overview: SurveyMonkey has a range of plans that allow for everything from basic 10-question surveys to highly controlled white label surveys offering A/B sampling, question and answer piping, randomization, and more.

Cost. Free to $67/month.

4Q (iPerceptions)

URL: *http://www.4qsurvey.com/*

Overview: 4Q is a very simple survey system that is successful because of its simplicity. You can ask up to four questions:

1. Based on today's visit, how would you rate your site experience overall?
2. Which of the following best describes the primary purpose of your visit?
3. Were you able to complete the purpose of your visit today?

   4a. (If yes) What do you value most about the [sitename] website?

   4b. (If no) Please tell us why you were not able to fully complete the purpose of your visit today.

Cost. Free to $399/month (depending on number of respondents).

Multiuse Tools and Sites

For an overview of this topic, see "Multiuse Tools and Sites" on page 14 in Chapter 1.

SEOmoz

URL: *http://www.seomoz.org/tools*

Overview: SEOmoz offers a terrific set of SEO-related tools. Several of these tools can be leveraged against SEM as well. Their offerings include:

- Open Site Explorer, as reviewed in "SEOmoz Open Site Explorer (formerly Link-scape)" on page 332
- SEO Toolbar, which provides an add-on to web browsers to get some information instantly while on a web page
- Trifecta, which pulls in competitor insights from multiple sources
- Juicy Link Finder, which can provide you with leads on other websites to approach for back links
- Historical PageRank Checker, which can provide PageRank data as far back as 2007

These tools can all be accessed with a $99/month Pro Service membership; in addition, you will be able to ask unlimited questions of the pro staff.

Cost. Starting at $99 per month.

Web CEO

URL: *http://www.webceo.com/*

Overview: Some of Web CEO's features are outlined in "Other options" on page 340. The company offers online and desktop versions of the software that are both worth looking at. Beyond checking rankings, you also have access to:

- Keyword research and suggestions
- SEO advice based on automated reports
- Web page auditing
- Search engine submissions
- Link building tools, to find related sites to foster link building
- Pay per click (PPC) management
- Link popularity tracking, to see if you are building links well
- Automated page audits of page issues

Cost. $499 plus optional subscription bases.

SEO Book

URL: *http://tools.seobook.com/*

Overview: SEO Book offers a variety of free tools as well as a selection of premium tools available to monthly subscribers. The $300 monthly fee also gets you access to training videos and the community forum. The available tools include:

- Keyword Research Tools—aggregate data from Google, Yahoo!, and Bing (free with signup).
- Competitive Research Tool (requires paid access)
- Duplicate Content Checker—looks for duplicate content that may be splitting rank in the search engines across other sites, letting you know if your content is original or if others are also using it (requires paid access)
- Website Health Check—lets you know if your website has any issues to do with canonical URLs 404 error headers/messages, and indexability/crawlability (requires paid access)
- HubFinder—allows you to look for close neighborhoods and good neighborhoods based on links (requires paid access)

Cost. Free to $300 per month.

ClickEquations

URL: *http://www.clickequations.com/*

Overview: ClickEquations offers a highly detailed analysis of your paid search campaigns, from copy creation through to bid management and user engagement and interaction. Further, ClickEquations allows you not only to track on-site conversions but also to import data on external conversion, improving your ability to track all aspects of your paid search campaigns, from end to end. It can generate alerts when issues such as poor Quality Scores arise and can segment data to allow you to target and refine your programs. ClickEquations is an excellent enterprise-level solution to look at.

Cost. $2,000 + 3.75% of spend to $30,250 + 2.5% of spend. See website for more details.

Enterprise options

Several "one-stop shopping" options for large enterprises are available, and are rapidly improving. Enterprise-level sites are likely to have additional issues that smaller sites may not have, such as the need to scale and to consolidate data from many more data points than a small business needs to deal with. Further, the enterprise issues bring about complexity amongst internal team management: it's important that the right data gets to the right team or person.

Large-scale enterprise options enable you to tie together search, other digital marketing, and offline marketing measurement points. All of the following products are excellent tools. If you are in need of an enterprise-level solution, these are some of the top-tier choices:

- Covario Insight: *http://www.covario.com/what-we-do*
- Brightedge: *http://www.brightedge.com/*
- Conductor Searchlight: *http://www.conductor.com/searchlight*
- Adobe SearchCenter, SiteCatalyst, Test&Target, Discover, and Search&Promote: *http://www.omniture.com/en/*

Keep in mind the 90/10 rule of investing 90% in smart people and 10% in the tools. Understand what business objectives you are truly trying to measure, and how these programs will help you. The biggest benefit for most of them is their ability to scale to much more complex campaigns and not simply measure but perform rapid optimization and provide alerts. Basically, these tools, if configured correctly, should operate as multiple sets of eyes on your data, allowing you to jump through multiple segments quickly. The enterprise options allow for seamless integration, using pixels and code already implemented on your site; they also do an excellent job of importing data from and exporting it to multiple integration points.

Index

We'd like to hear your suggestions for improving our indexes. Send email to *index@oreilly.com*.

The Long Tail: Why the Future of Business Is
    Selling Less of More (Hyperion), 48
LPO (landing page optimization), 3, 82–92
    A/B testing for, 84
    keyword clusters for, 82
    multivariate testing for, 85–91
    testing effects of, 169
LSI (latent semantic indexing), 122

M

macro metrics, 15, 16
Majestic SEO, 184, 331–332
    API for, 319
    back links, analyzing, 194
    link diversity, 205
    neighborhood tracking, 203
malware alert, 268
management (see executives)
market share (see share of voice)
marketing, xiii–xiv
    (see also SEM)
    budget for, justifying, 305
    identifying campaigns in URLs, 10
    keyword research applied to, 3
    of competitors, tracking, 185–187
    off-line campaigns, 192–193, 208–209
    purchasing stages aligning with, 77
    value of, 30
media websites, 20
    (see also news and information websites)
meta descriptions, 138, 257, 316
metadata
    for images, 152
    mining, 181
    in XML files, 152
metrics, 8
    (see also data; specific metrics)
    baselines for, 28
    challenges measuring, 9
    importance of, survey regarding, 8–9
    privacy issues regarding, 21
    types of, 15–17
micro metrics, 15, 16
Microsoft AdCenter, 47
Minify, 281
mining
    footers, 182
    keywords, 179–181
    links, 182

metadata, 181
mobile searches
    conversion rates from, 232–233
    location affecting, 220–224
    paid search, tracking, 228–229
    repeat searches from, 224–228
    SEO compared to paid search traffic, 107
    software for, 14, 353
    types of devices used, 229–231
    unique characteristics of, 215–220
Morville, Peter (author)
    Search Patterns (O'Reilly), xvii
most linked pages report, Google Webmaster
        Tools, 202
mozRank, SEOmoz, 12, 206, 334–335
mozTrust, SEOmoz, 12, 336
multiple-click attribution, 52
multivariate testing, 85–91, 137–138, 163, 167,
        168

N

neighborhoods, tracking, 203–205
news and information websites, xiv
    (see also media websites)
nonbranded words, 3, 23

O

objectives (see goals and objectives)
objectives and key results (see OKRs)
off-site trends, 191–194
    diversity of links, 205
    diversity of off-site links, 194–203
    domain rank, 205–206
    external campaigns, 208–209
    neighborhoods, 203–205
    page rank/authority, 205–206
    SERP position changes, 211
    social media, 209–211
offline sales
    cost of, 8
    estimating, 29
    tracking, 68–69, 75–76
OKRs (objectives and key results), 15
Omniture Sitecatalyst (see Adobe SiteCatalyst)
on-site search (see site search)
Open Site Explorer, SEOmoz, 328, 332

About the Author

Brent Chaters, a former member of Hewlett Packard's worldwide search team, worked across multiple regions and countries to establish SEO programs based on solid metrics foundations, evangelizing the need to always be improving results. Brent helped to create and implement some of HP's first SEM and SEO programs in Canada. Brent is currently with SapientNitro, where he works with many Fortune 500 companies to improve their search or analytics programs across the company.

Colophon

The animal on the cover of *Mastering Search Analytics* is a burrowing owl (*Athene cunicularia*), which nests and roosts on the ground. Though capable of digging their own burrows, these birds usually use holes already created by prairie dogs or other animals. They range widely throughout North and South America, in open habitats with low vegetation like grasslands, desert, agricultural fields, and even golf courses.

Burrowing owls have round heads with no ear tufts, white eyebrow markings, and yellow eyes. They also have long legs (longer in proportion to their bodies than other owls) and brown plumage with white spotting. On average, these birds are about 10 inches long and weigh 6 ounces. Though both sexes of this species are roughly the same size, males often appear lighter because they spend more time outside the burrow during the day and their feathers become bleached by the sun.

This species is unique among owls in that it hunts during the day as well as at night, especially if there are nestlings to feed. The burrowing owl's diet mostly consists of insects and small mammals, though they also eat fruit and seeds. In addition to living in the ground, these owls also hunt close to earth—to catch prey, they run across the ground or swoop down from a perch (such as a fencepost or mound of dirt). Another hunting technique used by this owl is to collect mammal dung to line the walls of its burrow—this attracts dung beetles, which the bird can then easily catch and eat.

The cover image is from *Wood's Animate Creations*. The cover font is Adobe ITC Garamond. The text font is Linotype Birka; the heading font is Adobe Myriad Condensed; and the code font is LucasFont's TheSansMonoCondensed.

CPSIA information can be obtained at www.ICGtesting.com
Printed in the USA
BVOW081659271011

274628BV00003B/4/P